Andrew Mueller was born in Wagga Wagga, and lives in London. He is a contributing editor at *Monocle*, and a regular presenter on its radio arm, Monocle 24 – including hosting the award-winning *The Foreign Desk*. His byline also appears in *GQ Australia*, *Smith Journal*, *New Humanist* and *Uncut*, among others. He has reported from more than 80 countries, and done his best to keep up with Geelong's progress from all of them. His country band, The Blazing Zoos, have made two albums: *I'll Leave Quietly* and *Chocks Away*. He also collaborated with Luke Haines and Cathal Coughlan on the acclaimed *The North Sea Scrolls* concept album.

www.andrewmueller.net

Also by Andrew Mueller:

Rock & Hard Places
I Wouldn't Start from Here
It's Too Late to Die Young Now

CARN

carn /kan/ INTERJECTION *Australian* contraction of *Come on!*, as rendered by a football fan in transports of passion, the exclamation possibly distorted by a mouthful of meat pie: *Carn the Saints!*

ANDREW MUELLER

HarperCollins*Publishers*

HarperCollins_Publishers_

First published in Australia in 2019
by HarperCollins_Publishers_ Australia Pty Limited
ABN 36 009 913 517
harpercollins.com.au

HarperCollins_Publishers_
Level 13, 201 Elizabeth Street, Sydney NSW 2000
Unit D1, 63 Apollo Drive, Rosedale, Auckland 0632, New Zealand
A 53, Sector 57, Noida, UP, India
1 London Bridge Street, London, SE1 9GF, United Kingdom
Bay Adelaide Centre, East Tower, 22 Adelaide Street West, 41st floor, Toronto,
   Ontario M5H 4E3, Canada
195 Broadway, New York NY 10007, USA

A catalogue record for this book is available from the National Library
of Australia.

ISBN: 978 14607 5194 7 (paperback)
ISBN: 978 14607 0676 3 (ebook)

Cover design by Darren Holt, HarperCollins Design Studio
Cover image of John Dugdale of North Melbourne taking a mark against
St Kilda in 1961 by News Ltd/Newspix
Typeset in Minion Pro by Kirby Jones
Printed and bound in Australia by McPherson's Printing Group
The papers used by HarperCollins in the manufacture of this book are a natural,
recyclable product made from wood grown in sustainable plantation forests.
The fibre source and manufacturing processes meet recognised international
environmental standards, and carry certification.

For Nick and Katriina

Life-cycle (for Big Jim Phelan)

When children are born in Victoria
they are wrapped in the club-colours, laid in beribboned cots,
having already begun a lifetime's barracking.

Carn, they cry, Carn ... feebly at first
while parents playfully tussle with them
for possession of a rusk: Ah, he's a little Tiger! (And they are ...)

Hoisted shoulder-high at their first League game
they are like innocent monsters who have been years swimming
towards the daylight's roaring empyrean

Until, now, hearts shrapnelled with rapture,
they break surface and are forever lost,
their mind rippling out like streamers

In the pure flood of sound, they are scarfed with light, a voice
like the voice of God booms from the stands
Ooohh you bludger and the covenant is sealed.

Hot pies and potato-crisps they will eat,
they will forswear the Demons, cling to the Saints
and behold their team going up the ladder into Heaven,

And the tides of life will be the tides of the home-team's fortunes
– the reckless proposal after the one-point win,
the wedding and honeymoon after the grand final ...

They will not grow old as those from more northern States grow old,
for them it will be always three-quarter time
with the scores level and the wind advantage in the final term,

That passion persisting, like a race-memory, through the welter of seasons,
enabling old-timers by boundary-fences to dream of resurgent lions
and centaur-figures from the past to replenish continually the present,

So that mythology may be perpetually renewed
and Chicken Smallhorn return like the maize-god
in a thousand shapes, the dancers changing

But the dance forever the same – the elderly still
loyally crying Carn ... Carn ... (if feebly) unto the very end,
having seen in the six-foot recruit from Eaglehawk their hope of salvation.

Bruce Dawe

Contents

INTRODUCTION
Geelong 18.8.116 Essendon 18.14.122
Kardinia Park
ROUND 19, 1976

This wasn't the first game of football I saw. It was too late in the season for that – this was Geelong's second-last home fixture of 1976, and Dad had taken me to Kardinia Park[1] at least half a dozen other times during the year. I was seven years old, and my family were living in Point Lonsdale; Dad, a soldier, was on a 12-month posting to the Australian Army Staff College at Fort Queenscliff.

But this is the only game of my first season as a football fan of which I have any single clear memory. It is of getting lost, and being helped down towards the fence, and over it into the hands of a police officer, and being led along the boundary until Dad spotted me from the crowd. I'm pretty sure I recall an Essendon player marking quite close to me on the run, and drawing up more quickly than he otherwise might have, before looking upfield and taking his kick.

If this occurred, as I seem to remember, on Essendon's left half-back flank, it might have been Ken Roberts, or Gary Foulds, but for all the use the human memory is at this distance, it might not even have been this game. It's possible that I've misfiled the colour of the sash on the visiting team's guernseys: perhaps I actually got lost at the Richmond game in Round 2, and therefore nearly got collected by Francis Bourke or Kevin Sheedy, which would be a slightly cooler story – especially as that would have been the first game I saw, being Geelong's first home match of 1976 – but I'm pretty certain I can still see scarlet amid the black.

---

1   Throughout this book, football grounds will be referred to by their original and proper names, regardless of whatever sponsor-mandated nonsenses they might have been lumbered with at any point.

Reading contemporary accounts of the Essendon game now, I can't retrieve what I'm sure was genuine anguish on the day, as Geelong tossed away a 21-point half-time lead. But I suppose it was a useful introduction to the defeat-from-the-jaws-of-victory ethos which Geelong would make an institutional speciality during my first three decades as a supporter.

Nor, grasping back towards 1976, can I reconnect with the consolatory pleasure of witnessing Larry Donohue kick five goals – Donohue, a lumbering, curly-haired full-forward, on his way to leading the year's VFL goalkicking with 105, was an unimaginative choice as my first favourite player. I would also have seen, this afternoon, several future occupants of space on childhood bedroom walls: 'Jumping' Jack Hawkins, an aristocratic aerialist; Robert 'Scratcher' Neal, a ginger-thatched winger who appeared half-man, half-lurcher; Ian and Bruce Nankervis, dauntless overseers of an often otherwise fragile defence, watchtowers amid disarrayed sandbags.

I'd have had a copy of the weekend's *Football Record*, a reasonable outlay of 20 cents of pocket money. I can read it again now online. Advertisements included spots for Craven Mild and Winfield cigarettes, Trans Australia Airlines and their rivals at Ansett, Four'N Twenty pies, Carlton Draught, a collection of country and western covers by The Hawking Brothers ($4.99 record, $5.99 cassette), Kellogg's Corn Flakes (the slogan 'For All Sorts of Reasons' recognisable to my adult writer self as the it's-Friday-afternoon-this'll-do work of someone having a long week), the Toyota Corolla, and the Datsun 180B ('The Australian motorist knows value for money when he sees it', apparently, even if Australian copywriters had not grasped that it had for some time been perfectly legal for Australian women to drive cars as well).

Among the team lists and previous round's match reports in this edition of the *Record* was a feature explaining the 'checkside' or 'boomerang' kick – a recent import from South Australia – and the surreal Ampol/VFL 'Football Girl of the Week' feature, for which the *Record*'s photographer stalked a ground in search of 'the most attractive girl'; if she saw her picture in the following week's *Record*, and presented herself at VFL House on Jolimont Street, she would be entitled to bounty including a Prue Acton cosmetics collection, a style and blow-wave at her choice of Edward Beale salon, a pair of Polaroid sunglasses, a $20 voucher for Just Jeans and $20 worth of Ampol petrol (to be responsibly turned over, presumably, to an appropriately male motorist).

As if this were not sufficient enticement, claiming these treasures also entitled the woman so honoured to entry in the 'Football Girl of the Year' quest, and a crack at the week for two in Surfers Paradise that accompanied this title. In this edition of the *Record*, it was noted that the previous week's winner, 22-year-old typist, Carlton barracker and 'very attractive lass' Cheryl Twomey, had responded to her summons; she was, regrettably, 'the fourth married girl this year, but she is still eligible (as they all are) to take off our major prize'.

There was also an application form for finals tickets, which would prove some use to Geelong supporters in 1976, if less than we might have liked. Geelong finished the home-and-away rounds fourth, but after squeezing past Footscray in the qualifying final, were swatted aside by North Melbourne in the semi-final, Wayne Schimmelbusch scoring six goals for the Kangaroos. Dad drove us to Melbourne for the grand final anyway. I wouldn't have known that Hawthorn were playing, as they saw it, for Peter Crimmins, their teammate who was struggling with cancer – and who would die a couple of days after the newspapers ran a picture of him, surrounded by Hawthorn players, beamingly clutching the premiership cup they'd brought to his house. I might, I suspect, have taken umbrage at Leigh Matthews' flagrant and unsparing up-roughing of North's Keith Greig, one of my favourite non-Geelong players, who gathered 18 possessions in a losing cause despite being treated by Matthews as a one-man whack-a-mole game.

We left Point Lonsdale at the end of 1976, but I took Geelong – and Australian football – with me. Other than the signifiers of identity that are conferred at birth or shortly after – I'm someone's son, someone's brother, the citizen of a particular country – I've been a football fan, and a Cats barracker, longer than I've been anything else. I could waste a lot of time wondering what might be different, had Dad been posted somewhere else that year (though there was Geelong in the family: Dad's mother, coincidentally, had grown up there, and before her memories became scrambled by a fall late in life, could recall the crowd at the station in 1937 waiting, to the accompaniment of the St Augustine's Boys Band, for the train bringing the team and the cup back from Melbourne after dispatching Collingwood in that year's grand final).[2]

2   Any Port Adelaide fans reading are asked to interpret all jokes at their club's expense as affectionate homages to the author's grandmother, who spent her adult life in Adelaide. As her second- and third-favourite teams were Norwood and later the Crows, she grew to regard Port Adelaide as an

It's possible, I guess, that one of the reasons Australian football enthrals me is that I was as bad a player as has ever tripped over his own bootlaces. This is no attempt at endearing self-deprecation, but a simple statement of fact. As a kid, I was all the wrong things to be on a football field: scrawny, slow, maladroit, not altogether keen on dispensing or absorbing violence, and short. A late growth spurt propelled me to a decent height, but endowed me with none of the other requisites. Were I to meet Larry Donohue now, I could look him in the eye, just about, but I'd still pick him ahead of me at full-forward, 14-year age difference or not.

I played four seasons in my early teens for a Canberra club called Weston Creek, nicknamed the Wildcats; we wore green guernseys yoked with a gold V. Our coach was of the old school, which is to say that he secreted a pure-hearted passion for the game and protective love of his players behind a facade of raging bellicosity; there are umpires of the period who can probably still hear him. He led us to no success, a record to which I contributed nothing. On trophy nights, I only ever won the Best Clubman award – the one they give that poor bastard who is no good at all but keeps turning up. The only impressive thing that happened to me on a football field was once getting shirtfronted by Brett Allison, then of Belconnen South, later of North Melbourne and Sydney: a perfectly fair bump, though it can only have been an accident that I was close enough to the ball for Allison to have thought me worth unloading.

In my later teens, having accepted my limitations as a footballer, I umpired junior football in Sydney, figuring it freighted less chance of getting me concussed than playing – though only just; those parents could be ornery – and a more agreeable way of raising money to buy records than stacking supermarket shelves. I officiated in the North Shore-Warringah League, a sprawling beat from Seaforth's ground adjoining Curl Curl beach, to Willoughby's next to Royal North Shore hospital, to East Sydney's at Trumper Park amid the terraces of Paddington, to the Volvo-ringed ovals of Pittwater and St Ives further north, where if I called 'Your kick, Nathan,' half the home team would turn around. My family's arrival in Sydney coincided more or less with South Melbourne's, and

---

unfathomable sink of depravity, and Port barrackers as legions of darkness: a cruel, swingeing judgement of a body of people far from exclusively comprised of feral barbarians with wantonly unmown lawns.

though I often went to see the Swans at the SCG – and on a couple of occasions umpired the junior game at half-time – switching allegiance from Geelong seemed no more an option than changing my eye colour.

I left Australia in 1990, so was away for Geelong's losses in the 1992, 1994 and 1995 grand finals. From those days to this, I've never seen a minute of any of them. My parents refused to send tapes of the games because they didn't want to depress me, and I haven't sought the footage for the same reason. But I saw the grand finals of Geelong's 21st-century imperial period. I watched the 2007 grand final against Port Adelaide on television in London, live in the small hours, in one of those ghastly Australian theme pubs decorated to look like the inside of John Williamson's head. It says much about the psychological damage done by years of disappointment that, at three-quarter time, with Geelong 90 points up, when one young Cat was observed ordering champagne, those of us with a couple more decades' service all but wrestled him to the floor to prevent him tempting a Martian invasion or some other calamity which might see the game abandoned. I watched the 2008 grand final against Hawthorn at the same venue; I have no wish to discuss this one further.

I saw the tense 2009 victory over St Kilda in a hotel room in Macon, Georgia, where I was on assignment – the city in which Little Richard first whooped, 'Awopbopaloobopawopbamboom!' I may have exclaimed something similar, to the vexation of other hotel guests, as Paul Chapman's third goal sailed between the sticks. In 2011, I was at the MCG for the win over Collingwood. I found the day pretty well unbearable until the last few minutes, when the margin stretched past any realistic prospect of Geelong blowing it, but those last few minutes were worth waiting a damn long time for.

I'm sure homesickness is a factor. I know that part of the reason I like watching a couple of games every weekend during the northern hemisphere summer in my lounge room in London is that it gives me the means and the excuse to spend a few hours listening to Australians talking (or, if Brian Taylor is commentating, yelling, like he has set his trousers on fire and is trying to beat it out with a wasps' nest). The game has become my way of keeping up with the country from which I come.

Hence *Carn*. It is, first and foremost, an episodic history of the game, told through studies of noteworthy matches – a definition expandable to cover anything from obvious importance to plain weirdness. And/but I hope it also serves as a story of the country that has played the game, and watched it, and loved it – and as an illustration of the extraordinary degree to which Australia's game, in Melbourne especially, has, for better and worse, become the fixed point around which orbit such relative fripperies as politics, business, music, the arts, popular culture and crime.

Carn covers the period from the foundation of the Victorian Football League in 1897 to the present day, charting the game's evolution from a tribal tournament among Melbourne's inner suburbs to a professional national competition. I'm aware that this neglects several decades of pre-VFL Australian football history, but one has to start somewhere, and I like the near-symmetry of the beginnings of Australia's national football competition and the federation of the Australian nation. Nor does *Carn* address the AFLW, the professional women's competition launched in 2017: the story of the women's game deserves better than being an appendix to a book about the men's game.[3]

Publishers are fond of asking authors who they think a book is for. Authors are just as fond of responding 'Anybody in possession of convertible currency, after the exchange of which they can use the bloody thing to start their barbecue, for all I care.' But I do have in mind an ideal reader for *Carn*. It's someone who loves the game in a way that acknowledges its importance while admitting its frivolousness.

Late in the third quarter of the 2015 grand final, in which Hawthorn proceeded untroubled past West Coast to their third consecutive flag, the Hawks' Isaac Smith dribbled a delectable goal from a tight angle in a pocket, making an already foregone result six points more inevitable. As Smith wheeled along the boundary in celebration, a West Coast fan in the front row offered a high five, which Smith accepted. The Eagles barracker – one Ilario Dichiera of Leederville, we later learned – wore exactly the expression of wry resignation which might be expected in one who has travelled across a continent only to see his team get unmercifully flogged. Nevertheless, he had found a way to enjoy the experience: such is the perversity embraced by anybody the game has seduced.

---

3   There is also nothing in here about AFLX, the fatuous short-form variant introduced as a pre-season diversion in 2017, which barely even deserves this footnote.

1

The Opening Bounce
Geelong 3.6.24 Essendon 7.5.47
Corio Oval
ROUND 1, 1897

At 3 p.m. on 8 May 1897, balls were bounced at Victoria Park, Brunswick Street and the Lake Oval in Melbourne, and at Corio Oval in Geelong. So began the first season of the Victorian Football League.

Essendon would have dismounted their train from Melbourne reasonably confident. Not yet the Bombers – Australia's skies were still 13 years from hosting a powered aircraft[1] – their contemporary nickname, 'The Same Old' (or 'Same Olds'), was cribbed from their victory song of the time, and emphasised a reputation for consistency. The previous September, in the last appearance in the Victorian Football Association for both clubs, Essendon had made the same trip to Corio and beaten Geelong by four goals. The Same Olds had finished the 1896 VFA season third on the ladder, and still included in their ranks several veterans of the side that had racked up four consecutive VFA flags between 1891 and 1894, among them the man they'd elected captain for the first VFL season. This was George Stuckey, who had also played cricket for Victoria, and who just a few weeks previously had won the 1897 Stawell Gift, off a 12-yard handicap, returning from the Grampians a hundred sovereigns richer.[2]

---

1   Flown by Harry Houdini at Diggers Rest near Melbourne on 18 March 1910. It was a 60-horsepower Voisin biplane purchased in Germany for the purpose of enthralling the simple folk of the South Seas: the great Hungarian-American escapologist made 18 flights during his tour of Australia. A rival claim is staked by some for the English pilot Colin Defries, who flew a Wright Model A at Sydney's Victoria Park Racecourse on 9 December 1909 – but whether he did so with a sufficient degree of control is hotly debated by the kind of people who hotly debate these kind of things. Australia Post honoured Defries in its 2010 series commemorating aviation pioneers, although only on the cheapest stamp, worth 55 cents. Houdini graced the $2.10.

2   The Stawell Gift was first run in 1878. Stuckey was the first of three Essendon players to win it, followed by Clarrie Hearn in 1929 and Lance Mann in 1952. Mann, indeed, became the first

George Stuckey looked pretty much how every white male of the 19th century looks to 21st-century eyes: severe and straight-backed, acutely aware of the camera pointed at him. He flaunted the splendid moustache popularly associated with the period, though an Essendon team photo taken that year suggests an even split between thatched and clean-shaven upper lips. Footballers of the time played in long sleeves, and knickerbockers stuffed into striped socks. Essendon's guernsey design had already reached the endpoint of its evolution: black, with a red sash from left shoulder to right hip.

Alongside Stuckey in that portrait were some formidable players and/or characters: Charlie 'Tracker' Forbes, a towering pillar of Essendon's VFA glory years and a pioneer of the high mark; Edward 'Son' Barry, an accomplished rover; Norman Waugh, who had topped the VFA's goalkicking table the year before with 29. Waugh's immediate destiny, along with those of at least three of Essendon's 1897 team, lay abroad: he moved to South Africa to pursue a career in insurance. It can only be wondered if he caught up with teammates Charlie Moore, Bert 'Baron' Salkeld and George Cochrane, all of whom would debut for Essendon later in 1897, and all of whom would end or interrupt their football careers to fight in the Boer War.[3]

Moore, who would be Essendon's leading goalkicker in 1898, became the first VFL player to die on active service, at Kwaggashoek on 12 May 1901. Salkeld went on to Scotland to study medicine. Cochrane came home, resumed his career with Essendon between 1901 and 1904, and hanged himself on New Year's Eve, 1914, aged 37. The terse death notice in *The Weekly Times* described him as a railway employee who lived on Pelham Street in Carlton. It made no mention of his 23 League

---

sprinter to complete the Stawell, Wangaratta and Bendigo Gift treble in a single year. Other notable footballers to have won the Stawell Gift include Carlton's Norm Clark (1899), Collingwood's Bill Twomey (1924), Geelong's Jack Grant (1938) and Fitzroy's Treva McGregor (1971).

3   The Boer War would, in turn, interrupt the 1900 football season, after a fashion. Round 3 that year, due to be played on 19 May, was postponed following days of heavy rain. That same sodden weekend, Australia heard of the Relief of Mafeking – the lifting, by the British Army, of the 217-day Boer siege of the South African town. This prompted immense jubilation in Melbourne: Swanston Street was a-heave with crowds waving flags, blowing trumpets, jangling bullock bells and roaring 'God Save the Queen' and 'Soldiers of the Queen'. On the Monday morning, *The Argus* exulted: 'We know the freedom and righteousness of British rule, and are absolutely sure that the British flag in South Africa is a pledge of political equality, of pure administration, of justice to all races' – a declaration that did not age well. The VFL decided to restage the delayed games on the public holiday promised in honour of Mafeking's deliverance, but with the Queen's Birthday games looming, clubs weren't keen on playing so many matches so close together. Eventually, Round 3 of 1900 was shoehorned in at the end of the season; the Essendon versus Collingwood Queen's Birthday fixture was played on the Mafeking holiday, preceded by patriotic observances.

appearances or his war service, noting merely: 'He had been drinking heavily for about a week.'

At Corio Oval, the only consolation for Geelong, as they braced for their first VFL fixture, was the absence from Essendon's line-up of Albert Thurgood, popularly and accurately known as 'Albert the Great'. Thurgood would be a three-time Champion of the Colony before he was done,[4] a prodigious goalscorer with a freakish boot, able to punt 80 yards, drop-kick 90, and place-kick over 100 if the wind was with him. In 1895, Thurgood had headed west to seek his fortune, and had profited in front of goal, at least, for his new club, Fremantle, topping the West Australian Football Association's goalkicking that year and the next. He would do so again in 1897, before resuming his career with Essendon in 1899.[5]

Geelong wore blue and white hoops, but more of them and closer together then than later. (Had they also sported black eye-masks and carried sacks marked with dollar signs they'd have resembled a convention of pantomime burglars; berets, bicycles and strings of onions would have turned them into a chorus of comedy Frenchmen.) They were led by Jack Conway, about to stake a minor claim on footballing immortality as the only player in League history to captain his side in every game he played (all 51 of them).

Other eventually noteworthy Geelong players this day included Teddy Rankin, incipient patriarch of a Geelong dynasty, three of whose sons would play for Geelong, two as captain; Eddie James, who scored Geelong's first goal this afternoon, on his way to becoming the VFL's joint

---

4   Or possibly not. The title of 'Champion of the Colony', allegedly bestowed upon Victoria's best player between 1856 and 1940, appears to have been the post-hoc invention of C.C. Mullen, who published football almanacs in 1950 and 1951, and a history of the game in 1958. These books referred to the Champion of the Colony as a prize conferred by a vote of club captains and journalists; other winners, by Mullen's account, included Australian football pioneers Tom Wills and H.C.A. Harrison, early and earlyish champions Charlie Forbes, Dick Lee, Bill Busbridge and Roy Cazaly, and pre–World War II titans Laurie Nash, Gordon Coventry, Dick Reynolds and Jack Dyer. Mullen clearly never envisaged the technology which would enable curious fans decades hence to rifle rapidly through reams of ancient newspapers; such a search yields no reference whatsoever to any such award. An 1897 edition of *The Weekly Times* refers to Albert Thurgood as having been 'the champion player of the colony', though this appears purely descriptive, rather than a formal title. It seems somewhere beyond likely that Mullen made the whole thing up, although his list still appears in the AFL's annual *Season Record*, beneath an introduction containing the key phrase 'it is believed' – which translates from journalese as 'we can't stand this up, but whatever'.

5   The primeval Fremantle Football Club, who played in red and white, started out under the name Unions. They disbanded amid financial difficulties in 1899, despite having won nine premierships in 11 seasons, and were effectively relaunched as the team since known as South Fremantle. Albert Thurgood died in a car accident in Melbourne in 1927, aged 52, having enjoyed a successful post-football career as a bookmaker and racehorse trainer: one of his charges, Amazonia, came third in the 1921 Melbourne Cup. *The Argus*'s report of the fatal crash described him as 'perhaps the greatest footballer of all time'.

first leading goalkicker, tying with Melbourne's Jack Leith on 22 at the end of the home-and-away season, 27 after the finals (James would repeat the feat in 1899, topping the table with 31); and Peter Burns, one of the game's early superstars, who'd joined Geelong in 1892 after winning four VFA flags with South Melbourne, where (at least according to the 1930 edition of *The Sporting Globe Football Book*) he so mesmerised fans that local children at their nightly prayers would ask God to bless 'Daddy, Mummy and Peter Burns' – doubtless no less than his 'unsullied reputation for manliness and grand play' merited.

At this point in their history, Geelong were labouring beneath one of the unwieldier nicknames ever bestowed on any club, in any code, anywhere. Having begun life as the Seagulls – reasonably, for a bayside town's team – Geelong had latterly traded as the Pivotonians, apparently a reference to Geelong's importance as a shipping and railway hub. Decades later, ideas this stupid would command considerable sums when proposed by people with the word 'marketing' in their job titles.

The weather at the first bounce was pleasant, but the ground tough, recent rain having done little to soften the surface. In charge was the most distinguished umpire of the period, Ivo Crapp, who would officiate in seven VFL grand finals, and ten more in Western Australia. Photos of this composed man with a sweeping fringe all seem to capture him in those seconds of resignation and resolve prior to enduring another joke about a 'Crapp decision' from some wag certain they are the first to make it. Crapp pioneered the conventions of naming the earners of free kicks and giving instant explanations for his judgements. Among the new VFL rules Crapp was called upon to enforce were the abolition of the 'little mark', whereby the ball barely needed travel any distance from the boot to earn the recipient a free kick; it was generally agreed that this reform was sensible. The VFL had also abolished the push-in-the-back rule; it was generally agreed that this reform was completely insane. 'Such a practice always works for the shirker against the plucky man,' expostulated 'Observer' in *The Argus*; the rule was restored in time for Round 2.

Geelong were never really in this, failing to score in the first quarter, and managing just four behinds by half-time. The following Monday's match report in *The Geelong Advertiser* appeared adjacent to a Reuters dispatch from the Greco-Turkish War of the time, and glum Pivotonians must have reflected grimly on the parallels between the Kingdom of Greece and their football team. For 'the Greek Army was unable to cross the solitary bridge which barred their retreat before the arrival of the Turks and was decimated by the enemy's fire while crossing', read 'the Geelong players got disorganised and crowded into the centre, leaving their wings and opponents, with the result that Essendon prevailed, and kept the ball close up to Geelong's homestead'. Where 'the war correspondents describe the bravery of the Turkish soldiers as amazing. The baggage of the Duke of Sparta and Prince Nicholas was captured by the Turks,' so 'Essendon by a quick movement concentrated their forces in Geelong territory, [Tod] Collins from a place kick shot registering [a] seventh goal for Essendon'.

Back in Melbourne, Collingwood beat St Kilda, Fitzroy beat Carlton, and Melbourne beat South Melbourne. Geelong would finish the inaugural VFL season as minor premiers, Essendon as actual premiers, after winning the post-season round-robin playoff among the top four teams. In the 11 September 1897 edition of *The Australasian*, the composer of its Football Notes column, one 'Markwell',[6] became far from the last pundit forced to acknowledge their own fallibility, but one of the few to do so with such grace. After noting that Essendon's 'triumphant victory has been accomplished without any undue proportion of luck', and before lauding that 'they have, every man of them, played unselfish and whole-hearted football', Markwell, who had clearly been late aboard the Same Olds' bandwagon, declared with an almost audible whisking off of his hat that 'my congratulations upon their success are none the less hearty because of their having shown my estimate to be erroneous'.[7]

---

6   'Markwell' – and we can see what he did there – was the nom de plume of John Healy, also a schoolteacher and secretary of the Victorian Cricket Association.
7   The journalism of the game's early years was distinguished by a theatrically genteel tone, almost as if overcompensating for the indelicacy of what was being reported. At times, early football writers sounded like miffed opera critics: the sports pages of one edition of *The Argus* from 1910 included the headlines 'An Unsatisfactory Day: Several Games Spoiled', 'Another Uninteresting Game' and 'Bad in Every Feature: Unpleasant Game at Carlton'.

2

St Kilda Win

St Kilda 10.8.68 Melbourne 9.13.67

Junction Oval

ROUND 1, 1900

Between the beginning of the 1897 season and the end of the 1899 season, St Kilda turned out 48 times, for 48 losses. They scraped together 1014 points in those three years, and had 3612 heaped against them, for an average losing margin of just over nine goals.

At the start of 1900, there was little reason to imagine that things would get appreciably better. The concluding weeks of 1899 had seen the Saints suffer two of the most ignominious defeats ever endured, both to Geelong, both at Corio: 16.23.119 to 0.2.2 in Round 14, 23.24.162 to 0.1.1 in the post-season round-robin tournament which was still used to settle the premiership. Of the first of these massacres, *The Geelong Advertiser* was willing to concede that 'the game provided many laughable incidents even if it lacked attractive play, and the crowd were kept in good humour as a consequence'.

The second prompted something of the nauseous ennui that might result from an afternoon spent watching a seal-clubbing expedition. The *Advertiser*'s report noted, with sorrow verging on shame, that this merciless pile-on was a consequence of the daft finals system then prevailing: Geelong's only hope of making the grand final was to run up a colossal score and hope South Melbourne faltered against Essendon (they didn't). 'A better method than that in vogue must be devised by the League,' sighed the *Advertiser*. Geelong's Firth McCallum, a fine midfielder, had several teeth loosened by an accidental collision; 'he continued to play nevertheless,' the *Advertiser* noted, 'but during the last quarter went full-back, where he had absolutely nothing to do.'[1] This wretched affair was watched by barely 300 sadistic locals, who would have enjoyed seeing Jim McShane kick 11 goals, the first double-figure bag in League history.

St Kilda's early years of unremitting haplessness made them what they still are: everyone's second-favourite team, the indefatigably cheerful three-legged, one-eyed puppy following the big dogs around, wagging a mangy tail, slobbering tongue akimbo. 'The fact that they have remained together,' patronised the *Advertiser*, 'despite their long run of failure, speaks well for them as sportsmanlike footballers, and none would regret a turn in the tide for them.' Fittingly, when St Kilda's fortunes did finally improve, they did so in a manner both absurd and maladroit, denying them the final-whistle celebration that might have redeemed three years of misery for players and supporters alike.

In the 1899–1900 off-season, St Kilda had reinforced their threadbare playing list. They recruited heavily from Collegians, the Wesley College old boys team, then as now an immense presence in the Victorian Amateur Football Association, and from other schools. However, only one of the newcomers would end up having much impact, and that as a statistical curiosity: aged 15 years and 209 days, Claude Clough became, and remained, the youngest player in League history (and, as he didn't appear again after 1901, surely the youngest retiree).[2]

In the first half of the Saints' first game of 1900, the most influential player was the wind: St Kilda scored 6.2 to 0.2 in the first quarter, Melbourne 6.6 to nothing in the second. When the tempest abated after the main break, St Kilda played uncharacteristically nimble football, their youth policy paying better dividends than their dusting off of VFA veteran and occasional Victoria opening batsman Charles 'Gillie' Wilson for his first VFL match since St Kilda's first VFL match three years earlier. (It would be Wilson's last, as well: *The Age* chuckled that 'a veteran stepped

---

1   Firth McCallum died in 1910, aged 37, of tuberculosis – the 'white scourge', as the newspapers described it. At around this time, tuberculosis was the second-most common cause of death for Australian men, and the most common for Australian women.
2   A story in *The Bendigo Independent* from May 1904 reports a 19-year-old named Claude Clough, 'whose parents reside in Melbourne' and 'who only came up recently to gain an insight into mining to complete his theoretical studies', losing two fingers in an accident in the Clarence United goldmine at Eaglehawk. It wasn't Clough's first brush with misfortune, or with the media. *The Brighton Southern Cross* of 18 December 1897 reports the mugging of a Brighton Grammar boy called Claude Clough 'by two ruffians', who stole 'a hand camera' from him. Clough died in 1922, aged 37.

into the breach, whose exertion was not of much value to his side, though it had a very palpable effect on himself'.)

At full-time, the scoreboard recorded the scores as level: 10.8 to 9.14. The tie was applauded by a home crowd as startled as they were delighted. Somewhere on the premises, however, indignant representations were being made: St Kilda were seeking a greater prize than two points for the draw.

The controversial moment had occurred at the end of the third quarter. Melbourne winger Arthur Sowden had kicked to his captain, Dick Wardill,[3] who was paid the mark by umpire William Freame – despite the fact that the bell to end the quarter had sounded while the ball was in flight (to Melbourne's credit, they did not dispute this). It was from this dubious free kick that Wardill had scored the behind that had ultimately, as St Kilda saw it, levelled the scores.

The following Friday evening, the investigation committee of the VFL convened at League headquarters, behind the handsome arches and colonnades of the Port Phillip Club Hotel on Flinders Street, to consider the matter. The meeting was chaired by Carlton president Arthur Hewitt Shaw, a prosperous top-hatted businessman-about-town, active in the Freemasons and the Australian Natives' Association. Hewitt gave every appearance of being the sort of chap one could imagine later writing a weary letter to the editor of *The Argus* pointing out that the paper had mistakenly transposed his initials in their account of proceedings, in a manner liable to grievously waste the time of fact-checking authors many decades hence.

The meeting found in St Kilda's favour. Few people in Melbourne owned telephones,[4] so it has to be assumed that St Kilda's players read of their victory in their morning papers on Saturday, 12 May, before reporting to the Lake Oval, where they were beaten by an injury-ravaged South Melbourne, 6.21 to 3.7.

---

3   Dick Wardill's father, Richard Wardill Sr, had been a captain of the Melbourne Cricket Club's first football team, co-author of the first rules of Australian football, maker of the first century scored in first-class Australian cricket (for Victoria against New South Wales at the MCG on Boxing Day, 1867), a tolerably well-reviewed stage actor, an erratically successful gambler and – not tangentially to the latter – a fraudster. In 1873, on the verge of being rumbled for embezzling more than £7000 from his employer, Victoria Sugar, he threw himself into the Yarra River and drowned. He was 32. The Wardill Stand opened at the MCG in 1912 was named for Richard Wardill Sr's rather more upstanding brother, Ben Wardill, a long-serving secretary of the MCC.

4   The first telephone line in Australia had been established in Melbourne in 1878, between the Elizabeth Street premises of ironmongers McLean Brothers & Rigg and their depot in Spencer Street.

Melbourne, despite conceding their opening match to St Kilda, would go on to win the 1900 premiership, defeating Fitzroy in a grand final which any remotely sensible finals set-up would have kept Melbourne well out of. At the end of the home-and-away season, Melbourne lay sixth out of eight teams; the following season saw the imposition of the final four, the genesis of the system that endures today. St Kilda would continue upon one of the most protracted yomps through the wilderness ever undertaken in any sports league anywhere. The Saints would not win another game until Round 12 of 1901, and wouldn't win another one after that until Round 6 of 1903. Over ensuing aeons, the three wooden spoons already in the Saints' trophy drawer would be joined by 24 more, offset by a single, lonely premiership flag – won by a last-gasp behind of their own, Barry Breen's snapped, wobbled point in the dying seconds of the 1966 grand final.

St Kilda would be followed on this forlorn trudge by as stoic and obdurate a band of cultists as ever donned cowls and plodded chanting up the hill once more on the word of an augur insisting that this time – no, really – deliverance is truly at hand. In 2006, the Saints would lose a match in nigh identical circumstances to those of 1900, when Steven Baker[5] scored a tying behind against Fremantle after a siren unheard by the umpires; the Dockers were (correctly) awarded all four points on appeal. The two points St Kilda were denied would have put them in the top four at season's end, ahead of eventual grand finalists Sydney. As it was, they lost the elimination final to Melbourne by 18 points, after leading almost all day. No St Kilda barracker has ever required instruction in the relationship between sainthood and martyrdom.

---

5   Steven Baker, a combative tagger, was suspended for a total of 28 weeks during his 203-game career with the Saints. He was eventually banned from football for life in 2013 while representing the Sorrento Sharks in the Mornington Peninsula Nepean League: the six weeks he got for breaking an opponent's jaw in his first practice match with Sorrento put him over the threshold of career misdemeanours tolerated by Victorian Country Football League rules. However, the ban was rescinded on appeal. 'I think it's his first win at a tribunal ever,' quoth the startled club president.

3

Dick Condon Returns
Melbourne 4.10.34 Collingwood 8.3.51
Melbourne Cricket Ground
ROUND 2, 1902

'Your girl's a bloody whore!'

Some players – indeed, some people – spend their lives apparently determined upon self-destruction. They are forever railing against whatever authority governs them, daring the punishment which will confirm their belief that the world is out to get them. They are often – though not exclusively – people possessed of transcendent, if volatile, talent. They sometimes seem to be demanding, even if they do not themselves realise it, assistance to help tame what rages within.

Twenty months before Melbourne welcomed Collingwood to the MCG in 1902, Magpies star Dick Condon, enraged by the decisions of field umpire Ivo Crapp[1] during another match against Melbourne, had marched up to the distinguished official and cast the above aspersion upon the virtue of Crapp's daughter. It was, as far as all concerned were concerned, the final straw. Season 1900 alone had seen Condon, a fate-tempting choice as Collingwood's captain, suspended for three weeks for berating another umpire, fighting with a teammate during a three-quarter-time interval, and trying (and failing) to lead his team off the field in protest against still further hostile officiating; Condon, sadly, does not seem to have been the type given to wondering whether they might themselves be the problem.

---

1   Ivo Crapp was christened Henry. 'Ivo' was a family nickname, probably a reference to Ivo Bligh, who by 1902 was the 8th Earl of Darnley, but who some years prior to that had captained England's cricketers during the first ever Test series contested for what had become, following Australia's surprise victory in England in 1882, the prize known as the Ashes. England won 2–1 in Australia in 1882–83: Bligh is the 'Ivo' mentioned in the poem, cut from Melbourne magazine *Punch*, which adorns the side of the Ashes' container, and begins: 'When Ivo goes back with the urn, the urn ...' One really has to wonder whose side the Crapp family were on.

You couldn't speak to Ivo Crapp like that, though. The VFL suspended Condon for life. This apparent sensation – Condon was one of the most famous players in the game – was barely reported by the Melbourne papers, who covered it in brief, matter-of-fact paragraphs. Perhaps *The Age*, *The Argus* and others wished to rise piously above such indecorousness. Perhaps they just weren't surprised, or realised that their readers would consider Condon's intemperance catching up with him no more startling a headline than 'Cloud Produces Rain'. All things considered, the eventual rescinding of Condon's ban after three appeals was more of a turn-up than its imposition.

We cannot know how mixed were the feelings of his teammates at Condon's reappearance in 1902. Nor can we be sure what was circulating in the heart and head of Condon, now 26, as he laced up his boots in the visitors' dressing-room at the MCG, and shrugged himself back into black and white stripes. Just as Condon did not play like other men, so he did not think like other men. In the manner of many endowed with a singular vision, he was impatient with those who couldn't see what he could. Back in 1896, 'Follower' in *The Age* had harrumphed that 'this remarkably fine player would be of double the value to his side if he could be induced to remember that C-o-n-d-o-n does not spell "Collingwood"'.

Even after resuming his career this May afternoon, Condon would remain in a state of war with his club, the League, his teammates and – a fair assumption with such preternaturally tempestuous characters – himself. Condon would play 181 games, for Collingwood and Richmond, and feature in two Pies premierships, including that of 1902. He'd also coach – and fall rancorously out with – both teams. It would take Collingwood until 2013 to award Condon life membership, by which point he had been safely dead for 67 years. He did, however, live long enough to read, in *The Age* in 1944, a profile of Jock McHale, the Collingwood oracle who had coached more games, and more premierships, than anyone else.[2] McHale, it reported, replied 'unhesitatingly' to the hack question about the greatest player of all time: 'Why, Dick Condon, of course!'

Condon was the foundation of an archetype: the brooding, volatile maverick at least as likely to confuse and infuriate his own side as the opposition. Later decades would be as transfixed and bewildered by the

---

2   Jock McHale still holds the record for most premierships coached – eight – and the medal awarded to premiership coaches is named after him. His record of total games coached – 714 – was broken by Mick Malthouse (Footscray, West Coast, Collingwood, Carlton) in 2015.

likes of Phil Carman, Ben Cousins and Gary Ablett Sr. Condon was a gawky, gangly sort: big nose, jutting ears, curly hair. Surviving images suggest a gaze both sceptical and irritable. Anything you might say to a man like that might well be the wrong thing. For his teammates on the day of his comeback, it was probably best just to leave Condon to do what he did, try to keep up, hope that he didn't thump a spectator, or knock a policeman's hat off, or challenge someone to a duel, and perhaps be grateful that Percival Devine, not Ivo Crapp, was umpiring this match.

Condon had a good game on his return – 'steady' and 'solid' were the adjectives chosen by 'Old Boy' in *The Argus*.[3] He played up forward and kicked two goals. Condon was outshone, however, by Ted Rowell, who kicked three, and moved 'Follower' in *The Leader* to commend: 'Nothing finer than Rowell's marking, running and kicking in this match has been seen for a long time.' In 1907, Rowell would (briefly) replace Condon as Collingwood's coach, before relinquishing the role to settle into a playing career that would last almost until his 40th birthday.[4]

Melbourne, ironically, were undone on the day by their own resident loose cannon, Dick Wardill, rebuked in one account of the match for 'his inordinate indulgence in the old fault of nearly always holding onto the ball too long', and heckled in another for playing 'with such a lack of system and such a degree of recklessness that the value of his work was altogether discounted'. Wardill, the captain-coach of Melbourne's 1900 premiership side, was nearing 30, and may have arrived at the past-caring stage of complacent genius. He would play just once more for Melbourne, in a loss to Essendon the following week.

As season 1902 unfolded, Condon's disregard for the Corinthian niceties would redound to Collingwood's ultimate benefit. Bored by weak opposition during a summer exhibition match in Launceston, Condon amused himself by chipping the ball short to teammates, rather than drop-

---

3   'Old Boy' was the nom de plume of Reginald Wilmot, whose sports journalism spanned more than half a century – and who also played for Essendon in the pre-VFL 1890s. Wilmot's son was the legendary war correspondent Chester Wilmot, who during World War II reported for the ABC from North Africa, Europe and Papua New Guinea, eventually having his accreditation revoked by Field Marshal Sir Thomas Blamey, who was not a fan of Wilmot's journalism. Chester Wilmot covered D-Day for the BBC, arriving in Normandy by glider with the British Army's 6th Airborne Division, and after the war wrote the superb history *The Struggle for Europe*. He died in 1954, aged 42, when the BOAC de Havilland Comet airliner he was travelling in between Rome and London broke up over the Mediterranean.

4   Rowell's career was distinguished by three flags and two of the less likely mishaps in the game's history: one, in 1911, when he was bitten by a dog while kicking in from a behind in a match against Richmond; the other, in 1912, conceding a goal to Essendon when one of his boots became somehow stuck in a Victoria Park drainpipe.

kicking or otherwise hoofing it long to contests or open space. Condon's inadvertently invented stab-pass system would help the Magpies cruise past Essendon in the 1902 grand final, the first held at the MCG, drawing a gate nudging 35,000 and a take of £901 (sixpence into the ground, a shilling extra into the grandstand). Despite the appointment of Crapp to umpire the grand final, Condon kept it civil, and Crapp bore no grudges: Collingwood won by 33 points. Condon, in the estimation of 'Follower' in *The Age*, had 'seldom played better'.

It is a dreadful cruelty of life that we tend to learn lessons only when it's too late. In August 1914, Condon, by then living in Sydney, wrote an open letter to 'Old Timer', football correspondent of *The Referee*, collecting some of his views on the game and how it should be played. 'Football,' Condon sermonised, 'has a tendency to develop the good and bad qualities in a man.'

One imagines Ivo Crapp reading this over breakfast at home in Melbourne, adjusting his monocle and leaning inwards. Could he have had a word with Condon? A few weeks earlier, Crapp had been in Sydney, umpiring at the 1914 Sydney Carnival, at which Condon had helped former Carlton and Collingwood great Billy Strickland coach the New South Wales side. Perhaps Condon and Crapp had met, sunk a schooner or two, shaken hands. Perhaps an older, more philosophical Condon had been in a likelier mood to listen.

'Some players,' continued Condon's editorial, 'stand many bumps, and never attempt to retaliate. Such men do credit to the game and themselves, while others, with little provocation, lose their heads, and resort to many things not in the rules.'

'By George,' Crapp is now exclaiming, 'I think he gets it!'

'To these men I say,' hectored Condon, 'it is the time for coolness.'

At which point Crapp mutters something to the effect of: 'These men?'

'Try and think before you act,' wrote Condon, now flinging stones around the glasshouse with impressive abandon. 'Do not bring discredit on yourself, and after all is over you will feel contented, and retain the respect your club and comrades desire. I know it is British pluck to defend oneself; but retaliation on the field brings condemnation and stigma.'

One has to hope that Crapp's monocle survived its fall – landing safely, once unmoored from a precipitously arched eyebrow, on a cushion of marmalade.

Ivo Crapp was a byword for fair play, good manners and the common courtesies. It is no slight upon his memory to hope that he consumed the subsequent 834 words of Condon's sanctimonious disquisition, anticipating Condon's concluding, redeeming, self-aware admission of the disreputable means by which this wisdom had been won – and, upon not finding it, because it was not there, downing the newspaper, sighing, and saying, 'Well, Dick, fuck your daughter, as well.'

4

Charlie Pannam's 100th
Carlton 2.3.15 Collingwood 7.10.52
Princes Park
ROUND 14, 1902

It was one of the most important milestones in the history of the game, and it languished unremarked upon, at least by the League's professional observers. On a windy, wintry August afternoon at Princes Park, Collingwood winger Charlie Pannam became the first player to turn out in his 100th VFL match. No newspaper preview or review of the match made any reference to the feat, which Pannam had accomplished by missing only two games since the League was founded. It's not even clear whether Pannam was aware of it himself.

Certainly, Pannam had attracted considerably more press attention a few weeks previously when, wearied of the persistent heckling of Fitzroy supporters at Brunswick Street, he'd climbed over the fence and belted one of them. Pannam's victim had declined to press charges, possibly recognising that it might be a struggle to assemble a jury willing to convict. In the following weekend's edition of *The Leader*, 'Follower' wrote: 'In the abstract, of course, Pannam was guilty of misconduct, but it must be remembered that a hiding is but mild punishment for the abusive and filthy language used by some of those disgusting people whose sole object in attending matches seems to be to create a disturbance, and who cannot be fair to the side for which they are not barracking.'[1]

---

1   The dynamic was echoed at Selhurst Park in London 93 years later, when Manchester United's Eric Cantona launched himself over the hoardings at a Crystal Palace fan who had uttered imprecations pertaining to Cantona's Frenchness. The more that was subsequently learned about the target of Cantona's kung fu manoeuvre, one Matthew Simmons, who turned out to have a criminal record for attempted robbery with violence and a history of attending far-right rallies, the more sympathy

Modern Australian football is largely unblighted by the tribal hooliganism which plagues European and South American soccer; this was not always the case. In the late 19th and early 20th centuries, Melbourne's streets were roamed by gangs known as pushes. Some pushes were serious criminal enterprises, others merely unruly troupes of annoying young men – pelting the Salvation Army with flour was one popular pastime – and many pushes identified with football clubs. The crowded, working-class, inner-city suburbs of Collingwood and Fitzroy, and the games in which those two teams were involved, were especially notorious for push-related larrikinism, though North Melbourne, still playing in the VFA, attracted the favour of the Crutchy Push, a posse of scofflaws whose members were distinguished by missing limbs (a consequence of previous mishap rather than an initiation rite, although the latter would certainly have weeded out time-wasters). In 1899 the Crutchies, wearing bell-topper hats adorned with blue and white streamers, had stormed the field at half-time in a North Melbourne versus Footscray match and given a surprisingly vigorous account of themselves in a confrontation with police.[2]

If correspondents covering Pannam's 100th match had known of his century, or been interested in it, they'd have mentioned it, as the game itself offered them little to work with. According to *The Sportsman*, 'it was absolutely lifeless, and possessed no attractive features whatever'. *The Age* at least approved of the new banked spectator accommodation around the Princes Park perimeter, which 'afforded them the means of obtaining a splendid view if there had been anything to look at – but unfortunately there was not'. It was one of those mismatches between a team who can't do anything right and a team who can't do anything wrong: '[Collingwood] all played so well as parts of a piece of well-constructed machinery it is almost invidious to particularise,' wrote *The Age*'s reporter, frantically deploying the instantly recognisable orotundities of an anguished hack desperately stretching a hopelessly thin story to a daunting word count.

---

the fractious footballer attracted, to the extent that Richard Williams, writing for the impeccably liberal broadsheet *The Independent*, concluded that 'Cantona's only mistake was to stop hitting him,' and that 'the more we discovered about Mr Simmons, the more Cantona's assault looked like the instinctive expression of a flawless moral judgement.'

2   The pushes dwindled during and after World War I, for obvious reasons, but as late as 1920, newspapers covered a large-scale dust-up between Carlton's Woolpacks and Fitzroy's Checkers, abetted by the Checkers' youth wing, the Red Roses. A dispute over the affections of a local woman resulted in a huge brawl in Nicholson Street – featuring, as *The Sun*'s correspondent reported, with exquisite deadpan, 'fighting and cursing to such an extent that peaceful citizens in the neighbourhood were thrown into a state of alarm, which was not lessened when the reports of four revolver shots rang out'.

Carlton could advance the excuse that they were missing the player who would lead their goalkicking in 1902: 19-year-old rookie Fred Webber,[3] who was absent following the death of his mother; his teammates wore black armbands in her honour. However, leading Carlton's goalkicking in 1902 was not the accomplishment it would be in later years – Webber would finish the season with 11 – and besides which, Collingwood were down some big names of their own. Jack Incoll, George Angus, Ted Lockwood and the great Dick Condon were all absent, but this did not stop the Magpies winning comfortably while playing well within themselves. Carlton, like many a team strapped for ideas, were driven to pointless footling up and down the wings.

Pannam's 100th game might not have mattered much in 1902, but it mattered, eventually. It became the foundation of one of the AFL's most cherished rituals: the observances of the promising 50th game, the solid 100th, the respected 200th, the nigh sacrosanct 300th, the barely fathomable 400th. It took time for the significance of such accomplishments to be recognised, however. When Carlton captain-coach Fred Elliott, a colossus of the time, became the first to 200 games in 1911, nobody noticed, or nobody cared: no newspaper remarked upon it.[4] When Collingwood's Gordon Coventry became the first to broach the 300 barrier, in 1937,[5] this was briefly noted by the press, and acknowledged by three cheers from the day's hosts, Footscray, and the subsequent presentation of the match ball, signed by all who played in the game.[6] When Richmond's Kevin Bartlett became the first to 400, in 1983, 81,966 people near-filled the MCG for an otherwise meaningless late-season game against Collingwood, and the match was bracketed by

3   Fred Webber played 23 times for Carlton before giving football away in 1904 to become an itinerant stockman. In 1917 he won the Military Medal while serving with the 45th Australian Field Artillery in France, for helping to extinguish a burning gun pit while under fire.
4   Fred Elliott's nickname, 'Pompey', apparently a reference to the Roman city buried by Mount Vesuvius in AD 79, and awarded in affectionate tribute to a volcanic temperament, was later applied to Major General Harold Elliott, one of Australia's outstanding officers of World War I: his battalion won four of the seven Victoria Crosses earned at Lone Pine. Elliott the soldier (and later senator) never cared for the soubriquet, and Elliott the footballer couldn't have liked where it ended up: he was a conscientious objector who eventually enlisted in 1916, aged 37, one of many reluctant warriors goaded into khaki by white feathers in the post. Fred Elliott attempted suicide at training camp and was discharged as unfit to serve. Carlton paid the mortgage on his family home while he was later institutionalised.
5   If you ever fancy starting a fight with a Collingwood historian, you could float the name of Peter Burns, who played his 300th top-flight game in 1902, towards the end of a career which began in the VFA with South Melbourne in 1885 and continued at Geelong. Only his last 89 games were VFL fixtures, however. 'He has been a splendid player, always fair and chivalrous,' approved The Argus upon his retirement, hastened by a leg injury.
6   Coventry was also the first to score 1000 goals, still a feat accomplished by just four others.

days of commemoration which would make subsequent North Korean state funerals look ascetically unassuming.

Charlie Pannam was also a pioneer of another tradition which would take some while to be properly appreciated: Australian football as an engine of assimilation for Australian immigrants. The Pannams had arrived in Victoria as the Pannamopolouses, in the vanguard of a Greek influx which would eventually turn Melbourne into a staple pub quiz trick answer as the world's third-biggest Greek-speaking city (after Athens and Thessaloniki), as well as a staple pub quiz argument involving hotly advanced claims for Nicosia, New York and Chicago, and then a general row, possibly resulting in upturned tables and sundering of lifelong friendships, about how anyone would measure these things anyway.

In 2013 the AFL named Charlie Pannam on the bench in its Multicultural Team of the Century. Though Pannam earned his guernsey on merit, the recognition was also for the dynasty he founded. His sons, Charles Jr and Alby, both played for Collingwood, as did two of his grandsons, one of whom would not merely represent the club, but personify it: his name was Lou Richards.

In many respects, Pannam's principal stake on immortality, as the VFL/AFL's first centurion, is a raffle win – if he'd missed a couple more games along the way, or someone else had missed a couple fewer, history would recall another name in his place. The following week, for example, Pannam's teammate Jack Monohan played his 100th VFL game; if that wasn't agonising enough, one of the handful he'd missed was the 1901 grand final, from which he'd been bafflingly omitted despite playing every game that season, including one in which he'd blanketed Albert Thurgood, the most potent weapon wielded by Collingwood's grand final opponents, Essendon; in Monohan's absence, Thurgood ran riot and the Magpies were crushed. Monohan's luck didn't improve in 1902: a knee injury, sustained in the semi-final, forced him out of that year's grand final, again against Essendon, although his half-time advice to take Con McCormack off Thurgood and replace him with Fred Leach was crucial to Collingwood's victory.

Monohan eventually won a flag with Collingwood in 1903, and played in a grand final loss in 1905. He died in 1934, aged 61, well before the recognition of landmark games became a ritual, and therefore oblivious to his status as Australian football's own Buzz Aldrin.

5

The First Game in Sydney
Fitzroy 7.20.62 Collingwood 6.9.45
Sydney Cricket Ground
ROUND 4, 1903

The relative reluctance of portions of Australia to embrace Australia's game is an eternally confounding conundrum. It can only be wondered how different things might be, in the rugby league realms north-east of the Barassi Line,[1] if the VFL had made greater exertions earlier. In 1903, when Fitzroy and Collingwood travelled north for the first League game to be staged in Sydney, it was still all to play for. New South Wales was not at all inhospitable: Australian football had long been played in the state, flourishing to the extent that at one point in the late 19th century, there were reckoned to be 22 functioning clubs, before the code withered (or, as *The Argus* fretted in January 1903, in the rueful tone of a disappointed missionary retreating beneath a hail of angrily flung Bibles, 'There have certainly at times been efforts made to educate the people of the northern states in the mysteries of the Australian game, but the movements were of mushroom growth, and soon languished and died').

In the early years of the 20th century, however, a resurgence appeared afoot – a patriotic embrace, perhaps, of the indigenous code encouraged by the coming together of a newly federal nation. The New

---

1   The Barassi Line is an unofficial border between Australian Rules Australia and Rugby League Australia, descending approximately from the northern tip of Queensland's border with the Northern Territory to the eastern end of New South Wales' border with Victoria. The Barassi line was a coinage of Professor Ian Turner, in the 1978 iteration of his annual Ron Barassi (Sr) Memorial Lecture, which he would deliver at Monash University during grand final week. Turner was co-author, with Leonie Sandercock, of 1981's *Up Where, Cazaly?*, one of the first books to take Australian football seriously. In 2005, aluminium goalposts were erected alongside the highway near Wahgunyah, which lies on the Barassi Line on the south bank of the Murray, across the border from Corowa. In 2014, Ron Barassi attended the unveiling of a plaque explaining the installation.

South Wales Football League was founded in 1903, comprising clubs including North Shore, East Sydney, West Sydney, Sydney, Redfern, Summerhill, Balmain, Ashfield, YMCA and Newtown.[2] Serious people were involved: the NSWFL's inaugural patron was the state's governor, Sir Harry Rawson,[3] its first president the premier, Sir John See,[4] and among the vice presidents the state minister for works, Edward O'Sullivan.[5] The club founded in Paddington boasted as honorary secretary Victor Trumper, no less. Though it was early in Trumper's stellar cricketing career, Australia revered few names more ardently: it was only months since he had become, against England at Old Trafford, the first batsman to score a century before lunch on the first day of a Test.

Emissaries from New South Wales descended to Melbourne to present their credentials to the game's authorities. The VFL, keen to conquer new realms, promised to send reigning premiers Collingwood and their fierce rivals from the other side of Smith Street, Fitzroy, to show Sydney how the Australian game was played. It would not be the first such expedition – Carlton had visited Sydney in 1877 to play the Waratahs at both Australian Rules and rugby union, and New South Wales and Victoria had played an interstate Australian Rules match at the SCG in 1881 – but the visit by the Maroons and the Magpies would be the first game played for VFL premiership points in the Harbour City.

The VFL promised to allocate all gate takings to the fledgling New South Wales league, and both Fitzroy and Collingwood generously offered to underwrite their own travel expenses. The VFL's pre-season annual meeting, at the Port Phillip Club Hotel, expressed hope that the fixture 'should establish the Australian game firmly in New South Wales'. Proceedings then became sidetracked by a discussion of a lack of uniform discipline among the VFL's teams, especially pertaining to the caps still

---

2   East Sydney were the inaugural premiers, defeating North Shore in the grand final.

3   Prior to being punted out to the colonies, Sir Harry Rawson was a Royal Navy officer who rose to the rank of admiral. He commanded British forces in the Anglo-Zanzibar War of 1896, the shortest military conflict in history, which consumed less of his afternoon than watching this game of football would have. Less quaintly, in 1897 Rawson oversaw the capture and destruction of Benin City, and with it Britain's annexation of the Kingdom of Benin.

4   Sir John See, a shipping tycoon, was premier from 1901 to 1904. To his credit are New South Wales' extension of votes to women, in 1902, and the establishment of the State Clothing Factory, which did much to undermine Sydney's sweatshops.

5   Edward O'Sullivan, born in Tasmania, was a journalist who launched newspapers in three states, before becoming a combative trade-union leader and politician described by *The Bulletin* as 'a combination of Samuel Plimsoll, Cicero, John L. Sullivan and Gaius Gracchus'. Within a few years of helping found the NSWFL, O'Sullivan was president of the New South Wales Rugby Football League. His other most notable bequest to posterity is Sydney's Central Railway Station.

worn by many players: VFL president Alexander McCracken declared of the widespread sartorial disarray that 'he had never seen anything more extraordinary, except in a coal-heaving contest at Aden'.[6]

Organisation of the Sydney fixture did not go altogether smoothly. A cohort of Collingwood members objected, on the grounds that they wouldn't be able to see the game. It was briefly feared that this revolt might scupper the match, or reduce it to an exhibition kickabout, but – emboldened by letters of support – Collingwood's committee overruled the malcontents. It may have smoothed some self-ruffled Magpie feathers that Collingwood won the lot drawn to determine the location of the return fixture.[7]

Collingwood arrived in Sydney on the Tuesday morning before the Saturday game, and Fitzroy on the Wednesday; both were met off their trains by local football grandees, then escorted to their respective lodgings at Grand Central and Petty's hotels. The Grand Central even flew a black and white pennant from its flagpole in Collingwood's honour. The pre-eminent whistleman of the era, Ivo Crapp, arrived on the Friday with his goal umpires.

As the visitors were there attempting to impress Sydney, efforts were made by Sydney to impress the visitors. There was an official reception, at which Edward O'Sullivan made some patriotic remarks about how, 'since that muddy stream the Murray had been bridged over by Federation', all present were Australians, and that there should therefore be no further sectarian chatter about 'the Victorian game'. The teams were taken to a performance by Fitzgerald's Circus, to dinner at the Trocadero, on a drive to Sandringham, to an evening's entertainment at the Lyceum theatre, to the Tooth's brewery, and on the inevitable harbour cruise, aboard the ferry *Aleathea*. Collingwood planned to leave Sydney on the Monday following the game, in order to fulfil a friendly fixture against Rutherglen on the way home. Fitzroy, who were sticking around to play a New South Wales

---

6   Alexander McCracken had either endured a traumatic stopover in the Ottoman port, now part of Yemen, en route to a visit to the United Kingdom, or had read of such exotics in the popular prints.

7   Collingwood won this return match, which – as luck would have it – proved the difference between first and second at year's end, putting the Magpies a game ahead of Fitzroy. Collingwood then beat Fitzroy by two points in the 1903 grand final, after Fitzroy's Gerald Brosnan shanked a set shot with the last kick of the game. Among Collingwood's best was Bill Proudfoot, playing under the nom de footy Bill Wilson in order to evade a brief ban on serving police officers playing in the VFL, imposed by Chief Commissioner Thomas O'Callaghan, who believed such uncivilised pursuits inappropriate for his men. Such lofty moralising was somewhat ripe coming from O'Callaghan: readers of Frank Hardy's *Power Without Glory* a few decades later might have sensed something familiar about the hilariously bent top cop character Thomas Callinan.

side on the Wednesday, looked forward to spending Tuesday evening at a smoke night at the Grand Central.[8]

Matchday dawned bright, and around 20,000 people rolled up to the SCG for a spectacle which, newspaper advertisements promised, would be 'Fast, Brilliant, Scientific and Exciting'. Among the crowd were Australia's governor-general, Hallam Tennyson,[9] Governor Rawson, as well as the local MP, the walrus-like George Reid, also leader of the opposition; he would become Australia's fourth prime minister the following year. H.C.A. Harrison, who along with his cousin Tom Wills had more or less invented and codified the game's first rules, was also in the stands.

To help bring neophytes up to speed, cards were issued listing the names of the players, corresponding to numbers which had been stitched onto their guernseys – the first time this had been done (the practice was adopted across the VFL in 1912). The crowd were keen, notwithstanding lack of tribal allegiances: *The Argus*'s correspondent likened the atmosphere to a rugby union match between New South Wales and New Zealand or, even more impressively, a cricket match between Australia and England.

The two squads arrived with more ceremony than would usually have attended Round 4, borne in horse-drawn carriages festooned with ribbons in team colours. Collingwood got the jump on Fitzroy – Dick Condon was especially impressive early – without managing to spring clear: the Magpies' 11-point lead at quarter time was ground down to put Fitzroy two points clear at the half, as the Maroons adjusted more quickly to the SCG, a smaller playing surface than either team were accustomed to. During the main interval, inaugurating an enduring tradition of incongruous half-time entertainments, the local League of Wheelmen conducted bicycle races. The third quarter was, as so often, decisive, Fitzroy's three goals to one giving them a lead Collingwood could not claw back. Fitzroy's roving combination of Percy Trotter and Bill McSpeerin between them constituted the difference, finishing with two goals each.

---

8   Despite the state of their lungs, Fitzroy beat New South Wales, 8.22 to 7.5. Among the New South Wales team was the remarkable Ralph Robertson, who had played for St Kilda before moving to Sydney, where he became the biggest star of the local competition, playing for East Sydney, then North Shore, and captaining the state on many occasions. He was killed in Egypt in 1917, aged 34, serving with the Royal Flying Corps, when his Bristol Scout collided with another aircraft.

9   Hallam Tennyson was the 2nd Baron Tennyson, and son of the famous Alfred, Lord Tennyson, whose poem 'Charge of the Light Brigade' unwittingly presaged generations of Geelong sides more concerned with all-out attack than the consequences thereof.

In itself, the game had to be reckoned a success, drawing a good crowd, not entirely grudging notices from local press ('The play went along at a very fast rate,' marvelled *The Sydney Sportsman*, 'and is quite different from Rugby or British Association rules ... the ball is kept on the go the whole of the time') and raising £600 for the New South Wales league. Such was the excitement that a Round 2 game between Geelong and Carlton, which had been postponed due to a railway strike that scuppered Carlton's train to Corio, was opportunistically rescheduled for the SCG and played on a bank holiday on Monday, 3 August. The following year, Essendon and Melbourne played their Round 4 clash in Sydney – perhaps significantly, it attracted a crowd of just 6000 or so, a fraction of the attendance of the 1903 Fitzroy versus Collingwood match.

The expansionist zeal faltered, limited to sporadic exhibition fixtures and interstate carnivals, though there would be some talk of amalgamating Australian football and rugby league to create a unified – and unifying – national code ('It is believed by many,' reflected *The Age* in 1914, 'that the public would grow up with the new game.') But little came of this, and there would not be another VFL game played for points in Sydney until 1952, and not another one after that until 1979. And so the field was ceded to rugby, the dominance of which was cemented by the establishment of the New South Wales Rugby League in 1907; serving as its honorary treasurer, and as an avatar of the wavering loyalties of his fellow New South Welshmen, was Victor Trumper.

Australia's state identities, such as they are, have always been largely bogus constructs, drawing heavily upon sport for what little meaning they have. For all the satisfaction that one might derive from a victory for one's home state in a Sheffield Shield cricket match, or a State of Origin rugby league contest, there are no meaningful cultural differences between a Victorian and a West Australian, a Tasmanian and a Queenslander – and certainly nothing comparable with those between, say, a Texan and a Californian, or a Scot and a Londoner. Even our accent has developed almost no regional variations.

The deepest cleft dividing us remains the one, geographical and spiritual, between rugby league and Australian football: the rupture which has prevented Australia's national game, nigglingly and intriguingly, from ever quite becoming Australia's national game.

6

The League Expands
University 14.10.94 Richmond 12.4.76
East Melbourne Cricket Ground
ROUND 2, 1908

This was canny scheduling by the VFL. Whatever other struggles the League's two newest members might have faced in their debut seasons, one of them would – give or take the slender possibility of a draw – win at least one of their first two games. As it turned out, Richmond didn't need the help. Since decamping to the VFL from the Victorian Football Association, where they'd been semi-finalists in 1907, Richmond had acquired as coach the brilliant, turbulent Dick Condon, who'd spent the previous season in exile as an umpire in Tasmania. (Given Condon's troubled relationship with authority, it is tempting to interpret this as an act of penitence.) A consiglieri for Condon was already installed as the Tigers' captain: his former Collingwood comrade Charlie Pannam. In Richmond's first League game, they beat Melbourne by 11 points, inspired by centreman Billy Schmidt, who kicked four goals.[1]

University's opening fixture, against Essendon, suggested that there might be a greater gulf between the VFL and University's alma mater, the Metropolitan Junior Football Association, than existed between the VFL and the VFA. Though University had played with some dash ('In seeking promotion to the seniors,' enthused *The Argus*, 'they are not in the least presumptuous'), and boasted some real talent in the shapes of domineering ruckman George Elliott[2] and the three

---

1   Later in life, Billy Schmidt would coach Warracknabeal to three premierships in the Wimmera League. On the strength of these endeavours, he was appointed coach of Richmond in 1933, leading them to grand final defeat in his only season.
2   George Elliott, like many University players a doctor, would captain the team in 1911 and 1912. He was the brother of Major-General Harold 'Pompey' Elliott, the distinguished World War I

Fogarty[3] and two Cordner[4] brothers, they kicked just three goals, and lost by 66 points.

There was nevertheless great goodwill for the University experiment, especially from the big end of town, where it was hoped that the refined student amateurs might have a civilising influence. '[It] has,' pronounced 'Markwell' in *The Australasian*, 'been hailed with satisfaction by all who earnestly desire the raising of the social status of the game … there can be no doubt their inclusion amongst leaguers will improve the general tone.'

The addition of Richmond was recognised as a more ruggedly commercial consideration: '[Richmond] has,' noted 'Markwell', 'a big unified district at its back, and a very strong and enthusiastic following.' Richmond's accession was, however, a significant blow to the VFA, especially given that the VFA had responded to a separate bid for defection by a combined West Melbourne and North Melbourne proposition by expelling both clubs. A reconstituted North Melbourne were accepted back into the VFA for 1908, but West Melbourne never played again: the last trace of their existence was a red sash, in homage to their red and white hooped guernseys, added to North's colours for one season.

Richmond wore gold and black vertical stripes,[5] University black with a blue V-neck, cuffs and cummerbund-ish hoop. University were the home side, though they'd been the away side on the same park the week previously: they were now sharing the East Melbourne Cricket Ground, more or less adjacent to the MCG, with Essendon, who'd been based there since 1882.[6] Richmond nevertheless started clear favourites, not just because they'd won their opening match, and had arrived in the VFL from the tougher competition: they were a proper football club, with an already storied heritage, a proud suburban identity, and a large and rowdy following.

---

commander. George Elliott served overseas as a surgeon with the Australian Army Medical Corps. He was killed at Chateau Wood in September 1917, aged 32, and posthumously awarded the Military Cross.

3   Chris Fogarty was killed at Gallipoli in November 1915; his death was only confirmed because Joe Fogarty, also serving at Gallipoli, recognised a distinctive bunion on a severed foot. Tom Fogarty, University's captain, had played previously for St Kilda and South Melbourne. A solicitor by trade, he threw himself off St Kilda Pier in 1922, after being suspended by the Law Institute.

4   Harry and Ted Cordner had both previously played for Melbourne, as would four of Ted's sons – Edward, Denis, John and 1946 Brownlow medallist Don. In 2017, Harriet Cordner, granddaughter of Don, played for Melbourne in the inaugural season of the AFLW.

5   After a flirtation with all-black with a single gold horizontal band, Richmond's sash appeared in 1914, initially from the right shoulder, before moving to the left in 1919, where it has remained since.

6   Essendon moved to Windy Hill in 1922, the year the East Melbourne Cricket Ground was knocked down to make way for a holding yard for Victorian Railways.

University were – by definition – students, a cohort saddled, then as now, with a reputation for effete milquetoastery, contemporary judgements of which were robust. One critic of the time damned University as 'the kind of blokes what cleaned their teeth and wore pyjamas', and their fans were also routinely dismissed as simpering, floppy-fringed Fotherington-Thomases, pilloried for the decorum of their applause and the demureness of their barracking. On some occasions during their tenure in the VFL, University would be outright bullied: in 1910, Fitzroy fans, aggrieved at how a match against 'the Professors' – a nickname pronounced with derision more often than not – was unfolding, seized the ball whenever it went out of bounds, and hoofed it petulantly into the railway reserve opposite the East Melbourne ground.

University did not, however, play like a bunch of dainty, consumptive flaneurs, reluctantly venturing outside in between sipping absinthe and composing unbearable sonnets for women cruelly unaware of their existence, or uninterested in it. Though priggishly committed to a creed of gentlemanly propriety – only one University player would ever be suspended for an on-field misdemeanour – they could play, as they demonstrated to Richmond. Richmond scored first, but that goal was swiftly equalised by University's freshly unsheathed new blade, Leo Seward, a ruckman down from Ballarat.[7] He would be widely judged best afield, especially in a first half during which University ran up a 30-point lead, abetted by witheringly accurate goalkicking: they were 11.2 at the main break.

The second half had something of a tortoise-and-hare dynamic: University became careless, scoring 3.8 for the rest of the match, while Richmond plugged consistently away, answering their 6.2 in the first half with exactly the same return in the second. But Richmond were caught between a natural inclination to gum matters up, to slow down University's runners, and Dick Condon's impatient insistence that Richmond play swift and flowing football, as he always had encouraged at Collingwood. Condon would not be the last coach whose strategic vision outran the capacities of his players.

It would take Richmond a while, but they'd get there. They reached their first VFL grand final in 1919, and won their first flag the year after

---

7   Leo Seward was a talented all-rounder, who in a club cricket match in Western Australia in 1920 would take ten wickets for 34 for Pingelly against Returned Soldiers; nine of his victims were clean-bowled, the last four in successive balls.

that (and their second the year after that). Of those who turned out against the Professors this afternoon, a few would get a taste of the Tigers' first imperial period. Bill Mahoney would return after a five-year absence to play three games in the 1920 premiership year, and Billy Schmidt would be back after six seasons at St Kilda for a four-game cameo in 1921. By then, two of their 1908 teammates already knew the delirium of winning a grand final, or the disappointment of losing one: Thomas Heaney, then with Fitzroy, and Bob Bowden, who'd joined St Kilda, were on opposite sides in the 1913 decider.

University would go on to have a better debut season in the VFL than Richmond, finishing sixth of what was now ten clubs, while Richmond finished ninth, kept off bottom only by an unusually hopeless Geelong combination who, after trouncing Collingwood on opening day, won one match thereafter – against Richmond. Unfortunately for University, their first VFL season was about as good as it got (they also finished sixth in 1910, though with a couple more wins). But this afternoon, they had won some admirers along with the match. 'In the literal sense,' said *The Argus*, 'University will never make a great noise in the football world – they have not the "barrackers" – but if they continue to play such football as on Saturday they must add greatly to the pleasure of the game as a skilful spectacle.'

Such was University's remit, whether they understood it or wanted it or not: to render the game more acceptable to polite society, on and off the park. The club's admission to the VFL was the beginning of the gentrification of football – which, like all such processes, would be substantially soundtracked by people complaining that things were much better, back when things were much worse.

7

The First Game Filmed
South Melbourne 4.14.38 Carlton 4.12.36
Melbourne Cricket Ground
GRAND FINAL, 1909

Charles Cozens Spencer, proprietor of the Chilco ranch in British Columbia, had been at large for just under a month when his body was found in the Chilcotin River, on 9 October 1930. An indigenous tracker named Little Charlie, from the nearby Anaham reserve, spotted something catching the sun amid logs piled up by the current: upon closer inspection, it proved to be a gold ring throttling one finger of a cold, white hand. The shotgun with which Spencer had killed one man, and wounded another, was recovered upstream.

Spencer was well known in the district, dapper in his suit and vest, moustache and goatee. Local reaction to his crime was as much confusion as grief, speculation swirling around possible financial tribulation, either the cause or result of some psychological disturbance – although assessments of Spencer's estate would confirm him an extremely rich man, a multi-millionaire by 21st-century measurements. Mystified witnesses reported seeing Spencer unloading a truck at Deer Creek Ranch, another of his holdings, with Deer Creek storekeeper Edward Smith and Deer Creek foreman Walter Stoddard. With little in the way of warning, Spencer had seized a rifle and shot the pair of them, the former fatally.

Spencer had bought the Chilco about seven years previously, a prodigal son returned. He'd originally come to Canada from his native England back in the 1890s to prospect for gold, but had become entranced by the new technology of motion pictures – an entertainment he then pioneered in Australia in the early years of the century, earning considerable fame and fortune.

Spencer opened the Great American Theatrescope at the Lyceum in Sydney, and established a film studio, a production company and a chain of theatres. He became best known for a sequence of well-loved bushranger films: *Captain Starlight, or Gentleman of the Road*; *The Life and Adventures of John Vane, the Notorious Australian Bushranger*; *The Romantic Story of Margaret Catchpole*. Other productions included *Australia Calls*, a propagandist fantasy of invasion by 'Mongolians', which featured marauding extras recruited from Sydney's Chinatown, and a heroic cameo by pioneer aviator Bill Hart, Australia's first licensed pilot.[1]

Spencer also recorded, in collaboration with cinematographer Ernest Higgins, the oldest known motion-picture footage of top-flight Australian football. It's 2 October 1909, grand final day at the MCG, South Melbourne versus Carlton. Spencer's decision to film this grand final seems to have been impulsive: under the finals system then employed, the season would have ended had South Melbourne won the final against Carlton the previous week. Having finished the home-and-away rounds as minor premiers, however, South were entitled to a rematch.

Carlton, reigning triple premiers, started favourites. South were missing key players – full-back Bill Dolphin, injured in the final, and rover Jim Caldwell, suspended for nine weeks for thumping Carlton's George Bruce. The Blues also anticipated the return of defender Norm Clark, who possessed the rare and treasurable combination of speed and heft – a former Stawell Gift winner, his teammates addressed him as 'Hackenschmidt', after the world-famous wrestler of the same name.[2]

South had some popular sympathy, at least. 'Feeling would indeed be overpoweringly for red and white,' observed 'Observer' in *The Argus*, 'were it not for a few little mannerisms in their play, which the great mass of neutrals do not quite like.' 'Observer' was the pen name of Donald Alaster Macdonald, one of the most influential Australian journalists of that or any age: a sportswriter, novelist, nature columnist

---

1   William Ewart Hart also won Australia's first air race, in 1912, against the American aviation pioneer A.B. Stone, between Botany Bay and Parramatta (Stone got lost, confusing the Parramatta and Georges rivers). Hart was seriously injured in a crash of his self-built two-seater monoplane at Richmond in Melbourne later that year, and never flew again.

2   George Hackenschmidt, though popularly known as 'the Russian Lion', was born in Estonia to German and Swedish parents. He was the pre-eminent global superstar of wrestling's golden age, and the author of several books on diet and development – all at once the Charles Atlas, Muhammad Ali and Arnold Schwarzenegger of his day. Hackenschmidt toured Australia in 1904 and 1909. He 'created a good impression on the large attendance assembled to receive him, and quite upheld the reputation he has established of being the finest physical example of present day masculinity,' approved *The Age* of his Christmas Eve 1904 appearance at Melbourne's New Opera House (later the Tivoli).

and foreign correspondent. As Macdonald's fingers hovered over the keys prior to tapping out a military analogy, they need not have been stayed by self-consciousness: he knew of what he wrote. A few years previously, Macdonald had covered the Boer War, been besieged at Ladysmith, and had his collected dispatches published as the bestselling *How We Kept the Flag Flying*. To win the grand final, he declared, South would have to 'play the game of the guerrillas against the heavy dragoons'.

The South Melbourne men in Spencer's film certainly had the appearance of a brigade of irregulars, in that they lacked uniform discipline. South were yet to adopt the red V – this adjustment would be made in 1932 – and wore white guernseys with a red sash. There was, however, either disagreement or indifference about whether this should drop diagonally from the left shoulder or the right. Carlton were beset by an even more entrenched internal dispute about their colours: some players wore the navy blue with the white club crest, others a paler guernsey with a chamois yoke, lending the team the appearance of two rival factions united against a common foe.

The shots of the crowd in Spencer's film demonstrated that the transfixing effect of being on camera is not a new phenomenon. As the lens collected the faces, delirious smiles erupted beneath the bowlers and boaters atop the men, and the fabulous confections adorning the women: human narcissism, perhaps, has merely expanded to fill the space technology permits it. The 37,759-strong crowd was down by 5000 on the final played seven days previously, but they got to witness what was by all accounts a fine game – yet by some hunches a shameful travesty.

South Melbourne had tried to rough Carlton up in the final; 'They were,' sniffed 'Follower' in *The Age*, 'distinctly inferior to the winners in system, coolness and judgement, and again frequently handicapped themselves by rushing their opponents instead of playing the ball.' This had possibly cost South the game, and certainly cost them Jim Caldwell's services in the grand final.

South had done their best to get Caldwell off the hook at the hearing which followed the final. Representations were made by the club doctor that Caldwell had been concussed, and was therefore not responsible for his actions. South's president, George Elmslie – later Victoria's first Labor premier, albeit for just 13 days in December 1913 – emphasised, according to *The Argus*, that Caldwell was 'knocked silly, and didn't know what he was doing'. With a politician's guile, Elmslie concluded by expressing confidence that the VFL's investigation committee 'would not notice the hysterical effusions of anonymous correspondents in the newspapers'. Here, Elmslie may have overplayed his hand. The first instinct of bureaucrats is to protect themselves: the League suspended Caldwell until the following June. He would wait nearly a decade for redemption, captaining South to the 1918 flag.[3]

The 1909 grand final was umpired by Jack Elder, who by the time he was done would officiate in 20 semi-finals, five preliminary finals, seven finals, and seven grand finals. Writing for *The Sporting Globe* in 1935, he rated the 1909 decider 'the most brilliant grand final ever played, and certainly one of the most stirring'. By Elder's account it was a stout attritional struggle. He apportioned particular praise to South's Albert Franks, 'at his top in the ruck'. This was generous, given that Franks was hardly known as an umpire's pet. Franks had missed the 1907 grand final through suspension, and would be at the centre of even greater sensation in 1910, after accosting umpire (and previously 1902 Collingwood premiership captain) Lawrence 'Lardie' Tulloch, after a League hearing against a teammate. As Tulloch left the League's rooms in the Block Arcade, Franks swore at him and kicked him. Franks was suspended indefinitely, and would not play again until 1912.

Elder recalled being most impressed, however, by South's Bill 'Sonna' Thomas, the half-back who 'smashed attack after attack', none more crucially than Carlton's last attempt to overcome the two-point margin deep in the last quarter. 'It seemed odds on that [Carlton] would snatch their fourth successive pennant,' waxed Elder, 'but Thomas held the bridge for South like Horatius of old ...' Elder was either a keen Roman scholar, or had endured as a schoolboy Thomas Babington Macaulay's interminable poem about the defence of the Pons Sublicius from the onrushing Etruscans.

Even *The Age*'s previously sceptical 'Follower' parted with praise, though he couldn't resist letting South know that he'd told them so: 'They apparently realised that after leading in the first round they had been handicapping themselves in the semi-finals by their bad judgement and impetuosity, as I had pointed out. On Saturday they changed their tactics completely; instead of knocking opponents about they devoted their

---

3   Jim Caldwell coached Carlton for one indifferent season in 1925. He returned to South Melbourne as coach in 1929, but died suddenly that year, aged 41. His older brother Arthur Caldwell, who played briefly for St Kilda in 1908, died of wounds sustained at Gallipoli in 1915.

attention to the ball, and in consequence they gave the vast multitude assembled a splendid and exhilarating entertainment, and won the premiership after having striven unsuccessfully to do so for 19 years.'

The South players were chaired from the ground by the crowd. Carlton slunk off to recrimination, and eventual scandal. At Princes Park, suspicions festered that the 1909 grand final had been a fix – that Carlton players had taken bribes to play dead. These innuendos erupted towards the end of 1910's home-and-away rounds, when Carlton, then on top of the table, contrived to lose their last match to the hitherto winless St Kilda – an occurrence upon which one might indeed have got decent odds, akin to those available on the half-time brass band being scattered by the descent of the returning Christ. In the MCG dressing-rooms on the morning of the 1910 semi-final, also against South, Carlton officials confronted three of their own players: triple premiership star Alex 'Bongo' Lang, newcomer Doug Fraser and recruit Doug Gillespie.

Gillespie would be exonerated by the club, and would play in the grand final, lost by Carlton to Collingwood. Lang and Fraser remained dropped by Carlton, and on grand final eve the VFL announced that the pair would be suspended for five years (incredibly, Lang returned to the Blues briefly in 1916; Fraser never played again, and died in 1919, aged 32, one of around 15,000 Australian fatalities of a devastating post-war global influenza pandemic).

A week before the VFL passed judgement, an intriguingly embittered letter appeared in *The Age*. Signed 'Carltonian', it read, in full: 'I hope the South Melbourne Football Club is proud of the alleged premiership it won last season. For it is well known that there was more than one Carlton "stiff 'un" in the [Grand] final last season. To my mind South's position in the matter is despicable. It is equal to "Please, Carlton, let us win. And if you do, Mr. ——— will pay you well." And isn't it enough to make the angels weep to see Andrew Fisher and Frank Tudor slobbering South Melbourne over such a glorious "premiership"?'

Andrew Fisher and Frank Tudor were, respectively, the prime minister and the minister for trade and customs. The public record contains no reference to either man 'slobbering' ostentatiously in South's direction, though it would be unsurprising if either had conveyed their congratulations to the premiers – and extremely startling if either had been directly involved in any match-fixing skulduggery, as appears to be the implication. The identity of the alleged kingpin whose name

The Age redacted is lost to history. It is impossible to discern whether 'Carltonian' was indeed an informed insider or a forerunner of those seething troglodytes who fill online newspaper comment sections with audaciously punctuated assertions about the complicity of the Illuminati in the manipulation of their mortgage interest.

In the closing scenes of Charles Cozen Spencer's film, the victorious – or, as 'Carltonian' might have had it, 'victorious' – South Melbourne players are carted off by exultant supporters, followed by small boys dressed up for the big day in suits and caps, capering and waving for the camera. They're maybe nine or ten years old. It's a good age to be an Australian in 1909 – probably too young for the next war, likely too old for the one after that – but a portentous one to be a South Melbourne fan: only two more premierships to look forward to in the next 91 years of the 20th century, and about on track to have their dotage ruined by their club being uprooted and packed off to Sydney.[4]

---

4   This bereavement was considered in song in 1987 by Weddings Parties Anything in 'The Swans Return', narrated from the point of view of a mournful South Melbourne–supporting pensioner. It appeared on the B side of 'Hungry Years'.

8

University Bow Out
University 7.10.52 St Kilda 13.15.93
Melbourne Cricket Ground
ROUND 18, 1914

The possibility would have been among the last things on the minds of the men in the black guernseys with blue Vs, as they trudged from the MCG after this last game of 1914, the claps and cheers of fewer than 5000 spectators drowned out by the squawking of seagulls, but they had entrenched a record which might well stand forever.

University had lost their 51st consecutive match, in a streak dating back to Round 3 of 1912. A couple of weeks previously, they'd overtaken St Kilda's inglorious genesis, of 48 defeats on the bounce between joining the VFL and the Saints' first victory. For University, however, there would be no opportunity for redemption. In his match report in the following Monday's *Argus*, 'Observer' was righter than he knew when he wrote: 'The long lane has had no turning for University.' University withdrew permanently from the League a few weeks later.

It wasn't just the recently declared war. Though many students had already joined the newly formed 1st Australian Imperial Force by the end of 1914's home-and-away rounds, University had more prosaic reasons for retreat. The club had been defeated by logistics, in that exams fell in the middle of the football season, and money, in that they could not keep up with the payments to players which were now commonplace. University's vice-president, Irish-born X-ray pioneer Professor T.R. Lyle,[1] told a meeting of the League that the club's footballers thought

---

1   The Thomas Ranken Lyle Medal is awarded biannually by the Australian Academy of Science to an outstanding physicist or mathematician. Lyle had played rugby for Ireland before migrating to Australia.

it unfair to the public and the VFL to continue. In return, League president Alexander McCracken acknowledged the difficulties the club had faced, and congratulated them on their courage, and a 'retirement with honour'.

University's last game was far from the most abject tubbing the club had suffered; that mark had been set, or at least equalled, the week before, in an 89-point loss to Fitzroy. Against St Kilda, indeed, University held a five-point lead at half-time, though the Saints were at less than full strength. With no hope of reaching the finals, St Kilda were giving some younger players a run, recruits from Port Melbourne Railway United, who'd just won the Victorian Junior Football Association premiership for the second year running.

More significantly, St Kilda were without captain Dave McNamara, and the goals he provided with his left-foot place kicks, which had been known to clear 100 yards. (A few weeks previously, McNamara had bested rivals from different codes, including rugby league idol Dally Messenger, in a long-kicking competition at the Sydney Cricket Ground, with a mark of 89 yards and 2 feet.) In Round 17, McNamara had been booked for elbowing Geelong's champion half-back Joe Slater during a hectic encounter at Corio Oval. *The Argus* reported that, following this concussion-inducing assault, McNamara 'was fumed at from all parts of the ground, and the hot mood of the crowd appeared to infect the players'. The intervention of police had been required to restore order on the field at one point, and the League had made an example of McNamara, suspending him until June 1915. By then, Joe Slater had sailed for Egypt as a lieutenant with the 22nd Battalion of the AIF; he'd survive Gallipoli, earn a mention in dispatches at Pozières, and die at Bullecourt in May 1917, aged 28.

Either the Students just couldn't keep up in the second half or the Saints resolved to quit clowning around; possibly both. University posted just one more goal for the match, while St Kilda helped themselves to eight, 'practically doing as they liked', as *The Malvern Standard* reported. St Kilda's stolid half-back Gordon Dangerfield was widely reckoned best on ground; a young Roy Cazaly had a quieter day, failing to get among the goals.

Roy Park, who today as so often was University's leading goalkicker – in 44 appearances for University, he was held goalless only twice – ended his time in black and blue without ever walking off a winner. He would experience better luck with Melbourne the following year, leading their goalkicking with 35, but his VFL career would end in ignominy and rancour. In Melbourne's Round 15 match against St Kilda in 1915, before barely 6000 people at an echoing MCG, Park was reported for striking the Saints' Gerry Balme as field umpire Harry Rawle appeared to lose control and/or interest during an unruly final quarter. ('Rawle umpired as only Rawle can,' sniffed Gerald Brosnan[2] in *Winner*, 'seeing things that no one else sees, stopping the game for imaginary breaches, and allowing serious faults to go unpunished … while his umpiring could not be held responsible for the roughness of the second half, it certainly did not have the slightest effect towards checking it.')

Park was suspended for four matches. Outraged, he retired from the VFL before going to war. He returned from service with the 5th Australian Field Ambulance to play for Footscray in the VFA – he kicked five goals as they won the 1920 grand final[3] – and then composed perhaps the least glorious Test record in Australian cricketing history, playing just once, against England in 1920's New Year's Eve Test, conceding nine runs from his only over with the ball, and making a first-ball duck in his only innings with the bat.[4] Legend insists that Mrs Park missed her husband's entire career at a Test crease in the act of reaching down from her seat to retrieve dropped knitting.

For St Kilda, the last home-and-away game of 1914 was a different kind of farewell. The Saints' red, black and white guernseys would be mothballed for the duration of hostilities and beyond, due to an unhappy

2   This was a weirdly damning indictment of an umpire taking charge of only his 15th match – although, perhaps even more weirdly, of the six matches Harry Rawle had umpired in 1914, one of them had been the grand final. Rawle does appear to have tended towards officiousness. He awarded 108 free kicks between Melbourne and St Kilda on the afternoon in question, and in 1923, his performance in an up-country match between Ballarat and Golden Point resulted in protests – according to *The Sporting Globe*, 'his free use of the whistle [was] one of the chief objections urged against him'.

3   Roy Park refused payment from Footscray, but at a club picture night at the Barkly Theatre in November 1920 he was presented with a roll-top desk and chair, a cricket bat and a trophy of a silver football donated by club president David Mitchell, the excitement heightened further by Park's recent cricketing heroics in Adelaide, where he'd made 152 for Victoria against South Australia. 'Although he has been in Footscray only about nine months,' approved local rag *The Independent*, 'Dr Roy Park has won the esteem and affection of the people to a degree hitherto unknown in this locality … his sterling worth as a citizen, his skill and sympathy as a medical man, and his innate modesty at all times are the foundation upon which his popularity rests.'

4   The most plausible rival to Roy Park as the holder of the most lamentable record in Australian Test cricket history is Victorian leg spinner Bryce McGain. Given a debut against South Africa at Cape Town in 2009, he was plastered for 149 runs for no wickets at worse than eight an over by the Proteas' unsentimental batsmen. His two visits to the crease yielded a duck and two, and he never played for Australia again. In 2016 McGain was appointed director of football and under-19s coach at Waverley Blues, in the Eastern Football League.

coincidence with the colours of the flag of the German Empire. St Kilda played in 1915 and 1918 – they were among the clubs who sat out 1916 and 1917 – in the red, black and gold stripes of an ally. ('The colours of gallant Belgium,' approved *The Argus* of the new look's first outing, 'showed up strongly.') It was a noble gesture of solidarity, if one which would have prompted widespread nonplussedness, if news of it ever reached the Low Countries.

University would mourn more than the loss of their place in the VFL. Of the 94 VFL players who died on active service in World War I, 17 had played for University.[5] Two played in University's last game. Percy Rodriguez, from Broome and of Filipino descent, turned out a couple of times for Melbourne in 1915, and died on the Somme in 1918. Cyril Seelenmeyer joined the Australian Army Veterinary Corps, won the Military Cross for his devotion to the animals under his care, and died at Fouilloy in 1918, aged 26, while treating an injured horse under shellfire.

Another veteran of University's last game, Bill Hinman, lost a brother at Gallipoli – Arthur Hinman, also a former University player – but came home wearing a Military Cross won at Pozières, and a Croix de Guerre and knighthood awarded by King Albert I of Belgium; he became a lawyer in his native Launceston, and was later president of the Hobart Chamber of Commerce. Another former University player, Keith Doig, added another Military Cross to this team's remarkable collection of decorations, recognised for persistent heroics while serving in France as medical officer to the 60th Battalion of the AIF. After the war, he worked as a doctor in Colac.

Football itself would become a casualty of the war. Though the nine remaining VFL teams would play on in 1915, only four would show up for 1916, six for 1917 and eight for 1918; Melbourne, in 1919, were the last to rejoin. The conflict in Europe did not seem quite real to Australians just yet. Whichever University and St Kilda players took *The Argus* on matchday mornings read, on 29 August 1914, a newspaper riddled with

---

5   An 18th, Ken MacLeod, was killed during World War II. MacLeod, who played 54 games for University between 1910 and 1913, was a lieutenant commander in the Royal Navy serving aboard HMS *Glowworm* when it engaged the German cruiser *Admiral Hipper* off Norway in April 1940. With the outgunned *Glowworm* already battered by several direct hits, the ship's captain, Lieutenant Commander Gerard Broadmead Roope, deliberately rammed the *Admiral Hipper*, damaging the German craft but finally sinking his own. Roope was awarded, posthumously, the first Victoria Cross of World War II – partially on the strength of a letter of commendation sent to the British Admiralty by the *Admiral Hipper*'s commander, Kapitan-zur-See Hellmuth Heye. Ken MacLeod was among 109 men who went down with the *Glowworm*.

the names of places that still seemed a long way away: Ostend, Boulogne, Arras, Namur, Danzig. But they also read that their countrymen were on the move, an Australian fleet sailing for operations in the Pacific. By the time the 1914 season ended, with Carlton defeating South Melbourne in the grand final, Australian troops had won their first victory, capturing German colonies in Papua New Guinea, and suffered their first losses, including all 35 men aboard the Royal Australian Navy's first submarine, HMAS *AE1*, which disappeared off Rabaul.

As the realities of war became apparent, so did unease about the continuation of organised football. Some thought it a vacuous indulgence and/or a dereliction of duty, or even vaguely treasonous; Lawrence Adamson, headmaster of Wesley College and president of the Victorian Amateur Football Association,[6] spluttered that players who chose football over their country's call should be presented with Iron Crosses. Others considered it a vital morale boost and/or crucible of warrior spirit, or even that it would be vaguely treasonous to stop. 'It would be a sign,' thundered an editorial in *The Australasian* in May 1915, 'of decadence and funk to show the white feather in stopping all sports and amusements in this critical part of our nationhood,' further suggesting that 'the abolition of football would drive more men to drink than to the war'.

The arguments went on, but so did the game, if only just.

---

6   Among the VAFA's current clubs are University Blacks and University Blues, descendants of University.

9

The Recruitment Games
Fitzroy 6.9.45 Carlton 6.9.45
Brunswick Street
ROUND 1, 1917

Lieutenant Rupert Maskell was not having a glorious war. A 22-year-old clerk when the conflict began, Maskell enlisted in October 1914; boasting previous military experience in the Victorian Rangers and Brighton Rifles, he'd swiftly acquired three stripes on his sleeve. After completing basic training at Broadmeadows, he'd sailed for Egypt on 22 December 1914, aboard HMAT *Ulysses*, as a quartermaster sergeant with A Company of the 14th Infantry Battalion of the Australian Imperial Force, leaving his wife, Ruby, back in Mentone. Unlike many fretful spouses of the time, Ruby didn't have to wait all that long to see her husband again: Maskell was discharged as medically unfit in early April 1915, and was on his way home when the rest of the 14th stormed ashore at Anzac Cove.

Still keen to do his bit, and perhaps tiring of life as a storekeeper for Victorian Railways, in 1916 Maskell applied for, and received, an officer's commission, and was set to work recruiting. By that time, the war had become a tough sell, the length of newspaper casualty lists from Pozières and Fromelles advancing rather faster than any of the front lines on the Somme. In October 1916, after returning from a long visit to Europe, Australia's prime minister, Billy Hughes, held a referendum seeking agreement that Australian conscripts could be sent overseas: it, and a second similar referendum in December 1917, prompted bitter, vicious and frequently unruly public debate, and the proposal was defeated both times.[1]

---

1   The 'conscription referendums' of 1916 and 1917 weren't really about conscription, which Australia had imposed on males since 1911, and weren't really referendums, as they had no legally binding

Football fans were nevertheless regarded as potentially bountiful recruiting fodder, and appeals were regularly made to their patriotic ardour, their fondness for a tear-up, and/or their guilt. One early recruiting poster juxtaposed a bandaged Anzac and a dead comrade with a hallucination of a crowd enjoying a football match, the caption asking, 'Will they never come?' Another featured Maskell's *Ulysses* shipmate Albert Jacka VC against a backdrop of gambolling athletes – including a footballer – and urging, 'Play up, play up and play THE game.'[2] In 1917, it was decided that the opening day of the new VFL season would be a providential opportunity to address large numbers of young men who might still be interested in being pulverised into unrecognisability by German artillery in some glutinous French hellscape before it was too late.

Round 1 is always exciting: no hopes yet dashed, no dreams yet shattered. It was perhaps more giddying than usual in 1917, as there was a sense that football was, if not properly back, then getting there. After the nonsense of 1916, in which only four clubs had competed, and in which Fitzroy had earned pub quiz immortality by winning the wooden spoon and the premiership in the same season,[3] South Melbourne and Geelong had rejoined the League. At Brunswick Street, 6000 people – a decent crowd by wartime standards – had turned out to see Fitzroy host Carlton, a rematch of the 1916 grand final.

Lieutenant Maskell was due to make his pitch at half-time. While he had not been greeted effusively by Fitzroy's committee, whose hospitality had extended no further than admitting him to the grandstand, Maskell could not have complained that the game had not warmed the crowd up nicely. The first two quarters had been a keen contest, Fitzroy's captain-

---

power. But 'advisory plebiscites on whether or not to send people already conscripted to serve outside Australia' was never as catchy.

2   This was a line from Sir Henry Newbolt's 1897 poem 'Vitae Lampada', a bumptious doggerel equating sport and warfare. In fairness to Newbolt, he wearied of his best-known work in later life, complaining that it had become 'a kind of Frankenstein's monster', and lamenting: 'In vain do I explain what is poetry: they roar for "Play up", they put it on their flags and their war memorials and on their tombstones.'

3   Fitzroy won twice and drew once during the truncated 12-round season of 1916, but finishing last still meant finishing in the final four, there being only that many teams competing. Inexplicably, Fitzroy beat Collingwood in the semi-final, Carlton – who'd lost two games all year – in the final, and Carlton again in the grand final rematch to which the Blues, as minor premiers, were entitled. The best Australian Rules game of 1916 was almost certainly played at the Queen's Club in London on 28 October – an exhibition match between Australian Training Units and the 3rd Australian Division, among the sides such greats as Bruce Sloss, Dan Minogue, Bill Sewart, Charlie Perry, Percy Trotter and Jack Cooper. It drew a crowd of 8000 and raised £300 for the Red Cross. At least six of the players involved were subsequently killed in France, including South Melbourne superstar Sloss, and Fitzroy captain Cooper.

coach George Holden putting on an especially glittering exhibition, Carlton debutant Frank Martin catching the eye for the visitors in defence ('Time and again,' approved *The Age*, 'Martin stalled the Maroons'; he would go on to play 87 games for the Blues). When the bell rang to end the second quarter, there was only a point in it, the home side ahead 3.4 to 3.3.

Lieutenant Maskell was accompanied by a recruiting sergeant called Gordon Carpenter, who'd been wounded at Gallipoli and subsequently invalided home after falling ill while recuperating in Egypt.[4] Carpenter had been learning the hard way for a while that the bugle's call was falling on increasingly deaf ears. At a recruiting rally at the Mechanics' Hall in Coleraine the previous year, he'd had to resort to offering a pound note from his own wallet to the first man to step forward; the headline of *The Coleraine Albion & Western Advertiser*'s sadistically extensive coverage of the event had been 'Effort Big, Result Little'.

We do not know whether Lieutenant Maskell had laboured long on the text of his patriotic oration. We must hope that he did not. The Brunswick Street crowd were unreceptive, men and women alike heckling and insulting him, and then setting physically about Maskell and Sergeant Carpenter as they beat a tactical retreat down the grandstand steps. In a subsequent report of his day's endeavours, Maskell whimpered, 'I am not keen on again being sent to these matches. My staff also request that they should not be sent.'

Maskell and Carpenter's experience was not exceptional. Recruiters at all other League grounds on this Saturday afternoon were left reflecting that the last comparably hostile reception they'd experienced had been flying Turkish flags above its machine-gun nests. At the Lake Oval, where South Melbourne hosted Geelong, Sergeant Charles Kilpatrick, another wounded Gallipoli veteran, was shoved and jostled, and escaped just ahead of a proper hiding; he later said he wouldn't attempt another such venture without protection.[5] At Victoria Park, where Collingwood played Richmond, Sergeant-Major Harry Durand was merely jeered and abused,

---

4   A newspaper report of the time identified the illness as 'septic poisoning'. Gordon Carpenter's war records list it as orchitis, an inflammation of the testicles which can be associated with mumps, but which can also be associated with careless visits to Egyptian nightspots of questionable repute.

5   In 1918, Charles Kilpatrick was convicted of bigamy. Though already married with eight children under 13, he nevertheless wed a widow named Elsie McDonald. Kilpatrick's interesting defence – that he was drunk at the time, and had no idea what he was doing (a line confirmed by his actual wife, and by the vicar who conducted the fraudulent ceremony) – resulted in a suspended gaol term of three months.

rather than actually assaulted, perhaps in recognition of his relatively advanced years,[6] but he nevertheless abandoned his address early.

Polite opinion was scandalised by this treatment of soldiers. 'Heartless, vicious and detestable actions,' raged *The Age*, 'on the part of individuals who class themselves as sports people … it is another big blot on football.' News of the deriding of a nation's heroes reached Australia's opposite coast, where Perth's *The Sportsman* called the hecklers 'truculent shirkers', before reflecting – not inaccurately – that 'football crowds are notoriously intolerant of plain facts. Good barrackers are bad losers. The average habitual punter is a philosopher who will listen to reason – after the race – but the football barracker is a different sort of ass. He fastens his mind to his club colours or party dogma and reckons it his duty as a man to howl the opposition down.' The kerfuffle even made headlines across the Tasman, where *The Press*, of Christchurch, described Australian football fans as 'a loud-mouthed, stupid, hooligan class, quite insensible to all the prevalent ideas of national decency'.

Maskell and Carpenter took the hint and left Brunswick Street at half-time – a shame, as the second half delivered on the considerable promise of the first. The game came down to a ferocious defensive tussle in the final quarter, for 15 minutes of which nobody could find a way to score. A behind by Charlie Fisher gave Carlton a six-point lead; a goal from Fitzroy's Tom Heaney, who'd kicked seven in the two games against the Blues which had landed the absurd 1916 flag, made it 6.8 each. The Maroons scored another behind, the Blues another, and at the death Fred Moore had a set shot which could have won it for Fitzroy: he shanked it out of bounds. In the clearly unlikely event that many present were given to metaphysical cogitation, they might have discerned a certain symmetry in the fact that a game which had framed an effort to recruit participants for an attritional stalemate had ended in precisely such a result. (Decades later, the first Collingwood versus Essendon Anzac Day match, on the 80th anniversary of the Gallipoli landing, would furnish an equally apt outcome.)

---

6   Harry Durand, an accountant at the state bakery, gave his age as a curiously punctilious '44 and 5/12' when enlisting in 1915. He embarked from Sydney on HMAT *Suffolk* in November that year, and was sent back from Egypt on the same ship eight weeks later, on the grounds of poor eyesight and old age. In July 1916 he told a crowd at Albury Town Hall that he was 53, but also claimed to have 'participated in several skirmishes' while overseas. At one especially miserable recruiting event in Ballarat in 1917, Durand offered to go two rounds with one of the evening's star attractions, American welterweight Harry Stone, if five more men would come forward. They didn't, but one has to wonder if Durand – who was clearly what might be charitably described as a raconteur – nevertheless regaled subsequent crowds with a breezily embellished fiction of the night he put the great 'Hop' Harry down for the only time in his career.

Maskell was, if nothing else, a trier. Though his resolve to steer clear of football grounds did not waver, he spent the rest of the war doggedly hosting recruiting meetings, sometimes organising entertainments to pull the crowds, often enjoining his sergeants to belligerently question the manhood of the assembled, rarely to much avail. In May 1917, a report on the work of recruiters in a short-lived newspaper called *The Graphic of Australia* ran – along with a handsome photograph of Maskell – figures showing that Australia was barely contributing every four months the recruits that Great Britain wanted every four weeks.

It seems to have become too much for Rupert Maskell. In 1924, Ruby Maskell sought a divorce, her affidavit alleging that her husband had lost his position, his rank and frequently his temper, due to an overfondness for the bottle. She also appeared to explain the brevity of his service overseas: he had 'contracted a disease, but she forgave him'. The range of illnesses for which one might require a spouse's absolution is a narrow one. (The street at the heart of Alexandria's red-light district was called Rue des Soeurs, which should have been warning enough.)

Fitzroy nearly backed up their improbable 1916 triumph with another flag they had little right to win. At the end of 1917's home-and-away rounds, the Maroons scraped into fourth position, two points ahead of the returned Geelong, but then beat Carlton in the semi-final and – incredibly – saw off minor premiers Collingwood in the final. But Collingwood, exercising their right as table-toppers to a rematch, restored order by 35 points in the grand final.

The war would outlast one more VFL season, and would consume many more players. The last – Albert Gourlay, briefly of Melbourne and Carlton – died of wounds sustained while serving in France with the Wellington Infantry Regiment of the New Zealand Expeditionary Force, ten days before the guns fell silent.

10

Up There, Cazaly
St Kilda 10.6.66 South Melbourne 9.13.67
Junction Oval
ROUND 1, 1921

We know who first uttered one of the most resonant exclamations in Australian sport – indeed, it would turn out, in Australian popular culture. He was Fred 'Skeeter' Fleiter, a burly follower who played for South Melbourne between 1919 and 1925, and briefly coached the club in 1929. What we don't know is precisely when Fleiter first encouraged the ruckman he was shepherding into the contest with a cry of 'Up there, Cazaly!' But it might have been this afternoon. It was Roy Cazaly's first game for South Melbourne, therefore his first in the same team as Fleiter, Cazaly's former schoolmate and fellow Albert Park native.

South Melbourne wore the striking all-red guernseys with white SMFC logo that they'd taken to the previous season.[1] St Kilda were still working out their World War I–induced identity crisis, as if wondering when it might be acceptable to wear once again the red, black and white which evoked the vanquished German empire (1923, was the eventual answer). The simple red, black and gold stripes in which the Saints had spent the war years had evolved – possibly in recognition of the fact that Germany's national flag was now itself simple red, black and gold stripes – into a scarlet monstrosity with black sleeves, with a gold and black V-neck and gold and red cuffs.

St Kilda were the team Cazaly had captained the season before. He'd wearied of the dysfunction on the field, where the Saints had won just twice in 1920, and off it: notwithstanding the beatings the Saints sustained

---

1   The white with red sash would be resumed in 1923, before being abandoned for the red V in 1932.

on Saturday afternoons, the players found no opposition more hostile than their club's own committee. Some players, led by Wels Eicke,[2] had threatened to strike rather than play alongside prima donna centreman Billy Schmidt, who had himself attempted to leave to return to his old club, Richmond, along with another Saint, Norm Turnbull. Cazaly had been further tempted by an offer from South Melbourne of £6 a week – £6 a week more than St Kilda were paying him.

South's investment in Cazaly proved shrewd. This was not merely because it was at Albert Park that he properly blossomed in the long term, becoming part of a domineering ruck combination, along with Fleiter and Mark Tandy – the latter christened 'Napper' by Cazaly, due to a deceptively somnolent demeanour. It was also because in the extremely short term, i.e. this afternoon, Cazaly was a decisive factor in a game that South should have won much more easily.

Both teams started brightly – uncharacteristically so, in St Kilda's case. At quarter time the Saints, with a strong southerly at their backs, led 6.0 to 5.1, one of their goals a 60-yard place kick from the famously potent boot of Dave McNamara. The pace dipped in the second quarter, South scoring 2.6 to 0.3 for a ten-point half-time lead, before St Kilda clawed back in the third. At the last change the Saints were nine points clear, and looking comfortable.

The last quarter was a bicep-bulging, vein-straining arm-wrestle, yielding just a behind to South, before Cazaly, with one goal already to his name, took charge. His fine mark on the forward line laid on Edwin Marsh's[3] third goal of the afternoon, bringing South within two points – a deficit then erased by behinds from South's Bobby Allison and Artie Woods. With scores level, and time expiring, it was Cazaly who kicked the goal which put South ahead; another behind for South by Allison furnished a margin which Ted Collins' last-minute goal for St Kilda could not quite cover.

---

2   Wels Eicke made his debut as a 15-year-old in 1909. An outstanding defender during a period when St Kilda needed one, he played 218 games for the club, was best and fairest three times, and the first captain in League history to call for a head count of the other team – against Carlton in Round 12, 1924. A pleasing but uncheckable legend has it that, on being informed by field umpire Vincent Maguire that his opponents had the correct 18 men afield, Eicke replied: 'You forgot to count yourself.'

3   Edwin Marsh is one of those maddening enigmas who lurk in the shadows of the game's history. He kicked three goals on debut, at age 21, and seems to have impressed all who saw him. He played in the following week's loss to Richmond, thereafter never again, and the trail runs cold until what appears to be the announcement of his funeral in 1968. One can only hope that he did not spend the intervening interregnum boring to tears unwary patrons of his regular pub with the tale of the day he scored three in the same side as Roy Cazaly.

If Fleiter did make his famous outburst of 'Up there, Cazaly!' this afternoon, it took a while to lodge in the public consciousness. It seems to have become common currency at Melbourne football grounds during the 1920s, but the first discussions of the phrase did not begin appearing in Melbourne newspapers until the early 1930s, by which time Cazaly had retired from playing in the VFL (he still loomed in football's consciousness, however, as a player and/or coach in Tasmania and the VFA, and would return to the VFL in due course).[4] Though the expression was by then well known, its origin myth was not.

A short piece in *The Sporting Globe* in September 1931 wondered, 'Who was the first to use the phrase "Up there, Cazaly?",' observing that 'throughout Australia, everyone knows the cry', and relating the tale of a recent voyager to the outback who had heard it from jackaroos who had never seen a game of football, or heard of Roy Cazaly. In 1935, the same publication received a letter from a reader who'd worked during the 1920s at Vickers' Shipbuilding Company in Barrow-in-Furness, England: the phrase had been used, he reported, as a password by Australian colleagues, then taken up by the workforce in general, and the town as a whole. That same year, Cazaly himself told *The Sporting Globe* that he'd heard of it being said in India, where the locals had apparently picked it up from visiting Australian horse-breakers. A 1936 story in South Melbourne's local newspaper, *The Emerald Hill Record*, reported hearing it in a Queensland shearing shed.

More sensationally, in April 1937 both *The Age* and *The Argus* covered a cockatoo which had learned the phrase. *The Age*'s story suggested that the bird had learned it organically while nesting near Albert Park, while *The Argus*, a day later but with a photo, gave the feathery squawker's age as five months, implying a measure of domestic supervision – and, therefore, human tuition. Neither newspaper got the creature's name: an inexcusable dereliction that, in a properly old-school newsroom, would have seen the reporter in question fleeing for the door beneath a barrage of teacups.

In 1944, Hyde Park in London echoed to the exclamation of 'Up there, Cazaly!', as two XVIIIs drawn from the Royal Australian Air Force

---

4   Roy Cazaly, an extraordinarily durable athlete, was 48 when he played for the last time, for Camberwell against Sandringham in the VFA. He also coached Hawthorn for two seasons, in 1942 and 1943. The principal legacy of this otherwise uninspired stint is Hawthorn's nickname, which was changed, at Cazaly's insistence, from the hilariously unintimidating 'Mayblooms' to the more satisfyingly predatory 'Hawks'.

played a scratch match of Australian football before a crowd of bewildered Allied airmen. Their comrades in khaki in North Africa bellowed it as a battle cry, and employed it as a wry greeting. It also jumped armies: Chester Wilmot, the ABC war correspondent whose father, Reg, covered football for *The Argus* as 'Old Boy', heard it yelped by Scottish anti-aircraft gunners defending besieged Tobruk. The phrase also appeared, in a context which suggested common understanding, in Ray Lawler's 1955 play *Summer of the Seventeenth Doll*.

Roy Cazaly died in 1963, aged 70, having spent his post-football years mostly in Tasmania, coaching, breeding trotting horses (he won the inaugural Tasmanian Trotting Championship in 1956), exploring often eccentric and/or remarkably progressive ideas about diet and movement, and opening a fitness centre in Hobart with his son, Roy Cazaly Jr.[5] Cazaly also stood, unsuccessfully, as a Liberal candidate for Tasmania's House of Assembly in 1950; the campaign slogan should have taken care of itself.

The phrase 'Up there, Cazaly!' continued to embed itself in the colloquial lexicon: a 1967 article in *The Australian Women's Weekly* referred to it passing 'from Australian Rules into the idiom', and pondered that 'people might well find that one a little hard to account for in a couple of thousand years' time'. In 1973, the *Truth* newspaper launched its own regime of footballing awards. Taking a cue from the Logie Awards, which acknowledged television stars with gongs named for a pioneer of that medium, *Truth* called its prizes the Cazalys. A silver Cazaly was presented to the year's best player in each position, and to the player in each team voted most popular by their supporters; the Gold Cazaly honoured the best player in the League. The trophies were statuettes of Cazaly, airborne in the ruck, frozen in Perspex.[6]

In 1979, Channel Seven went looking for a jingle to promote its coverage of the VFL. Earlier that year, World Series Cricket had scored

---

5   Roy Cazaly Jr won the Distinguished Service Medal for his actions as an anti-aircraft gunner aboard HMAS *Shropshire* during the Lingayen Gulf campaign of World War II; he may have saved the ship when he brought down a Japanese kamikaze in January 1945. He played for New Town in the Tasmanian Football League after the war, under the coaching of his father.

6   The Cazaly Awards ran until 1981, by which time the Gold Cazaly was accompanied by a cash prize of $6000. The Gold Cazaly was won twice each by Kevin Bartlett, Leigh Matthews and Gary Dempsey, and once each – there were two ties – by John 'Sam' Newman, Graham Moss, Garry Wilson, Kelvin Templeton and Rod Ashman. The Cazaly Awards were broadcast on Channel Nine, which laid on a production which may be credited/blamed as inspiration for the interminable circus now attending the presentation of the Brownlow Medal. The Cazalys' other ambiguous legacy was the inadvertent launch of Newman's broadcasting career, after he was deputised at one ceremony to stand in as a presenter for Jack Dyer, who had been waylaid by a car accident.

a number-one hit with the theme 'C'mon Aussie C'mon', an oafish bray composed by Alan Morris and Allan Johnston of the Mojo advertising agency, also responsible for such obstinate plagues as Meadow Lea's 'You Oughta Be Congratulated' and Tooheys' 'How Do You Feel?'.[7] The VFL commissioned Mike Brady to come up with something similar for the football.

Brady had been famous-ish, briefly, in the 1960s, as part of MPD Ltd, a punchy beat group who were approximate sonic kin – and touring partners – of The Easybeats, before flaming rancorously out. Since then, Brady had applied his knack for a catchy chorus to advertising; the song he delivered to the VFL, which was released under the name The Two-Man Band, swiftly beguiled hundreds of thousands, many of whom were hearing Cazaly's name for the first time.[8] 'Up There Cazaly' became 1979's biggest-selling single by an Australian artist. The second-biggest, indicative of the grip sport exercises on the Australian imagination, and/or the philistine tastes of the period, was 'C'mon Aussie C'mon'.

Brady's 'Up There Cazaly' was both boilerplate populist sentimentality and audacious pop masterpiece. It became so familiar so quickly that few noticed what a strange record it was. The verses glided on a breezy arrangement of almost-muzak piano and organ, evocative of an early 1970s Billy Sherrill or Al De Lory production for some Nudie-suited Nashville balladeer. The chorus, cued by fusillades of timpani, was an exultant, soaring paean, lifted above the prosaic chant it might have become by a preposterous key change from D major to F major – approximately the musical equivalent of changing from first gear straight into fifth, and somehow executed by Brady without causing the engine to vault through the bonnet.

It was the video that really made it, though. Illustrating 'Up There Cazaly' with archive footage of high marks was the first (and only) thought that anybody should (or could) have had, but two brilliant subsidiary decisions were made: to run them in slow motion, emphasising the balletic graces of the game at its best, and (though this may have been necessitated by the fact that colour TV had only arrived in Australia four years previously) to include vintage black-and-white clips, which lent 'Up

---

7   Mojo was later responsible for Paul Hogan's offer, in the name of promoting Australian tourism, to 'slip another shrimp on the barbie for you', despite the fact that shrimps are called prawns, and only a barbarian would barbecue them.

8   The author recalls his parents, both born in Australia in the mid-1940s, being perplexed by the expression.

There Cazaly' a spurious but persuasive historical anchoring, as if this was a song we had always sung (which, in a way, it was). Along with football's beauty, the clip also admitted its terror,[9] with merciless, funereally paced studies of Carlton's Alex Jesaulenko being ironed flat by Collingwood's Stan Magro,[10] and Carlton's Mike Fitzpatrick getting an ear warmed by St Kilda's Jeff Sarau,[11] among other transgressions.

Brady, not one to abandon a winning formula, wrote further songs about football, though with incrementally diminishing returns. In 1981, 'One Day in September' featured another slow-mo highlight-reel video, and troubled itself so little to distinguish itself from 'Up There Cazaly' that the chorus thereof was actually quoted in the coda. In 1982, 'There's a Little Bit of Cazaly in Us All' retrod the familiar theme and melody – the verses chronicled the workday grind of the football fan, the singalong choruses rejoiced in the redemption of an afternoon at the game, and the original 'Up There Cazaly' riff was evoked by a brass part buried beneath the bluster. 'Up There Cazaly' would itself be rewritten by Brady several times: as a Sydney Swans anthem ('Up There for Sydney'), as an England World Cup song ('Up There Old England')[12] and – catching up with the legend of its use as a battle cry – as an elegy to Australian troops serving overseas in early 21st-century campaigns in Afghanistan and Iraq ('Up There Australia').

Brady also released an astounding concept album, *The Songs of Football's Greatest Sons*, each of its 13 tracks a ballad in honour of a different player. Highlights included 'Those Cold Blue Eyes', a leaden blues for John Nicholls, not a million miles from early Bad Seeds; 'The Infamous Captain Blood', a demented sea shanty warning of the foolishness of crossing Jack Dyer; 'Big Gun from the West', evoking the

9   Educated readers will have spotted the seamless allusion to Dorothea Mackellar's patriotic poem 'My Country'. These subtleties are wasted on the rest of you.

10   In 1979 this was adjudged a free kick against Magro, who later assessed that in the modern game it would have seen him suspended for five or six weeks. One further punishment was imposed that day at Princes Park: Magro was uninvited to the post-match drink-up traditionally hosted by the home team.

11   It's not possible to determine whether or not hitting Carlton players was more popular than usual in 1979, but they won the flag that year, losing only three games en route, so it's plausible.

12   Mike Brady was English by birth, and arrived in Australia as a child. The England World Cup version was recorded in 1982 by Cliff Portwood, an English soccer player – Preston North End, Port Vale, Grimsby Town, Portsmouth – who became a minor pop star in Australia in the 1970s, and a regular on Channel Seven's bizarre Saturday-night variety-and-harness-racing show *The Penthouse Club*. 'Up There Old England' featured backing vocals by surviving members of England's victorious 1966 World Cup squad; it was scuppered by a licensing issue at the time, but released for the 2010 World Cup – not that many people noticed, least of all Portwood, who had died earlier that year.

unlikely occurrence of Marty Robbins considering the impact of Polly Farmer's revolutionary use of handball upon the VFL; and 'It All Sounds Like Football to Me', a knees-up featuring a self-mocking cameo by Ted Whitten. Less gloriously, Brady's Full Moon Records underwrote the mercifully brief recording career of Mark 'Jacko' Jackson – two singles which reduced music critics to the same state of floundering bewilderment Jackson engendered in umpires, but neither of which was quite the worst record for which Full Moon was ever responsible; this was Joe Dolce's 'Shaddap You Face', which displaced 'Up There Cazaly' as the all-time biggest-selling Australian-produced single.

Roy Cazaly would have been remembered even without the catchphrase and song he inspired: one is not ennobled a Legend in the Australian Football Hall of Fame merely because one's surname rolls easily as an exhortation, or possesses a mellifluousness that sounds good in a chorus. As a player, Cazaly extended the possibilities of the game's defining visual motif, the high mark. He insisted that his training routine, of inhaling a deep breath as he leapt at a ball hanging from the roof of his shed, literally converted his lungs into balloons, and gave him a reach far beyond what should be expected of a man of under six feet; Cazaly was not tall for a ruckman, even by the standards of the 1920s (at 180 centimetres, Cazaly was barely three centimetres taller than 21st-century 'small forwards' Cyril Rioli and Brent Harvey).

Cazaly had played 99 games for St Kilda before today, and he'd play 98 more times for South. In that second half of his VFL career in particular, Cazaly made a name for himself. Half a century or so later, 16 years after his death, his name made him all over again, the exotic, melodic 'Cazaly' becoming Australian football's own irresistible equivalent of the Nabokovian three-step tongue-trip down the palate.

11

James Bennett Comes Home
St Kilda 13.11.89 Essendon 15.7.97
Junction Oval
ROUND 7, 1922

It was a few minutes shy of three-quarter time, and first-year half-forward Cyril Gambetta[1] had just marked and goaled for the home team when the uniformed army bugler marched onto the field. It would not be the last time that an interruption of play would prompt speculation about its effect on the result of a match, or even the course of a season. But if this particular intrusion did somehow deprive St Kilda of an upset win, few Saints fans would have begrudged it, in the circumstances. From the centre circle, the bugler sounded 'The Last Post'. Around the field, players stood to muddy, bedraggled attention. In the stands, flags were hauled to half-mast, and de-hatted heads bowed. In the sky above, four aircraft of the Royal Australian Air Force,[2] black crepe streamers trailing from their wings, flew in crucifix formation.

Outside the Junction Oval, the funeral procession of Lieutenant James Bennett paused on its journey from Queen's Hall in Parliament House,[3] where his body had lain in state, to St Kilda Cemetery. The

---

1 Cyril Gambetta played 129 times for St Kilda, mostly as a hardworking defender during a period in which defending for St Kilda was mostly hard work. Gambetta's success, especially his renown as a high mark, was all the more remarkable given a childhood attack of polio, which bequeathed him a distinctively skewiff running gait. His teammates honoured him, and the Australian tradition of affectionate abuse among friends, with the nickname 'Jazz Legs'.

2 The RAAF had officially acquired this nomenclature the previous August, but the memo seems not to have reached the newspapers of the day, whose coverage of events still used the earlier name, Australian Flying Corps. The aircraft were likely Airco DH.9As, a single-prop two-seater biplane bomber flown by Bennett's No. 1 Squadron, 29 of which had been presented to the RAAF by the British government in 1920.

3 This was at the time Australia's federal parliament, which did not move to Canberra until 1927, at which point the building was returned to Victoria's state government, which had since 1901 been bivouacing in the Royal Exhibition Building in Carlton.

cortege was led by an array of braid-embaubled military aristocracy, including generals Sir Harry Chauvel[4] and Sir Brudenell White, and representatives of every tier of Australia's government: 45 cars had followed the aeroplane trailer bearing Bennett's flag-draped coffin, and crowds of thousands lined the route, four and five deep along Bourke and Swanston streets. Bennett was a national hero – possessed, as Prime Minister Billy Hughes declared, of 'those qualities of daring and courage which we know to be symbolic of the Australian nation' – but he was also a son of St Kilda, born in the suburb just over 28 years previously, and thereafter loyal to its football team.

Bennett had been killed on 13 April at the Brooklands aerodrome in England, along with the World War I ace and pioneer aviator Sir Ross Smith,[5] when the Vickers Viking amphibian biplane they were testing crashed shortly after take-off. Bennett had previously flown as a mechanic with Smith and his older brother, Sir Keith Smith,[6] when the pair became, in 1919, the first pilots to fly from England to Australia, spending 135 hours airborne in a Vickers Vimy biplane bomber over 28 days between London and Darwin, stopping in Lyon, Rome, Crete, Cairo, Damascus, Ramadi, Basra, Karachi, Delhi, Allahabad, Calcutta, Rangoon, Bangkok, Singora, Singapore, Surabaya and Atambua. The feat had made them superstars. While they'd been en route, indeed, one Melbourne couple had been moved to name their newborn son after the Smith brothers: Keith Ross Miller would later render sterling service to the St Kilda Football Club, the Australian cricket team and the RAAF.

The Smith brothers were more egalitarian than the mores of the time: they'd split the £10,000 prize which had been offered by the Australian government for an England–Australia flight evenly between themselves, Bennett and the crew's other mechanic, Wally Shiers.[7] Officialdom, however, favoured the Smiths, both officers, with knighthoods, while Bennett and Shiers, then both sergeants, received bars to the Air Force

4 General Sir Henry 'Harry' Chauvel, a veteran of the Boer War and Gallipoli, owed most of his considerable fame to his exploits commanding the Desert Mounted Corps in Sinai and Palestine later in World War I. He was among those who regarded sport and war as somewhat interchangeable, remarking in 1919 that the discipline necessary to win battles was 'the same discipline as that which wins cricket and football matches'.

5 Ross Smith served at Gallipoli as a sergeant in Chauvel's 1st Australian Light Horse Brigade, and elsewhere in the Middle East, before joining the fledgling Australian Flying Corps in 1917. By the end of the war, he'd won the Distinguished Flying Cross three times, and the Military Cross twice.

6 Keith Smith never saw active service, initially rejected by the AIF on medical grounds, before paying his own way to the war and becoming a gunnery instructor in the Royal Flying Corps.

7 Five other crews accepted the challenge. Four crashed, two with fatal consequences, while the other made it to Darwin after 237 days.

Medals previously awarded for similar work on the Smiths' 1918 flight between Cairo and Calcutta.

Inside the Junction Oval, *The Argus*'s correspondent at the match estimated the stillness and silence in Bennett's honour at not less than ten minutes: there can have been fewer more complete arrests of a team's momentum in the game's history. Bennett, a Saints barracker all his short life, would have been familiar with his club's tradition of baroque bad luck. He now became part of it. Gambetta's goal had followed one by St Kilda's Horrie Mason, and had brought the Saints within a kick of an unlikely lead – Essendon had arrived at the Junction unbeaten League leaders, while St Kilda had scraped together two modest wins for the year. When play resumed following the solemnities for Bennett, Essendon's Tommy Jenkins scored to give Essendon an eight-point lead, which St Kilda weren't quite able to overhaul.

Even by 1922, Saints barrackers were used to treasuring what meagre glimmering flakes of optimism they could pan from an unrelenting sludge of disappointment. St Kilda's 25 years in the League to date had left the trophy cabinet barren but for ten wooden spoons. The most recent had been seized in a two-win season in 1920, and they'd have repeated the feat in 1921 if not for a last-round, last-ditch, two-point win over Essendon, sealed with a goal two minutes from time by Bill Cubbins, widely reckoned one of the greatest full-backs of his era. (St Kilda had become, if inadvertently, a rigorous academy of the defensive arts, much as Hell could serve as a school for firefighters.)

Against Essendon today, the Saints' stoic fans might have perceived a chimera of salvation wearing the number 2 jumper – a new arrival from Western Australia, where he'd earned good notices with South Fremantle. Wal Gunnyon was in fact undertaking a homecoming: though he'd been raised in the west, he was a native of Stawell in western Victoria. A travelling salesman by trade, Gunnyon had moved to Melbourne for professional reasons. His footballing career, like many others, had been interrupted by the war – in his case, service with the AIF's Siege Artillery Brigade on the Western Front, where he'd been wounded four times (five, if one counts the substantially self-inflicted injury of syphilis).[8]

---

8   Gunnyon was far from alone in this ignominy. More than 60,000 men of the AIF – nearly one soldier in seven – were treated for, and/or discharged because of, venereal diseases during World War I. Some, embarrassed, re-enlisted under false identities after being returned to Australia. One, Maurice Buckley, deserted from the infamous VD hospital at Langwarrin and re-enlisted as Gerald Sexton, under which nom de guerre he won the Distinguished Conduct Medal and the Victoria Cross in France.

Gunnyon had debuted the week before, and been unspectacular in an unspectacular game. Moved to half-forward against Essendon, he took charge after a typically disorganised opening quarter left the Saints goalless at the first break. ('Of course,' sighed *The Australasian*, 'a team that commits such extraordinary blunders must pay the penalty, though strangely [St Kilda] never seem to learn anything by their mistakes.') Though there remained doubt as to whether St Kilda's most formidable opponents on the day were Essendon or St Kilda themselves, the Saints swashbuckled back into contention, despite having effectively lost the services, early on, of Harry Moyes,[9] their club's leading goalkicker of 1921, who was hit hard and late by Essendon's Ken Adam. (Substitutes were not introduced into the VFL until 1930, so injured players were often left on the field as long as they could stand unaided.) Essendon's more creative players were also contributing, notably a jockey-sized rookie called Jack Moriarty, who kicked two goals.[10]

In the last quarter, St Kilda edged within a point, aided by Gunnyon's fourth goal, from better than 60 yards, and a fifth from comparable range. The home fans, who should have known better by now, had struck up a hearty chant of 'Goodbye, Essendon' when Jack Garden – a nippy winger who would be one of the Same Olds' 'mosquito fleet' that would win them the 1923 flag – swooped from a wing to score, followed by another Essendon goal from Tommy Jenkins. Gunnyon got his sixth before the bell, but it wasn't enough, and St Kilda failed by eight points to win one for Lieutenant Bennett.

Australian football has become accustomed, in the decades since, to serving as a forum for public grief in times of collective loss: the 60 seconds of solemn silence around the centre circle before the bounce, the taut black armband taped around a brawny bicep. On rare occasions, play has stopped entirely. In 1910, Round 2 was postponed when news of

---

9   Harry Moyes was a twice-wounded veteran of the Western Front, and also played in the famous 1916 exhibition match in London. He later transferred to Melbourne, kicking three goals in the club's 1926 grand final victory.

10 Though Jack Moriarty led Essendon's goalkicking in 1922, he couldn't get a game in 1923, and in 1924 was allowed a move to Fitzroy, where his father, Geoff, had played in two premierships. This ranks as one of the most calamitous such blunders in football history – at least among clubs other than Richmond, whose consistent genius for transfer misjudgement is an unfair measure. Moriarty scored 21 goals in his first three games for the Maroons, led the League's goalkicking that season with a then-record 82, and Fitzroy's goalkicking nine times. In 1925, Moriarty was the target of a bizarre attempt to nobble him before a match against Carlton, when someone – an enterprising Blues fan, and/or someone with a few bob on the result – offered him chewing gum which turned out to be poisoned. Moriarty still kicked four goals – three of them in the first quarter, before whatever toxin properly kicked in – and Fitzroy still won.

the death of King Edward VII reached Melbourne. (The grim tidings did not make it as far as Arden Street, where North Melbourne were meeting Footscray in a VFA match, until 3000 people had already paid sixpence each to get in; after anguished discussion, the game was abandoned, and the takings donated to charity.) In 1997, a qualifying final between Adelaide and West Coast was delayed to avoid clashing with television coverage of the funeral of Diana, Princess of Wales. In 2015, Adelaide's game with Geelong was cancelled, and the points split, following the murder of the Crows' coach, Phil Walsh.

As is the case with all team sports, the rivalries underpinning Australian football are glorious only as long as everyone understands, somewhere beneath the spleen and spittle, that none of it really matters – that there's a reason why there's a white line around the playing surface, and a fence around the line, and a gate between the ground and the real world outside. On the day they laid James Bennett down, there were silences, too, at Princes Park, Victoria Park and the Lake Oval. 'These little acts of courtesy,' *The Australasian* had it, 'which mean so much to the relatives of the dead hero, and to the sentiment of the nation, make one optimistic of the future of the race.'

12

Fred Rutley Gets Life
North Melbourne 9.5.59 Geelong 22.22.154
Arden Street
ROUND 12, 1925

In their first season in the VFL, North Melbourne were half a century from their first premiership. Just 12 weeks into their debut campaign, however, North achieved something: participation in what was, in the estimation of 'Old Boy' in *The Argus*, 'the worst game for years' – and, not coincidentally, the longest suspension ever imposed on a player for on-field misdemeanours. He was Fred Rutley, a 23-year-old rover who would be banned forever for his contribution to the day's infamies. By the time his sentence was commuted five years later, he had sat out 89 games, a stretch exceeded only by the banishments of Carltonian bung-takers Doug Fraser and Alex Lang.

The Cats[1] arrived at Arden Street comfortable League leaders, having lost once all year, and that as far back as the opening round, but North had some grounds for optimism. Though they'd only won three games, one had been Geelong's first-week aberration, at Corio, where North had won by eight points, the game sealed with a goal by colossal ruckman Johnny Lewis. (Jack Dyer, for one, reckoned Lewis the best player North had ever produced; 'even with four top-class ruckmen,' he said, 'you could never be sure Lewis wouldn't beat the lot.') And North were at peak strength – having been unlucky with injuries all season, this was the first time they'd had a full squad to choose from.

---

1   Geelong had taken this nickname a couple of years earlier, after a run of poor results prompted *Herald* cartoonist Sam Wells to sketch captain Bert Rankin carrying a black cat. Geelong beat Carlton in their next game, prompting Rankin to suggest the club adopt the mascot permanently. The general relief at finally ditching the 'Pivotonians' monstrosity can only be wondered at.

Geelong had racked up ten straight victories since losing to North, and were further buoyed by the previous weekend's heroics by captain-coach Cliff Rankin,[2] representing Victoria against Western Australia at the MCG. He'd starred in an 85-point demolition of the Sandgropers; although Western Australia were described by *The Argus* as 'too bad to be true', you can only beat what's in front of you, and word was that the match ball which Rankin had hoofed ten times between the big sticks was to be affixed with a silver plate and presented to him in honour of the accomplishment.[3]

At Arden Street, the first quarter went as form predicted, and might have done more so had Geelong kicked straighter – they led 4.8 to 3.0 at the first break, North's backs struggling to contain Geelong's high-flying full-forward Lloyd Hagger,[4] on his way to becoming the League's leading goalkicker for the year, with 70 in the home-and-away rounds. It had been nasty and niggly, though. 'Old Boy' in *The Argus* had written of pre-game rumours of various scores to be settled – and, as usual, 'Old Boy' was well informed. Geelong's Eric Fleming had received a letter, signed 'Geelong Supporter', warning him that North would be gunning for him, and Geelong club secretary Ivan More had been sent something similar, a correspondent identifying themselves as 'Well-wisher' claiming: 'While viewing the Interstate match on Saturday last I happened to mention Eric Fleming's name, and a prominent North Melbourne player said "Don't worry about your Fleming. He won't be playing after Saturday next. We'll see to that."'

By the second quarter, this reckoning appeared to be underway, abetted by the laxity of umpire Bob Scott, who either failed to instate order or hoped the players would get the mayhem out of their systems organically. 'When attempting to stop that roughness later,' rued *The Age*, beneath the headline 'A Brutal Exhibition', '[Scott] found the players were so far out of hand that the task was well nigh impossible.' 'Players frequently went sprawling on the ground,' deplored *The Geelong Advertiser*, 'and there were cases where, upon arising, the men were

---

2 Cliff Rankin was the brother of Bert Rankin, and son of Teddy Rankin, who had been a mainstay of Geelong in the VFA/VFL crossover years; several other Rankins also played for the club. Cliff and Bert were an uncompromisingly solid fraternal pairing. In 1923, Cliff refused to play in a semi-final after Bert was dropped from the team – and Geelong were beaten by Fitzroy.

3 At least one of Cliff Rankin's vanquished opponents from the west could still snort dismissively at his ten-goal bag: East Perth's Hugh 'Bonny' Campbell only managed four against the Vics that day, but at the previous year's Australian National Football Carnival in Hobart he'd kicked 23 goals for Western Australia against Queensland, in a 264-point flogging which surely couldn't have been much worse if Queensland had gone home, or even actively collaborated with their opposition.

4 Lloyd Hagger also had artistic tendencies: he created a cat motif to be turned into a lapel badge for Geelong's players. The silhouette feline profile logo that Geelong began wearing on their guernseys in 2008 was based on the design.

too groggy to make anything like ordinary use of a free kick.' Players were tripped, punched and hacked. Even before the margin blew out in Geelong's favour, a high-minded cohort of the crowd were observed leaving, aghast at the unfolding barbarity.

Unpleasantries erupted properly shortly before half-time, when Geelong ruckman Arthur 'Bull' Coghlan was felled by a piece of concrete hurled from the grandstand, which struck him on one leg. This may have been a reaction to an earlier incident in which Coghlan had clouted North's Harold Johnston in a marking contest – *The Argus* drily suggested that the launch of the projectile was 'not resented by bystanders' – but so furious were Geelong's committee with North's lackadaisy in seeking the culprit that they refused to attend the traditional half-time tea.

Ill will dominated the second half, which grew more acrimonious as Geelong booted nine goals to two in the third quarter to extend their half-time lead from a reachable 16 points to an insuperable 62. Steering virtuously clear of trouble, as befitted the VFL's first reigning Brownlow medallist, was Geelong centre Edward 'Carji' Greeves.[5] The final change was marred by a melee also involving officials from both teams, and in the last quarter Cliff Rankin was knocked cold and stretchered off. The umpires reported six players – four from North, two from Geelong – and the tribunal braced itself for a long Thursday night.

It was past one in the morning before proceedings adjourned. Geelong's representative, Jim d'Helin, did his best to disrupt things, seeking to introduce the warning letters the club had received, and accusing the umpires of comparing notes before testifying. It was, he said, no doubt tucking his thumbs portentously into his lapels, his duty, no less, to bring out the 'dirt and filth' that had befouled the game.

D'Helin had misjudged his audience. Both Geelong defendants, Arthur Coghlan and Stan 'Dasher' Thomas, were adjudged guilty of elbows and fisticuffs, and suspended for the remainder of the 1925 season, and all of 1926. Coghlan would eventually return for six more seasons, and do two stints as Geelong coach. Thomas never played in the VFL again.

Rutley aside, North's miscreants had the book hurled at them with slightly lesser velocity. Bill Russ was suspended for the rest of the season for punching Rankin in the face. Rankin did his best to get Russ off the hook, muttering about a slight blow on the back of the neck – couldn't say from

---

5   Without much extra luck, Carji Greeves might have won the first five Brownlow medals: he was runner-up in 1925, 1926 and 1928, and equal third in 1927.

whom, etc. – but the tribunal were clearly sceptical of the traditional players' *omertà*. Tim Trevaskis got three weeks for striking Les Smith, and Harold Johnston escaped with a telling off after a charge of attempting to kick Stan Thomas was unsustained, despite Johnston's audacious gambit of informing the tribunal that the charge was 'below my dignity' and 'frivolous'.

As for Rutley, he hadn't had a bad game – he'd bagged three of North's nine goals. But an example had to be made of someone; it had been a rotten day for the VFL, with violence erupting among the crowd as well. At least one Geelong supporter, 20-year-old William Evans of 200 Verner Street, was admitted to hospital upon his return to town, for treatment for the battering he'd sustained from a larrikin mob of Shinboners barrackers.[6]

Rutley was an ideal scapegoat – not that well known, and accused of multiple charges of kicking, always a crime regarded as more contemptible than honest, old-fashioned thumping. Certainly, Geelong's Syd Hall and Eric Fleming did not feel compelled to observe the code of silence entirely strictly: while affecting vagueness as to the precise identity of the owner of the boot, both confirmed that the kicks aimed in their direction had connected. Rutley did not defend or explain himself, and confusion lingers as to whether he pleaded guilty (as reported in *The Geelong Advertiser*) or not (as reported in *The Age*). It probably wouldn't have mattered. Tribunal chairman and VFL president Sir Walter Baldwin Spencer[7] thundered: 'The tribunal is of the opinion that this is one of the most serious and worst cases that has ever come before it.' Rutley was disqualified for life.

The suspensions of Coghlan and Thomas caused uproar in Geelong: 500 people attended a protest meeting at His Majesty's Theatre called by local MP John Lister.[8] In the event, Geelong were unhampered by the

---

6   The olde-worlde North nickname 'Shinboners' derives either from the butchery trade that once flourished in the district, or from a predilection among early North Melbourne teams for hacking their opponents, as Fred Rutley was accused of doing.

7   Sir Walter Baldwin Spencer was a distinguished English-born anthropologist and biologist, who did pioneering work among Indigenous Australians in the early 20th century; it could be fairly said that his paternalistic conclusions were much as might be expected from a man of his background, time and moustache. He was a noted aficionado of Australian art, patronising – in the good way – Streeton, Heysen, Lambert and Lindsay, among others. When he passed judgement upon Fred Rutley, he had overcome a long struggle with drink, and was about to return to London to pursue a romance with a librarian 30 years his junior. He died in 1929, aged 69, on Navarino Island, Chile, while on an expedition, accompanied by his lover, to meet the Yaghan people of the vicinity of Tierra del Fuego.

8   John Lister had been a driver with the 2nd Light Horse Field Ambulance at Gallipoli, before being discharged as medically unfit with pneumonia and pleurisy. He had been one of those who heeded the call of then prime minister Billy Hughes – 'Let those who think like me follow me' – and deserted Labor due to the party's lack of enthusiasm for conscription. Representing Hughes' new Nationalist party, Lister won Corio from Labor in 1917.

losses – they won their first VFL premiership later that year, overcoming Collingwood in a close grand final thanks to five goals by a clearly recovered Cliff Rankin. But the suspended Coghlan and Thomas were defiantly invited to all the consequent celebrations, including a reception at City Hall, a team excursion to Jenolan Caves near Sydney, and a curious ceremony at Corio Oval. The plan had been to bury a dead magpie beneath the turf, but due to squeamishness, or a sense among the local magpie population that it would be a good day to be out of town, no such bird could be located. To the rescue came Ern Copeland, former Collingwood secretary,[9] part of a delegation down from Melbourne to participate, sportingly, in Geelong's premiership revelries; *The Geelong Advertiser* reported, implausibly, that the visitors claimed to be 'almost as pleased as if Collingwood had annexed the premiership'. Copeland lent Geelong a gold ring engraved with a magpie, which was interred with due solemnity.[10]

For Geelong, 1925 was quite a year. Aside from the club's first VFL premiership, Ford had selected the town for its Australian headquarters, and started building Model Ts in the disused Dalgety & Co woolstore on Gheringhap Street. Ford also began an association with the local football club which remains the longest continuously existing such sponsorship arrangement anywhere in the world. Henry Ford's efforts to have at least a portion of Geelong declared an alcohol-free dry area were rather shorter-lived.

Fred Rutley's suspension was commuted in 1930 – at the urging of Geelong secretary Ivan More, who persuaded the VFL towards mercy on the grounds that 'the ends of justice had been served'. Rutley would play four more games for North in the VFL, bringing his total to 11. He died in 1947, aged 44, after a long illness. In 1946, when North Melbourne announced a fundraising drive for him, newspaper reports noted that he had already been in hospital for four years, a man unduly punished in more ways than one.

---

9   Collingwood's best-and-fairest award, the Copeland Trophy, is named in Ern Copeland's honour.
10 This inaugurated a tradition whereby Geelong celebrated premierships by interring a representation of their defeated grand final opponent's mascot at their home ground: a cuddly toy tiger in 1931, a dead magpie in 1937, a toy bomber in 1951, another dead magpie in 1952, a hawk figurine in 1963. The ritual was not resurrected when Geelong beat Port Adelaide to win the 2007 premiership: a shame, as Geelong could have buried a bottle of port, or some avatar of 'power', or – ideally – whichever idiot thought 'the Power' was a good name for a football team in the first place. Ern Copeland's ring was returned to him in due course.

13

Bob Pratt Gets Hit by a Truck
South Melbourne 15.14.104 Collingwood 11.17.83
Melbourne Cricket Ground
SEMI-FINAL, 1935

The mood in South Melbourne's dressing-room afterwards can be estimated as exhausted relief. They had beaten their likeliest rivals for the 1935 premiership. They had booked passage to a grand final two weeks hence. They expected to face Collingwood again in the decider, but would have derived considerable succour from the fact that, while they now had a week off, Collingwood had to prepare for a preliminary final against a rested Richmond, who in the other semi-final, a week earlier, had surprised Carlton with free running and aggressive leading, scoring seven goals to two in the first quarter, and never looking troubled thereafter.

Most pleasingly for South, full-forward Bob Pratt looked in good touch: he'd kicked six goals, a slightly better than average afternoon's work, for him, and was uninjured. Pratt's 1935 season had been somewhat less prodigious than his 1934, in which he'd scored 150 goals,[1] but he was, for the second year running, the VFL's leading goalkicker. The third goal he'd kicked this afternoon was his 100th for the season, and while South Melbourne were obviously a good team, few disputed that Pratt was what made them potentially great. In his preview of today's game for *The Argus*, Ivor Warne-Smith[2] conceded the strength of the other components of

---

1   Wonderfully, Pratt did not win South Melbourne's best-and-fairest trophy in 1934, which was given instead to Terry Brain. When Pratt asked the committee to explain themselves, he was told, 'You're very spectacular, but not very effective' and 'You've won a lot – you can't get everything.' Pratt never won the award; there really is no pleasing some people.

2   Ivor Warne-Smith, formerly of Melbourne, had retired from football three seasons earlier, as the game's first dual Brownlow medallist. He was also a veteran of Gallipoli – he'd lied about his age to enlist at the age of 17 – and had been wounded and gassed in France; two brothers, Waldo and Spencer, were killed in World War I. Warne-Smith also served in Papua New Guinea during World

South's attack – Roy Moore and Austin Robertson – but still believed that 'if [Jack] Regan can subdue Pratt, Collingwood has nothing to fear from South's forward line'.

Jack Regan wasn't beaten often: Dick Reynolds described him as the best full-back he'd ever seen.[3] But Regan was beaten today. When he retired in 1942, he named Pratt as his most difficult opponent, citing his 'brilliant marking', 'fine kicking' and even 'his determined ground play – when beaten for a mark, he would dash for the ball like a terrier'. An echoing assessment of Pratt's completeness as a full-forward, nonetheless persuasive for its partiality, was offered in the mid-1990s by Pratt's wife, Olive, who told an interviewer that her husband 'led like Dunstall, marked like Ablett, kicked like Lockett, and best of all, looked like Modra'.

There was little doubt who'd been the difference in this semi-final. It had been an ugly scrap on a field sodden by violent thunderstorms: sawdust had been scattered on the most viscous bogs. The report in *The Australasian* said that South 'are just an ordinary good combination, no better than any of the other aspirants to fame, but for the fact that in Pratt they have a match-winner. On his day he is worth at least five goals to a side.' Pratt – and South Melbourne – started slowly, but improved as the ground dried. Collingwood expended a lot of energy early, and kicked poorly as the game went on. Aside from their 17 behinds, 12 shots at goal missed everything. Even the great Gordon Coventry, as Collingwood scrabbled to stay in touch during the third quarter, failed from point-blank range.

But today's work was satisfactorily done. South Melbourne would play their third grand final in three years. This was a team assembled with greatness in mind – the so-called 'foreign legion', recruited from all over Australia, including the mercurial Tasmanian Laurie Nash and so many players from Western Australia that *The Sporting Globe*'s Hec de Lacy joshingly suggested that South should adopt the state's emblem, the swan. This all-star team was a combination of the vision of club president Jack

---

War II, and was Melbourne's chairman of selectors when the Demons won four flags in the late 1950s. His Brownlow medals were stolen from his Ivanhoe home in 1951, and have never been recovered.

3   This was in 1942, when Jack Regan quit to join a Salesian community at Sunbury as a lay brother, telling the committee: 'While I have my regrets in severing my connection with football, I feel that I am doing something much better.' He returned to captain the side in 1943, however, and again briefly – following service in the RAAF – in 1946. The Jack Regan Trophy is now awarded annually to the player finishing fifth in Collingwood's best-and-fairest count.

Rohan, and the money of vice-president Archibald Crofts, who tempted likely-looking players with jobs at the chain of grocery stores which bore his name.[4] Led by captain-coach Jack Bissett, South were the VFL's glamour side.

The foreign legion's first date with destiny had gone well: in the 1933 grand final they had smothered and smited Richmond, 9.17.71 to 4.5.29. The following year's grand final featured the same two teams, and a very different result: with Pratt held to just two goals, Richmond cantered to a ten-goal lead by three-quarter time and won it easing up, amid mayhem as South realised that the game had gotten beyond them. South's vice-captain, Peter Reville, took the 1934 disappointment especially badly. Having already declared his intention to retire, Reville plumped for the blaze-of-glory option: he king-hit Richmond's Bert Taylor, broke the nose of Kevin O'Neill, and was repeatedly observed charging elbow-first or knee-first into packs. He was suspended for the entirety of 1935, for all that he would have cared.[5]

There would be further fisticuffs in South Melbourne's dressing-rooms after the 1934 grand final, as players accused each other of having taken a dive. Many years later Pratt would claim he had declined a bung of £100 to play dead, as part of a sting orchestrated by Melbourne gangster Joseph Leslie 'Squizzy' Taylor; whatever one believes about Pratt's story of a bribe, it cannot have been Taylor who offered it. He had been fatally wounded eight years previously in a gunfight with rival John 'Snowy' Cutmore in a Carlton boarding house.[6]

As the 1935 grand final loomed, things looked better for South. They believed they had Collingwood's measure, given the result of the semi-final, but the Magpies had also suffered some potentially helpful injuries as they'd seen off Richmond in the preliminary. Collingwood would be without two regular ruckmen for the grand final – Jack Knight was

---

4   In 1935, Archibald Crofts was elected to Victoria's Legislative Council as the member for Melbourne South.

5   *The Emerald Hill Record* mourned Peter Reville's announcement in verse, lines by local poet Harry Paull including 'No more the joyous impulse to come bursting through the ruck/With socks around his ankles and his heart aflame with pluck' and 'Honour from all to Peter; he has proved himself the peer/Of Burns, Cazaly, Franks and Sloss, those giants to memory dear'. Reville went on to captain-coach Coburg in the VFA. He returned to the VFL in 1938, for a couple of seasons with Fitzroy.

6   Persistent legend, encouraged by Frank Hardy's *Power Without Glory* and the attendant libel case, holds that Squizzy Taylor was set up for his final showdown by John Wren, the archetype of the 'colourful turf identity', and ardent Collingwood barracker and patron, whose horses raced beneath jockeys wearing black and white silks. Wren died in 1953, of a heart attack sustained in the delirious aftermath of Collingwood's grand final win over Geelong; an almost identical fate was suffered by Collingwood's greatest coach, Jock McHale.

out with a twisted ankle, Len Murphy[7] with a broken shoulder. South Melbourne had lost only once since Round 1, and although that had been to Collingwood, it had been away at Victoria Park, only by two points, and it seemed a long time ago.

Shortly after 2 p.m. on the Thursday before grand final Saturday, Bob Pratt was walking to board a tram on Prahran High Street when he was hit by a truck carrying bricks. The glancing blow shunted Pratt abruptly onto the footpath, leaving him with lacerations on both legs, and injuries to a thumb and an ankle. It could have been much worse, but there was little appetite for perspective in South territory. *The Emerald Hill Record* brooded that 'the initial attack on the inhabitants of Adowa by Mussolini's invading army could not have occasioned Emperor Haile Selassie a greater shock than that received by South Melbourne Football Club officials and players when they learned on Thursday afternoon, through the press, that Bob Pratt, the crack goalkicker, had been injured in a collision with a motor truck'.[8]

As late as grand final eve, South Melbourne's officialdom were still gripped by that delirious optimism with which our nervous systems inoculate us at moments of grief. That same counterintuitive insistence that the partner or employer who has tired of us will shortly realise the error of their ways could be diagnosed in club secretary Dick Mullaly, who hastened to Pratt's East Prahran home to assess the damage. 'Pratt had a wonderful escape,' Mulally beamed. 'He is not too bad, and he will probably be able to have a try-out on Saturday morning … the doctor examined him again this evening, and was hopeful that he would have recovered sufficiently to take his place in the side.' South's selectors, placing faith in the ministrations of club masseur Nat Powell, and a Friday appointment with a Collins Street specialist, named Pratt for the grand final. Hope, however, would prove an insufficient healer.

Collingwood captain Harry Collier would later tell the story of being accosted by a fan on Hoddle Street on the fateful Thursday, after Pratt's

---

7   Len Murphy, surely one of the most fantastically luckless players of all time, also missed Collingwood's 1936 grand final win through suspension, and was confined to the bench for the 1937 grand final loss to Geelong.

8   This reference to the Second Italo-Abyssinian War, which began that same week, while commendably erudite, was somewhat overplayed. The Ethiopian forces can scarcely have been as surprised by the Italian assault as South Melbourne were by Pratt's mishap. More than 700,000 Italian troops had been deployed in Eritrea and Somaliland over preceding months, and Ethiopian emperor Hailie Selassie had already announced a general mobilisation, concluding with the admonishment: 'Anyone found at home after the receipt of this order will be hanged.'

accident but before it had become public knowledge. Collier recalled that he was asked how he fancied the Magpies' chances, and replied: 'If Pratty wasn't in that bloody side, I think we'd win.'

As it happened, Pratt wasn't, and Collingwood did, recovering from a slow start to beat South by 20 points, almost exactly a reversal of the semi-final result two weeks previously, and a margin comfortably within Pratt's average return. Pratt was not the only key player South had to do without: they lost Jack Bisset shortly before three-quarter time with a fractured skull. *The Emerald Hill Record*, fair to the point of self-parody, would not hear a word against the Collingwood player who'd whacked South's captain-coach. 'We express the opinion,' the *Record* said, 'shared by several of Bisset's teammates, that the bump administered was one of the fairest and most powerful stops ever witnessed.' (At least one teammate demurred: South's Austin Robertson announced his retirement after the 1935 grand final, declaring that the game had become too rough.)[9]

As had happened a year previously, a myth would develop that the result of 1935's grand final had been contrived by creatures from the murky depths of Melbourne's underworld, and that the driver of the brick truck which collected Pratt had been acting under instruction. But no evidence was ever advanced that the collision was other than an accident. The driver was a (doubtless mortified) South Melbourne barracker, one C.L. Peters of Armadale, who sought to make amends later the same day by bringing Pratt a pack of cigarettes.

Nor does there seem to have been, following the 1935 decider, any repeat of the previous season's post–grand final enmity among South Melbourne's players. Despite the loss to Collingwood, and the ill fortune which had deprived them of their spearhead, several Swans players, clad in novelty hats and garlands of flowers, were observed clinging jovially to the running boards of a car careening down Collins Street, regaling passers-by with the club song; suspicious minds may have wondered

---

9   Austin 'Ocker' Robertson, a chemist by trade, later reconsidered, playing another two seasons. Robertson was also a noted sprinter – he missed the 1933 grand final because he was visiting the United States to try to organise a head-to-head showdown at the Chicago World's Fair with Eddie Tolan, who'd won Olympic gold in the 100 and 200 metres at Los Angeles in 1932. A US$1000 bet was proposed but the race never occurred, scuppered by arguments about whether Tolan would be compromising his amateur status. Robertson eventually raced Tolan in Melbourne in March 1935 for the World Professional Sprint Championship: Robertson won the 130-yard race, but Tolan beat him over 75, 100 and 220 yards. Robertson's son, Austin Robertson Jr, played briefly for South Melbourne in 1966, between two longer stints with Subiaco. He was eight times the WAFL's leading goalkicker, and at time of writing the leading goalkicker in WAFL history. Robertson Jr was later involved in Kerry Packer's establishment of World Series Cricket, and managed several prominent cricketers, including Dennis Lillee and Shane Warne.

whether this was behaviour less in keeping with crushing sporting disappointment than with the receipt of a gangster's largesse.

Collingwood's celebrations, which continued all weekend, peaked with Harry Collier driving his car through the fence of Raheen, the residence of Daniel Mannix, the Catholic archbishop of Melbourne. Mannix, though probably professionally obliged to forgive Collier anyway, was also a Collingwood barracker, and therefore unminded to press charges after the Magpies captain sheepishly presented himself at the police station in Kew to retrieve his front bumper.

14

Two Heroes
Fitzroy 16.9.105 St Kilda 19.15.129
Brunswick Street
ROUND 11, 1936

Matches like this get played every year: the mid-to-late-season encounter between two mediocre teams aware that thoughts of finals, if not delusional, are fanciful. They are matches played, as the vernacular has it, 'for pride', it apparently being some consolation that you're not quite as bad as the bad side you've beaten. These encounters are generally forgotten quickly: sometimes, indeed, while they're under way. Posterity generally only exhumes them if they are blighted by a crucial injury, or a noteworthy stoush, or distinguished by some statistically freakish individual performance. The 7000 or so people who set out towards Brunswick Street on this fine winter's day, afternoon sunshine scattering the morning fog, would have done so with little expectation of seeing anything likely to attract the attention of historiographers decades hence.

Fitzroy were having a dreadful season: they had won one game all year, and would only win one more before it was over. This was despite looking pretty handy, on paper. The Maroons[1] fielded arguably the greatest footballer of all time. Captain-coach Haydn Bunton looked like a hero from a Boys' Own annual, and by every account was like a hero from a Boys' Own annual. ('The embodiment,' purred *The Referee* in 1932, 'of all that is clean, clever and courageous in football.') Bunton had just turned 25 and

---

1 The following season, Fitzroy abandoned the 'Maroons' nickname in favour of the more belligerent 'Gorillas'. 'Freak names for football clubs have been increasing lately,' sniffed Percy Taylor in *The Argus*, 'but it is doubtful whether many will stick.' Taylor was correct in at least this instance – Fitzroy became the Lions in 1957.

was already a triple Brownlow medallist.[2] His teammates included dashing winger Wilfred 'Chicken' Smallhorn, who'd won the Brownlow in 1933, and unflappable centre half-back Denis 'Dinny' Ryan, who'd win it in 1936.

St Kilda weren't having quite as bad a season, certainly not by the standards they'd struggled to overcome since joining the VFL. The Saints had six wins from ten games, but were nevertheless eight points adrift of the final four, with matches against top teams South Melbourne and Richmond to come in the following fortnight. But they'd have been confident about today. Full-forward Bill Mohr[3] was in splendid fettle, en route to becoming the first Saint to kick 100 goals in a season, and Smallhorn was absent, injured, from Fitzroy's line-up.

The game itself went much as might have been anticipated: the home team started brightly, as underachieving home teams sometimes do, before the visitors' superiority eventually told. St Kilda were 20 points up at the half, then withstood a third-quarter rally by Fitzroy, before knocking in six goals in the final quarter to win by 24 points. Mohr contributed four, as did half-forward Alby Weiss.

Whatever aspects of the match the spectators might have contemplated as they left Brunswick Street, they couldn't have discussed the most – indeed, the only – interesting thing about it, as they couldn't have known. On the field had been two men whose lives would assume heroic proportions, beyond the boundaries of any football ground.

They'd have noticed Fitzroy winger Doug Nicholls, of course. Though in his fifth year with the club, and playing his 48th game today, Nicholls remained a novelty in terms of his colour, and his stature: the Yorta Yorta man from the Cummeragunja mission in New South Wales stood just 158 centimetres.[4] Nicholls was quick, though: in the late 1920s,

---

2   Haydn Bunton is one of four players to have won the Brownlow Medal three times, along with Ian Stewart, Dick Reynolds and Bob Skilton. However, in a subsequent stint at Subiaco, Bunton also won the West Australian equivalent, the Sandover Medal, three times. He was killed in a car accident near Gawler, South Australia, in 1955, aged 44. His son, Haydn Bunton Jr, toting a burden of expectation unmatched except perhaps by Ted Whitten Jr and Gary Ablett Jr, had a fine career in the SANFL and WANFL, winning the Sandover in 1962, and premierships as a player and/or coach with Swan Districts and Subiaco.

3   Bill Mohr was the inspiration for Sir Sidney Nolan's 1946 painting *Footballer*, although Nolan – a St Kilda barracker – depicted his player in red, gold and white hoops, not colours St Kilda ever wore. When the National Gallery of Victoria bought *Footballer* in 2002, premier Steve Bracks presented the painting to the NGV on *The Footy Show*. Later the same year, the NGV opened the Ian Potter Centre for Australian Art in Melbourne. At an open day before the exhibits were installed, *Footballer* was the only work displayed; thousands came to see it.

4   Doug Nicholls remains one of the smallest men to have played in the VFL/AFL. The record is held by Jim 'Nipper' Bradford, all 155 centimetres of him, who had brief spells at Collingwood and North Melbourne, between longer careers with Camberwell in the VFA, and West Torrens in the SANFL.

when he played for Northcote in the VFA – the only Aboriginal in that competition – he'd made some of his living as a professional sprinter, winning £130 a go for victories in the Warracknabeal and Nyah gift races in 1929, money worth having at a time when the average adult male wage was around £250 annually.

Nicholls was tough, as well: before joining Fitzroy, he'd spent time with Jimmy Sharman's boxing troupe, touring showgrounds in Victoria and New South Wales, taking on local champions and punters who fancied their chances. (A notice in *The Sporting Globe* in 1932, ahead of a Sharman engagement at the Wangaratta Carnival, described Nicholls as the 'great little aboriginal footballer-footrunner', every word of which was accurate in isolation, but which in combination sounded immensely patronising.)

Nicholls had first come to town at the invitation of Carlton in 1927, but left the club without playing a game: other players were unwilling to countenance an Aboriginal teammate, and claimed that Nicholls smelled bad,[5] though it is difficult to imagine many working men of the period being compared to a rose garden in spring in this regard. Nicholls went to Northcote instead, spending five seasons in the green and gold of the Dragons before Fitzroy came calling. Neither Nicholls' Aboriginality nor his ardent Christianity were issues at his new club: Fitzroy employed him as groundsman, and Haydn Bunton himself made a point of changing alongside Nicholls in the dressing-room, lest any lesser player – which was to say, any player – doubt whether a black man was part of their side.

On Saturdays, Nicholls played football. On Sundays, he preached in Melbourne churches, having converted a few years previously under the guidance of Pastor W.W. Saunders at the Northcote Church of Christ. ('I get quite a thrill out of it,' Nicholls explained to *The Sporting Globe*'s readers in 1935, 'I feel I'm doing good.') But as the VFL neared the end of its fourth decade, Indigenous players remained a rarity. The first, Joe Johnson, had also played for Fitzroy, between 1904 and 1906, winning two premierships, but not even enough to fill a goal-to-goal line had followed his example: Nicholls' only Aboriginal contemporary was Alf Egan, who played for Carlton and then North Melbourne from 1931 to 1935.

Press profiles of Nicholls written at the time were inadvertent masterclasses in awkward condescension. In 1934, 'Spectator' in *The*

---

5   In 2016, Carlton held an acknowledgement ceremony, by way of atonement, with members of Nicholls' family present.

Argus, beneath the headline 'A Flying Aborigine', lauded Nicholls in the same incredulous terms one might apply to a wallaby that had learned to eat with a knife and fork, calling him 'a most remarkable type, a studious and lovable character', and praising Fitzroy for 'giving him the opportunity to make good' – as if selecting a clearly superb footballer was some virtuous sacrifice. It would be pleasant – though it is difficult – to believe that 'Spectator' was reporting accurately when he asserted that 'a single word of disparagement is never heard from spectators'. (The memoirs of Jack Dyer, to name one source, confirm that racist abuse of Nicholls by opposition players was routine.)

Nicholls would go on to further acclaim, all of it merited, for subsequent years of diligent campaigning, patient agitation and unstinting pastoral service. Among many other honours, Nicholls would be named Father of the Year, crowned King of Moomba, knighted, appointed Governor of South Australia, and have his name affixed both to a suburb in Canberra and the AFL's annual Indigenous Round. At the risk of echoing the unctions of *The Argus*, few are the Australians who have led more commendable lives.

But something of the sort could also be said of the kid making his debut on the wing for St Kilda. Leslie Allen 'Peter' Chitty, wearing number 36, was a 24-year-old down from near Albury, where he'd played for Border United and Walwa on weekends away from the Chitty family dairy farm at Corryong. The Chittys could afford to indulge the odd attempt by one of their mob to try their luck in the big city: Mr and Mrs Allen Chitty had nine sons and three daughters. The following year, one of Peter's younger brothers, Bob, would play his first game for Carlton, beginning the forging of a formidable career, and a monstrous reputation.

Peter Chitty would have little such luck, at least as a professional footballer, but his first game was sufficiently solid to suggest that St Kilda's efforts to lure him to Melbourne, which had included finding him work in a box factory, would be rewarded. He came off second-best when playing directly against Doug Nicholls on the wing, but so did most people, and he made the great Haydn Bunton work for it when he followed play into the centre – and he'd been part of a winning combination first time up.

From St Kilda's perspective, there was a lot to like about Chitty off the park, as well. He was a devoted fitness fanatic – far from a given at the time – and was already married and expecting his first child; conventional wisdom, then as now, had it that settled family men were likely to be less prone to unhelpfully dissolute personal habits.

Chitty missed St Kilda's next match with a leg niggle, but reappeared the following week, as the Saints faced South Melbourne's famous, fearsome foreign legion. Eight goals from Bill Mohr weren't enough to win it for St Kilda, and though Chitty started opposite the great Herbie Matthews,[6] he played well enough to begin imagining a regular place for himself.

Careers cut short by on-field injury attract widespread sympathy: the applause as the stricken player exits the arena on a stretcher is perhaps some consolation. Careers cut short by off-field injury attract less, especially when they're cut so short that few would have noticed they'd started. Peter Chitty was just these two games into his VFL career when a log at the box-cutting plant rolled into one leg. The injury was initially thought merely season-ending, and Chitty trained with Brunswick in the VFA early in 1937, but realised that his time in the big leagues was over. He took his family back to the bush and played for Cudgewa, captain-coaching them to two successive Upper Murray Football League premierships. In Melbourne at the same time, Bob Chitty was on his way to his first VFL flag with Carlton.

Peter Chitty might not have been heard from again, except as a footnote to the eventful career of his diabolical brother. But World War II did to him what it did to millions, scooping him up from an ordinary life and flinging him like dice. In February 1941, as an ambulance driver with the 22nd Brigade, he sailed from Sydney aboard the *Queen Mary*, one of four ships bearing the 8th Australian Division overseas. In February 1942 he was among upwards of 50,000 Allied soldiers taken prisoner by Japan when Singapore fell.

During their longueurs in Singapore prior to Japan's invasion, Australian soldiers had played Australian football. There was some proper talent among them, including Wilfred Smallhorn, who'd seen Chitty's debut for the Saints but hadn't played in it, and Melbourne's 1940 premiership ruckman Harold Ball. Play continued after all were confined to the Selarang barracks adjoining Changi prison, although without Ball.

---

6   Herbie Matthews won the Brownlow Medal in 1940, in a tie with Collingwood's Des Fothergill. After the two could not be separated by the countback system then in use, each was presented with a replica medal, while the VFL kept the real one. Matthews and Fothergill were finally presented with the real things in 1989.

On 9 February, as the Japanese onslaught began, Ball had been with an ambulance crew evacuating wounded from Tengah airfield when they were stopped by a Japanese patrol. Though Ball and his three comrades were unarmed, and wearing red crosses denoting their non-combatant status, all four were bound, tortured and beheaded. Their unburied remains were discovered by a working party of Australian prisoners three months later.

Two seasons of football appear to have been played in Changi. The first, beginning in August 1942, was described by *The Sporting Globe* in October 1945, on the basis of a Changi Football League season report compiled by a Private Jim Makeham, a prisoner in Changi, and posted home to his brother Bob, who'd played 157 games for Collingwood, including a best-afield performance in the 1930 grand final. The Changi Football League, as Jim Makeham described it, comprised four teams, named after the 1941 VFL finalists: Carlton, Melbourne, Richmond and Essendon. (In the 1941 VFL grand final, Melbourne had comfortably beaten Essendon, despite having lost several stars from their 1940 premiership side to active service. One, Ron Barassi Sr, had already been killed. Three more members of the 1940 team – Harold Ball, Keith Truscott and Syd Anderson[7] – would be.) In the CFL grand final, Richmond defeated Carlton.

The Changi Australian Football Association seems to have been formally inaugurated swiftly afterwards; a measure of confusion occludes how completely the two competitions were separate. Six teams were organised, named after VFL clubs: Melbourne, Geelong, Richmond, Collingwood, Carlton, Essendon. Wilfred Smallhorn, anxious to ensure that the matches boosted morale, rather than providing excuse for all-in brawls and possible overreaction by Japanese guards, appointed himself chief umpire, leg injuries having long since curtailed his playing days. In a further effort to encourage fair play, Smallhorn retrieved from British stores a soccer medal, and had it engraved 'Geelong FC', in honour of Charles Brownlow, the Geelong administrator whose named adorned the

---

7   Syd Anderson was initially rejected by recruiters due to a leg injury sustained playing football. He persisted, and was accepted by the RAAF. He was the navigator on a Bristol Beaufort bomber shot down near Wom Point, New Guinea, in May 1944. Anderson survived the ditching, but was killed when Japanese soldiers opened fire on the aircraft's life raft. One member of the crew made it back home: wireless operator Ray Graetz, who spent eight days wandering the jungle, largely without food, evading capture by avoiding Japanese soldiers or pretending to be one, feigning insanity to explain his lack of language skills. Along the way, he opportunistically sabotaged several Japanese vehicles and weapons. Eventually rescued by American patrol boats, he was later awarded the Military Cross.

medal Smallhorn had won himself nine years earlier. This would be the Changi Brownlow, awarded to the competition's best-and-fairest player – and to be decided, like the actual Brownlow, by votes from the umpires.

The CAFA was a rigorously orderly competition: players could only be transferred between clubs on payment of three bowls of rice, plus a small serving of vegetables. Balls were commissioned from Chinese craftsmen, made from the skin of boars the soldiers shot themselves on illicit excursions with local hunters. Uniforms were sourced from Singapore tailors. Goalposts were easier, the vicinity hardly lacking tall, straight bamboo. The games were played on a paddock alongside the Selarang barracks. Chitty was recruited to the Geelong team by Lou Daily, who'd played briefly for the actual club of the same name.

The CAFA never finished its first season. Allied officers became concerned about the number of injuries to bones and muscles already rendered vulnerable by poor diet – the weekly allowance of meat was just two ounces per man – and chronic disease. There was further concern regarding the corrosion of discipline by interclub rivalries and betting on games (cigarettes were the primary currency). The players' Japanese captors worried about the same things, for different reasons: the men hurling themselves at a football and each other with scant regard for consequence were the labour pool they intended to force to build a railway from Ban Pong in Thailand to Thanbyuzayat in Burma. When the season was abandoned, the undefeated Geelong were declared premiers, but it felt unsatisfactory. Permission from the guards was sought for a contrived but hopefully gratifying climax: Victoria versus The Rest, on 24 January 1943.

Chitty captained Victoria, Daily led The Rest, qualifying via his birthplace of Perth, and 92 games – and the 1935 Sandover Medal – with Subiaco. Victoria wore blue guernseys with a white V, The Rest white guernseys with a red V. More than 10,000 men surrounded the field, watched by wary Japanese guards, some from towers, some on the ground among the crowd. Before the bounce, Smallhorn mounted a bench to address the assembled. He was in considerable pain, ill with appendicitis, but determined to umpire the match. He summoned another league organiser, Ben Barnett, who had kept wicket for Australia on the 1938 Ashes tour of England. Barnett handed Smallhorn a velvet purse, which Smallhorn passed along to Captain John Frew,[8] who plucked from it the

---

8   John Frew, a doctor, survived the Burma Railway, and was knighted in 1980 in recognition of a distinguished career in medicine. The Royal Melbourne Hospital maintains a fellowship in his name.

Changi Brownlow, and announced that, upon counting of the season's votes, it had been won by Peter Chitty. In his acceptance speech, Chitty told the crowd that he would not trade it for all three of Haydn Bunton's real ones. In the game that followed, Chitty led Victoria to victory, 14.9 to 10.3.

The Changi Brownlow wasn't the only medal Chitty would have to show for his war service. In 1947, he was awarded the British Empire Medal, in recognition of the further leadership he exhibited during what followed the final Changi football game: the grotesque hell of the Burma Railway, amid which Chitty routinely nursed, protected and even carried men struggling with exhaustion and disease. 'An outstanding example,' said his BEM citation, 'of unselfish conduct and courage, continuously helping the sick by carrying their kits as well as his own and helping them along and constructing shelter for them when halted. By these means he undoubtedly saved lives.' Chitty may have carried one comrade, James Downie, as far as 300 kilometres, only for him to die. On another occasion, Chitty toted an unconsciously drunk Japanese guard 15 kilometres back to his camp to spare him what would doubtless have been uncompromisingly brutal punishment for falling, literally, down on the job.

Peter Chitty led a quiet post-war life. He died in 1996, aged 84. In 2004, his family donated the Changi Brownlow to the Australian War Memorial; Ron Barassi, whose father had fallen in North Africa a year before one of Chitty's brothers – Arthur Chitty, killed at El Alamein in July 1942 – spoke at the ceremony. Chitty's opponent on his St Kilda debut back in 1936, Doug Nicholls, died in 1988, aged 81, a properly admired public figure. Of Nicholls it may be said that he accrued, in life and death, the recognition he deserved. Chitty, at least, seems to have received all the acknowledgement he wanted, though it does seem odd that no room has ever been found on an Australian postage stamp for the first, last and only recipient of the Changi Brownlow. We have no way of knowing if these two remarkable men – neither of whom yet realised how remarkable he was – shook hands after the match, but they both seem like the type who would have made a point of it.

15

Keith Miller's Day Out
St Kilda 16.18.114 North Melbourne 21.10.136
Junction Oval
ROUND 17, 1941

In the last Wednesday edition of *The Sporting Globe*[1] prior to the 1941 grand final,[2] Hec de Lacy ruminated on the passing season's best players, with affectation of reluctance. 'There have been,' he wrote, 'so many men in camp, so many men working in munitions, and carrying on their football without proper opportunities to train, that the honours seemed somewhat hollow.' He nevertheless struggled valiantly onwards, deploying the time-honoured deflection of blaming his public for any perception of unseemliness. 'Many readers,' continued de Lacy, 'have written asking that a list be prepared, so that list is given for what it is worth, in view of wartime football conditions.'

As is usually the way of such things, de Lacy's choice of 1941's best players was pretty predictable. At full-back, totemic Carlton ogre Bob Chitty. In the middle, Melbourne's captain Allan La Fontaine, about to lead the Demons to a third consecutive premiership.[3] In the ruck, Footscray's captain-coach, and 1941's Brownlow medallist, Norm Ware. At full-forward, Melbourne's Norm Smith ('perhaps the greatest man of his type the game has produced'). Even ahead of this stellar cast, however,

---

1 The pink-papered *Sporting Globe*, established in 1922 by Keith Murdoch, appeared twice weekly – on Wednesdays and on Saturday evenings; the Saturday edition carried reports of the afternoon games. The weekend paper was discontinued in 1979, the Wednesday in 1996.

2 Melbourne coasted to victory over Essendon, 19.13.127 to 13.20.98. Seven of Essendon's 13 goals were scored in the last quarter, when Melbourne's cue was firmly back in the rack.

3 Allan La Fontaine would later coach Melbourne for three seasons, to markedly less success. In between, he served as a pilot with the RAAF in New Guinea during World War II: a 1944 *Sporting Globe* report had him among cricket enthusiasts who'd cleared an oval from the jungle surrounding their base, and also noted that 'the RAAF boys have been putting up records for bombing attacks on the Nips', with the cheery racism of the period.

one player commanded the sub-headline, and the bold-type opening paragraph. In nominating Keith Miller, a St Kilda player in his second season, as 'the best all-rounder I saw', de Lacy was more right than he can have known.

St Kilda were having a(nother) bad year. As the Saints prepared to welcome North Melbourne for 1941's second-last game, they'd won just three matches. The only answer they appeared to have to anything was 'Keith Miller'. St Kilda had signed him early the previous season, after club officials had seen him play at full-back for Brighton in the VFA, and hold the great Bob Pratt, then playing for Coburg, to six kicks and a single goal.[4] Miller had started 1941 as the Saints' full-back, but been moved steadily up the ground – from half-back flank, to centre half-back, to centre, to centre half-forward – as if in the vague hope that an equally commanding clone would self-deploy in every position he vacated. Miller can't have been surprised when captain-coach Jack Knight told him he'd be playing full-forward against North.

Coaches can claim greater credit for some tactical decisions than others: opting to play Keith Miller in any position merited little more than the sort of applause one might garner for remembering to put on one's trousers before leaving the house. Miller scored a goal with his first kick. By the first change, St Kilda held a 22-point lead. As the game went on, however, North were able to contain everything but Miller – who, despite St Kilda's dearest wishes, couldn't be everywhere. When the final whistle went, St Kilda had 16 goals, of which Miller had kicked eight, but North had shredded the threadbare Saints, piling on 14 of their own in the second half, to win convincingly ('St Kilda tired considerably during the closing stages,' lamented Donald Don[5] in the *Globe*, 'and had no counter for North's amazing accuracy.') For North, captain Bill Findlay finished with seven goals, and Sel Murray, who would lead the VFL's 1941 goalkicking, with six.

For most men, kicking eight goals in a League match, losing side or not, would be the defining boast of their lives. Even as early as this game,

---

4   Bob Pratt decamped to the VFA in 1940 when the VFL denied him a clearance from South Melbourne to Carlton: he kicked 263 goals in 40 appearances for Coburg. He played one more game for South in 1946, after returning from military service overseas.

5   Donald Don, a former captain of Richmond, and twice a premiership player, is best remembered for an incident in the 1921 grand final, in which he chinned Carlton's Jack Greenhill. Don was subsequently suspended for eight matches; more immediate retribution was enacted shortly after the match by an enraged Carlton barracker, who split Don's lip, necessitating stitches, before being laid out in turn by another Richmond player.

it might have struggled to make Miller's personal top ten. An exemplar of the earliest idea of football – as a means for cricketers to keep fit during winter – Miller had been famous his entire adult life, since making 181 on debut for Victoria against Tasmania at the age of 18. In his first Sheffield Shield match, in 1939, he ran out Donald Bradman in Adelaide, and he made 108 at the MCG in the return engagement against South Australia, whose attack was led by the era's pre-eminent leg spinner, Clarrie Grimmett. And Miller still hadn't figured out that he could bowl at least as well as he could bat.

By the time he was done, Miller's bag for the Saints against the Shinboners can barely have seemed worth recalling. The great English cricket writer Neville Cardus described Miller as 'the Australian in excelsis', a description which flattered Australians more than it did Miller. Keith Ross Miller seemed an idealised archetype: ruggedly handsome, raffishly charming, named after two national heroes – pioneer aviators Keith and Ross Smith – and all but preordained to become one himself. His first cricketing mentors were Bill Woodfull, the unbowable Australian captain of the Bodyline wars, who taught Miller mathematics at Melbourne High, and Keith Truscott, another sporting and martial paladin in the making, who captained the school team.

Miller's haul against North Melbourne occurred in the 32nd of just 50 games he played for the Saints. It is self-evidently preposterous to regard Miller's as a life unfulfilled, but a wistful what-if can be permitted to shroud his thwarted career as a footballer. This was interrupted, first and foremost, by World War II, in which Miller served as a pilot – most significantly, flying a de Havilland Mosquito over Europe in the late stages of the conflict, with 169 Squadron of the Royal Air Force. It was this experience that informed Miller's celebrated dismissal of the notion of 'pressure' as a factor in sport. 'Pressure,' he snorted, 'is a Messerschmitt up your arse.' He flew light bombers with the same jaunty disregard for convention that characterised his performances on various sporting fields. Once, returning from a raid on Germany, Miller detoured over Bonn, so he could see where Beethoven was born. On other occasions he infuriated his commanding officers by buzzing race meetings at Goodwood and Royal Ascot.

After bidding farewell to the war by starring in the Victory Test cricket matches between England and an Australian Services XI, Miller went back to the Saints in 1946. He was only 26 when he played his last game for the club, scoring a goal at full-forward in a 15-point loss to Carlton. He ended his season early to travel to Boston to marry Peggy Wagner, an American woman he'd met en route to his service in Europe. (Miller's personal life, which might be decorously described as 'eventful', also included some variety of relationship with Princess Margaret, at least according to persistent rumour, which Miller never hastened to deny.) And the Victorian footballer Miller might have been gave way to the New South Welsh – and Australian – cricketer Miller became.

Miller had already made his Test debut for Australia, and excelled in one home Ashes series, before relocating to Sydney in 1947 to play cricket for New South Wales – and to take a helpfully flexible job as a travelling salesman for Cawsey's Cordials, jacked up for him by the company's manager, and captain of the North Sydney Cricket Club, Ron Eaton. Approaches were made by a couple of rugby league clubs sensing a drawcard, but Miller attempted to maintain his parallel career in Australian football. In April 1947 he played in a practice match for Sydney against Eastern Suburbs at Trumper Park. He missed the first half of the game – he'd been at the races – but atoned for his dereliction in the second, scoring two goals, one a drop kick from 60 yards, another punted from beyond 70.

Miller wore the blue and red of Sydney[6] in the New South Wales Australian National Football League, and was elected vice-captain. Sydney had been NSWANFL wooden-spooners in 1946, and didn't improve much during Miller's stint, kept off bottom only by the RAAF side. Later in the year Miller played for New South Wales against Canberra at Trumper Park – where he saved the day with a last-ditch mark at full-back, with the hosts three points ahead – and against Queensland in Brisbane, and at the interstate football carnival in Hobart.

In 1948, with an Ashes tour of England looming, the man who could have been anything – indeed, had been most things before his 30th birthday – chose to be a cricketer. Miller was certainly one of the reasons that Donald Bradman's 'Invincibles'[7] were not vincible, but he

---

6 Sydney were also known as Sydney Naval, due to the presence in their squad of a contingent of sailors from the Garden Island base. The League's official *Football Record* referred to the club merely as 'Sydney', but newspaper reports preferred the longer moniker, perhaps keen not to echo the eternal oddity of Melbourne, a city of (then) 11 teams, one of whom laid claim to the whole city's name. Sydney/Sydney Naval folded in 1970.

7 There was another St Kilda alumnus among the Invincibles: Sam Loxton, who made his debut for the Saints in 1942, played 41 games and kicked 114 goals. Loxton was later a member of Victoria's parliament, and a cricket administrator and Test selector.

bristled at Bradman's – and, some might argue, Australia's – predilection for annihilating sporting opponents rather than merely beating them. At Southend, where Australia piled up 721 runs in a day against Essex, Miller declined to participate in the slaughter: coming in at number four with the score already 2 for 364, he stepped back to a straight first delivery and allowed the ball to hit the stumps. (He was less conscience-stricken when called upon to bowl, taking 3 for 14 in Essex's first innings.) It wasn't Miller's first rebellion against Bradman's choke-their-rivers-with-dead ethos. In his first Ashes Test, in Brisbane in 1946, Miller had argued with Bradman's instruction to bowl short at England's Bill Edrich: Miller understood something of what Edrich had endured while flying Bristol Blenheims for RAF Bomber Command,[8] and had no wish to add to his traumas.

Miller's legendary insouciance was not a product of his war service, but does seem to have been amplified by it. He once claimed – implausibly, given the flair he later exhibited as a cricket columnist – only to have read one book, Monty Noble's memoir, *The Game's the Thing*. If true, it was surely the title that appealed. For some men, confrontation with mortal danger makes them withdrawn and serious. Miller was one of those upon whom it had the opposite effect; the English cricket commentator John Arlott described Miller as someone who lived life like he was running out of it. In the Fourth Test of that first Ashes series he played in, Miller ended the third day in Adelaide on 33 not out. Resuming the following morning, he belted the first ball of the day's play into the grandstand, and swaggered to an undefeated 141.

Miller never lost his love for Australian football: as late as 1987, he served a season as commissioner of the New South Wales Football League. His truncated career as a footballer is unique among such cameos as being the game's loss, rather than the player's.

---

8   Bill Edrich won the Distinguished Flying Cross for his service. Like Miller, his survival of the war turned him into an existential boulevardier: the obituaries which followed his death in 1986, aged 70, made much use of such telltale terms as 'convivial', 'bon viveur' and 'ladies' man'.

16

Bluey Truscott's Last Game
Melbourne 18.9.117 Richmond 30.16.196
Punt Road
ROUND 2, 1942

Rarely has a goal scored in a losing cause received such applause.

Early in the third quarter, field umpire Percy Hutchinson blew for a free kick, about ten yards from the posts Melbourne were attacking. He signalled a push in the back, and pointed at the player wearing the Demons' number 1 guernsey. It did not look like a turning point: after a ten-goal second quarter, including five in the last seven minutes, Richmond had gone into the rooms at half-time 52 points up. Not even the most enraged and/or depressed Melbourne fan would have left early, however, for fear of missing what they were about to see: Keith Truscott, slathered in mud, walking back to his mark, socks around his ankles, wiping the filthy ball on his shorts, running up and scoring for his old club. It was the day before Truscott's 26th – and, it would turn out, last – birthday.

Truscott's previous game for the Demons had also been against Richmond: the 1940 grand final win, in which he'd also kicked a goal. A year before that, he'd scored two as Melbourne sank Collingwood to win the 1939 flag. Truscott had missed the 1941 season, however: he had been otherwise occupied. When he'd left Melbourne – and Australia – a little over a year previously, Truscott was known by the leadenly ironic honorific 'Bluey', as Australian redheads often are, and regarded as a solid half-forward. He had returned as Squadron Leader Keith Truscott, holder of a Distinguished Flying Cross and bar, a world-famous Spitfire ace with 452 Squadron of the Royal Australian Air Force, credited with at least 16 victories over the Luftwaffe.

Truscott had arrived unannounced in Melbourne on the Thursday before the match, enjoying the idea of surprising everyone. Having given his family no advance notice before embarking from Britain, he had to spend the day scouring the city for his mother; he eventually found her lunching in a café. By the time they got home, word had spread. The Truscotts' house in South Yarra was overrun by players and officials from Melbourne; this may have been where the plan for his return was hatched. The last guest called at 1.30 in the morning. Newspapers recorded both Mrs Truscott's delight at having her son back, and her concern about the quantity of laundry he'd brought with him.

The mania would not dissipate while Truscott was in town, and would compel him to relocate to a carefully guarded address under an assumed name. The press were agog at news of his plans to marry. The much-envied woman was named as Margaret Rees, a 22-year-old typist at the Food Ministry back in London, where *The Evening Standard* had run her picture on the front page.

The game against Richmond was a home fixture for Melbourne, but it was played at Richmond's ground, the MCG having been repurposed as a military barracks for the duration. Truscott arrived just ten minutes before the bounce, accompanied by his friend Flight Lieutenant Clive 'Bardie' Wawn, also of 452 Squadron, and also a holder of the DFC.[1] Truscott was not finding the attention altogether disagreeable. Earlier that day, he'd told *The Sporting Globe*'s Hec de Lacy that he had no interest in a brief, applause-milking cameo. 'What, pull out of a football game?' he'd scoffed. 'No, I'll keep playing as long as I can stand up.'[2]

Reaching the Melbourne dressing-room was a challenge, involving the negotiation of ranks of handshakers, back-patters and hair-rufflers – many wearing khaki, taking advantage of the half-price admittance on offer to servicemen in uniform during the 1942 season. Once Truscott was inside, and squeezing a not entirely match-fit frame into his kit – he had worn the number 5 during his seasons with Melbourne, but was

---

1   Clive 'Bardie' Wawn was decorated for completing 'a large number of operational sorties'. One was the mission on which Truscott earned the bar to his DFC: an attack on three German battle cruisers – *Scharnhorst*, *Gneisenau* and *Prinz Eugen* – attempting the 'Channel Dash' run from Brest to Germany's northern ports in February 1942.

2   A substitute, the 19th man, had been introduced in 1930, but was intended as a replacement for an injured player, rather than a tactical option – once a player was swapped out of the game, he was done for the day. A 20th man was added in 1946, but interchange was not permitted until 1978.

presented with the number 1 for today[3] – any efforts by captain-coach Percy Beames[4] to address his players were rendered farcical, as the locked doors were continually belaboured by well-wishers, journalists and telegram-deliverers. One messenger, recently retired Melbourne coach Frank 'Checker' Hughes, bore an especially interesting envelope: it contained a letter of congratulation from prominent businessman – and 'prominent businessman' – John Wren, and a cheque for £1000.

The day's edition of *The Football Record* did not stint on the patriotic unction, devoting a page to Truscott's return. 'He proved himself,' approved the text, 'a grand fighter on the playing fields here, and he proved himself a veritable "Demon" on the fields of battle over Britain.' Lest any reader fail to spot the subtle elision between football and warfare, the *Record* continued: 'He was a playing member of the team that won the premiership in 1939 and 1940, but was playing the grander game of shooting down the Hun over England when the 1941 pennant was gained.' The tone was as jovial as Truscott's return was welcome, but Melbourne did not require reminding of the reality of the war: by early 1942, the club's honour roll already ran to Jack Atkins, Harold Ball, Ron Barassi Sr and Barney Wood,[5] and they wouldn't be the last. Richmond were yet to lose a player on active service, but would lose Bill Cosgrove[6] and Bill Garvie.

Beames deferred to Truscott as captain for the day, and so Truscott led the Demons onto the ground. It being Melbourne's first 'home' game

---

3 The number 5 guernsey Truscott had worn the last time he'd played was owned by one of today's opponents, Richmond's Bernie Waldron, with whom Truscott had swapped after the 1940 grand final. 'I will never part with it,' Waldron assured *The Argus* in the build-up to Truscott's return.

4 Percy Beames played in three Melbourne premiership teams, and also played cricket for Victoria. After retiring from sport in 1945, he combined his twin sporting expertises in a 30-year career as *The Age*'s chief football and cricket writer.

5 New Zealand-born Percival Barnes 'Barney' Wood played five games for Melbourne in 1928. He was also a respectable boxer who fought (unsuccessfully) for the welterweight championship of Victoria in 1923, and a decent cricketer, playing once for his adopted Western Australia (he also played football for Perth). In the late 1920s, Wood and a friend, Alan Mackay, set several Australian speed records for long-distance motoring in their Essex Super Six, including Darwin to Adelaide (six days, 18 hours, 13 minutes), Darwin to Melbourne (six days, three hours, 58 minutes) and Fremantle to Sydney (four days, 23 hours, 51 minutes). Wood was killed 39 years into an eventful life on 9 June 1941, while serving as a sergeant with the 2/16th Battalion of the 2nd Australian Imperial Force during the Battle of Litani River in Lebanon, where Australian troops clashed with Vichy France forces.

6 Bill Cosgrove played just three games for Richmond in 1940 before joining the RAAF, but nevertheless painted a tiger on the fuselage of each of his sequence of Bristol Beaufighters, all of which he named after Jack Dyer. He flew missions in Africa and the Middle East, and in 1942 was one of a dozen airmen who escaped occupied Java in an open boat, reaching Fraser Inlet, in Western Australia, after nearly seven weeks at sea. Cosgrove was killed in a crash off Goodenough Island, Papua New Guinea, in 1943. His nephew, General Sir Peter Cosgrove, became chief of the Australian Defence Force, and governor-general of Australia.

of the season, the scheduled official formality was the unfurling of the 1941 premiership pennant, but that had been upstaged by the guest. Truscott was handed sprays of orchids, to present to his mother, and to the wife of Melbourne's president, Joe Blair. Richmond's players crowded around Truscott in search of a handshake, and the Tigers' captain, Jack Dyer, not known for a charitable attitude towards opponents, demanded three cheers for Truscott from the crowd. (A legend would develop that Truscott's goal was sportingly gifted to him via a theatrical fumble by Dyer – whose wife, Sybil, was a cousin to Truscott – but all contemporary reports recall the free kick.) Truscott was presented with a special medal, struck for the occasion, by VFL president William McClelland.[7]

Truscott won the toss, and Melbourne initially held their own, ahead by a point at quarter time. Truscott started on a half-forward flank, opposite Bill Perkins. A coldly pragmatic coach might have benched Truscott at the first break – clearly out of condition and practice, he was slow to the ball, late to packs, and when he did finally take a mark, scuffed the resulting kick straight into the MCG mud. However, a coldly pragmatic coach would have needed to consider the possibility of being chased out of the ground by a mob armed with umbrellas and fence pickets. Besides which, any disadvantage to Melbourne from carrying Truscott was offset by Richmond's care not to dent the national treasure: Bob Bawden, Richmond's second ruckman, was seen to pull out of a potentially bruising contest as Truscott was fumbling for possession and vulnerable, and Truscott was heard to thank him.

The ten-goal second-quarter blitz by Richmond didn't quite break Melbourne. Truscott's goal in the third inspired something of a revival, and by three-quarter time the Demons had reeled the deficit in to 12 points. Richmond stopped toying with them in the last, piling on another 12 goals. By the time the bell rang,[8] Dick Harris had seven for the Tigers, Jack Titus six,[9] Jack Dyer four. It was the highest score Melbourne had

---

7   William McClelland, captain of Melbourne in the early years of the 20th century, was president of the VFL from 1926 to 1955 – and also president of the Melbourne Cricket Club from 1944 to 1957, making him more or less the king of Melbourne. The trophy awarded to the AFL's minor premiers is named in his honour.

8   A siren replaced the bell at the MCG in 1946, and at all grounds in 1950.

9   Jack Titus remains Richmond's all-time leading goalkicker, with 970 goals from 294 games. Several decades later, Titus's number 12 was worn by Matthew Richardson – who, although rightly regarded as one of the great forwards of his time, scored 170 fewer goals from 12 fewer starts. Though Titus was short (175 centimetres) and slight (66 kilograms) and played when the game was at its roughest, he put together one run of 204 consecutive appearances, a record that stood for decades, until broken in 1996 by Melbourne's Jim Stynes.

ever conceded. It would be a significant win in the context of Richmond's season: the Tigers would finish in second spot on percentage ahead of three other teams on 48 points (though would lose the 1942 grand final to Essendon). But today was Truscott's day, no question, and not just because £667 was taken at the gate, reckoned to be £300 more than had he not been playing: all club profits, along with some allocations from the League, were earmarked for patriotic funds.

In the days following the match, a brouhaha gathered around Wren's gift to Truscott.[10] It was a lot of money – in 1942, £1000 would have paid for a house in Truscott's home suburb of South Yarra. Wren intended this fortune to be split between Truscott and another 452 Squadron alumnus whose reputation he admired: the Dublin-born ace Wing Commander Brendan 'Paddy' Finucane. Aside from the unseemliness of chucking such sums about during wartime, it was unclear whether King's Regulations permitted such donations; Wren offered the compromise of paying the pilots' mothers. Eventually, it was decided that while Finucane was bound by King's Regulations and couldn't take the money – though Finucane's mother could hold it in trust until hostilities were concluded, and her son demobbed – Dominion pilots such as Truscott were not, and were therefore permitted to fill their boots. In Newcastle, workers at a coalmine owned by Wren downed tools, taking the not unreasonable view that if their boss had that kind of cash to fling at flyboys, a rise in their wages might be in order.

The newly minted Truscott left for his new posting, to 76 Squadron in Papua New Guinea, two months later. Although 76 Squadron flew American-built Curtiss P-40 Kittyhawks, the change from Spitfires didn't trouble him. Truscott served with distinction in the Battle of Milne Bay, taking charge of the squadron after the loss of its commander, and was mentioned in dispatches. Later in the war, after 76 Squadron was posted to Darwin, he shot down a Japanese bomber.

Truscott had never been good at landings, though. His training had been hampered by a habit of levelling out a few metres too high on approach; had the enlistment of a dual VFL premiership footballer

---

10   John Wren had form for this sort of thing. During the previous World War, he had presented the AIF's first Victoria Cross winner, Lance Corporal Albert Jacka, with £500 and a gold medal. If Truscott knew how that had panned out, he'd have taken Wren's money with forceps. Jacka used his bounty to go into business with Wren, only for Wren to pull the plug when their electrical goods importer went bust: Albert Jacka, VC, MC and bar, found himself obliged to earn a living as a travelling soap salesman, before dying of kidney failure at 39.

been less of a sensation, he might have been quietly diverted to desk duties. In the dusk of 28 March 1943, Truscott was escorting a US Navy Catalina, returning to 76 Squadron's latest base, at Exmouth Gulf in Western Australia. To relieve the tedium of this workaday mission in the Kittyhawk, Truscott practised some dogfighting manoeuvres around the lumbering flying boat. As the Catalina came in to land, Truscott made a dive underneath it. He misjudged the gap between the American plane and the flat sea, and ploughed into the water. His body was found the next morning, still strapped into the Kittyhawk's mangled cockpit.

Paddy Finucane never got to spend Wren's money either. His Spitfire, distinguished by the shamrock painted beneath the cockpit window, crashed into the English Channel on 15 July 1942, two months after Truscott's one-match comeback. Finucane had shot down more than two dozen Luftwaffe aircraft, won the Distinguished Service Order, the Distinguished Flying Cross and two bars, and was the youngest Wing Commander in the history of the RAF. He was 21.

17

Captain Blood Poses for Posterity
Richmond 16.12.108 Essendon 12.15.87
Junction Oval
PRELIMINARY FINAL, 1944

Everybody who has ever played or watched Australian football wishes there was a picture like this of us.[1] It's the photograph of Richmond's Jack Dyer taken during the last quarter of this, the 1944 preliminary final. Dyer is a few weeks from his 31st birthday, 222 games into what will be a 312-game career, and captain-coach of the reigning premiers.[2] He looks like he's enjoying himself, his expression more amused smirk than determined rictus, and well he might. As the strapped left thigh and bandaged left thumb attest, he has been in the wars,[3] but he's still standing. He has the ball grasped between both mighty mitts, and is leaning into a purposeful sprint upfield. In his wake, three Essendon players flail haplessly. He has bossed this game, kicking nine goals.

It's an absolute image of confident command, perhaps Australian football's equivalent of Steve Powell's photo of Diego Maradona at the 1982 World Cup, ball delicately caressed by his left instep as half a dozen Belgian defenders regard him like a huddle of hedgehogs interrupted by

---

1   Efforts to identify the photographer have been as extensive as they have been fruitless.
2   In the 1943 grand final Jack Dyer kicked three goals, including two in the last quarter, and spoiled a shot for goal from Essendon's Norm Betson near the end, as Richmond won by five points.
3   Not the war, though. Due to Dyer's own extravagant fabulising, it is difficult to know for certain what is true and what is not about his life, but one yarn has it that he arranged a meeting with Prime Minister John Curtin to discuss his angst about not serving in the military. Curtin is said to have replied that Dyer was not only performing vital duty in his day job as a police officer, but that tales of his footballing exploits were valuable for morale at the front. Curtin apparently put in a solicitous word for his nephew, Claude Curtin, who played for Fitzroy – and whom, at the next available opportunity, Dyer made a point of flattening.

an impending truck.[4] The Dyer photo is the model for Mitch Miller's bronze statue of Dyer at Punt Road, and for the logo of *The Footy Show*. In one image, it depicts Dyer doing what he did for Australian football as a whole between 1931 and 1952: taking charge, leaving everyone else to chase and flounder. After Dyer died in 2003, the Richmond cheer squad's run-through at the Tigers' next game used a representation of the picture, alongside the caption 'Heaven's football team can now take the field, because your captain has arrived'. Even former opponents, their scars still visible, who might have disputed this prediction of Dyer's immortal destination, would have forgiven the sentiment.

When Dyer began his bolt towards the lake end of the Junction Oval in the last quarter of the 1944 preliminary final, Richmond were already thinking about the following week's grand final. The game had been effectively over since quarter time: at the first break, having kicked with the wind, Richmond led 8.2 to 0.5. Dyer scored four of them and helped set up another three. Richmond would have been nearly as surprised as Essendon clearly were. It had been an even season, with just six points separating the first five teams at the end of the home-and-away rounds. In the first semi-final, Essendon had thrashed Footscray, while Richmond had lost the second semi-final to Fitzroy.[5]

The last time Richmond had played Essendon, at Punt Road in Round 14, Essendon had won by four points, despite a seven-goal haul by Tigers rover Dick Harris, replicating his feat against the same opposition in the previous year's grand final. But in Round 14, Dyer hadn't been playing – he was serving what was (incredibly) the first and (even more incredibly) only suspension of his career. In Round 11, Richmond had hosted Collingwood, a team – a thing – Dyer loathed with a passion unusual in its fervour, if not its subject. 'You couldn't like them,' he later wrote, 'they think they are God's gift to football, they shun all outsiders and the only time I like to think of Collingwood is when they lose, because it hurts them so much … I wouldn't drink anything they offered, you wouldn't know what they had done to it.'

---

4   This celebrated image is something of a swizz. It was taken from the side of the pitch, just after Diego Maradona had received a short free kick from Ossie Ardiles: the Belgian players, rather than being the terrorised defence they appear, are in fact the wall which had assembled in anticipation of a longer free kick, dispersing. Also, Maradona had a pretty ordinary game, and Argentina lost. Jack Dyer, very much a 'print the legend' kind of guy, would have approved.

5   Keith Stackpole Sr kicked five goals for Fitzroy in this match: after retiring from the VFL after 118 games with Collingwood and Fitzroy, he played cricket for Victoria. His son, Keith Stackpole Jr, played 43 Test matches for Australia in the 1960s and 1970s.

If there was one thing Dyer hated more than Collingwood – and that was an 'if' big enough that one would require yaks and Sherpas to scale it, Dyer having once claimed that his abhorrence of Collingwood was such that he wouldn't watch black-and-white movies – it was Collingwood's embodiment, Jock McHale. By 1944, McHale had been a Magpies player, and/or the Magpies' coach, for 41 years – long enough that his son, Jock McHale Jr, was playing for the team. This proved too tempting a target for Dyer, who lamped McHale. ('So it wasn't the old boy,' Dyer later shrugged. 'So what? It was the fruit of his loins.') McHale, suffused with filial loyalty and fortified by a few drinks he'd downed at a wedding earlier in the day, hit Dyer back. Both men subsequently claimed, when fronting the tribunal the following Tuesday, not to recall anything of the incident, if indeed incident there was, etc., but both got four weeks.

As Essendon learned on preliminary final day, Richmond were a different team when Dyer was on the park: of the four matches Richmond lost during the 1944 home-and-away season, three were during Dyer's suspension. There are many pre-television superstars we can only imagine in action, but the lack of footage of Jack Dyer seems especially cruel. This is not merely because he was (clearly) a splendid and spectacular footballer – in 1947, in the twilight of Dyer's career, his knees completely shot, and exiled to full-forward, where he never led further than 30 yards from goal because he could no longer kick beyond that, former Melbourne premiership captain Allan La Fontaine still rated Dyer the best player in the VFL. In an article in *The Sporting Globe*, illustrated with the famous 1944 image, La Fontaine wrote: '[Dyer] is the only player I have known who can successfully combine calculated robustness with extraordinary football skill. When he moved upfield, either to turn the tide from his own defence or to start something on behalf of the Tigers, then Jack plays with a purpose and a fire that has never been outdone in my experience.'

The dearth of moving pictures of Dyer in his prime is yet more regrettable because of the subsequent decades of mythologising – much of it by Dyer himself – of what La Fontaine referred to in the same article when he wrote: 'I don't like some of his methods.' Dyer's indubitable relish for mayhem, and a post-football career in which he cultivated the image of an affable duffer doing to the English language what he had done to many opponents, means that we have seen much more of Jack Dyer as

Australian football's own Yogi Berra[6] than we have of the player whom Bob Davis, who valued skill and grace like he valued little else, called 'a far better footballer than most modern fans realise ... Most fans, who did not see him play, have an image of a big, brawling ruckman who was more rugged than skilled ... Nothing could be further from the truth ... He was a brilliant mark, and clever on the ground ... strong, balanced and an excellent kick.'

Dyer was a tough man playing a tough game at a tough time: when he made his debut for Richmond in 1931, aged 17 and already three years out of school, the Great Depression was as deep as it got. Unemployment was nudging 30 per cent nationwide, and was much higher in inner-city neighbourhoods like Richmond – which acquired, and took pugnacious pride in, the nickname 'Struggletown'. The effects of the Depression were felt everywhere, even on the football field, where older players with families to feed wouldn't pass the ball to an obviously talented up-and-comer like Dyer, for fear that he might eventually cost them their place in the team, and the money that went with it. The other part of Dyer's footballing apprenticeship was served in the even less forgiving milieus of the Metropolitan Junior League, where he played for his neighbourhood team, Richmond Hill, and the Wednesday League, where he turned out for his then employer, Yellow Cabs. Games sometimes ended in riots; indeed, were sometimes barely distinguishable from them.[7]

Dyer claimed that his rumbustiousness was an adjustment to his physical limitations. In 1932, Dyer's second year with Richmond, a shattered knee ended his season early. It cost him a place in that year's grand final–winning team, and damned him to a lifetime's agony, the joint swelling angrily at the end of every game he played. In 1933, he damaged the other leg, if not quite as severely. So playing straight at the ball, and straight through opponents, was the last option left to a man who could not easily turn or baulk. But even if the number of opposition collarbones Dyer claimed to have broken – 64, give or take – was embroidered, the soubriquet 'Captain Blood', awarded in homage to the 1935 Errol Flynn movie, was one he grew gratefully into.

---

6   Yogi Berra was a catcher with the New York Yankees in the post–World War II decades, who became a celebrated, if debatably intentional, aphorist. Among Berra's many bequests to the language are 'It ain't over till it's over', 'When you come to a fork in the road, take it' and – possibly most sagely of all – 'I never said most of the things I said'.

7   The Wednesday League was a competition of teams from professional organisations; other participants included Railways, Metropolitan Fire Brigade, Telephone Exchange, Postal Workers, Police, Press and Victoria Market. The Wednesday League folded after the 1934 season.

Dyer's position in the pantheon would have been assured had he not booted nine goals against Essendon on preliminary final day in 1944, and had he never been photographed making the difficult game of Australian football look like something which had been designed for his personal convenience. But the picture might never have been taken: for some of the week preceding the match, there was doubt as to whether the 1944 preliminary final was going to be played.

On the Tuesday night before the game, the tribunal sat in judgement of Richmond half-forward Jack Broadstock, reported for hacking Fitzroy's Noel Price as Richmond lost the second semi-final. Broadstock, aghast at the accusation – he had never been reported for anything, either in Victoria or during his years with West Adelaide in the SANFL, never mind for so discreditable an act as kicking – was even more aghast at the verdict: guilty, and eight weeks. 'Thank you, gentlemen,' he told the tribunal. 'It is obvious that you have not played the game.' This was inaccurate – tribunal chairman Jack Brake had starred in the ruck for University before World War I, played in the famous 1916 London exhibition match during it, and had a sporadic career with Melbourne after it – but Broadstock, with a readily imaginable turn on his heel, declared, 'You have helped me make up my mind,' and announced his retirement.

Dyer thought Broadstock the most talented player he'd ever seen. The 1943 grand final against Essendon had been only Broadstock's sixth game for the Tigers, but he'd kicked a goal and held down the centre half-forward position against the great Wally Buttsworth – although only after Dyer had talked military police out of arresting Broadstock upon his arrival at the ground; he'd gone absent without leave from the army in order to play.[8] On the Wednesday afternoon at 5.30 p.m., a conclave at Punt Road discussed forfeiting the preliminary final in protest at Broadstock's suspension. Thirteen Richmond players, Dyer and vice-captain Dick Harris among them, took part in the meeting;

---

8 Jack Broadstock was one of those people who regarded the law more as a set of flexible and forgiving guidelines. On the day of the preliminary final for which he'd been suspended, he went to the races, taking a portable radio to follow the game. On hearing that Dyer had kicked four goals in the opening minutes, Broadstock bolted to the bookmakers' ring, arrived before the news from the Junction Oval, and plunged 60 quid on Richmond at 3/1. Contrary to his threat to retire, he played for Richmond again in 1946, before returning to his native South Australia to continue at West Adelaide – where, in 1947, he missed another grand final after being suspended for kicking an opponent in a preliminary final. Also in 1947, he was convicted of attempting to burgle an Adelaide garage, and entered into a bond which compelled him to live further than 25 miles from Adelaide for three years; contemporary reports do not record whether he was offered six years for good behaviour.

others were kept away by military duties or work in industries essential to the war. The Tigers eventually agreed to play, with two provisos: a formal registration of the club's disgust at the sentence in Broadstock's case, and a commitment that Richmond's delegates to the League would press for the establishment of a mechanism by which tribunal findings could be appealed.

The 1944 premiership decider would be Jack Dyer's last grand final, and a match he would not care to remember – either for the result, as Richmond fell to Fitzroy, or for his own contribution to it. He'd been ill all week, had barely slept or eaten for some days, and, though he kicked one goal, was a pallid and peripheral figure. His final seasons in football were nevertheless formidable – Dyer was club best and fairest for the sixth time in 1946,[9] and Richmond's leading goalkicker in 1947 and 1948. He signed off in style at the end of 1949, with six goals in a huge if meaningless win over Geelong, including one with his last kick in football.

In subsequent seasons as non-playing coach, Dyer couldn't rally the Tigers as he'd been able to from amid the fray. Dyer was a warrior, not a strategist; a sergeant-major, not a general. His footballing career ended in the most melancholy fashion imaginable, certainly to Dyer: not merely dumped as Richmond's coach, at the end of the 1952 season, but dumped in favour of Alby Pannam, a Collingwood man. 'I should have spat in his eye,' Dyer later fumed.

But Jack Dyer understood, as did his great friend (the whole 'Collingwood' thing notwithstanding) Lou Richards, that not only was the fame he'd earned on the football field something that could be leveraged into a media career, but that he really only had to show up and be himself – radio, television and newspapers being, like football fields, arenas open to dominance by those able to inhabit and impose a caricature of themselves. Dyer was prolific in broadcast and print; his column in the scurrilous but buccaneering tabloid *Truth* rejoiced in the masthead 'Dyer 'Ere'; for some time, it ran opposite one by Billy Picken called 'Picken Knows'. Dyer settled into a role as football's uncle-in-chief, basically amiable, vaguely mischievous, affecting confusion and contempt when confronted by the new of fangle, light on pads or limp of handshake. His trademark malapropisms became a treasured component of football's lexicon.

---

9   Richmond's best-and-fairest medal is now named in Dyer's honour.

Many of these were just silly or inadvertently surreal, but some were remarkably – if possibly accidentally – astute aperçus of universal zen. We all have days like the player having an off game, who is 'where the ball ain't'. And moments when, recognising that some battles are likelier won by not fighting them, we decide: 'I won't say anything in case I say something.'

18

The Bloodbath
Carlton 15.13.103 South Melbourne 10.15.75
Princes Park
GRAND FINAL, 1945

'The game's greatest blot and the most repugnant spectacle football has ever known,' seethed *The Weekend Truth*. 'A disgusting exhibition of larrikinism,' harrumphed *The Sporting Globe*. 'VFL must stop savagery,' thundered *The Argus*. As is so very often the case, the response of the sporting establishment to scandal was a purse-clutching, lemon-sucking contrast to the reaction of the sporting public. There is nothing in the historical record to indicate that the crowd at the infamous 1945 grand final thought it other than a marvellous day out.[1] Decades after the dust settled, the 1945 grand final remains one of the game's most cherished folk memories: compare the gallons of wistful ink slung over the 'Bloodbath', as it became known, with reverential elegies to the 1944 or 1946 grand finals, should you be able to find any. There cannot be a football fan alive who, upon their successful assembly of a time machine, would not set the controls for 29 September 1945, and a good seat at Princes Park.

A celebratory mood gripped the match, above and beyond the fact that it was grand final day. It was less than a month since Japan had signed its surrender, ending World War II. The packed grandstands – fully 62,986 people somehow squeezed into Princes Park, 20,000 more than when the same ground had hosted the 1943 grand final – included

---

1   An eyewitness report printed in South Australia's *Port Pirie Recorder* exemplifies the contradiction. The introduction to the recollections of local man W.J. Thomas, manager of Sharples Printers, vapours: 'To use [Thomas's] own words, it was the most disgusting exhibition of brawling and spleen ever he had seen on the football field.' Yet Thomas's own testimony concludes: 'an afternoon of real entertainment, and all for half a dollar – plus tram fares'.

many khaki-clad returnees from the conflict.[2] The choice of venue was itself an exigency of war, the MCG still under requisition for military use. The apparent home-ground advantage this conferred upon Carlton was less than it might have looked: South Melbourne's Lake Oval had also been commandeered, so the Swans had roosted at Princes Park in 1942 and 1943, before moving to the Junction Oval in 1944.

Carlton appeared to need all the help they could get. Having been as low as ninth as late as Round 11, the Blues had just clambered into the final four in the last home-and-away game, summoning an immense performance to pull down third-placed Footscray. South Melbourne, in insouciant contrast, had strolled through 1945, finishing as minor premiers with a game and percentage to spare. The Swans had only needed to play once in the previous four weeks to get into the grand final, in a semi-final against Collingwood, while Carlton had slogged past North Melbourne in a semi-final, and Collingwood in the preliminary final, thoughts of which would have preyed menacingly upon the mind of grand final umpire Frank Spokes as he changed into his whites.

Years later, some would insist that the Bloodbath had in fact been a parasol-twirling saunter through a pastoral arcadia of tulips, daisies, butterflies, squirrels and faeries, when compared to the match which preceded it. The 1945 preliminary final was a wild one, even by the unreconstructed standards of the era: 'one of the hardest and roughest games for some time', winced *The Argus*, not suspecting that it was merely a curtain-raiser for the main event.

The violence of the 1945 preliminary final overshadowed a remarkable comeback. When Collingwood scored against the wind early in the last quarter to reach what would be their final score of 12.8, Carlton had just 6.9, with heavy rain and greasy turf conspiring against them. But suddenly the Blues put a game together. Vin Brown began breaking up Collingwood's attacks. Lance Collins found space on the forward line. Jim Mooring started anticipating the tap-outs. Carlton's barrackers regained their voices.

It had been ugly all day: *The Argus* chronicled 'elbow jabs, sly kicks on the ankle, not-so-sly kicks in the packs, and a good deal of slinging

---

2   The author's grandfather, Corporal Mervyn Mueller of the RAAF, was one of them. Before the war, he twice opened the batting for South Australia, in a team captained by Sir Donald Bradman. Also at the game were a coterie of students, all Carlton barrackers, who would later become better known as the philosopher Brian O'Shaughnessy, the film director Tim Burstall (responsible for *Alvin Purple* et al.) and the artists John Perceval and Arthur Boyd.

and jostling'. Collingwood had targeted Carlton's legendarily pugnacious captain, Bob Chitty – specifically, the bandage on one hand, where he'd severed a finger a couple of weeks previously in an accident at the Maribyrnong explosives factory where he worked. Chitty, for his part, had repeatedly used his good fist against the head of Collingwood's leading goalkicker, Des Fothergill, loosening several of Fothergill's teeth.

Matters erupted properly in the last quarter. Collingwood ruckman Len Hustler, a surprise selection at forward pocket,[3] king-hit Vin Brown, and Carlton winger Fred Fitzgibbon sprinted 80 yards to remonstrate, earning (amazingly) the day's only report – and (less amazingly) a suspension of four weeks; Fitzgibbon would nevertheless find a way to play a part in the grand final. But the punch-up energised his Carlton teammates, who kicked seven unanswered goals in the last ten minutes to stun the Magpies by ten points. Carlton would play South Melbourne for what was being spruiked, in those heady post-war days, as 'the Victory Pennant'.

On grand final day, the footballing establishment did its best, as it always has and always will, to apply a veneer of family-friendly decorum while absolving itself of any responsibility for anything. The editorial in *The Football Record*[4] sniffed that the preliminary final 'could not be classed as a good display of football … not enough concentration on the ball … players were skittled like ninepins and, frankly, had the officials done their duty at least half a dozen players would have had to face the tribunal … unseemly incidents and rough play will never be stamped out whilst the umpires are so lax in their duty … the League has come in for criticism in this matter, but it's pertinent the public should know that the League itself is not wholly to blame …' The League had not seen anything yet.

In those undomesticated decades, most clubs had reason for bearing a grudge against most clubs, and Carlton and South Melbourne were no exceptions. When they'd met in the first round of 1944, South Melbourne's captain, Herbie Matthews, had suffered a broken leg – blamed, accurately or not, on Ron Savage, Carlton's graceful but determined blond ruckman.

---

3   Len Hustler was playing just his eighth game for Collingwood since debuting in 1942, prompting speculation that coach Jock McHale had deployed him as a knuckle-man – a suspicion that Hustler's behaviour on the day did nothing to alleviate. He never played for Collingwood again. In 1947, while representing Victoria Brewery in the Saturday Morning League, Hustler was reported on three striking and two kicking charges in one match against Raymonds, and suspended for life.

4   This issue's back-page advertisement was for the Discharged Servicemen's Centre, a department established to provide 'Back to Civvies' outfits at Manton's, of Bourke Street.

In the same match, a number of spectators had climbed the fence to square up to Bob Chitty after he'd levelled another South Melbourne player; the intervention of police had been necessary to restore what passed for order. Matthews had missed the rest of the season as he recuperated.

The first quarter of the 1945 grand final was, relative to what was to ensue, uneventful. The only notable unpleasantness was exchanged between Carlton's 20-year-old half-back, Jim Clark, and South's grizzled, half-crocked 35-year-old full-forward, Laurie Nash. Clark, like many of his generation, grew up idolising Nash. Nash had been a superstar footballer since the early 1930s: a member of South's 1933 premiership side, and a prodigious goalkicker for Camberwell in the VFA from 1938 to 1941, and he'd once, in 1934, scored 18 in a single game for Victoria against South Australia. Nash had also been a Test cricketer,[5] and had won further public esteem during the war by refusing the soft options available to someone possessed of his fame and arthritis-riddled knees, and served in Papua New Guinea. Jim Clark had been a South Melbourne supporter as a boy, and hollered, 'G'day, Laurie!' to his hero, who was playing in his fifth grand final. 'Up your arse,' came the reply.

At quarter-time Carlton were ahead, 2.4 to 0.5, but wondering if they'd done enough with the breeze. They also had injury worries: against Collingwood the week before, Chitty had added a broken bone in one foot to his severed finger, and Lance Collins, whose four goals against the Magpies had been crucial, had torn tendons in one ankle and could barely move. South were also effectively down a man, defender Brian Kelly limping on a damaged knee. But they had the wind in the second quarter, and they had Nash, who wasn't what he'd once been, but who hadn't been held goalless all season. Plus, South seemed to have settled down faster.

They had. Though Carlton kicked the first goal of the second term, their lead still looked the product of a few determined individuals winging it, while South were a team with a plan. Goals to Keith Smith, Laurie Nash and Reg Richards brought South level; another from Vic Castles

---

5   Laurie Nash, son of early Collingwood star Bob Nash, played two Tests for Australia, the first against South Africa in 1932, the second in the decisive fifth Test of the 1936/37 Ashes series, in which Nash took 4 for 70 in the first innings. He was bizarrely omitted from the Australian team for the 1932–33 'Bodyline' series, despite his boast that his tempo of chin music would have persuaded the Poms to knock their nonsense off within two overs; Keith Miller later damned the under-selection of Nash as the greatest waste of talent in Australian cricketing history. Not known for a lack of self-confidence, Nash once responded, when asked who was the greatest footballer he ever saw, that he saw him in the shaving mirror every morning. He is the only person to have played Test cricket for Australia and in a VFL/AFL premiership side.

gave them their first lead of the afternoon. Ken Baxter goaled for Carlton, Castles again for South Melbourne, and then Ron Clegg,[6] a 17-year-old centre half-forward earning rave reviews in his first season with South, drifted into the sights of Bob Chitty. Chitty hit him under the chin. Clegg, clearly concussed, shaped up to take his free kick facing the wrong way. Bert Deacon,[7] who'd lined up on Clegg for Carlton, sportingly attempted to turn him in the correct direction. 'I don't knock them down,' Chitty informed his teammate, 'for you to pick them up.'

Minutes later, as if to underline the lesson, Chitty singled out South's other rookie prodigy, Billy Williams, a busy rover a couple of weeks past his 20th birthday.[8] Chitty and Williams were acquainted: Williams had grown up a Carlton barracker, and as an even younger boy had volunteered to carry Chitty's bags. Chitty, though no further evidence was required that he wasn't the sentimental sort, caught Williams with an elbow to the head that sent him careening into the fence pickets, and prompted an all-in brawl of such length that umpire Spokes resolved to sit on the ball until everyone got hold of themselves. When hostilities ceased, Spokes informed Chitty that his number had been taken, which Chitty absorbed as an implicit suggestion that if he was going to the tribunal anyway, he might as well make an evening of it. He played the rest of the match as if on a mission to render South Melbourne's red-and-white guernseys all-red.

South collectively determined that if Carlton wanted a fight, they could have one. South's Jack Williams – no relation to Billy – who hadn't acquired the nickname 'Basher' for nothing, apparently inferred from Chitty's example that it was open season on any callow teenagers who'd been foolish enough to place a tender foot onto the increasingly gore-drenched arena. As the boundary umpires returned the ball to the centre after a Carlton goal, Williams dropped Carlton's 18-year-old centre half-forward, Ken Hands. To the enquiries of umpires about what had befallen the unconscious Blue, Williams offered the implausible explanation of sunstroke. Another melee ensued, during which Williams squared up to any Carlton player who fancied his chances, and umpire Spokes. Amid

---

6   Ron Clegg recovered from Chitty's king-hit to play 231 games for South Melbourne; he won the Brownlow Medal in 1949.
7   Bert Deacon won Carlton's first Brownlow Medal, in 1947.
8   The Bloodbath occurred, regrettably, nearly two decades before the publication of Ian Fleming's *Chitty-Chitty-Bang-Bang*, which might have furnished an appropriate subheading for the sections of newspaper reports chronicling this pair of infamies.

considerable outraged clamour in the crowd, one voice in the rainswept outer sounded familiar to those in earshot. 'That was atrocious,' bellowed Robert Menzies, leader of the opposition, and former and future prime minister, 'absolutely atrocious. That man should be rubbed out for life.' Retorted a fellow Carlton supporter, 'I agree with you for once, Bob.'

Chitty acknowledged the half-time bell by waving his maimed hand, now further bloodied against the skulls of his opponents, to a crowd that was also growing restive: around the ground, police struggled through thickets of barrackers to break up fights. The rain grew heavier as the players left the field. Basher Williams, his name already in the book, further pursued his dispute with the umpires, and was reported again. The race into the dressing-rooms was surrounded by Carlton fans; South's players had to negotiate a barrage including, but by no means limited to, bottles and rocks.

At half-time, Carlton were two points up, but a player and a half down. Lance Collins' ankle was wrecked, and 19th man Charlie McInnes, a chunky, ham-thighed half-forward,[9] had taken his place – which meant that Ken Hands, badly bloodied, head ringing with concussion, would have to continue. In South's rooms, it was decided to send the equally stupefied Clegg back on.

In the third quarter, with the rain making play even harder and tempers even shorter, umpire Spokes resorted to the tactic often leant upon by officials fearing a loss of control, and paid several free kicks in succession, to break up rucks and assert authority. It seemed to work, especially for Carlton. The Blues kicked five goals in the quarter, two of them by Hands, who may no longer have known which way was up, but still knew where the posts were. South were floundering, having lost whatever drive they might have had from a still-bewildered Clegg and Williams, and having overinvested in the creaking knees of Laurie Nash, who was being beaten to contests by Carlton's nimble defenders. At the three-quarter interval, Carlton led by 23 points, and looked more than three quarters home.

Nash had made no announcement, or indeed decision, that the 1945 grand final would be his last game of VFL football.[10] But he played – or,

---

9   Lou Richards would later enjoy telling the story of how he'd played his first game, in 1941, opposite Charlie McInnes – who, as soon as the ball was bounced, turned around and punched Richards square in the face by way of welcome to the VFL.

10 Laurie Nash accepted an offer to coach Wangaratta in the Ovens & Murray League, taking the club to a flag in his first season. The same year, in his spare time, he coached Greta in the Ovens & King League, and won the premiership with them as well. He coached South Melbourne for one season in 1953.

at least, behaved – like it was. Early in the final quarter, Nash led out of the forward line for a mark – perceiving, as he did so, the spectre that haunted the nightmares of his generation of players: Bob Chitty, charging on a collision course. Nash saw him coming, and Chitty didn't see that Nash had seen him coming. Nash caught Chitty with a fist above the left eye, splitting Chitty's head so wide that 27 stitches would be required to close the wound. ('A perfect left hook,' Nash beamed to *The Argus* a decade later, taking care to emphasise that it had not significantly tarnished his friendship with Chitty, and that they'd enjoyed a few drinks together after the match.) Half a dozen police were needed to break up the consequent to-do. Chitty, upon regaining consciousness, waved away the trainers, and leant against a behind post to compose himself.

The game was effectively over. Despite or because of this, the fight wasn't, especially as South Melbourne saw things: Chitty may have started it, but Nash and others appeared determined to finish it. When another rumpus flared, amid a hail of bottles from the other side of the fence, Carlton's Fred Fitzgibbon, confined to the bench by the suspension he'd incurred for his previous week's transgressions, could contain himself no longer: his gabardine coat flapping about his elegant blue suit, he sprinted to the scrap and hurled himself in, before being dragged away by cops, who'd deputised themselves to assist the despairing umpires.

Nobody appeared able to rise above the madness, not even South Melbourne's Jim Cleary, whose renowned decency had earned him the nickname 'Gentleman Jim': his number went into umpire Spokes' over-filled notebook for another hit on Hands, who would end the day with a split lip, a broken nose, his allotment of teeth reduced by two – and, somehow, three goals. South winger Ted Whitfield, meanwhile, appeared completely past caring. Possibly emboldened by a matchday ritual carefree even by the cavalier standards of the era – Whitfield favoured six pints of beer before the bounce and a couple of sharpeners at half-time – he clobbered several Carlton players, and took a swing at goal umpire Les Whyte.[11] When Spokes made to note his number, Whitfield pulled his

---

11 Les Whyte had seen worse. In 1914, he'd made his debut as a field umpire in the Round 2 clash between Carlton and St Kilda at Princes Park. Blues fans blamed Whyte's indecisive officiating for a surprise loss, and a mob estimated at 2000-strong rushed him when the game ended, overwhelming the police officers trying to protect him. One Stanley Oliver was subsequently convicted of assault and fined £5 with 12 shillings costs, even though the arresting constable vouched for his innocence. Whyte, intriguingly, claimed to have lost his job as a draper's clerk over the incident; history does not record whether his employers were Carlton barrackers. The report of the day's indecencies in *The Argus* also noted that the St Kilda players, making their exit down the race, had been compelled

jumper up over his head and ran away. Bob Chitty kicked the last goal of the game, and was carried from the ground by his ecstatic teammates; confounded and covered in blood, not all of it his own, he didn't know who'd won.

The tribunal sat the following Tuesday. Wisely, separate waiting rooms were designated for Carlton and South Melbourne. Nine players had been charged, although one had decided that he had better things to spend his evening on than a foregone conclusion: Ted Whitfield, not wishing to waste his tickets to South Melbourne's end-of-season ball, scheduled for the same night, sent apologies by telegram. He was suspended for two weeks for kicking the ball away after an opponent's mark, and for the entirety of 1946 for insulting, and attempting to strike, goal umpire Whyte.

Whitfield's teammates who did deign to face the music fared little better. Basher Williams went for 12 weeks for shaping up to field umpire Spokes, among other misdemeanours. Gentleman Jim Cleary got eight for decking Hands.[12] Don Grossman got eight for striking Carlton's Jim Mooring, and Herbie Matthews was reprimanded for throwing the ball away after having a free kick paid against him. Keith Smith was acquitted on a separate charge of striking Mooring – who, as he had during Grossman's hearing, did his best to spring his assailant, offering evidence sufficiently vague as to enrage the tribunal's chairman, VFL president W.C. McLelland, who sighed at Mooring: 'You are a very unreliable witness. You want to brush up on your memory.'

Bob Chitty's first victim of the grand final, Billy Williams, valiantly affected similar amnesia when Carlton's cases were heard, but Chitty nevertheless got eight weeks, as did Ron Savage, adjudged guilty of striking Grossman. Ken Hands, possibly benefiting from sympathy prompted by the state of his face, and by the fact that he told the tribunal he could remember almost nothing of the game, never mind the incident in which he was alleged to have jumped into Ron Clegg, was acquitted. The following week, the VFL's investigation committee met to consider the case of Fred Fitzgibbon, who'd sloshed through the mud in his Saturday best to join the fight in the last quarter. They declined to believe

---

to take evasive action: 'Some of the women were so mad with anger that they poked at the players with their umbrellas through the iron bars of the fence, and their impotence only made them madder.'

12 Ken Hands would always gallantly insist that Cleary simply mistimed an attempt to spoil a mark. He played 211 games for Carlton, and coached the Blues for six seasons between 1959 and 1964.

Fitzgibbon's recollection of a public-spirited attempt to effect a citizen's arrest upon a pitch-invading hooligan, and added four weeks to the suspension he was already serving.

The 1945 grand final ended careers, and made names. Ted Whitfield,[13] Herb Matthews and Laurie Nash never played another game for South Melbourne; Jim Cleary threatened to join them in exile, but was talked out of it. For Carlton, the most notable departure was Ron Savage, just 28, and the club's reigning best and fairest, who quit to become captain-coach of Hobart. Bob Chitty returned in 1946 to play six more games before retiring, his stature as folkloric bogeyman assured.

None of the game's participants, however, were as damned or as celebrated as the Bloodbath itself, which remains the most famous/infamous match ever played. It has been interpreted as a macho psychodrama – of players who (mostly) hadn't served in the recent war seeking to demonstrate their warrior credentials to an audience who (substantially) had worn khaki. This theory focuses especially on Bob Chitty, who'd had one brother killed overseas, and three more taken prisoner[14] – Peter Chitty, winner of the Changi Brownlow, listened to the game on a radio on a base in Darwin, where returning PoWs were awaiting the last leg of their repatriation.

A measure of nostalgic longing also attaches to the Bloodbath, for a less regulated and more nakedly gladiatorial age – although just as modern health and safety regulations are most loudly decried by those who've never done a dangerous day's work, this is roughly nine-tenths delusional. It may just be that the Bloodbath, with its glorious characters and cartoonish grotesqueries, endures like the ballads of Banjo Paterson endure, as a yarn reinforcing an image which we Australians enjoy having of ourselves: unbowed by threat, uncowed by authority, and willing, once the final siren has sounded, to slap an opponent on the back and shout them a beer.

The tiny surviving scrap of newsreel footage of the match reminds that there was some football played, some of it decent: in scratchy, flickering black and white, we see Ted Whitfield outmarked by Carlton's Herb 'Stumpy' Turner, a dash across half-back by Carlton's vice-captain, Rod

---

13   Ted Whitfield was also declared persona non grata by South Melbourne, who informed him that he was no longer welcome even as a spectator – though he would eventually be admitted to the Past Players' Association.

14   This debatable analysis underpins the song 'Bob Chitty's Blues', by the author's scandalously underrated country band, The Blazing Zoos.

McLean,[15] a baulk, swivel and kick by Jim Mooring. But it's the violence that earns the Bloodbath its place in the game's mythology. Somewhere in those rammed grandstands, straining over sardined shoulders for a view of the mayhem, was an impressionable 12-year-old from the western suburbs of Melbourne. Ted Whitten – for it was he – later called it the greatest game he ever saw.

15　Rod McLean, another noted hardman of the era, was rarely far from the trouble that besmirched the Bloodbath, but managed to escape the attention of the umpires. He had missed the beginning of the season due to a suspension incurred late in 1944, despite advancing the novel defence that his victim, Footscray's Ron Grove, had been unscathed. 'I can hit hard, believe me,' he told the bemused judges, 'and if I had hit Grove he would not have been able to take his kick.' McLean's son Ricky, and grandson Brock, both played for Carlton.

19

Fred Fanning's Big Bag
St Kilda 10.18.78 Melbourne 27.9.171
Junction Oval
ROUND 19, 1947

It looked a barren pasture for anyone seeking to harvest immortality. Final game of another lean season for St Kilda, with just a two-point win over North Melbourne and a draw with Footscray to give fans reason to continue living. Last match of a disappointing year for Melbourne, from runners-up in 1946 to mid-table becalm in 1947, an initially promising season scuppered by a six-game losing streak starting in Round 10. Three consecutive wins since – including one against their eternal nemeses Collingwood, by less than a kick at Victoria Park – had improved the Demons' morale, but not their chances of playing in 1947's finals.

Nevertheless, Fred Fanning, Melbourne's 25-year-old full-forward, had the football world at his feet – his bountiful right foot, in particular. He'd had a good year – 79 goals from 15 games, benefiting from the injury-enforced absences of a waning Norm Smith, and establishing himself on the Demons' forward line as anointed apprentice to ageing sorcerer Jack Mueller, also selected today.[1] Fanning was hopeful of ending the season as the VFL's leading goalkicker – only Geelong's Lindsay White and Footscray's Bill Wood[2] were in touch, and neither had the enviable advantage of a game against St Kilda in hand. But Fanning had further reason for wanting to dominate this game: he was playing his last match of League football.

---

1   No relation to the author. Though past his best by this point, Jack Mueller would limp through three patchy further seasons with the Demons, finishing with 378 goals from 216 games. Mueller's renowned marking ability was unhindered by his possession of just eight fingers, having lost two in 1934 in a mishap at the rope factory where he worked.

2   Bill Wood, originally from Albury, could claim one imagination-boggling goalkicking feat of his own: while playing for South Sydney in 1943, he kicked 28 of his team's 31 goals in a match against Sydney Naval.

Towards the end of the 1947 season, reports had begun surfacing that Fanning had been offered a coaching job by Hamilton, in western Victoria. For Fanning, the lure was twofold: a substantial hike in salary, from three quid a game to 12, and, having married into a Hamilton family, the chance to use his engineering training as partner in his father-in-law's bicycle business. Fanning foresaw no problems: in his nine years at Melbourne, he had rejected offers of £500 a season and then £750 from his original club, Coburg, to leave the VFL and return to the VFA, and he expected his loyalty to be rewarded. As it turned out, he might have saved himself considerable headache by going missing for the St Kilda game, or perpetrating some other infraction, like showing up drunk or declaring himself a communist. It proved an inopportune moment to remind Melbourne how good he was.

Fanning, an imposing Lockett-like unit of 193 centimetres and more than 100 kilograms, had already reaped some hefty hauls in 1947: nine each against Richmond and Collingwood, ten in a previous encounter with St Kilda in Round 8,[3] another ten against Footscray a week before today's match against the Saints at the Junction Oval. He would have approached this game as the prowling lion approaches the herd of sleepy wildebeest. Melbourne had nothing to play for but confirming Fanning as the VFL's leading goalkicker for the fourth time in five seasons, and St Kilda, if not quite winless, were certainly hapless and hopeless.

Fanning kicked four straight in the first quarter, but must have wondered when his teammates were going to join in: at the break, Melbourne led by just seven points. The second quarter was what Demons barrackers anticipated, neutral observers expected, and Saints supporters feared. Melbourne piled on 11 goals, seven of them from Fanning. At half-time, Melbourne had run up an even 100 points, and a 66-point lead – which precisely equalled Fanning's contribution so far of 11 goals. In the third quarter, St Kilda's captain-coach, Allan Hird Sr,[4] ordered his inexperienced team to mark Fanning more tightly, nominal full-back Stan Le Lievre needing all the help he could get, but the big forward kicked three more – and, between his 13th and 14th goals, his only behind of the afternoon, from a set shot 15 yards out.

---

3   Fred Fanning's direct opponent that day was St Kilda's Alan Stretton, later Major General Alan Stretton, named Australian of the Year in 1975 for his role in supervising the evacuation of Darwin following Cyclone Tracy.

4   Allan Hird Sr was the father of Allan Jr, and grandfather of James. Allan Sr resigned as St Kilda coach the day after this debacle; it was his last game of VFL football. He subsequently coached Essendon's reserves, and became president of the club. Allan Hird Jr played four games for the Bombers in 1966–67.

At three-quarter time Fanning was poised to join two of the most fabled figures of the VFL's first half-century: the only two men who'd scored more than 14 goals in one game. South Melbourne's Bob Pratt had managed 15 against Essendon in 1934. Collingwood's Gordon Coventry had kicked 15 against Essendon in 1933, 16 against Hawthorn in 1929, and 17 against Fitzroy in 1930. Fanning reached 15 from another easy mark, 16 from something similar, and 17 from a 40-yard set shot. His 18th, establishing a new benchmark, was greeted with applause – or at least as much as might be generated by 6000 people, most of them home fans glumly watching their useless team getting filled in by 93 points. St Kilda later presented Fanning with the match ball – on the face of it a sporting gesture, but keeping it would probably have felt as wise a decision as the purchase of a mummified monkey's paw from a black-eyed fakir.

As season 1948 loomed, Fanning's portmanteaus were packed for his new life in Hamilton, but Melbourne decided, on reflection, that they'd prefer it if Fanning stayed. Possibly, they'd run the numbers, and noted that of the 250 goals and 242 behinds Melbourne had scored in 1947, Fanning had contributed 97.38. Melbourne announced that they would refuse Fanning's application for a clearance.

Uproar ensued in country football circles, where this was perceived as lordly high-handedness from the grandees of the big city – perhaps even something worse. At the Victorian Country Football League's annual conference in April, VCFL president Stan Freeland described the VFL's attitude to League players who wished to pursue their careers in the bush as 'fascist', no less – an imprecation possessing thunderous resonance in 1948. One delegate from Murray Border District Football Council made leaden humour of a movie known to be in production. 'There is a moral,' he fumed, 'in the film now being made of the Kelly Gang, in which a former Carlton player takes the lead.'[5] Hamilton's local newspaper, The Spectator, fulminated: 'The Melbourne [Football] Club has a chance to yield Fanning gracefully and say a practical "thank you" to the Hamilton Football Club. It was from Hamilton some years ago that Melbourne

---

5   This was The Glenrowan Affair, starring none other than Bob Chitty as Ned Kelly. Released in 1951, it is, by common consent, one of the worst films ever made in Australia – worse even, perhaps, than Moulin Rouge! As The Sunday Herald reported: 'The script is dreary, the photography more often out of focus than in, the editing is unimaginative and the acting petrified. It would be a misplaced kindness, in fact, to try and ferret out a single redeeming feature.' It was narrated by Charles 'Bud' Tingwell, recently returned from distinguished service as a fighter pilot, and shortly to embark upon a lengthy and splendid career in cinema, of which this would remain the lowlight. 'It was the first time Chitty ever needed armour,' quoth Jack Dyer, inadvertently anticipating the reviews.

obtained the services of Colin McLean, the local side's brilliant young half-back flanker, who has been a tower of strength to the Redlegs in recent years and is still one of their most dashing and consistent players. It is up to Melbourne!'

Melbourne declined to budge. Coach Frank 'Checker' Hughes[6] and club secretary Alex Gray travelled to Hamilton to visit Fanning, and plead, cajole and/or threaten; Fanning replied that he would stay in Hamilton whether he was permitted to play for the local club or not. Melbourne nevertheless selected Fanning for the opening match of 1948, against Essendon at the MCG, and requested that he advise the club of his preferred travel arrangements. Fanning advised that he preferred not to make any.

Melbourne tried to lure Fanning towards compromise, offering to clear him to Hamilton for 1949 if he'd play for Melbourne in 1948, with employment and accommodation guaranteed. No sale. They offered to clear him if he'd just suit up for the first two games, against Essendon and – Melbourne may have thought this an enticement, akin to loading a hunter's rifle for him and staking out a drugged zebra on a treeless plain – St Kilda. No dice. Finally, at a special meeting of the Melbourne committee after the match against the Saints – a cantering five-goal win – it was decided to let Fanning go, with a splendidly sanctimonious statement that the club felt obliged to do so 'because, to a large degree, the successful future of Fanning was dependent on the granting of the clearance'.

Celebrations in Hamilton were other than universal, however. Jack O'Keefe, who'd played for Melbourne, Hawthorn and South Melbourne, had been caretaker coach during what had looked like being a disappointing 1947 season, but – vexingly, for those masterminding the Fanning coup – had hauled Hamilton into the grand final of the Western District League, where they'd beaten Casterton by a point. The winning behind was bundled through by Ted Kenna – a local hero who, less than two years previously, had won the Victoria Cross in New Guinea.[7]

Some now sought to reverse Fanning's appointment, and retain O'Keefe. The consequence of this stramash was the formation of a new

---

6   Frank 'Checker' Hughes won two premierships as a player and one as a coach with Richmond, and four more as a coach with Melbourne. Hughes also imposed the 'Demons' nickname on Melbourne, who had previously been known, less menacingly, as the Fuchsias. While serving on the Somme in World War I, Hughes helped stage a match between the 57th and 60th battalions of the AIF's 15th Brigade on a stretch of mud near Mametz Wood.

7   Ted Kenna died in 2009, aged 90, Australia's last surviving recipient of a VC in World War II. At least one obituary suggested that he considered his vital part in the 1947 WDFL grand final the greater achievement.

club, Hamilton Imperials, and the cleaving of a schism which would divide the town for decades. With remarkable speed, the black-and-white-striped Hamilton became the club for landed gentry and/or Protestants, and the red, white and blue Imperials the home, somewhat confusingly, of workers and/or Catholics. The Imps' resentments can only have been fuelled by the fact that Fanning coached Hamilton to a flag at his first attempt. (After more than six decades of crosstown sectarian and class enmity, the clubs amalgamated in 2012, becoming the Hamilton Kangaroos, of the Hampden League.)

In the 40 remaining years of his life, Fanning witnessed some creditable attempts to surmount football's most daunting individual single-game feat: Peter Hudson's 16.1 against Melbourne in 1964, Peter McKenna's 16.4 against South Melbourne in 1969, Kelvin Templeton's 15.9 against St Kilda in 1978 – and, most threateningly, Jason Dunstall's 17.5 against Richmond in 1992.

It is possible that Fanning's record will never be broken: full-forwards are no longer the tip of the spear, merely now one prong on the pitchfork, and defences are better organised. Fanning has, therefore, a surer claim on immortality than almost any other player in the game's history, but still seems something of a could-have-been. If the six seasons he ended up playing in the bush had been played for Melbourne, League history might have been very different.

Melbourne won the 1948 premiership, although not without requiring a replay after the grand final against Essendon was drawn; Jack Mueller kicked six goals in each game. But those next six years without Fanning – and without Checker Hughes, who retired after securing the 1948 flag[8] – were years of mediocrity and disappointment for Melbourne, descending to a gruesome nadir with the one-win wooden spoon of 1951, before the renaissance of the Norm Smith era. Fanning's 18 goals in a nugatory match at the end of a lost season are the game's strangest chimera, both deathless and meaningless.

---

8 The actual 1948 flag went missing for decades, before being advertised on eBay in 2014, with a starting price of $80,000; police recovered it from a house in Moama. The 1982 flag, won by Carlton, also drifted awhile in Melbourne's underworld. After Mark Moran, of the well-known Melbourne family, was shot dead on his Aberfeldie doorstep in 2000, Carlton responded in the affirmative to a request to borrow the 1982 pennant for coffin-draping purposes. (Mark Moran's grandfather, Les Brooks, had for many decades been a doorman at Carlton; Moran's wake was held at Princes Park.) The Morans were, however, tardy in giving the flag back, and Carlton officials possibly nervous about asking too forcefully; its return was confirmed in 2007.

20

John Coleman Crash-lands
Carlton 9.10.64 Essendon 16.12.108
Princes Park
ROUND 18, 1951

John Coleman kicked seven goals this afternoon, slightly better than an average afternoon's work, for him.[1] Heading into this, the last home-and-away game of the year, Coleman's Essendon had been comfortable in third place, fancying themselves for a sixth consecutive grand final – or a seventh, if you count the two necessitated by the draw with Melbourne in 1948.[2] Carlton had been adrift several weeks in there's-always-next-year territory. It was a match between the team with everything to lose and the team with nothing to play for; these often go badly for the former.

Coleman, in his third season with the Bombers, hadn't quite replicated the prodigies of his first two. As a 20-year-old in 1949, Coleman had kicked 12 on debut against Hawthorn – including five in the first quarter[3] – and finished with an even century for the year, including six in a grand final win. He'd followed that up with 120 in 1950, including four in another victorious grand final. In 1951, Coleman had missed a couple of games, and been relatively well held in a few others,[4] but he arrived at Princes Park with 68 goals for the season, and hope that another century might still be on, given a decent finals run. As things turned out,

---

1   Coleman's career average was 5.48 goals per game; among players who kicked 500 goals or more, only Peter Hudson's average (5.64) is superior, and very few are even comparable.
2   Essendon lost the replay, 13.11.89 to 7.8.50.
3   A record on debut. During this match, Coleman also joined the coterie of players who scored a goal with their first kick, but fell a way short of the record-holder in this category: Carlton's Clen Denning, who scored with each of his first six kicks in League football, against South Melbourne in Round 4, 1935.
4   Coleman was held goalless just once in his 98-game VFL career, by Fitzroy's Vic Chanter at a swamp-like Brunswick Street in 1952.

Coleman might more usefully have considered coming down with a cold, or twisting an ankle, or getting lost on the way to the ground.

Coleman – and Essendon – had survived a big scare two weeks previously. Late in an undemanding demolition of Geelong at Windy Hill, in which Coleman had kicked five, the full-forward had lost a marking contest with Cats full-back Bruce Morrison[5] and raised a knee at his opponent, prompting a scuffle. Both boundary umpires had approached with a view to calming the situation, and Coleman, famously genteel in his interactions with all classes of person other than those clad in white and armed with whistles, had instructed one, 'Shut up,' and the other, 'Pull your head in,' and been reported by both for misconduct in disputing an umpire's call. He'd been cleared by the tribunal, on the interesting technicality that he had only disputed the boundary umpires' advice to leave Morrison alone, not the field umpire's decision to award Morrison the mark.

Maybe this escape had persuaded Coleman that he could do as he pleased: certainly, it hadn't taught him that he couldn't. Late in the second quarter at Princes Park, Essendon were struggling, in what was proving a bad-tempered game: Carlton's Jim Clark and Essendon's Jack Jones had clashed, as had Carlton's Fred Stafford and Essendon's Greg Tate. With half-time impending, Carlton repelled another Essendon attack. As the ball headed back downfield, Carlton ruckman Harry Caspar punched Coleman in the chest and the face, and Coleman retaliated in kind. Both had their numbers taken. As other players gathered about the pair in menacing packs, field umpire Bill Barbour stopped play for a few minutes in the hope that a pause might encourage the temperature to drop.

It did not. In the third quarter, the mayhem continued ('fists, elbows and knees were used at the slightest provocation,' lamented *The Age*), and Coleman narrowly avoided being maimed by a lemonade bottle launched from the crowd. At the end of the game, both Coleman and Caspar were booed off by their respective opposition fans; Coleman was pelted with orange peel, balled-up *Football Records* and other detritus as he entered the race. Umpire Barbour had to be escorted through an irate jostle of Carlton hoodlums by the cops, although this did not deter one assailant,

---

5   During a match against Footscray at the Western Oval on an absurdly gusty day in 1948 – of the 148 points amassed by the two teams, only seven were scored against the wind – Bruce Morrison suffered the ignominy of having a kick-in from a behind blown back over his head between the goalposts; it was recorded as a rushed behind to Footscray.

identified by *The Argus* as 'a soldier' – one can only assume in uniform, which must have been a surreal spectacle – from pushing through the phalanx and punching the beleaguered official.

Coleman reported to the tribunal hearing at Harrison House on Spring Street the following Tuesday night with some cause for optimism. He'd been the retaliator, not the instigator. During Caspar's case, which was heard first, both umpires who'd booked the pair confirmed as much – one going so far as to aver that if he'd been in the same position as Coleman, he'd have walloped Caspar as well.

Caspar, while denying striking Coleman, did admit to some argy-bargy by way of remonstrating vis-à-vis a previous incident, which he said he would 'rather not mention unless I have to'. Bizarrely, nobody pressed him on this; suggestions later emerged that Coleman had taunted Caspar about a traffic accident in May that year, in which Caspar, a plumber by trade, had knocked down a pedestrian with his ute in Lygon Street, and killed him. Coleman denied striking Caspar: he put any contact down to defensive reflex, and added, logically enough: 'With the finals coming on I knew what consequences I could expect if I deliberately punched an opponent.'

The tribunal found Caspar guilty and suspended him for four matches, then took 12 minutes to reach the same verdict, and same sentence, for Coleman, ruling him out of the finals. He was – literally, to judge by his reaction – stunned. In the immediate aftermath of judgement being passed, he slumped in a corner with his eyes closed, refusing to speak to commiserating Essendon officials. When helped through the crowds waiting outside Harrison House, Coleman looked weak-kneed, tearful and pale in his baggy suit, woollen vest, tie and scarf, unable to stay on his feet as the mob (which included 'a score or more of 16- and 17-year-old bobby-soxers', as *The Argus* noted) surged forward: Coleman banged his head against a traffic signal-box and collapsed onto the footpath, before being loaded, barely conscious, into a waiting car. Rumour – plausible, in these fevered circumstances – had it that the 22-year-old had declared he'd never play football again.

A team good enough to make a grand final – never mind six in a row – is obviously a very good team. But however good a team, a great player still makes a difference. Disarmed of their freakish spearhead, Essendon limped through the finals. In the semi-final, they beat Footscray by eight points – despite the intervention of the prime minister, Robert

Menzies (possibly significantly, a fanatical supporter of Harry Caspar's Carlton), who importuned the minister for the army, Josiah Francis, to reverse his earlier refusal to allow Private Ted Whitten weekend leave from national service duties so that he could turn out for the Bulldogs. In the preliminary final Essendon fell over the line against Collingwood by two points.

On grand final day, it looked like the fates might gift Essendon a matinee ending after all. When teenage rookie ruckman John Gill reported sick, Essendon coach Dick Reynolds – the club's beloved totem, a triple Brownlow medallist who'd led them to four premierships before retiring in 1950 – decided to lace up, aged 36, for one last step into the breach. It wasn't enough: Geelong won by 11 points. Essendon's mood was not improved by the fact that the Cats' full-forward, George Goninon, booted four goals to reach 86 for the season, and end 1951 as the VFL's leading goalkicker.[6] Before joining Geelong, Goninon had spent three seasons at Essendon, where he'd played just nine games, unable to establish himself against John Coleman.

Coleman returned to Essendon in 1952, notwithstanding wishful delusions, reported in South Australian newspapers, that he was pondering offers from Port Adelaide and West Torrens. Though never temperamentally inclined towards the philosophical, Coleman might have reflected that, notwithstanding the previous season's setback, he wasn't in a bad place: he was three times the VFL's leading goalkicker, twice a premiership player, still only 23, and able to look forward to that spindly, wiry frame, shrouded by the trademark long-sleeved guernsey pushed up to the elbows, filling out a bit, perhaps making him a less tempting target for the League's knucklers and hackers. In Coleman's first game back, he scored seven against North Melbourne, including the goal that sealed a seven-point victory, scuffed off the turf in the final quarter.

The 1951 fiasco hardened Coleman, however. He was more willing to treat opponents as they treated him, and even more contemptuous of umpires, who, as he saw it, neglected their duty to protect him. In Round 15 of 1952, against Collingwood, Coleman erupted at field umpire Max Blumfield, suggesting that Blumfield avail himself of a rulebook, and that perhaps the pair might meet to discuss their differences in the street sometime.

---

6 This title belongs formally to Coleman, who kicked more during the home-and-away season.

The consequent tribunal hearing had less riding on it than the previous year's – Essendon were nowhere near the finals – but dozens of Coleman's voluble young female devotees nonetheless turned up at Harrison House to mourn or celebrate the verdict. Chairman W.C. McClelland was clearly unimpressed, wigging Coleman to the tune of 'We hope you realise the seriousness of what you have done, and also the uselessness of it', but Coleman was let go with a reprimand. Outside, Coleman's fans mobbed him, and then – less appreciatively – umpire Blumfield. The sole remaining interest of Essendon's 1952 season – the possibility of another century for Coleman – was just about still in play. In the final four weeks, Coleman obliged with five against Carlton, nine against St Kilda, 13 against Hawthorn and nine against Richmond, to reach the ton with three to spare.

In the first three games of 1953, Coleman kicked 31 goals – ten against Fitzroy, 11 against South Melbourne, ten more against St Kilda. Among the near-30,000 watching the game against South at the Lake Oval, which Essendon lost by ten points – aside from Coleman's contribution, they managed only two other goals – was Bob Pratt, whose judgement of a full-forward's greatness was to be respected. 'If I was better than Coleman,' he said, 'then I was twice as good as I thought myself.'

Pratt was less impressed by Coleman's teammates, who he believed were failing to take care of their most valuable asset: 'He's got to beat an army to get the ball. The rest just stand around. If he had good support instead of the pack of statues which are hindering rather than helping him, he'd get even more goals.' Victor Belcher, the former South Melbourne captain and Fitzroy premiership coach, quoted in the same *Sporting Globe* article, declared: 'Essendon should be locked up, the way they let Coleman battle on his own.' In fairness to Coleman's teammates, their fiery full-forward was very much of the if-you-want-it-done-right-do-it-yourself school of thought, regularly ordering the forward pockets to clear out to the flanks, which left the ball exclusively to him, but also two generally vindictive defenders free along with it. Either way, Essendon were about to learn – or, given the 1951 disaster, relearn – a severe lesson about over-reliance on one man, however lavish his gifts.

Essendon finished fourth at the end of 1953's home-and-away rounds, and faced a semi-final against Footscray. Coleman seemed in good touch – he'd bagged ten in the last game against Richmond, making it 96 for the season and confirming him as the League's leading goalkicker for the fifth year running. But on the Monday before the game, Coleman fell ill with a cold, sufficiently severe that he failed to front the ceremony at which the year's All-Australian blazers were being presented. He couldn't train on the Tuesday night. The Wednesday papers called it influenza, and Thursday's gave him little chance of making the game. The back page of Friday's *Age* blared: 'Essendon Takes Risk with John Coleman for Semi-Final'.[7]

Coleman had averaged better than 5.6 goals a game throughout 1953, just a little less than his Essendon teammates were able to muster between them against Footscray on a blustery day. Coleman kicked one, but he was never really in it, despite the ministrations of a trainer, who was rebuked by umpires for running medicine out to the wheezing forward. Coleman dropped several marks, and missed easy shots. *The Age* noted his 'lack of enthusiasm for movement, and apparent disinterest'. In *The Argus*, Hugh Buggy said that Coleman's 'arms were still from penicillin injections' and 'his face had an ashen pallor'. Footscray won by eight points, and Essendon's season was over.[8]

But there was always next year, and there was still Coleman, and so there was hope. In the opening game of 1954, he scored ten against Hawthorn, and afterwards – to the delight of the retinue of shrieking teenagers which had become a feature of his tribunal appearances – beat a charge of striking Hawks full-back Len Crane. By the time the Bombers welcomed North Melbourne to Windy Hill in Round 8, Coleman might have been in the best form of his career. 'He's a witch-doctor, not a forward,' gabbled Hec de Lacy in *The Sporting Globe*. 'He deals in spells, not football.' Though Essendon were struggling, with two wins for the season, Coleman was not: he had 37 goals from five appearances, including 14 the previous week against Fitzroy.

Hosting North Melbourne, Coleman started quickly, with two goals in the first quarter, but Essendon less so: at half-time the Bombers trailed by 25 points. They turned it around and overran North in the last to

---

7   Alongside this article was a photo of Footscray captain-coach Charlie Sutton, smiling uncertainly from his sickbed, where he too had been waylaid by flu: the selection committee picked the semi-final team at his home, Sutton being too ill to come to the club. Sutton, like Coleman, played in the match; unlike Coleman, he was among his team's best, and was chaired from the field afterwards.

8   A few minutes of film of this match was unearthed in 2014. The snippets of Coleman show him being beaten thoroughly by Footscray full-back Herb Henderson. Other cameos include Essendon's captain (and 1953 Brownlow medallist) Bill Hutchison, a youngish Ted Whitten, and Lionel 'Nappy' Ollington, who played five games for the Bulldogs but won greater fame as the proprietor of an infamous floating two-up school, which he ran for more than 30 years before selling out to colourful Melbourne identity Mick Gatto. In 1991, Ollington won the right to conduct legal two-up games at Flemington Racecourse on Anzac Day.

win by 23 points, but Coleman, who'd contributed three further goals to the fightback, wasn't there to celebrate. He'd landed awkwardly from a marking contest, dislocated his right knee, and been stretchered away to an ambulance. As he received bouquets, telegrams and well-wishers at Sacred Heart Hospital in Moreland, he understood that, aged 25, he might have played his last game.[9] 'I certainly want to play again,' he told *The Argus*'s Michael Armit, 'but if the doctor advises against it ...'

The doctors did advise against it, and though Coleman trained with Essendon before the 1956 season, he heeded their counsel. But he burnished his legend at Windy Hill after returning as coach in 1961, leading Essendon to premierships in 1962 and 1965. His loathing of umpires never abated. As a coach, Coleman was reported three times for misconduct in their general direction; persistent legend has it that he refused to serve umpires in the pubs that he ran, and shunned conversation with anyone wearing a white shirt, in any circumstances.

The what-if of the 1951 premiership was dwarfed in turn by the what-if of Coleman's career. Even allowing for a slight decline of pace in his late 20s and early 30s, if he'd played 300 games he'd have bolted past Gordon Coventry's 1299 career goals. And both were dwarfed by the what-if of Coleman's life as a whole, ended by a heart attack in 1973, at the age of 44. Few figures have contributed as much to football's folklore; fewer still have left it wanting so much more.

---

9   Incredibly, Coleman still led Essendon's goalkicking for 1954, with 42 from five and three-quarter games.

21

The Television Era Dawns
Collingwood 8.10.58 Essendon 13.15.93
Victoria Park
ROUND 1, 1957

There was always going to be a decent crowd. It was Collingwood at home – and a Collingwood who had played in the last two grand finals, even if they'd been roughed up pretty badly in both by arch-nemeses Melbourne. It was Round 1, and a Round 1 which fell on an Easter Saturday. The Weather Bureau's best guess was a cool April afternoon with little prospect of rain. Around 30,000 people turned out at Victoria Park. Shortly after three-quarter time, with the Magpies working harder than they might have anticipated to stay ahead of the visitors, that audience swelled considerably: for the first time, top-flight Australian football was about to be broadcast live on television.

This was not quite the great event originally portended. As late as the Thursday before the Saturday, the TV guide in *The Age* had promised that the three channels available in Melbourne would each broadcast the last quarter of one of the three games scheduled for Easter Saturday (the rest of the round was due to be played on Easter Monday). GTV-9 would show Collingwood versus Essendon, HSV-7 would carry St Kilda versus South Melbourne, and ABV-2 would have Carlton versus Hawthorn; the listings promised 'final quarter and dressing-room scenes'. The channels had each paid the VFL £50 per match for this access.

GTV-9 was the newest addition to Melbourne television schedules, having made its debut covering the Melbourne Olympic Games the previous November, and begun full-time broadcasting on 19 January.[1]

---

1   GTV-9's opening night extravaganza would, boggled *The Argus* the day before, attract an audience
     of 200,000, 'some of them as far away as Ararat, Bendigo, Traralgon and Mansfield'. It opened

By way of illustration of the attrition and angst attendant upon all media revolutions, 19 January 1957 was also the date on which Melbourne newsstands were graced for the last time by *The Argus*, which closed after 111 years of publication. *The Argus* had not merely covered football, it was woven into the game's fabric: a format of finals used in the VFL's early decades was known as the Argus System, in acknowledgement of the paper's championing of it. After more than a century of chronicling Australia's game, from its primordial rucking in the paddocks along the Yarra to the dawn of its role as a television spectacle, the last football-related item *The Argus* ran was a small notice that Collingwood were seeking an assistant secretary, under the age of 40, with accountancy or bookkeeping experience, salary £1000 to £1250.

GTV-9 hired former Australian cricket captain Ian Johnson[2] to front its VFL coverage. Channel Seven favoured a professional sportscaster: Tony Charlton, who came up through radio before being lured in front of the cameras by Channel Nine for the Olympics, and then poached by Seven. At the ABC, it was a double act of Ken Dakin and Ray McDonald. In theory, Channel Nine had the top drawcard of the season's opening day: 1956's beaten grand finalists[3] at home, in the sort of atmosphere that only a wounded and vindictive Victoria Park could conjure, while none of the teams playing in the day's other two fixtures had featured in 1956's finals. Channel Nine also planned to premiere, at 7.30 p.m., the first edition of *The Pelaco Football Inquest*,

---

with a two-hour variety show featuring stars of stage and radio, along with an Aboriginal choir led by Harold Blair, the performing ponies of Bullen's Circus, the ventriloquist Ron Blaskett and an orchestra conducted by accordionist Lou Toppano. The opening address was given by Victoria's English-born governor, Sir Dallas Brooks – for some years the number-one ticketholder at Richmond – whose limousine was driven directly into the studio. Clearly wondering how his career had descended to this from surviving Gallipoli, winning the Croix de Guerre and Distinguished Service Order in World War I, captaining the Combined Services' cricket and hockey teams, and rising to commandant-general of the Royal Marines in World War II, Sir Dallas gravely reminded viewers: 'If you're not happy with what you're seeing, you don't like it, or it just frankly bores you, put the switch to off.'

2   A considerable body of opinion has never understood why Ian Johnson was preferred as captain to the swashbuckling Boys' Own hero Keith Miller. Johnson, widely perceived as the diplomatic, establishment choice, became the first 20th-century Australian captain to oversee consecutive Ashes defeats.

3   Collingwood had been thoroughly towelled by Melbourne in the 1956 grand final, 17.19 to 6.12. A few Collingwood supporters brought further opprobrium upon the club by flinging a bunch of actual magpies onto the arena as the team took the field. Their wings having been cruelly and crudely clipped, the birds flapped helplessly about until retrieved by kindly members of the crowd or police. A then-record 115,802 people officially saw the match, but many more forced entrance, perching perilously atop grandstand roofs and perimeter fences. A ruffian mob estimated at 5000 stormed the members' gates, while others smashed windows at the back of the stands to gain access. 'A national disgrace,' grizzled *The Argus*, agonising about the imminent Olympics.

which promised contemplation of the day's big game by Ian Johnson, Jack Mueller and Phil Gibbs.[4]

When the great day dawned, however, a headline on *The Age*'s front page mourned 'TV for Only One League Game'. The accompanying story explained that an obscure dispute between the VFL and a body called the Ground Management Association had forced a scaling down of plans; as Victoria Park was not a member of the GMA, all three networks now planned to carry Collingwood versus Essendon.

A full-page advertisement in Round 1's edition of *The Football Record* recognised the potential of football fans as a market for television sets. Suttons of Elizabeth Street spruiked their Admiral TV consoles, boasting 'all Admiral's 1957 American features', which included a 'super-cascode chassis', 'top-front tuning' and 'aluminised picture tube', demonstrating that vapid technological jargon on advertisements for consumer electronics is not an exclusively modern blight. An editorial in the same edition of the *Record* pondered the potential downside, once televisions became a common household fixture. 'In mid-winter,' it fretted, 'when cold and wet conditions often prevail, attendances always fall away. To what extent they will be further affected by the persuasive appeal of a television receiver and a warm fireside remains to be seen.'

Few Melburnians, perhaps only 5 per cent, owned a television set in 1957. The new contraptions were a considerable investment: a 21-inch black-and-white TV on a fancy swivelling stand could run past £250, and however tempting the baroque hire-purchase arrangements advertised alongside the devices, that was still three months' wages for an assistant secretary at Collingwood. But whatever percentage of that percentage tuned in to their preferred channel at around 4 p.m. would have found – once they'd waited for their TV to warm up, and slapped the shadows and stripes out of the picture – that a grandstand finish was shaping up at Victoria Park.

To the surprise of many – especially Collingwood – the Bombers had given the Magpies a game. A batch of new recruits – identified by the subsequent report in *The Age* as 'Ken Timms in the ruck, John Birt,

---

4   This was simulcast as a radio programme on 3KZ. Pelaco's advertisements in *The Football Record* were adorned with the slogan 'It is indeed a lovely shirt, Sir', having moved mercifully – though not that recently – on from 'Pelaco Bill', a grinning cartoon Aboriginal dressed in one of Pelaco's pristine shirts with what was doubtless intended as hilarious incongruity, alongside the pidgin caption 'Mine tinkit they fit'. Pelaco Bill was based on Mulga Fred, an Indigenous showman buckjumper, who deserved better.

roving, and Col Hebbard on a half-forward flank'[5] – had stiffened Essendon's previously suspect spine. The centre half-back, Jeff Gamble, and his flankers, Bob Shearman and Mal Pascoe, had repelled all but Collingwood's most determined efforts. At three-quarter time, as football fans across Melbourne joined the audience, Collingwood were in front, but only by two points.

Collingwood's us-against-the-known-universe persecution complex was already well established by 1957, and had been further inflamed by those humiliating losses of the 1955 and 1956 grand finals to their silver-spoon-sucking rivals from Melbourne. It can have done Collingwood's precarious psychological equilibrium little good that on Easter Saturday 1957, people's first sight of live football on television, whether watching at home, or huddled before the windows of the stores which sold the things, was the Magpies getting overrun at Victoria Park, giving up six goals to one in the last to lose by 35 points. Here, perhaps, lay the true genesis of the Colliwobbles, that institutional tendency to disintegrate under pressure, and scrutiny.

Collingwood were not all bad. Ruckman Ray Gabelich, winger Brian Gray and half-forward Bill Serong were among the few able to penetrate Essendon's formidably fortified half-back line; they finished with seven of Collingwood's eight goals between them. Gabelich and Gray did have some experience – indeed, all the experience there was – of playing football live on television. They had been members of the combined VFL/VFA team which had played a Victorian Amateur Football Association side in an exhibition match at the Melbourne Olympic Games on 7 December 1956; both sides wore long-sleeved guernseys emblazoned with the Olympic rings, the VFL/VFA in green, the VAFA in white. But Gabelich and Gray had lost that afternoon as well, 12.9 to 8.7, as the amateurs scored an unlikely but appropriately Olympic victory. Among the VAFA's best was ruckman Dick Fenton-Smith of Ormond Amateurs, who contributed four goals; he was signed by Melbourne, to whom he was more or less destined by his double-barrelled surname alone, made his debut against Collingwood in Round 2 of 1957, and played in two premierships.

On Easter Monday, Channel Nine showed the last quarter of Geelong versus Footscray, live from Kardinia Park – another venue free of the iron

---

5   Ken Timms and John Birt would be members of Essendon's 1962 premiership side, and Birt of 1965's as well. Birt coached Essendon for one wretched season in 1971.

grasp of the Ground Management Association. It had been believed that no such broadcast would be possible, as Geelong lay beyond the 50-mile reach of Channel Nine's outside broadcast equipment. However, a team of engineers had reconnoitred a height in the vicinity and were able to direct a signal to Channel Nine's transmitter at Mount Dandenong. 'We are satisfied,' the station's general manager, Colin Bednall,[6] told *The Age*, '[that] the quality of pictures made in the tests justifies the telecast, but I would not like to promise the pictures will be as good as those taken at a Melbourne ground.' Those *The Age* referred to as 'televiewers' squinted through the static at a treat: the climax of a seesawing draw between the Cats and the Bulldogs, Geelong full-forward Fred Wooller finishing with seven.

Round 1 of 1957 was the most significant Round 1 since the first Round 1, 60 years previously. Television would not change the game itself much, in terms of rules and tactics, but would utterly transform the culture surrounding it. In the short term, some of *The Football Record*'s worries about attendance appeared justified: crowds were down slightly in 1958, down slightly further in 1959, and slightly further still in 1960. In 1961, the VFL bailed out of the final-quarter broadcast experiment, despite an offer of £225 per game from Melbourne's three channels, and also forbade TV replays[7] – and crowds came roaring back to pre-television levels and beyond.

Only the most obdurate Luddite could have imagined that this rigid protectionism was tenable in the long term, however – and more visionary folk could see that television was a gateway to bigger audiences, more money and a more dominant position in Australia's sporting landscape. Within half a century of the first flickering live broadcasts of the VFL, through various increments of liberalisation – there was for a time a restriction on broadcasting live matches in the cities where they were being played – it was possible to watch any AFL game as it happened from pretty much anywhere in the world, and live crowds were nevertheless

6   As air correspondent for *The Daily Mail* in the United Kingdom between 1942 and 1944, Colin Bednall regularly flew aboard bombers on raids. Other career highlights included being managing editor of *The Argus*, a brief stint at UNESCO, and serving as media consultant to Prime Minister Gough Whitlam.

7   Arrangements were made, once all tickets were sold, for a delayed telecast of the 1961 grand final, in which Hawthorn beat Footscray to win the Hawks' first flag. Victoria's premier at the time, Sir Henry Bolte, had interceded, saying: 'I feel as a private citizen that the VFL should allow the grand final to be televised. The League has, I think, an obligation to the thousands of football supporters who would not be able to attend the match.' The grand final would not be broadcast live in Victoria until 1977 – when, thanks to the draw between North Melbourne and Collingwood, viewers got to see two.

such that the AFL was, by some estimates, the fourth-best attended football competition on Earth, behind the United States' NFL, Germany's Bundesliga and England's Premier League.

The televising of Essendon's overwhelming of Collingwood on the first day of season 1957 was the beginning of the end of the VFL as a semi-regulated civil war among Melbourne's suburban tribes. It would grow less and less necessary to be raised within a club's geographical catchment area to develop an attachment to it, or to watch one's preferred team play. It also marked a significant acceleration of the transition from game to industry. Television money would make football professional, and players richer. Television cameras would make football cleaner, to the regret of those who believed that this arena of unfettered, unashamed machismo had become effetely bowdlerised – and to the likely relief of those who actually played in it, who would have to worry less and less about getting their heads busted by an elbow thrown 50 yards behind the play.

22

Lou Richards Loses a Bet
Footscray 12.8.80 Melbourne 10.11.71
Western Oval
ROUND 15, 1959

It seemed a safe wager to lay. Home ground advantage and Ted Whitten notwithstanding, there was little reason to fancy Footscray (one win all year, 12 points adrift at bottom of the ladder) against Melbourne (top of the ladder, participants in the last five grand finals, winners of three). It was certain wooden spooners versus premiership favourites,[1] and for most judges there seemed little to do but tip Melbourne to win, then speculate about the margin. On form and personnel, Footscray versus Melbourne shaped as a contest between the blancmange and the sledgehammer.

Writing in *The Sun News-Pictorial*, Lou Richards decided, as he often did, to liven things up a bit. The former Collingwood premiership captain[2] was four seasons retired, and establishing himself as a new sort of football pundit – one who regarded commentating on the game as a game in itself. He had inherited his column in *The Sun*,[3] and a persona of larrikin pontificator, from his friend and rival Jack Dyer, who was taking a year-long sabbatical in the United Kingdom. Photos of 'Captain Blood' arrayed in top hat and tails for Derby day at Epsom Downs had caused

---

1 Melbourne were indeed 1959's premiers, and indeed 1960's. That great Demons team of the 1950s would play in seven consecutive grand finals for five premierships.

2 Lou Richards led Collingwood to victory in the 1953 grand final, in which his goal early in the third quarter prompted the flurry which saw off Geelong. Richards played 250 games for Collingwood, and kicked 423 goals. He received a state funeral upon his death in 2017, aged 94.

3 *The Sun News-Pictorial* was launched in 1922. It was absorbed by *The Herald*, to become *The Herald Sun*, in 1990, on the Monday after that year's grand final. Beforehand, Richards – who also claimed 'the Colliwobbles' among his coinages – forecast that 1990 was going to be 'the year of the Pies. The champagne is already on ice, and the caviar has been ordered.' This recklessly fate-tempting prediction proved accurate, however.

considerable merriment in the tabloids back home. Richards negotiated a weekly retainer of £10 – four quid more than Dyer had been getting.

Richards, like everyone permitted to leave their residence unsupervised, thought Melbourne would beat Footscray. But he and/or his ghostwriter[4] searched themselves for an excitingly hyperbolic means of conveying the sun-to-rise-tomorrow inevitability of such an outcome. 'Do you ever think,' Richards asked *The Sun*'s readers, 'you will ever see the Bolshoi Ballet break into rock'n'roll during a performance? Well, you're the kind who'll believe anything – even that Footscray can beat Melbourne today.' This was a pretty laboured set-up, as these things go, and 50 years from being rendered invalid by the Bolshoi's collaboration with Lady Gaga – though it would have been expecting a great deal of Richards to see that coming from a year in which the biggest Australian single was 'Oh Yeah Uh Huh' by Col Joye & The Joy Boys.[5] 'If Footscray win,' Richards concluded, 'I'll sweep Collins Street with a feather duster.'

Footscray's 1954 grand final win – against Melbourne – seemed a long time ago, if not as long a time ago as it would grow to seem over ensuing decades, before the drought was broken in 2016 in supremely unlikely, Bolshoi-does-Black Sabbath style by a Western Bulldogs team who'd finished the home-and-away season seventh, with an injury list like that of General George Custer's 7th Cavalry on the evening of 25 June 1876. When Melbourne came to the Western Oval in 1959, just three veterans of Footscray's 1954 triumph remained: half-back Jim Gallagher, ruckman Arthur Edwards and talismanic captain-coach Ted Whitten.

At 26, Whitten was the second-oldest man in the side. He'd had plenty of practice at getting beaten since taking over as Footscray's captain-coach in 1957 – this was his 38th game in charge, of which the Bulldogs had lost 29 – but had not developed any appetite for it. Whitten would certainly have thought Richards' article less amusing than Richards did. The historical record does not tell us if Whitten removed a crumpled copy from his sock at a climactic moment in his pre-match speech, and brandished it at his spittle-drenched players as he conjured

---

4   Far from commonly among athletes turned columnists, Lou Richards was never shy about collaborating with ghostwriters, mentioning several in generous terms in his autobiography, *The Kiss of Death*. The book's ghostwriter, Stephen Phillips, was given equal billing on the cover.

5   Col Joye has a claim to having been Australia's first proper home-grown rock'n'roll star, or is at least entitled to arm-wrestle Johnny O'Keefe for the title. 'Oh Yeah Uh Huh', the first Australian chart-topper by an Australian artist, was a pleasant if insubstantial shuffle which had previously been a hit, in more up-tempo form, for American R&B duo Mickey & Sylvia. In Col Joye's version, in a doubtfully intentionally Dadaist touch, Joy Boys drummer John Bogie played a typewriter.

a sublime vision of its humiliated author being jeered by townsfolk as he performed his rite of atonement, but it would be surprising to learn that Whitten did not.

The preview of the match in *The Football Record* gave the home team little hope, noting the clobbering Footscray had received the previous week from Hawthorn. The only cheer that the red, white and blue–bedecked contingent at the Western Oval would have found in the *Record*'s pages was the promise of a post-match dance in the club rooms.[6] Organisers of this wingding, who would surely have been planning a wake for a massacre foretold, found themselves having to re-cater swiftly for a celebration of an entirely unanticipated victory. Led by the dauntless Whitten, with characteristic brio and three goals, the young Bulldogs – 11 of Footscray's team were aged 20 or under – stayed with Melbourne for the first half, got 14 points ahead in the third quarter, and hung on to win, astoundingly and confoundingly, by nine.

Lou Richards, no fool, must have realised as soon as his bet was lost that he'd won a much bigger prize. Had the game proceeded as expected, and had the Demons bludgeoned the Bulldogs, the column containing his pre-match prediction would have embraced one of the proverbial undignified fates of most newspaper journalism – wrapping fish, lining budgerigar cages – and been little thought of thereafter. But Footscray's upsetting of Melbourne had turned Richards' hubristic prediction into a story, and therefore an opportunity. On the Monday after the game, Richards, watched by a tittering crowd of passing pedestrians, and a heckling delegation of players and officials from Footscray, crossed Collins Street on his hands and knees, swishing at the bitumen with a feather duster. On the Tuesday, a photograph of Richards undertaking his penance consumed *The Sun News-Pictorial*'s entire front page.

Richards understood that if his footballing skills were not transferable to the world beyond Victoria Park, his personality might be. On the field, Richards was a masterly rover, distinguished by a penguinish

---

6   A highlight of *The Football Record* of the period was the letters column, 'Your Side of the Fence', putatively edited by a certain Philip Morris, who offered a carton of the eponymous tobacco company's cigarettes for the best weekly submission. In Round 15 of 1959, the Letter of the Week was one noting that the Brownlow Medal tended to be won by good players in average sides, and citing South Melbourne, who hadn't played finals since 1945 but had two Brownlow winners in their line-up, in Ron Clegg and Fred Goldsmith, who could shortly be joined by a third, Bob Skilton. (Skilton would indeed win the first of his three Brownlows in 1959.) The author of this observation, Danny Wilson of North Fitzroy, gave his age as 11, presenting the page's sponsor with an ethical dilemma. 'Good work, Danny,' read the reply. 'A carton of Philip Morris is on its way to Dad.'

gait presaging the later, if much quieter, Collingwood midfield mainstay Dane Swan, and he led his club's goalkicking three times. But Richards was also a professional pest – a chirruper, a sledger, a stirrer and an upsetter, usually able to wriggle out of trouble with a swift wit and guileless charm. Off the field, Richards realised, he could do much the same. In the profession of football punditry, there was a general tone of beard-stroking, pipe-sucking, finger-steepling seriousness, almost as if the trade's practitioners were desperately seeking to compensate for doing something so footling for a living. Richards resolved to remind everybody that it was only a game.

Richards had earned the nickname 'Louie the Lip' as a player – goading, mocking and annoying opponents and umpires over 15 seasons, during which the hardest men of a hard era had not been able to shut him up, though many served suspensions for trying. It was a short evolutionary step from that to the 'Kiss of Death': the set-up-to-fail forecast loaded with a forfeit that would earn the self-sabotaging anti-sage yet further publicity.

In 1961, Richards once again tipped a star-studded Melbourne side to crush a youthful Footscray led by Ted Whitten, this time in the preliminary final. It was a less sure bet than Footscray and Melbourne's 1959 encounter – Footscray were clearly much improved, and strange things happen in finals – but Richards declared not only that Melbourne would win, but that he would trim Whitten's front garden with nail scissors if they did not. Upon arriving at the MCG, Richards encountered the prime minister, Robert Menzies, who informed him: 'All I want to see is Melbourne get beaten here this afternoon, so you can cut that lawn.' Whitten once more dragged his Bulldogs over the line; by the following Monday, a temporary grandstand had been erected outside Whitten's Yarraville home to accommodate the crowd, estimated in the low thousands, who came to watch Richards perform his absurdist horticulture.[7]

Richards' wilfully unreliable prognostications occasioned many further misadventures. He painted the flagpole atop the T&G building with a nail polish brush. He jumped off St Kilda pier on a winter's morning. He bathed in the horse trough outside the pub he owned, the Phoenix

---

7   Ted Whitten would himself later undertake at least one similar expiation, walking Adelaide's Rundle Mall clad in a Croweaters guernsey after South Australia beat Victoria by two points at Football Park in 1994. 'Go on, have a laugh, you bastards,' he instructed onlookers, and retorted to one derisive blast of car horn with: 'Shut up, dickhead.' Whitten's single-handed efforts to pound life back into interstate football were nothing if not wholehearted.

on Flinders Street, as Hawthorn full-forward Peter Hudson performed back-scrubbing duties. He rowed Geelong's coach, Billy Goggin, across the Barwon River in a bathtub, as the Geelong players whose prospects he'd doubted pelted him with eggs from a circling speedboat; thousands of spectators lined the Barwon's banks. He cleaned Dermott Brereton's Ferrari with a cotton ball on the steps of Hawthorn Town Hall before involuntarily wearing the bucket, had an assortment of Italian cuisine tipped over him by various Carlton players, wheelbarrowed Blues ruckman Warren Jones down Lygon Street while wearing a dinner suit, and carried up a stretch of Errol Street, to North Melbourne Town Hall, all 114 kilograms of cumbersome Kangaroos ruckman Mick Nolan, one of many players who owed his nickname – in his case, 'The Galloping Gasometer' – to Richards' ebullient columns and commentary.[8]

Richards had grown up almost literally in the shadows of Victoria Park, in the Collingwood of the 1920s and 1930s, where the Great Depression bit hard: the footballs of Richards' childhood were fashioned from bundled-up newspapers, and kicked with bare feet. As is often the case with people who escape poverty, the thought of returning to it terrified him; Jack Dyer once said of Richards, 'He's been like a rat in a famine, and he still has those characteristics of native cunning. If he went to the Moon, he'd find five cents there, for sure.' Richards' trademark self-mockery was always astutely tuned so that nobody could forget that his was a self worth mocking.

It would be a sensationally profligate waste of time to fossick for subversive subtext, let alone dissident doctrine, in Richards' stunts and pranks – though some did seem, in retrospect, like physical enactments of yet-unwritten TISM songs ('Wheelbarrowing Wow Jones', for example, could readily be imagined as a B side to 'I Rooted a Girl Who Rooted a Guy Who Rooted a Girl Who Rooted a Guy Who Rooted a Girl Who Rooted Shane Crawford', not that the latter was ever a single.)[9]

---

8   Others so ennobled included 'Lethal' Leigh Matthews, Bruce 'The Flying Doormat' Doull, Rene 'The Incredible Hulk' Kink, Robert 'The Big Dipper' DiPierdomenico, 'Slammin'' Sam Kekovich, Peter 'The Macedonian Marvel' Daicos, 'Fabulous' Phil Carman and 'Delicate' Des Dickson. The last of these may have been the wittiest: Dickson was a notorious ruffian who arguably cost his team, Hawthorn, the 1963 flag. In the second-last home-and-away game of that year, Dickson was suspended for striking North Melbourne's Noel Teasdale, ruling Delicate Des out for games including the last home-and-away game, the semi-final and the grand final – all, by happenstance, against Geelong, and in each of which Dickson would have been tasked with nullifying, one way or another, Geelong's peerless ruckman, Graham 'Polly' Farmer. Geelong won all three matches.
9   TISM – an acronym for This Is Serious Mum – were a strange, angry band who formed in Melbourne in the early 1980s. Australian football was a recurring preoccupation of their work: TISM's singer, anonymous beneath the group's menacing masks, styled himself Ron Hitler-Barassi.

Richards' escapades were straightforward slapstick knockabout, things to be done because they seemed like fun things to do. They made people laugh, which appears to be pretty much all Richards wanted to do with his life, and there are worse ambitions to have. But all nonsense is disruptive, especially to those whose position depends on maintaining a veneer of gravitas. Richards was crowned King of Moomba in 1981,[10] but a more appropriate honour had been bestowed in 1972, when he'd been designated court jester to that year's Moomba monarch, John Farnham.[11] Richards was for Australian football what the curly-shoed, silly-hatted joculator was for medieval courts: a licensed trickster, engaged to remind all concerned of the follies of pomposity.

But there were, it turned out, limits to how far Richards would abase himself. In 1989, Richards declared that if Carlton beat Collingwood at Waverley, he would permit his head to be shaved by Blues winger Mil Hanna, whose own gleaming noggin, denuded by alopecia, had earned him the nickname 'The Cranium'.[12] It is irresistibly tempting to read a measure of personal vendetta into Hanna's 20-possession performance, which earned him three Brownlow votes as it helped the Blues to a six-point win. Richards reported to Lygon Street for his appointment with Hanna's razor, and photos of the bald pair were duly snapped for the newspapers. Observant readers noticed, at Richards' temples, the giveaway wrinkles of a swimming cap.

Explicitly football-related TISM songs included 'The Back Upon Which Jezza Jumped', a homage to Graeme 'Jerker' Jenkin, the Collingwood ruckman ascended by Carlton's Alex Jesaulenko for his unforgettable mark in the 1970 grand final, and the self-explanatory 'Shut Up – the Footy's on the Radio', which won a 1997 competition seeking a theme for Triple M's AFL coverage. However, TISM's entire oeuvre was riddled with obtuse football references. Part of TISM's video for 'Greg! The Stop Sign' was filmed in St Kilda's locker room, and the cover of TISM's 1991 compilation *Gentlemen, Start Your Egos* featured a portrait of Ted Whitten, whom TISM also credited with the sleeve notes on their 1990 album *Hot Dogma*. That TISM were never asked to perform at a grand final is a dark, shabby stain upon the game.

10 In 1982, Lou Richards also became the first human to be designated a living national treasure by the National Trust, who gave him a badge which he declared a satisfactory substitute for the Brownlow Medal he never won.

11 John Farnham – or Johnny, as he then was – has since figured in or as the grand final entertainment more than any artist bar Mike Brady. Farnham's best-known hit, 'You're the Voice', remains, however, a terrible song, being basically Australia's equivalent of John Lennon's 'Imagine', which is the worst song ever written.

12 Mil Hanna was the first Lebanese-born player in the VFL/AFL. He wrecked a knee early in his debut game in 1986 but restarted his career the following season. He was a member of Carlton's 1995 premiership side.

23

Big Nick versus Polly
Carlton 7.16.58 Geelong 7.22.64
Princes Park
ROUND 6, 1963

John Nicholls was five years younger than Graham Farmer when Geelong came to Princes Park in 1963, but Nicholls was the better-known quantity, at least to Victorian crowds, and Victorian opponents. At 23, Nicholls was already in his seventh season with the Blues. He had played his 100th game the week before, steadying the nerves of a team who looked determined to find a way to lose to Richmond, and kicking the goal that preserved Carlton's undefeated start to his first season as captain.

Graham 'Polly' Farmer – the nickname had lingered since his childhood in a Perth orphanage, bestowed in recognition of a talkative disposition, akin to that of a parrot – was playing his second season with Geelong, but only his twelfth VFL game since arriving, amid great ballyhoo, from Western Australia the year before. Farmer had won three flags with East Perth, two Sandover Medals for himself,[1] and had attracted plenty of interest from Victorian clubs. In one of those what-ifs liable to induce picturesque conniptions in St Kilda fans of fragile disposition, he'd seriously considered the Saints, who'd made a generous offer, including a sales job at a Holden dealership.

However, while Farmer was being given the grand tour by St Kilda after the 1961 season, Geelong club secretary Leo O'Brien staked

---

1   Polly Farmer won the 1956 and 1960 Sandover Medals, but tied with East Fremantle's Jack Clarke in 1957, and it was awarded to Clarke alone under the countback system. In 1997, when the countback system was abolished, Farmer was retrospectively declared joint winner of the 1957 Sandover. He joined Barry Cable, Merv McIntosh and Haydn Bunton Sr as triple medallists; Bill Walker of Swan Districts won four.

out Farmer's lodgings, waiting in a car parked outside the George Hotel.[2] O'Brien intercepted Farmer on his way out one day, and whisked him to a rendezvous with Geelong coach Bob Davis in Laverton, who drove Farmer the rest of the way to Geelong[3] for a furtive daytrip to Kardinia Park, and the big sell about the relaxed pace of life in a smaller town.

It was a lure Geelong utilised often, though it didn't always work. Five years earlier, the Cats had failed to entice a promising centre from Maryborough by the name of Don Nicholls. He went to Carlton, and his younger – though emphatically not littler – brother, John, followed him. John Nicholls had looked the goods immediately, although his 1960 season was truncated by a brief prison sentence for embezzling the hefty sum of £5558 from his then-employer, the English, Scottish & Australian Bank; Nicholls told the court he had become indebted to illegal bookmakers, not known for their indulgent attitude towards defaulters, whoever they played for.

The first showdown between John Nicholls, the VFL's supreme ruckman of the age, and Polly Farmer, the WANFL challenger for that title, was supposed to have been Farmer's first game for the Cats – Round 1, 1962, when Carlton opened the new season by hosting Geelong at Princes Park, in front of nearly 42,000 people. But Nicholls was a late withdrawal, hobbled by an ankle niggle. Between that absence and a recent hot spell that had cooked the ground into a deck of positively West Australian dusty hardness, conditions seemed to have conspired to encourage a dream debut for Farmer.

Conditions had, to the extent that Farmer took complete charge of the ruck, bewildering Carlton – and occasionally Geelong – with his reflexive playing on after marking, and his Brobdingnagian handballs, almost as far as some of his teammates could kick. He also kicked four goals while resting up forward, as Geelong won by 39 points.

And conditions hadn't. In the opening minutes, Farmer limped away from a boundary throw-in contest with Carlton's Graham Donaldson

---

2   The George Hotel is now an upscale delicatessen with an extensive range of craft beers, like everything else in Melbourne.

3   Probably at some speed. Though Bob Davis's nickname of 'The Geelong Flyer', after the Melbourne-Geelong express train, was principally a homage to his swiftness as a player, various contemporaries have shuddered at the memory of his driving. He is reputed to have once completed the trip from Geelong to Melbourne in 27 minutes.

and Maurie Sankey.[4] He played the rest of the match with a damaged left anterior cruciate ligament, an injury which should have finished his game, and could have finished his career. He played the next two matches as well, best afield for Geelong in both, before being stretchered off in agony against Richmond in Round 4. The rest of Farmer's debut season for Geelong consisted of abortive comebacks, against Essendon in Round 9 and North Melbourne in Round 17. After the latter collapse, beneath the headline 'An Operation Now', *The Age* ran a melancholy photo of Farmer limping off Kardinia Park, each arm around a supporting trainer, left knee bandaged, looking back towards the playing field, wondering if he'd ever dominate one again.

Geelong didn't wilt without Farmer in 1962, reaching a preliminary final against John Nicholls and Carlton – two preliminary finals, indeed, after the first was drawn. In the grand final, Carlton, exhausted, were jumped early by a well-rested Essendon, and never recovered. But both Carlton and Geelong thought themselves chances in 1963, and by the time the two clubs – and Nicholls and Farmer – met in Round 6, both looked like they had reason to. Geelong had lost only once, to the reigning premiers at Windy Hill. Carlton hadn't lost at all. And Geelong had Farmer back, minus one removed ligament, and he'd been beating the best: Footscray's John Schultz, North Melbourne's Noel Teasdale, and a wild-haired and wilder-tempered teenage St Kilda rookie called Carl Ditterich.[5] But the return to Princes Park would be the stiffest test yet of Farmer's talents, and of his rickety knee.

The front page of *The Age* on the Monday after the game was dominated by two pictures of the latest victim of Hawthorn's 'Delicate' Des Dickson – North Melbourne captain Allen Aylett.[6] One photo showed Aylett being stretchered from Glenferrie Oval, the other captured him recovering at home, dapper in a silk dressing gown, as if composing terse satires in between sips of absinthe, rather than attempting to recall what had hit him. On the back page, the battle between Nicholls and Farmer was assessed as a reflection of the game itself – an even contest,

---

4   Maurie Sankey played 100 games for Carlton, and should have played more. On 21 November 1965 he was one of three people killed in a head-on car accident on the Hume Highway near Wangaratta. He was 25.

5   Carl Ditterich would be reported 19 times in a 285-game career with St Kilda and Melbourne, a record which stood until overhauled by 1980s nuisance David Rhys-Jones, booked 25 times in 182 appearances. One of the 30 games Ditterich missed through suspension was the 1966 grand final – St Kilda's only ever premiership victory.

6   Allen Aylett would later serve as chairman of the VFL, from 1977 to 1984.

Geelong just shading it. *The Sporting Globe* concurred, calling it 'a vigorous, but fair and entertaining tussle'. The real difference between the sides was Geelong's full-forward, Doug Wade,[7] who found four goals on a day when they were hard to come by. Carlton's Tom Carroll could have tied it at the death, just as he had the previous year's preliminary final, but his hopeful hoist from 60 metres fell short.[8]

Carlton and Geelong's 1963 seasons diverged sharply subsequent to this encounter in Round 6. When the two clubs and the two ruckmen met again in Round 17, Nicholls had the better of Farmer, but he was about the only Carlton player who beat his man as Geelong won by 61 points, without playing especially well. Carlton floundered thereafter, and missed the finals. Geelong finished second on percentage behind Hawthorn. The Cats and the Hawks finished the year playing each other three times in four weeks: in the final home-and-away game at Glenferrie Oval, the second semi-final and the grand final.

Bob Davis had built this Geelong team in his own image: expressive, exuberant and joyous. At Hawthorn, John Kennedy had fashioned a dour, ruthless and nasty opposite: the players revelled in the nickname 'Kennedy's Commandos', and played with the approximate joie de vivre of a bandolier-swaddled guerrilla militia.

Davis saw those three games against Hawthorn as a triptych depicting the eternal struggle for football's soul: between flair and ferocity, style and surliness, beauty and beastliness. In Round 7, Geelong and Hawthorn had played a bitter draw at Kardinia Park, during which – among other infamies – Geelong half-forward John Sharrock had been knocked wobbly-legged, prompting an all-in that required the assistance of police to placate. Davis was typically forthcoming in his opinion of Hawthorn: 'The worst and dirtiest team I have ever played against.' It was around this time that Kennedy, according to some, coined the 'handbaggers' nickname that Geelong would spend decades shaking off.

---

7   In 1963, Doug Wade and all Geelong barrackers were still seething – some have not stopped – at an umpiring decision which might have tipped the 1962 preliminary final replay the other way. With Geelong five points behind, Wade – who'd kicked six already – marked 25 metres in front with seconds to play, but umpire Jack Irving penalised him for grabbing the shorts of Carlton full-back Peter Barry. Barry punted the ball safely upfield with the last kick of the game.

8   Tom Carroll was the VFL's leading goalkicker in his first season in 1961, with 54 goals. He played just 55 games for the Blues before retiring from the League aged 23, having failed to acquire a taste for city living. After returning to the family's Riverina turkey farm, he became something of a rural football legend, enjoying success with both Ganmain and Grong Grong-Matong. Dennis and Wayne Carroll, of South Melbourne and/or Sydney, were his nephews.

For the aesthetes – i.e. Davis and his ilk – 1963 concluded as an unalloyed triumph. Geelong beat Hawthorn by 38 points in the last home-and-away fixture, by 19 points in the semi-final and by 49 points in the grand final – before which, in a characteristically eccentric touch, Davis enlisted children's entertainer Happy Hammond to play some inspiring piano-accordion in Geelong's dressing-room.[9] At three-quarter time in the grand final, with the Cats just ten points in front, Davis made an audacious speech, in the circumstances, telling his players: 'We've got 'em beaten. This quarter, I want you to show 'em what genuine football is. Just show 'em how you pass the ball to one another. Just run straight over the top of them.'

Davis's Cats did exactly that. Hawthorn scored only three points in the last term as Geelong piled on six goals, one of them a glorious coast-to-coast bravura linking Roy West's kick-in from full-back to Ken Goodland's deft tap-down to Farmer's adroit roving and handball to Bill Goggin's short stab to John Sharrock's handball back to a still-running Goggin's handball to John Yeates' pass to captain Fred Wooller on the edge of the square for his third goal of the afternoon. On the sidelines, Davis was captured by television cameras laughing with undisguised delight at the twinkling play of his team, not a leader in command, but a fan in thrall. Davis later cheerfully admitted, 'I was the last of the non-thinking coaches. All I had to do was find the right positions for each of them, keep them fit and happy and send them out on the field to strut their stuff. Seriously, that's all I did.'

There was widespread agreement that Farmer had been best afield in the 1963 grand final. That evening at Geelong Town Hall, where thousands converged to greet the returning conquerors, the loudest chant was: 'We want Polly!' *The Geelong Advertiser* compared Farmer's domination of football to Sir Donald Bradman's of cricket. It was forgivably overwrought: about the only award Farmer did not win in 1963 was the Brownlow Medal, for which he was runner-up to South Melbourne's Bob Skilton, winning his second.

Farmer's 1963 was an extraordinary year by any standards, never mind the standards of people with only one completely functioning knee.

---

9   Happy Hammond's *The Happy Show* was an afternoon fixture on HSV-7. Hammond, a Geelong native, also ran onto the ground with the 1963 grand final team. One later cast member of *The Happy Show*, a simpering ingenue known as 'Lovely Livvy', became better known as Olivia Newton-John.

After one full season in the VFL, his innovative rucking and prodigious handballing had changed Australian football; Davis later insisted that Farmer was 'the only player to have made an original contribution to the game', an assessment echoed by his awestruck apprentice John 'Sam' Newman, who estimated that Farmer was 'about one decade, one century ahead of his time'. But Farmer was a pioneer in another respect. In 1963, there were still fewer Aboriginal players in the VFL than there are laces on a Sherrin. By the time Farmer went back to Western Australia at the end of 1967, he was certainly the best-known Indigenous Australian in two states, possibly the entire country.

There was, in contemporary coverage of Farmer, remarkably little discussion of his Aboriginality: a combination, perhaps, of ignorant indifference to his heritage among observers of the game, and the mesmeric effect he had on them as a player. He was generally accepted by other players, not merely as a teammate, but as a captain – and, later, a coach.[10] Where Aboriginals had mostly appeared in Australian advertising as exotic kitsch, if they were lucky, Farmer was seen as a bankable, aspirational brand – soft drink manufacturer Tarax sponsored a board game named after him.[11] In 1963, a new football magazine, *Footy Fan*, put Farmer's picture on the cover of its first issue, albeit bleached whiter and blonder than Barry Crocker. (Given that *Footy Fan* favoured a palette which also made Milky Bar Kids out of Ron Barassi and Murray Weideman, this may not have been as crass as it now looks.) Farmer certainly experienced racist abuse, on and off the field, but wasn't the retaliating type: he took the view that such slights reflected only on the deliverer, not the recipient. He was right, but it's a tough creed to live by, requiring Herculean reserves of self-possession.

A photograph was taken of Farmer and Nicholls at Princes Park in 1963. They're airborne in a ruck duel, Farmer doing to Nicholls what he did to any number of lesser ruckmen: jumping early into the contest from the side to deny his opponent a run-up, leading with a hip to ensure that

---

10 Back home in Western Australia, Farmer won two premierships as captain-coach of West Perth – both times defeating his former club, East Perth, in the grand final. Subsequent coaching stints at Geelong and East Perth were less successful.

11 With due acknowledgement that there is no lower-hanging fruit than vintage advertising when harvesting cheap, smug shots at the expense of bygone mores, particular kudos is due the Twisties ad which appeared in *The Football Record* of the period. It depicted a man offering a woman his bag of Twisties at the football, above the promise: 'You'll score for sure with Twisties!' More importantly, the boast of the '3 beaut flavours' of cheese, 'chick'n' – vowels were presumably still subject to post-war rationing – and bacon prompts wistful outrage that bacon-flavoured Twisties are no longer a thing.

the other guy pays a price in pain, left arm raised to either paw the ball down to a waiting rover, or gather it into his chest and play on himself. Nicholls, nudged into the rear position, mimics Farmer's pose, and has his right arm across Farmer's left shoulder, balancing himself and spoiling the other ruckman's view, but the expressions on their faces anticipate the result: Nicholls hopes he's got this, Farmer knows he has.

There is a case to be made for Nicholls over Farmer (there's a case to be made for Nicholls over anyone). Nicholls played more games in football's premier competition (328 against 101), and won more VFL flags (three against one). It was not, however, a case that was ever made by John Nicholls. 'There was only one Polly Farmer,' he once said, 'and he was the best.'

24

Ron Barassi Faces His Demons
Carlton 6.22.58 Melbourne 13.17.95
Princes Park
ROUND 8, 1965

Ron Barassi was not the first player to trade one guernsey for another in pursuit of better money and/or greater opportunity, not the first to choose ambition over loyalty. He was not the first to find himself playing his first match against former teammates. But in 1965, when Barassi welcomed his old club to his new, he was the biggest name to have made such a switch. (In 1965, Barassi was the biggest name to have done anything, on the basis that he was simply the biggest name in the game.) And the trauma of Barassi's departure from Melbourne had been amplified by the fact that for many – many Melbourne fans especially – Barassi and Melbourne were indivisible. Barassi was no mere employee, but family.

Everybody knew the story: how, after Barassi's father, Melbourne player Ron Barassi Sr, had been killed at Tobruk in 1941, when his son was five years old, Melbourne had pitched in to help his mother raise the kid. Everybody knew the Barassi nativity legend, of Melbourne lobbying the League for the introduction of the father-son rule so Barassi could wear the old man's colours, of coach Norm Smith accommodating the teenage Barassi in a backyard outbuilding, teaching him football, and life, the Melbourne way. (Norm Smith's older brother, Len Smith, who played for Melbourne and Fitzroy, and coached Fitzroy and Richmond, was another significant influence.)

And everybody, Melbourne and otherwise, knew Ron Barassi's playing record: 204 games, six premierships, five seasons as captain, twice club best and fairest, twice club leading goalkicker. At 28, Barassi surely had a few more seasons in him, before an inevitable coronation as

Melbourne's coach upon Norm Smith's eventual abdication. Ron Barassi could surely no more leave Melbourne than Sir Robert Menzies could leave the Liberal Party – although Menzies, a Carlton man, was among those delighted by the destination Barassi chose when he did.[1]

Those who walk out on their families to take up a better offer rarely do so to a chorus of hearty best wishes with their future endeavours, and Melbourne fans reacted to Barassi's departure to become captain-coach at Carlton as people do when they perceive betrayal, lapsing into melodramatics to articulate their rage. Some set to work unpicking the number 31 from their replica Demons guernseys; the less patient, or more enraged, burned them. Letters were written to newspapers seeking guidance vis-à-vis the protocol of renaming pet dogs called Barassi, and bewailing the difficulty of retraining parrots taught to squawk his name. Demands were made to know what one could possibly tell the children, much as if Santa Claus had been busted with a sleigh-load of guns and meth. Barassi himself received hate mail, some of it suggesting that his late father would deliver appropriate punishment in the event, obviously unlikely though it now was, that Barassi was ever permitted to join him in the eternal upstairs.

Initially, it was some consolation to the Demons that they still functioned without their departed mikado: Melbourne travelled to Princes Park undefeated after seven games. Carlton under Barassi were not doing as well, but they weren't doing badly: having started with a win followed by two losses, they'd put together four victories on the bounce. Carlton versus Melbourne was fourth versus first – and many tipped Carlton, seduced by the patricidal narrative, like *Hamlet* re-enacted in coloured vests, or assuming that Barassi would know Norm Smith's tactics as surely as his own name. In a year in which the average attendance at Princes Park was 25,933, more than 41,000 shoehorned themselves into the ground.

The larger contingent of these – Blues fans – were disappointed at quarter time, depressed at the half, vaguely hopeful despite themselves at the last break, and desolate at the finish. In the first half, Carlton couldn't find second gear, or the goal. By half-time they'd mustered 2.10,

---

1   Sir Robert Menzies, knighted in 1963, had been Liberal leader since founding the party in 1944, and prime minister – in his second stint – since 1949. At the 1970 grand final, Menzies – then four years retired – was among the hangers-on ordered out of the dressing-room by Barassi before he gave the speech which inspired Carlton to recover from a 44-point half-time deficit.

with rover Terry Board especially haphazard; he'd finish with 2.8.[2] John Nicholls bossed the ruck, as usual, but his hit-outs were falling to Melbourne players more often than to his own. Worse still, Barassi had a rotten game, tagged effectively by Bryan Kenneally. Ken Emselle and Hassa Mann led Melbourne's attack effectively – they'd finish with three goals each – ably supported down the wings by Brian Dixon[3] and 19-year-old second-gamer Stan Alves.[4]

Carlton had illusory glimpses of hope in the second half. The Blues got two points in front during the third quarter, an impertinence to which Melbourne replied with a fusillade of three goals. In the final quarter, Carlton had the temerity to advance within four points, which prompted a barrage, this time terminal, of five more goals. Norm Smith had toyed with his protégé, Melbourne had taunted their traitor, and Barassi knew it. 'On the way up,' he said afterwards, his words just about audible over grinding teeth, 'there are lessons to be learned, and this was one of them.'

As was often the case with Barassi, promises were indistinguishable from threats: he would coach Carlton against Norm Smith, at Melbourne and South Melbourne, ten more times, for nine wins. He would lead Carlton to two premierships, and North Melbourne to two after that. It would have had a cruelly inhibiting effect on Melbourne's celebrations after beating Carlton at Princes Park in 1965 had a time machine materialised in the visitors' dressing-room, and its pilot informed the Demons not only of the glories for which Barassi was bound, but that most of Melbourne's next grand final team had not yet been born. (And if the visitor from the future had really want to kill the buzz, they could have revealed that the 1988 Demons would lose to Hawthorn by what was then a grand final record margin of 96 points.)

---

2   This is not the worst case of the yips in League history. In 2007 Lance Franklin kicked 2.11 for Hawthorn against Western Bulldogs, and in 1969 Peter McKenna managed 1.10 for Collingwood against Hawthorn. The most behinds ever scored in one game is 12, by Alex Jesaulenko for Carlton against Hawthorn in 1969, though he also scored six goals. Carlton heaped up 30.30 that day – it must have been weird for Hawthorn to contemplate a 128-point monstering and reflect that it could have been much worse, if only Jesaulenko had kicked straight.

3   Brian Dixon had one of the stranger day jobs performed by footballers of the time. Since the previous June, he'd been a member of Victoria's parliament, representing St Kilda for the Liberal Party. Dixon held the seat until 1982, despite playing for Melbourne until 1968, and spending the 1971 and 1972 seasons coaching North Melbourne, to meagre success – after which he was replaced at Arden Street by Ron Barassi. Dixon later served as Victoria's minister for youth, sport and recreation, in which role he created the 'Life. Be in it.' campaign to encourage more active lifestyles.

4   Stan Alves would play 12 seasons with Melbourne, four as captain, and was runner-up by a point to Footscray's Gary Dempsey for the 1975 Brownlow Medal. He moved to North Melbourne in 1977, where he was part of that year's premiership team, coached by Ron Barassi.

Barassi's forsaking of Melbourne for Carlton has been praised and damned in the decades since as the formal acknowledgement of Australian football as a profession. There are those who believe that Carlton's £9000 over three seasons and a £10,000 loan are equivalent to 30 pieces of silver. (It's actually equivalent, in total, to about half a million 21st-century dollars.) There are those who argue that by 1965 it was long past time that a game getting 150,000 or so people through the gates every weekend, to say nothing of the audience on radio and television, started properly rewarding those who played it. As late as 1970, Collingwood were still able to placate Len Thompson and Des Tuddenham, both resentful of the $5000 a year splashed on Western Australian recruit Peter Eakins, with $105 and $125 per match respectively.[5]

Barassi's decampment, like all things that have happened, now seems inevitable, but it wasn't. Barassi was profoundly torn, by uncertainty as to whether he even wanted to coach – he'd knocked back an earlier offer from Richmond – and by his fealty to Melbourne; in opposition to the usual cartoon representation of such a dilemma, one has to imagine a demon on both Barassi's shoulders. In December 1964, newspapers were confidently reporting that the move was off. Norm Smith even offered to stand down as coach to allow Barassi to step up – at which point, the wisdom and bravery of Barassi's decision became apparent.

If Barassi had maintained Melbourne as a force, he'd have been the guy who inherited a fortune and turned it, perhaps, into a slightly larger fortune. Carlton, give or take the 1962 grand final (where they'd been soundly beaten by Essendon), had been obstinately mediocre for years: a team that could be improved on. And Barassi, consciously or otherwise, intuited that the old order, whereby the great coaches coached where they'd played, was ending. Jock McHale had played for Collingwood, so he coached Collingwood. Dick Reynolds played for Essendon, so he coached Essendon. Frank Hughes and Norm Smith played for Melbourne, so they coached Melbourne.

Within a couple of generations, that convention would be almost completely upended. The great (or very good) players who became

---

5   Len Thompson, who resembled a two-metre triffid inexplicably endowed with the speed, grace and agility of an Olympic hurdler, won the Brownlow Medal in 1972, and Collingwood's best and fairest five times. Des Tuddenham, a proverbially fearless on-field leader – 'as tough as an army biscuit', in Lou Richards' estimation – had several later-life run-ins with the law, including convictions for receiving stolen tyres, and for drink-driving. Peter Eakins, plagued by injury, played just 32 games for Collingwood.

great coaches – Leigh Matthews, Alastair Clarkson, Mark Thompson, Mick Malthouse, Kevin Sheedy, Malcolm Blight – did so where they hadn't played, where there was a lighter burden of expectation, and no awkward recalibration of relationships. By and large, the prodigal golden boys – James Hird, Michael Voss, Brett Ratten, Tony Shaw – would rank somewhere between disappointments and disasters. Barassi would succumb to this temptation, returning to Melbourne in 1981, and labouring for five years to turn a terrible team into an average one.

Between Ron Barassi's debut for Melbourne in 1953, and his departure from North Melbourne at the end of 1980, 29 VFL grand finals were played, if one counts both the draw and replay of 1977. Barassi figured, as player and/or coach, in 17 of those. Anyone who dominates a sport statistically tends to dominate it psychologically and spiritually: where Barassi once embodied Melbourne, he ended up embodying the game. Coaching was remade in his image – rigorous, macho and martial.[6] But, importantly, Barassi's teams were never indistinguishable ranks of remorseless automatons. Those who resent his imposition of professional discipline forget his paradoxical love for the players who most needed it.

A defining feature of Barassi's resume, other than all the winning, was an indulgence of mavericks and eccentrics whom a proper joyless martinet would have benched or exiled. At various points in his coaching career, Barassi put up with and/or actively encouraged all of the following: Sam Kekovich, Phil Baker, Malcolm Blight, Peter Keenan,[7] Mick Nolan, Stan Alves, Robert Walls, Mark Jackson, Robert Flower, Shane Zantuck,[8]

---

6   The author interviewed Ron Barassi for a profile in *Monocle* magazine in 2010. Asked the admittedly predictable question of which player he'd never coached that he would most have wanted in one of his teams, Barassi chose Leigh Matthews: 'Very tough, built like a brick shithouse, but had a tremendous brain and quite a bit of speed. But the thing that elevates him to number one in my head is: when needed, produced.' Afterwards, Barassi asked me what I was doing with the rest of my day, and I said I was getting the tram to the Alfred Hospital to visit my mum, who'd just started dialysis. 'Don't worry about the tram,' said Barassi, 'I'll give you a lift.' It was a moment I dearly wished I could somehow have flashed to the ten-year-old me, if I could have persuaded him to look up from his umpteenth rereading of *The Coach*, John Powers' chronicle of Barassi and North Melbourne's 1977 premiership season.

7   Peter Keenan's well-earned nickname, 'Crackers', proved commercially useful in his post-football life as a knockabout media identity, but somewhat at the expense of an equally merited reputation as one of the best ruckmen of the 1970s – as well as one of the game's most theatrical players, clenching fists and pawing the ground prior to every contest as if psyching himself up for his first parachute jump.

8   Shane Zantuck, famously, had to be restrained by teammates during what diplomats would describe as a full and frank exchange of views with Barassi at three-quarter time of a Melbourne game against Essendon in 1984. Significantly, for all that Barassi cultivated the aura of an iron-fisted tyrant, Zantuck was selected the following week.

Derek Kickett,[9] Dermott Brereton, Adam Heuskes and Tony Lockett. Which is to say nothing of Barassi's odd-couple relationship, spanning three clubs across three decades, with his apparent polar opposite, Brent Crosswell, the gifted but cavalier Launcestonian who once cheerfully described himself as 'ostentatious, lairising' on the field, and cultivated an aura of bohemian raffishness off it. It has been plausibly speculated that the relationship between Barassi and Crosswell inspired the central protagonists of David Williamson's play *The Club*: the old-school coach with the old-school moustache, struggling to corral the brilliant, but infuriatingly insouciant, floppy-fringed Tasmanian stoner.

Crosswell, whose later contributions to footballing literature were as brilliantly illuminating as they were tragically few, once wrote about playing chess with Barassi, which he described as 'the most arduous and excruciating contests I have ever experienced, ranking among the worst moments I have spent on Earth'. Barassi played chess, in Crosswell's telling, like he coached football: ferociously, relentlessly, with demented attention to the tiniest detail and a willingness to fight from the most apparently hopeless position, on the assumption that, as Crosswell saw it, 'if you placed a human being in a position of extreme discomfort for long enough, you'd win'.

Brent Crosswell, as an observer of the game, and indeed of life, didn't miss much – but he missed the fact that there were other, more pliable people with whom Ron Barassi could have been playing chess. Or football.

9   Derek Kickett, the leading example of nominative determinism in League history, would have won the 1987 Sandover Medal by fully 16 votes, had he not been ineligible due to suspension. In the VFL/ AFL he played for North Melbourne, Essendon and Sydney, joining Barassi's Swans after Kevin Sheedy omitted him from the Bombers' 1993 grand final squad.

25

Norm Smith Sacked, Unsacked
North Melbourne 11.15.81 Melbourne 9.6.60
Coburg Oval
ROUND 13, 1965

On the morning of the day before, Melbourne's players thought the biggest adjustment they would be making for this game was finding their way to the Demons' first ever fixture at Coburg Oval, to which North had relocated from Arden Street, for what would turn out to be a tenure of just this single season. By late evening on the day before, Melbourne's players had learned that this was the least of their worries. By the time the ball was bounced, the whole city knew. In the big, bold and forbidding typeface, stacked at one word per line, that Melbourne's newspapers would normally reserve for declarations of war, *The Sun*'s newsstand banners announced: 'Norm Smith Sacked'.

It was difficult to imagine a greater heresy, at least within the capabilities of Melbourne's committee – bulldozing the MCG to build a rugby ground, perhaps, or proposing a merger with Collingwood. Even Ron Barassi's recent departure for Carlton – a move received as akin to the Pope announcing that he'd had a better offer from the Methodists – seemed a mere hiccup, when measured against this foundation-rattling earthquake. It was no mere dismissal of an employee: it was regicide, if not deicide.

By 1965, Melbourne had won 12 premierships. Smith had played for the Demons in four of those, between 1939 and 1948, and between 1955 and 1964 had coached them to another six. Between that extraordinary record and his mentoring of Barassi, Smith had dominated – indeed, more or less invented – modern football. And it wasn't like Melbourne had lost their way. The team's defence of the 1964 flag was in decent shape. They'd fallen narrowly short against Richmond the week previously, but as the match against North Melbourne loomed, the Demons sat third on the ladder with nine wins, behind St Kilda and Geelong on paltry fractions of percentage. If they'd found another goal against the Tigers, Melbourne would have led the league.

Sacking Norm Smith in 1965 made as much sense as leaving Don Bradman at home for the 1948 Ashes, or giving Phar Lap a spell during the 1930 Melbourne Spring Racing Carnival.[1] The human urge to fix that which is not broken is a powerful thing, however, and daggers had been sharpening awhile behind Smith's back. Smith was never one of life's compromisers. He once suggested that his preferred model of a club committee was three people, with two of them off sick. He demanded – and generally received – total obedience from the players he coached, including a prohibition of the long hair and lairish moustaches common elsewhere by the mid-1960s. If Smith believed himself indispensable, he had reason – and the kind of people who enjoy sitting on committees do not enjoy being reminded that they are less necessary, or even, as Smith saw it, less than necessary.

Smith's falling out with Melbourne's complacent grandees had been simmering awhile, in particular over the club's reluctance to stoop to such indignities as spending money on new players. The Demons were, officially, still merely the football wing of the Melbourne Cricket Club, whose patrician panjandrums regarded the winter game as a secondary concern, and the flouting by less refined clubs of the Coulter Law[2] on player payments with the sort of horror usually reserved for people who passed the port the wrong way around the table as butlers cleared the dinner service.

This animus intensified in late 1964, when Smith took issue with the handling by field umpire Don Blew[3] of the Demons' Round 15 match against the Saints. Melbourne won comfortably, but Smith felt that Blew had been sympathetic towards the underdogs – or, as underdogs

---

1   In two weeks of October–November 1930, Phar Lap won the W.S. Cox Plate, the Melbourne Stakes, the Melbourne Cup, the Linlithgow Stakes and the C.B. Fisher Plate, clearly unfazed by an assassination attempt early on the morning of the second of those races: as Phar Lap was led back to his stables by handler Tommy Woodcock, a shotgun was fired at the peerless thoroughbred from a car on Etna Street in Glen Huntly. No arrest was ever made.

2   The Coulter Law, introduced in 1930, attempted to standardise payments to players, initially capped at £3 per match. Liberties were widely taken, via donations from wealthy fans, bonuses in paper bags left in lockers, or payments in the form of cars, discounted rent, or offers of employment overpaid and under-arduous. The Coulter Law was abolished prior to the 1971 season.

3   Don Blew later became a swimming judge, officiating at six Olympic Games.

were known in Victoria, St Kilda. Smith told 3AW that Blew had been 'subconsciously biased'. Blew, and the umpires' board, demanded an apology from Smith – but they, like everybody in football, must have known that this was like demanding a lullaby from a walrus. In March 1965, just prior to the beginning of the new season, Blew issued a writ against Smith.

Smith assumed that the Melbourne committee would support – and subsidise – his defence. They would not. Smith requested that the committee put in writing a decision one way or the other, warning that he would interpret anything less than complete fealty as a vote of no confidence; pointedly, if tactlessly, he said that the same would surely apply to Melbourne's club secretary, Jim Cardwell, who had heard Smith's remarks about Blew before 3AW aired them, and approved the transmission. (Smith had either not considered, or was pretending not to have considered, that Cardwell might have set him up.)

The committee agreed to support Smith, but refused to indemnify him against any loss in court. A couple of committee members made private offers to Smith, but his pride was wounded. Smith ceased even feigning politeness to the club's administrators, and they refrained from further expressions of gratitude for his accomplishments. Another layer in the clouds over the MCG was ongoing resentment at what some saw as Smith's insufficient efforts to keep Ron Barassi: suspicion festered that Smith had wanted to encourage his protégé at the expense of the club, or discourage a potential successor, ditto.

Efforts were made to locate a compromise. In the days before the game against North Melbourne, Smith agreed to the committee's request that he address the players, and reassure them that he and the committee were still on the same side. What was not agreed was precisely when Smith should make this declaration. The committee assumed that it was understood that Smith would do this as soon as possible, at training on the Thursday night, whereas Smith assumed that he was free to do it his way; he thought he might leave it until after North Melbourne had been dealt with.

At a meeting held in the late afternoon the Friday before the game, the committee voted 9–3 to sack Norm Smith. With all involved finding reason – some previous engagement, gout – not to tell Smith in person, a courier was dispatched to his house with a letter. Smith was on the phone to Melbourne's captain, Hassa Mann, when she arrived. After reading the letter, Smith called Mann back. Mann, confused by the choked and tearful voice on the line, assumed it was a crank call, the idea of Norm Smith being sacked scarcely less preposterous than one's refrigerator actually running.

By the time Melbourne's players emerged onto a boggy Coburg Oval shortly after two o'clock on this Saturday afternoon, they could hardly have been more disoriented if they'd been informed that, henceforth, they were to cease being a football team and retrain as a trombone orchestra. They had been commanded earlier to a meeting at the MCG, where Smith's removal was confirmed, and the players were told that their new coach was Frank 'Checker' Hughes – the 71-year-old overlord of Melbourne's first golden era, who hadn't coached a VFL game since the 1948 grand final replay. There were rumblings of mutiny, some players suggesting that they wouldn't go to Coburg, but this insurrection had been quelled by Mann, who reminded all present that Smith would want them to play, and to win.

It is perhaps crediting Melbourne's committee with overly generous helpings of Machiavellian cunning, but they had picked what looked a good time to sack a coach, if you wanted to demonstrate his superfluity. North hadn't beaten Melbourne for more than a decade, and were having a shocking season: the Roos had won two games all year, and lost every match they'd played at Coburg. After the – obvious, surely – formality of dispensing with North, Melbourne were scheduled to play Fitzroy, for which turning up looked sufficient to guarantee victory, and South Melbourne, lodged unmenacingly in mid-table. A month from now, the committee could have been forgiven for thinking, Norm Smith would be yesterday's man, and yesterday's actual man, Checker Hughes, could be three wins from three starts and basking in appreciative headlines about a heart-warming late-life renaissance, his walking stick acquiring the properties of magic wand.

On paper, Melbourne looked far the better team, the more so for welcoming back from injury third-year centre half-forward Ray Groom, to whom Smith had pointedly assigned Barassi's former number 31 at the start of the season.[4] A popular rejoinder to projections beginning 'On paper ...' is that football is played on grass. It may be even more potent a retort when football is played on a surface which looked

---

4 Ray Groom played 92 games for Melbourne, and was best and fairest in 1968. After retiring from football, he entered politics in his native Tasmania, winning the federal seat of Braddon for the Liberal Party in 1975. He was elected premier of Tasmania in 1992, and served until 1996.

muddy enough to swallow altogether any player buried at the bottom of a pack.

North Melbourne's coach, Alan Killigrew, was an excitable type whose half-time oratory was often evocative of a snake-handling, garment-rending, tongue-talking hot gospeller rousing a congregation of Baptist obscurantists in a clapboard church in some tumbleweed-strewn Alabama parish. Thinking more clearly than the bewildered visitors, Killigrew ordered his team to slosh onto the Coburg swamp well before the bounce, to acclimatise themselves to the morass by conducting kicking and handball drills with the sodden, slippery ball. North led Melbourne all day and won on merit, Noel Teasdale immense in the ruck despite conditions as helpful to an aerialist as leg-irons, Frank Goode decisive at full-forward with five goals. Afterwards, most of Melbourne's players and trainers visited Norm Smith at his Pascoe Vale home. Among Melbourne's committee, nerves jangled.

One can only wonder at the existential futility that must have enshrouded Ron Casey, Lou Richards, Jack Dyer and other denizens of Channel Seven's *World of Sport* as they prepared to go to air at midday the following day – even they can't have wanted to watch. On Channel Nine, at the same time, Norm Smith was making his regular scheduled appearance on *Tony Charlton's Football Show*.[5] Channel Seven offered Smith £1000 for the exclusive, roughly two-thirds of what Melbourne paid him in a season, but Smith, believing that a man's word was binding, never mind his signature, would not betray his contract with Nine.

From his redoubt in Charlton's studio, Smith pounded his enemies witheringly and mercilessly. 'I'm Melbourne through and through,' he declared, implicitly asserting that those conspiring against him were not. The class tensions which underpinned the standoff were uncorked when Smith banged Charlton's desk and recalled telling the committee, 'You went to a public school, I went to a state school, but they still spelt "principle" the same way.' (Later, Charlton would observe that the friction between the Melbourne committee and Norm Smith boiled down to 'old school tie versus no school tie'.) Asked by Charlton if he

---

5   Tony Charlton began calling football in 1952, co-presenting 3AW's first coverage of a VFL game – a post-season exhibition night match between Essendon and Richmond in tipping rain and inadequate lighting at the Melbourne Showgrounds. He was an enduring lesson that erudition need not be an impediment to a career in sports broadcasting.

thought he was being unreasonable, Smith hooted: 'Unreasonable? I reckon I'm being very reasonable. And I feel like saying a lot more.' And so he did. Smith referred to the committee as 'the 12 guilty men', then called them disloyal, jealous, weak and, in at least one instance, drunk. He incited revolt among Melbourne's fans. 'Get rid of these blokes,' he said, referring to his oppressors. 'That's the only way the club will progress.'

If any committee members anxiously watching Smith's *j'accuse* while their valets ironed their spats thought this couldn't get worse for them, they were mistaken. Three Melbourne players – Hassa Mann, Bryan Kenneally and John Townsend, which was to say Melbourne's captain, vice-captain and 1965's best-and-fairest-in-waiting – also appeared on Smith's behalf, as did Ron Barassi, who said, simply, 'He's been like a father to me.' Most damningly, Smith's wife, Marj, spoke plainly and sincerely on her husband's behalf. 'I've never known Norm to tell a lie, ever,' she said. 'Until he dies, he will be able to walk with his head up. But there's people at Melbourne going to have to walk with their head down.' If Smith's sacking was a football game, Melbourne's committee were ten goals down at quarter time, and preparing to kick into the wind.

Attempts were made by the Melbourne brass to strike back at Smith: newspapers were darkly briefed that there was more to the strife at Melbourne than had been made public, a shabby but often effective tactic, encouraging lurid imaginings of physical or moral infirmity. But the committee had not merely done a bad thing, they had done it badly. The devotion commanded by Smith, among players and public, startled them. Ron Barassi, still a Melbourne totem though no longer a Melbourne player, thundered across the hearth of secretary Jim Cardwell promising, at a volume that brought curious neighbours into the street, that any future return to coach Melbourne was off the table, for all time, unless Smith was reinstated.

Smith was hardly short of options. He was the reigning premiership coach, beyond question the finest football mind alive. He was only 49. At Richmond, there was great excitement at the possibility that Norm could seamlessly replace his brother, Len Smith, who had stepped down as Tigers coach for health reasons; as Richmond saw it, Norm Smith would merely switch one MCG dressing-room for another. (Richmond had moved from Punt Road to the bigger ground at the beginning of the season.)[6] But Smith had out-thought and outplayed many better strategists than the Melbourne committee. A coterie of splendidly stereotypical Demons supporters – i.e. grand and influential judges and solicitors – acted as intermediaries between the vindicated coach and the now-terrified club officials, who had been glumly fielding drifts of furious letters and incessant outraged phone calls.

The key interlocutor was Trevor Rapke. The son of feminist pioneer Julia Rapke, he was – aside from a red-and-blue-blooded Demons barracker – also Judge Advocate-General of the Royal Australian Navy, in which he'd served during World War II, an honorary Rear Admiral, and (probably) Victoria's first Jewish judge. In his days as a lawyer, Rapke had made many far more difficult cases than the one Smith had for unfair dismissal. By the next Tuesday night, Smith had his job back: the committee had not been the first or last officer corps to misjudge a coup against a civilian leader whose popularity they underestimated.

At Smith's return to the MCG the following Saturday, he drew louder cheers than those offered for Brian Dixon on the occasion of his 200th game. Melbourne won, holding off a fast-finishing Fitzroy. Smith, though not given to flights of romantic reverie, would have been more than human if he did not think even briefly of the complete victory that would now be represented by triumphant procession into the finals, and a seventh Melbourne premiership under his command. Instead, Melbourne lost their remaining four games, confirmation that they would miss the finals for the first time in 12 seasons delivered by the cruellest means possible: a seven-goal hammering by Collingwood at Victoria Park.

Smith never coached Melbourne in another finals series; nobody did, until John Northey, 22 years and seven coaches (including Ron Barassi) later. Smith resigned at the end of 1967, warned by doctors that his heart was no longer up to it, and warned even more brutally by the death of Len Smith the same year, felled by a similar condition. He made a comeback in 1969 with South Melbourne, getting them into the finals in his second season, but backed that up with a wooden spoon in 1971, and a second-last-place finish in 1972. After Smith left South, Barassi cannily poached

---

6   Len Smith was eventually succeeded by Tom Hafey, who'd had a modest 67-game career for the Tigers. Hafey blossomed into Richmond's greatest coach, winning four flags between 1967 and 1974; he later coached Collingwood, Geelong and Sydney. Hafey never won another premiership, but his post-Richmond career had its moments, notably taking Collingwood from the 1976 wooden spoon to the 1977 grand final replay. Hafey's influence on coaching may be gleaned from the fact that among those who played under him at various points were Kevin Sheedy, Mick Malthouse, Tony Jewell, Neil Balme and John Northey.

him as chairman of selectors at North Melbourne, but he had only months in the job: Smith died of a brain tumour in July 1973, aged 57.

At time of writing, Norm Smith remains the last man to have coached Melbourne to a flag. The Curse of the Red Fox, some call it, invoking the nickname Smith earned with his immaculate ginger barnet and his crystal-eyed cunning, and suggesting that Melbourne's treatment of its greatest chief has saddled the club eternally with an unshiftable karmic debt. Certainly, there are those who still believe that Gough Whitlam's dismissal was but the second in Australian history which demanded to be spelt with a capital D.

Nothing ever came of Don Blew's legal action.

26

Ted Whitten Waves Goodbye
Footscray 11.13.79 Hawthorn 11.10.76
Western Oval
ROUND 5, 1970

'It feels bloody awful, David. I don't feel very happy about it at all.'

A reporter from Channel Seven had joined Ted Whitten on his walk into the Western Oval to ask how he felt, approaching the ground to play his last game. Whitten was 36, in his 20th season as a Footscray player, and his 12th as the club's captain-coach.[1] He had come to be seen as the personification of his club, and the embattled district it represented. At Footscray, Whitten was not merely a player, nor even just a captain and/ or coach, but a tribal chieftain. A grandstand at the Western Oval already bore his name. The idea that the entire ground would one day do the same would have struck few as preposterous.

Neither Whitten's talent nor his ego – both substantial entities – could be confined to one guernsey. Aside from his role as the veritable Vercingetorix of Melbourne's western suburbs, Whitten was not only the embodiment of the Big V at a time when interstate football still meant something – still meant something, indeed, substantially due to Whitten's insistence that it should[2] – but of Australian Rules itself. Inside Footscray's dressing-room, a banner hanging on the wall waited to wish goodbye and good luck to both Ted Whitten, and Mr Football, the latter a nickname that only the former could have worn.

---

1   Ted Whitten was first appointed Footscray coach in 1957, aged 23, the youngest coach in League history. His tenure was interrupted in 1967 and 1968 by the return of Charlie Sutton, who had coached the Bulldogs to their first flag, in 1954.

2   Though state-of-origin football at the top level has fallen into abeyance, it is fitting that its surviving incarnation, the annual Legends game between teams of showboating veterans representing Victoria and the rest of Australia, is named after Ted Whitten. Launched in 1996, the Legends game raises money for the E.J. Whitten Foundation.

'But it has to come,' continued Whitten, 'and this is it.' He glanced up into weeping clouds. 'The skies haven't been too good to us either, really.'

Between Whitten and the grandstands lay an affable siege of autograph-seekers huddled under brollies. Whitten, in a sharp three-piece suit and tie, his combover immaculate, gleaming white Adidas kitbag in one hand, looked as much a 1970s television star as a footballer. This was fair enough, as Whitten was, by now, both – having long been wringing off-field celebrity from the instinctive larrikinism that underpinned and overshadowed his playing. His failure to win a Brownlow Medal, despite being exactly the kind of player who should, was attributed to his incessant in-game critiques of the umpires who apportioned the votes.[3]

But if Whitten had been quieter on the field, he might have had less opportunity to raise rumpus off it, and this was something he also enjoyed. That had been Whitten, in the commentary booth during the 1966 grand final, memorably shrieking, 'Hit the boundary line!' when St Kilda's Bob Murray marked at centre half-back, with the Saints a point in front with 28 and a half minutes on the clock in the last quarter. That had been Whitten appearing on *The Tarax Show* in a bracing advertising spot for Jonco football shorts, in which, for some reason, the garment in question was mounted on a plinth while Whitten was clad only in a guernsey, socks and briefs; his full-frontal kick to camera was eye-opening, especially for a Saturday-morning kids' show (or perhaps, such was Whitten's folkloric stature, nobody dared tell him he'd neglected to put the shorts on).

Whitten's signature on this day would be doubly valuable: it was his last game, and his 321st, which would overhaul the 19-year-old all-time games record of Essendon's triple Brownlow medallist Dick Reynolds, who was among the well-wishers milling in the rooms. Whitten's melancholy could only have been magnified by the knowledge that this landmark was the only reason he was playing. At the end of 1969, Whitten had appeared 317 times for Footscray. The committee, wanting a non-playing coach, told Whitten he could select himself until he had overtaken Reynolds, but no further. Whitten could not have enjoyed the suspicion that he was being patronised, especially given that he was still in decent touch – a fortnight previously, he'd kicked three goals as Footscray overran St Kilda.

---

3   Among the presentations made to Ted Whitten on the occasion of his last appearance as a player was one from the match officials: a VFL Umpire's Association tie, and a gold-plated whistle on a stand, in recognition of Whitten's manifold unsolicited contributions to their professional improvement.

The Western Oval was not as full as it might have been: just short of 20,000 had turned up, as opposed to the 26,596 who had come for the season's first game, four weeks previously, and seen Footscray briskly disassembled by Collingwood, a rampant Peter McKenna scoring 11.4 from 15 kicks.[4] The weather overhanging Whitten's last game could have been a deterrent, ditto the quality of the opposition: Hawthorn had four losses from four starts. It would also have been reasonable of any Footscray fan squinting into the rain from their front door to conclude that it wasn't like Whitten was really going anywhere; he would continue to coach the team, and probably intended to do so until the sun died. There would be other opportunities to say goodbye.

Whitten ended up among the day's spectators himself. In the first quarter, hurling himself into the fray with characteristic abandon, he clashed heads with Hawthorn's Michael Porter. It took a few minutes for Footscray's trainers and club doctor to decide to let him continue, though they may just have disliked their chances of persuading Whitten otherwise. But he barely got a kick afterwards, and by three-quarter time, Hawthorn had clawed back Footscray's early lead, and loomed two points astern. Peter Hudson, who'd kicked four for the Hawks in the third quarter, appeared especially unbothered by the prospect of ruining Whitten's farewell.

The last break called for a spot of rousing impromptu oratory, the sort of speech which would urge a bruised, mud-slathered team, huddled in their dressing gowns, cross-legged on miry turf, to draw one last great effort out of themselves to secure a valedictory victory for their departing liege. As captain and coach, it was Whitten's job to deliver it. As he leant over his team, one fist pounding against the other palm, voice a husky roar, hair disarrayed by the wind, he made it about them, not him.

'You had 'em in your hands, and you let 'em out,' bellowed Whitten. 'Now we've got to get back in there and close it up. They played attacking football, we went negative. And you can't afford to. I want attacking, purposeful football all the time. Now, we've got our backs against the wall, and we've got to fight, and fight hard. It's got to be a do-or-die effort.

---

4   That same opening round, Richmond and Fitzroy met at the MCG in the first Sunday game
     played in Melbourne. Guests of honour were Queen Elizabeth II, the Duke of Edinburgh, Prince
     Charles and Princess Anne. The royal family arrived at half-time, and were driven around the
     ground in a pair of Land Rovers. Sadly, they missed the brawl which had enlivened the second
     quarter – and in reports of which, according to newspapers, Princess Anne took particular interest,
     pressing Richmond and Fitzroy captains Kevin Murray and Roger Dean for details, and consoling
     Richmond's Kevin Sheedy on a gashed jaw.

You've got to show me all the guts, all the determination you've got in your body. You've got to inspire me, with this last-quarter win. You've been in front all day, and you've got to stay there.'

Whitten exiled himself to full-forward, recognising that the earlier bang on the head had rendered him surplus to the struggle about to occur, and/or entertaining hopes of sealing a fairytale finish with his last kick in anger. If any tactical means retrospectively justifies satisfactory ends, it was a masterstroke. The last quarter was a desperate grind, one of those spectacles in which football reverts to its primordial soup, evoking epic scrums of yore between the north and south sides of some ancient English mining town, with a hundred toothless villagers on each team and a greased pig as the ball. Hawthorn scored just two more behinds, Footscray just three, but it was enough. They'd won it for Whitten.

Few players have been more deserving of an elaborate formal acknowledgement of the end of their playing career; none has been less likely to leave the field without one. Not for Whitten the cursory chairing off aboard the shoulders of teammates. A microphone and a public-address system had been wrangled, a platform improvised. Speeches were made. Footscray's president, Jack Collins, who'd played alongside Whitten for most of the 1950s, began tactlessly, describing Whitten as a player the game could 'ill afford to lose'; he was booed. Footscray's number-one ticketholder, Victoria's chief commissioner of police, Noel Wilby, did better by asking for three cheers.

Whitten, when his turn came, spoke for some while to the thousands crowded around him and competing for space beneath umbrellas. He acknowledged the 'hundreds and hundreds and hundreds' of telegrams, telephone calls and cards he had received in the previous week. 'I love you all, and I hope you stick with us,' he concluded, or seemed to. 'I'm, ah, starting to feel a bit sad and sorry about it, um ...' Among those applauding the dropping of this heavy hint for a reprieve was a ten-year-old Bulldogs fan called Doug Hawkins. Footscray's overlords declined, however, to take this cue to spontaneously commute their edict against Whitten playing on.

And so Whitten didn't – and nor did he coach much longer, leaving Footscray at the end of 1971. He had done his best with a team about which he was usually the best thing, but only once in 13 seasons had Whitten coached the Bulldogs into September – in 1961, when they'd been beaten by Hawthorn in the grand final. Whitten did not, however, relinquish the Mr Football honorific, and nor did anybody challenge him for it, deliberately or otherwise. Over Footscray, he loomed sufficiently large that when Doug Hawkins, who had grown since 1970 into a dashing and splendidly mulleted winger, approached Whitten's 321-game mark in 1994, he considered not going through with it[5] – but as he bore down on the Footscray games record, Hawkins received a telegram from Whitten telling him he deserved the honour.[6] Whitten welcomed Hawkins onto the Western Oval for his 322nd game, where the pair exchanged ceremonial handballs (Whitten's was, technically, a flick-pass – the palmed handball of which he was famously fond, but which the VFL outlawed in 1966).

Ted Whitten said goodbye again on 17 June 1995. He was driven on a lap around the MCG in a white Saab convertible, soundtracked by Mariah Carey's 'Hero', before Victoria played South Australia in a state-of-origin match. Sitting on the car's boot, wearing his Big V blazer and tie, supported by his son, Ted Whitten Jr,[7] and accompanied by his young grandsons, Whitten saluted a crowd which knew, as he knew, that he was dying. The previous December, Whitten's cancer diagnosis had been revealed at a press conference: Whitten Jr had done the talking, his father too ill to utter a word beyond 'Sorry'.

At the MCG, Whitten, almost blinded by recent strokes, acknowledged the ovation with cheers, and with a gesture recalling his most famous celebration of a Victorian victory – in 1990, after Victoria defeated Western Australia at the WACA, unaware of the television cameras broadcasting live, Whitten, Victoria's chairman of selectors, transported by the victory, hoarsely extolled his players for having 'stuck it right up them'.

Whitten died in 1995, aged 62. His televised state funeral was held at a St Patrick's Cathedral heaving with past and present footballers, and

---

5 Had Doug Hawkins stood himself down after 321 games, it would have been the footballing forerunner of the gesture made by Australia's cricket captain, Mark Taylor, in 1998. Playing against Pakistan in Peshawar, Taylor equalled Sir Donald Bradman's Australian Test innings record of 334 by the end of day two, and declared overnight, denying himself the opportunity to erase Bradman's mark. Matthew Hayden suffered no such qualms five years later in Perth, scoring 380 against Zimbabwe.

6 Doug Hawkins played 329 games for Footscray, and 21 more in a single-season encore with Fitzroy. In 2013 he stood as a federal Senate candidate for the Palmer United Party, eponymous plaything of the boisterous mining magnate, and Footscray native, Clive Palmer. The Palmer United ticket, topped by former world super featherweight champion Barry Michael, fell short of a seat, finishing in fourth place overall, behind the Greens but ahead of the Sex Party.

7 Ted Whitten Jr's playing career might be better remembered had he been called something else, and cursed less by injury. He played 144 games for Footscray before being forced into retirement by persistent knee troubles, aged 25.

with the strata of dignitaries who show up at televised state funerals; thousands more listened to the service outside. The eulogy was delivered by Bob Skilton, who recognised both the 'brash, arrogant maniac' and the 'caring, compassionate, generous' mate. Ted Whitten had been, reflected Skilton, the kind of player who would cheerfully break an opponent's nose during a game, then offer, once the siren had concluded hostilities, to drive him to hospital, then take him out for a drink.

27

Sir Robert Drives In
Carlton 13.8.86 Footscray 11.17.83
Princes Park
ROUND 22, 1972

One attendee at Princes Park this afternoon had a more comfortable seat than any of the 24,618 others at the match – specifically, the white leather front passenger seat of a black 1963 Bentley S3, parked on a custom-built platform behind the goal at the Robert Heatley Stand end.[1] The occupant was Sir Robert Menzies, interminably serving former prime minister of Australia and lifelong Carlton barracker. In 1971, five years after he'd left office, a stroke left Menzies partially paralysed, and struggling to climb the stairs to his usual seat at Carlton; the club had made these arrangements for his vehicle to be driven straight into the ground.

This wasn't the first game Menzies had witnessed from this improvised eyrie of metal scaffolding and wooden planks, but it seems to be the only one at which someone had the wit to photograph it. If there was anything potentially gauche and imperious about the spectacle, it was offset by the easy informality of the crowd around the car, to which Menzies did not object: kids in flares and polonecks and haystack haircuts leaning on the pipes upholding the edifice, or sitting on spare corners of the platform. Inside the limousine, Menzies and his driver of many years, Peter Pearson, were more formally attired: Menzies in a houndstooth

---

1   Robert Heatley was a baker and bookmaker who served as Carlton president around the turn of the 20th century, before resigning in a row over allegedly creative handling of gate money by then-coach Jack Worrall. Worrall, who also played cricket for Australia – credited in some quarters with coining the phrase 'Bodyline' to describe England's short-bowling perfidy in 1932–33. Worrall's choice of second career was ironic, as journalism is a trade whose practitioners are proverbial for punctiliously honest accounting, especially where their expenses are concerned.

blazer, collar and tie, Pearson sporting two rows of service ribbons on the left breast of his jacket.

All had good reason for trying to secure the best view they could. The Blues went into 1972's last home-and-away round needing a win to nail down the minor premiership, but Footscray – who'd blown their theoretical finals hopes the previous week with a two-point loss to second-placed Richmond – made them work for the victory. Had the Bulldogs' Laurie Sandilands (0.4) and Bernie Quinlan (5.6, two others out on the full) kicked straighter, Footscray might have won handily. They'd kicked themselves out of it against Richmond, as well, turning 1972 into another chapter of Footscray's already burgeoning post-1954 saga of heartbreak. All who'd worn red, white and blue to Princes Park had already learned enough the hard way that they would merely have sighed resignedly if told that two of the players representing Footscray today would, nine years hence, tie for the Brownlow Medal, while wearing other colours.[2]

Menzies would have appreciated that he was watching a great Carlton vintage – a team that had played in three of the previous four grand finals, and won two of them, in 1968 and 1970, before narrowly missing the finals in 1971. With Ron Barassi replaced[3] as coach by esteemed paladin John Nicholls – still leading from the front in the ruck, at the age of 33 – the Blues had been revivified. There wasn't a line across the field that didn't feature at least one player who'd have been a walk-up start in any other team in the VFL: Bruce Doull, Brent Crosswell, Syd Jackson, Percy Jones, Geoff Southby, Robert Walls.

This was not a team which should have been unbalanced by a bizarre mishap befalling one of its stars, but such was the case when, early in the second quarter, Alex Jesaulenko – who had helped lay on three first-quarter goals for Greg Kennedy – trod on a tap rivet in the middle of the ground, injuring a foot, and was compelled to retreat,

2 These were Bernie Quinlan and Barry Round. Quinlan divided a 366-game career almost evenly between Footscray (177 games) and Fitzroy (189 games). At his first club, he was very good. At his second, doing nothing for Footscray's persecution complex, Quinlan was a superstar, leading the League's goalkicking in 1983 and 1984 with consecutive triple-figure seasons. Round was South Melbourne's captain when they moved to Sydney in 1982.

3 Ron Barassi left Carlton at the end of 1971 to concentrate on his business career, specifically Ron Barassi Office Furniture of La Trobe Street, opened in 1969 by Sir Robert Menzies. (At around the same time, by happy coincidence, Barassi received a contract to supply $23,499 worth of office furniture to the Commonwealth government.) In 1972, North Melbourne official Albert Mantello swung by the showroom in search of a second-hand desk, and correctly diagnosed the proprietor's itchy feet: Barassi was named North Melbourne coach in 1973, on $2000 a year plus a $50,000 loan for the furniture shop.

more or less immobile, to the forward pocket. This unshackled Footscray centreman Stuart Magee,[4] who took charge to the extent that by half-time, the Bulldogs had turned a 14-point deficit into an eight-point lead, despite their indiscriminate goalkicking. Menzies, as he contemplated the contents of his thermos, must have shuddered as the Bentley's radio broadcast the latest from Waverley, where Richmond, only two points behind Carlton on the ladder, were already eight goals clear of South Melbourne.

The established pattern continued in the third, Footscray all over Carlton, but unable to capitalise. Magee, along with Stephen Power and Denis Collins, ran the midfield. Up forward, Bernie Quinlan was too tall and too fast for Bruce Doull; though Doull had already begun compensating for a prematurely receding hairline with an unruly proto-mullet and sideburns like boot-brushes, he was yet to add the beard and the headband, and so could not be said to have yet gone full Flying Doormat. John Nicholls was getting thrashed in the ruck by Gary Dempsey, who would end the day with 26 hit-outs. But at three-quarter time, though Footscray had dominated the term, with seven scoring shots to three, they'd succeeded only in reducing their lead from eight points to seven. At Waverley, Richmond continued their saunter to victory. If Menzies had been the sort of man likely to lean on his car's horn and bellow encouraging obscenities out of the window – or even civilly request that his chauffeur do it for him – now would have been the moment.

In the last quarter Carlton, whose accuracy had kept them in the match, appeared to contract the yips from their opponents, but 3.5, against the Bulldogs' 2.1, was enough to get the Blues home by three points. Bob Rose,[5] Footscray's coach, lamented afterwards that 'we did everything right but win'. Menzies' Bentley reversed from its redoubt with its passenger secure in the knowledge that Carlton had clinched the minor premiership. Menzies saw his Blues win the '72 flag, though they got there the hard way, drawing the semi-final against Richmond, losing the replay, coming from behind against St Kilda in the preliminary final,

---

4   Stuart Magee played 216 games, for South Melbourne and Footscray. Born in Belfast, he later affably disputed Jim Stynes' claim to have been the first Irishman to have made 200 League appearances.

5   Bob Rose, a champion rover at Collingwood in the 1940s and '50s, could have done even better than his one premiership and four best and fairests had he not, aged 27, taken up the post of captain-coach of Wangaratta Rovers in the Ovens & Murray League, leading the club to two flags. He returned to Collingwood to coach in what became the early days of the Colliwobbles, taking the Magpies to grand final losses in 1964, 1966 and 1970, by a combined margin of 15 points. He coached Footscray until 1975, and returned briefly to Collingwood in 1985.

before beating Richmond in the decider: Alex Jesaulenko kicked seven goals each in the preliminary and the grand final.

Menzies' passion for football was no artifice of a lofty patrician affecting the common touch. Opening the 1958 Australian Football carnival – this iteration of the interstate tournament also known as the Centenary Carnival, acknowledging the hundredth anniversary of the primordial Melbourne Grammar versus Scotch College match – Menzies had said: 'I make no apologies for my firm belief that Australian football is the greatest winter game devised by mortal man.'

At least as much as he loved football, Menzies loved Carlton. In 1952, Hugh Buggy of *The Argus* had written of the prime minister: 'He makes no insincere pretence that he is interested in football in an academic way. He is an indefatigable supporter of Carlton, and he doesn't give two hoots who knows it. He goes to the football to see the Blues win.' The same article recalled a moment when, in September 1947, Menzies had campaigned for the Liberal candidate in a by-election for the safe Labor seat of Collingwood in Victoria's Legislative Assembly. At Collingwood Town Hall, Menzies, with the insouciance often displayed by people with nothing to lose, cheerfully informed the crowd that the Liberals would win Collingwood, and Carlton the premiership; both were heard by the locals as atrocious heresies, the latter more so. Menzies was, it turned out, half right – Labor retained Collingwood, despite a 10 per cent swing to Menzies' party, but Carlton won the 1947 flag, defeating Essendon by a point in the grand final, with a last-minute goal from Fred Stafford.

In 1958, while prime minister, Menzies contributed a foreword to Hugh Buggy and Harry Bell's history of Carlton, recalling how he'd first taken to the Blues as a teenager, when his family moved to Melbourne upon the election of his father to Victoria's parliament: Menzies' two elder brothers had been living with relatives in North Carlton. Menzies cited favourite players of decades past – Rod McGregor, Paddy O'Brien, Horrie Clover, astute choices each – and solemnly pronounced: 'Amid all my duties and burdens, I am proud to have my number-one members' ticket in so great a club.'

Though Menzies' passion for Carlton was genuine, he could afford to take a sanguine view about what it might cost him politically – the inner suburbs of Melbourne weren't going to vote for him anyway. In 1958, indeed, those serried terraces were represented in the federal parliament by Arthur Calwell, who would succeed H.V. Evatt as Labor leader in 1960. Calwell was a dyed-in-the-wool North Melbourne barracker who had served as club president from 1928 to 1934.[6] (Another Labor leader who never became prime minister, Simon Crean, was also number-one ticketholder at North.)

Australian football has always held an irresistible lure for Australian politicians, over and above any authentic affection for the game which many have possessed. In 1908, Prime Minister Alfred Deakin addressed the Australasian National Football Council, amid that year's Melbourne Carnival – an interstate tournament[7] convened to celebrate the 50th anniversary of the Scotch College versus Melbourne Grammar match.

Deakin's sporting passions were primarily directed towards cycling – a pioneer of the lycra-swaddled marauders who would later swarm Melbourne's thoroughfares, he was fined at least once for riding on the footpath – but he recognised the political and patriotic potence of football. Speaking at Melbourne Town Hall, Deakin declared: 'The game is Australian in its origin, Australian in its principle and, I venture to say, essentially of Australian development.' There were, at this point, few things besides the stump-jump plough of which this could be said, Australia being a seven-year-old nation which still thought itself a colony: Deakin concluded his address by musing on the martial virtues which the game might inculcate, to be drawn upon when the time came to 'stand by the old land'.

It is hard to be certain whether Menzies made more of a thing of his football allegiance than most prime ministers, or whether it just seemed that way because he was prime minister for so long. He was not the first to have adored the game. John Curtin filled a half-forward flank for Brunswick in the VFA as a youth, later supported Fitzroy and, during a period out of parliament in the 1930s, wrote football reports for *The Westralian Worker*. As wartime prime minister, Curtin was given to seeing the world as a football field. In December 1941, when the Royal Navy ships HMS *Prince of Wales* and HMS *Repulse*, two bulwarks of the defence of Singapore, were sunk by Japanese bombers, Curtin stoically remarked: 'Nobody squeals about being a few goals down at half-time.'

---

6   Arthur Calwell was an unyielding defender of the White Australia policy, and curiously proud of his quip that 'two Wongs don't make a white'. It is pleasing to think that his eternal slumber since his death in 1973 might have been disturbed somewhat by the appearance in royal blue and white stripes of Alex Ischenko, Majak Daw, Jose Romero and Nathan Hrovat, among others representing a more generous definition of 'Australian' than Calwell was willing to entertain.

7   The 1908 interstate carnival was technically an international tournament, given the presence of a team from New Zealand – who played in all black, and did pretty well, defeating New South Wales and Queensland. New Zealand were captained by Melbourne-born Tom Wright, who had played a few games for Collingwood before moving to Christchurch for work reasons. He was killed on the Somme in 1916.

Ben Chifley, who became prime minister shortly after Curtin's death in 1945, was a New South Welshman, and it showed. In 1948, Dame Enid Lyons – a Tasmanian – raised with Chifley in parliament her concern about the depiction of Australian football in a new Department of Information film. Dame Enid, the first woman elected to federal parliament and the widow of Australia's tenth prime minister, Joseph Lyons, fretted that the included clip of a VFL match showed only 'a very feeble piece of fumbling' rather than more enticing footage of the high marking which distinguished what she described as 'our national game'. Chifley cautioned that she was 'treading on dangerous ground', but Dame Enid was supported by the Australian National Football Council, which huffily telegrammed that 'the prime minister's obvious lack of knowledge of Australian sport is most regrettable'.

Chifley, at least, was not faking a fondness – a populist temptation that has beclowned far too many others. Paul Keating, who could not have made his indifference to sport more obvious if he'd mounted a billboard campaign featuring a football with a stake driven through it, agreed to be adopted as number-one ticketholder by Collingwood, and to pose for the awkwardly hearty photo-op with Lou Richards apparently compulsory in such circumstances. Collingwood had previously attempted to ensnare Gough Whitlam, organising the presentation of a Magpies guernsey by Ray Gabelich shortly after Whitlam became Labor leader in 1967. Some years later, Whitlam was persuaded into a Geelong guernsey for a picture with Graham 'Polly' Farmer, but neither ceremony persuaded him to abandon a lifelong disinterest in all outdoor recreations.[8]

Menzies aside, the only other prime minister to make such an ostentatious show of being a football fan was another Carlton barracker, and another Liberal – although, by at least one informed account, Malcolm Fraser swore allegiance to the Blues (initially, at least) out of political expedience. By the telling of brewing tycoon and then-Carlton president John Elliott, Fraser approached him in early 1975, shortly after he had deposed Billy Snedden to become Liberal leader, and said that he understood that he would now need to be seen following a football club. Elliott invited Fraser to watch Carlton from his box at Waverley Park, and arranged a photo with Alex Jesaulenko, which was duly splashed by *The*

---

8   A fine biography of Polly Farmer was written by Steve Hawke, son of Labor's next prime minister, Bob Hawke, who stood unsuccessfully for the federal seat of Corio at what was clearly an impressionable age in his child's life.

Sun; Fraser rang Elliott a few days later, having given the matter some thought, and declared himself for Carlton.

This sounds unlikely, if only because it is unusual for born-and-raised Victorians, as Fraser was, to decide their club allegiance in their mid-40s – though another source, the veteran journalist Alan Ramsey, corroborated it years later when he wrote that 'Fraser cares little about football, and less about John Elliott'. Even if Fraser was making a cold political calculation, he took to the Blues with a convincing impression of gusto. He frequently attended matches, and invited the 1981 and 1982 Carlton premiership teams to dine at the Lodge. On the former occasion, Fraser's wife, Tamie, gamely accompanied to hospital the plus one of Alex Marcou, a woman known only as Fabulous, who'd overdone it on the pre-prandial hospitality, fallen down the stairs and broken an ankle. After the latter visit, several Carlton players, apparently uncertain of their chances of a three-peat and another invitation, left the premises clinking with prime ministerial cutlery.

Australian prime ministers have been as divided as the nation they lead by the Barassi Line. John Howard, though obviously a sports fan, gave little indication of caring about the AFL, nor did his fellow Sydneysider Tony Abbott. Malcolm Turnbull proclaimed allegiance to the Swans, but suspicions that he regarded them principally as props for blokeish photo opportunities were not assuaged by his failure, in a 2016 radio interview, to recite the words to the team song. Kevin Rudd, a Queenslander, was able to join in on Brisbane's anthem when he appeared in the dressing-room following the Lions' elimination final win over Carlton in 2009; within a few years there were probably Brisbane players who hadn't heard it roared in victory often enough for the lyrics to have stuck.

Australian leaders have occasionally sought to deploy Australia's game as an instrument of soft power overseas. Turnbull mentioned Sydney defender Aliir Aliir, born in Kenya to displaced Sudanese parents, in a 2016 address to the United Nations, vaunting Australia's refugee programme. In 2011, Julia Gillard, on a visit to Washington DC, presented US president Barack Obama with a Sherrin, and conducted a handball lesson in the Oval Office. Gillard, a Western Bulldogs fan, had appealed for national unity during the 2010 election campaign on the basis that 'we can all hate Collingwood'. This prompted aggrieved uproar from Magpies barrackers – and the usual directly proportional amusement among everybody else – but the Division of Melbourne, amidst which Collingwood seethes, was lost by Labor for the first time in 106 years.

28

Peter Hudson's Helicopter
Collingwood 16.10.106 Hawthorn 13.10.88
Waverley Park
ROUND 21, 1973

As a season ebbs, there are three sorts of clubs. There are those who know they'll be playing finals: poised, determined, looking forward to the next few weeks. There are those who know they won't: resigned, thwarted, looking ahead to next year. And there are those on the threshold between glory and oblivion: fretful, preoccupied, possibly demented, unsure whether they're standing on a launchpad or a trapdoor. A couple more decent results, some other club's misfortune running your way – and, well, who knows? But there's no margin for error. Everything that can go right has to, and anything anyone can do to help, however bizarre it might seem, has to be worth trying.

By the second-last home-and-away match of 1973, Collingwood were in the first category. The Pies had started the season at the top of the ladder with a 76-point pasting of South Melbourne, and had descended from that eyrie only twice, in a couple of weeks when Carlton's percentage narrowly exceeded theirs. They were a team of the era's aristocrats – George Bisset, Ross Dunne, Barry Price, Max Richardson, Len Thompson, Ronnie Wearmouth – spearheaded by the League's leading goalkicker, Peter McKenna, a star on the field, who had also made faltering attempts to become a star off it. McKenna had been inaugural co-host of *Hey Hey It's Saturday* alongside Daryl Somers, before Collingwood suggested that he rethink his priorities; he was duly replaced, to lastingly successful effect, by a pink ostrich puppet. McKenna's ability to replicate the haircut of a Beatle or a Byrd had prompted someone, somewhere, to assume that he could sing like one, and he'd released two singles, neither hits, neither good.[1] But he was near his peak as a player: when Collingwood welcomed Hawthorn to Waverley, McKenna was two days short of his 27th birthday, with 735 goals at near five per game to his credit.

Hawthorn had started 1973 slowly, losing three of their first four games, the exception a 68-point demolition of Essendon in which Leigh Matthews amassed 41 disposals and kicked 11 goals. Since then, the Hawks had clawed their way to respectability, hauling themselves into fifth spot in Round 14 with a fine win at Glenferrie over second-placed Carlton, Matthews again uncontainable with 31 kicks and three goals.[2] Hawthorn occupied the same precarious perch for the next five weeks, just ahead of St Kilda. The Hawks met the Saints in Round 20:[3] something had to give, and it was Hawthorn. Hawthorn found themselves abruptly seventh, a game out of the five, with two rounds to go – away to Collingwood, at home to South Melbourne. Win both, and the Hawks were still a chance. Lose either, they were done.

A persistent legend, conceivably even true, holds that a church in the vicinity of Glenferrie in the early 1970s adorned the billboard outside with the admonishment 'What would you do if Jesus Christ came to Hawthorn today?', and that some anonymous graffitist added the reply 'Shift Peter Hudson to centre half-forward' – the implicit assertion that the son of God at full-forward would be good for better than Hudson's unparalleled 5.64 goals a game was a profound demonstration of faith. By this point in Hawthorn's sputtering 1973 season, Peter Hudson would indeed have seemed an answer to their prayers, but he'd left the club early the year before.

In the first game of Hawthorn's defence of their 1971 flag – to which Hudson's 150 goals had been the crucial contribution[4] – Hudson

---

1   Peter McKenna's two singles were 'Things to Remember', and 'Smile All the While'. The latter, written and produced by *Young Talent Time* host Johnny Young, was marginally less terrible. In 2004, Peter McKenna took a job with the government of Victoria as a chauffeur for senior politicians. Victoria's premier, Steve Bracks, a Geelong barracker, mused wistfully that 'it's just a pity that his stripes were vertical rather than horizontal'.

2   Leigh Matthews led the VFL's goalkicking in 1975, with 67 for the season. While 1975 clearly wasn't a vintage year for full-forwards, it remains an astonishing feat for someone who rarely played in that position. Matthews finished his career with 915 goals from 332 games – a goals-per-game average (2.76) which compares respectably with those of traditional spearheads like Matthew Richardson (2.84), Stephen Kernahan (2.94) and Michael Moncrieff (2.81), and comfortably outclasses such modern full-forwards as Nick Riewoldt (2.14), Jack Riewoldt (2.39) and Matthew Pavlich (1.98).

3   St Kilda were still, at this time, coached by Allan Jeans, who would later lead Hawthorn to three premierships.

4   Peter Hudson went into the 1971 grand final four short of beating Bob Pratt's 37-year-old record of 150 goals in a season. He was targeted early by St Kilda's Kevin 'Cowboy' Neale, who fetched Hudson a blow that left one of his ears almost split and his vision blurred. Hudson nevertheless kicked three goals to draw equal with Pratt, but in the last quarter fluffed two chances to beat Pratt's record, hoofing a set shot into St Kilda's Barry Lawrence, standing on the mark, and shanking out

had been stretchered off Glenferrie Oval just before half-time, his right knee wrenched in a clash with Melbourne's Barry Bourke. As estimates of three or four weeks on the sidelines became a season, then a career, the eight goals Hudson had rattled off against the Demons in the two quarters before his ligaments twanged seemed a melancholy coda to the reign of arguably the game's greatest ever full-forward. Aged 26, Hudson had retired to his native Tasmania, become the proprietor of the Granada Tavern in the Hobart suburb of Berriedale, and he wasn't available.

Unless, wondered Hawthorn's coach, John Kennedy, he was. Kennedy was accustomed to asking much of players, and accustomed to positive responses. Kennedy called Hudson at the Granada and asked how he was doing. Hudson replied that he hadn't played for nearly two years, hadn't trained, and that running a pub had not proved conducive to the upkeep of prime physical condition. Hudson had played at 90-odd kilograms; he was now a well-upholstered 100-plus. The good news was that the knee wasn't giving him too much trouble. Kennedy flew to Hobart and set Hudson to work, running him between the goalposts on the football field at Rosetta High School.

A few weeks of running up and down made as much difference to Hudson's fitness as it was ever likely to, but Kennedy was willing to resort to one of those desperate measures summoned by desperate times. Hawthorn offered to put Hudson on a plane to Melbourne the Friday night before the Collingwood game, and fly him back directly afterwards. Hudson demurred: that particular Friday night was due to be a big one at the Granada, with Norman Gunston playing to a full house.[5] Hawthorn secretary Ivan Moore suggested – having paused, one imagines, to scream into a handy cushion, or bite a chunk out of his desk – that Hudson get as much sleep as possible after shooing out the last punter and washing the last glass, fly from Hobart on the Saturday morning of the game, then be spirited by helicopter from Tullamarine to Waverley in time for the bounce at 2.10 p.m.[6]

---

on the full a running shot from 30 metres.

5 Norman Gunston, a character created by comedian Garry McDonald, was a showbiz reporter as oleaginous as he was inept, a twitching mess of gormless ego and self-inflicted shaving wounds, imposing his vanities and insecurities on (at best) half-suspecting celebrity stooges. Gunston appears, in retrospect, kind of the Elvis of the self-satirising chat show host genre, a spiritual godfather of Paul Kaye's Dennis Pennis, Steve Coogan's Alan Partridge and Sacha Baron-Cohen's Ali G, among many others.

6 The other most famous helicopter ride in football history was orchestrated by Geelong in 1981, by way of amplifying the deliverance narrative surrounding much-hyped midseason recruit Brian Peake, East Fremantle superstar. Thousands of fans awaited Peake's arrival by chopper at Kardinia

It was an audacious bet on Tasmania's capricious weather – and, it initially appeared, an ill-judged one. Hudson's scheduled flight was cancelled due to fog, but space was found for his party – Hudson, his wife, his father and father-in-law – aboard another aircraft which had been cleared to fly to Melbourne with only crew aboard. Upon arrival at Tullamarine, Hudson and family were ushered onto the waiting chopper, fed with quiche from lunchboxes someone had thought to bring, and whisked towards Waverley and a landing in the nearby grounds of St Mary's seminary – a drop-off point with divine portent that would have seemed appropriate to Hawthorn fans. Hudson's return had been a recurrent rumour, but here he was: back in that long-sleeved number 26 guernsey bunched up to the elbows, shaking hands with teammates he hadn't seen for almost two full seasons, and some, like a gangly 20-year-old named Michael Tuck, playing his 16th match, whom he'd never met.

Hudson could barely run, and he couldn't jump, and it didn't matter. It took two minutes for him to kick his first League goal in 17 months, a left-foot snap from inside a pack. It took another two minutes for him to kick his second, with one of his trademark right-footed flat punts after a mark on the boundary line. It took another few minutes after that for his knee to buckle, again, and that didn't matter either. Hawthorn continued to trust him as they always had, emptying their forward line, putting the pockets on the flanks, the flankers on the wings, isolating Hudson in one-on-one contests against whichever luckless short-straw-drawer was at full-back – which, today, was Jeff Clifton, then Lee Adamson, then Ross 'Twiggy' Dunne. Hudson beat them all, and finished with eight goals.

It was more than adequate, and not enough. Collingwood, though startled early by the mesmeric apparition on Hawthorn's forward line, pulled themselves gradually together, and won by 18 points; McKenna kicked four, while Len Thompson was best afield. The season was effectively over for Hawthorn, and actually over for Hudson, whose right knee had ballooned sufficiently to stretch the seams of his trousers. He'd try again in 1974, lasting two games before submitting to the surgeon.

As Collingwood learned in ensuing weeks, a superstar full-forward with two working knees is no guarantor of success, either. In the semi-

Park for his first training session. As credulous believers awaiting an airborne messiah often are, Geelong's legions were to be disappointed – although Peake was a better player than the cruel nickname 'Past 'is' suggested.

final, Peter McKenna was held to three kicks and two goals by Carlton's Geoff Southby, as Collingwood disintegrated in the last quarter and lost by 20 points.[7] In the preliminary final, McKenna wasn't even on the park. In a decision that should have prompted more discussion about what kind of mushrooms Collingwood's selectors were consuming with their breakfasts, McKenna was dropped in favour of a precociously burly 16-year-old called Rene Kink – which is to say that on the eve of a preliminary final, Collingwood binned the VFL's leading goalkicker, and replaced him with a teenager making his first full appearance for the club.[8]

McKenna had been ill earlier in the week, which Collingwood spun vaguely as the reason for his omission, but McKenna assumed he was playing until he read otherwise in Friday morning's newspapers. When journalists descended upon his Ivanhoe grocery store in search of a quote, the furious full-forward was disinclined to parrot the party line. 'I am disgusted with the way this business has been handled,' he informed the agog hackery. 'It staggered me because from what Collingwood said to me at training last night, I assumed I would be in the side. If they had come and said I would be dropped because of my poor form, I would have copped it on the chin like a man. I have played long enough at Collingwood to expect a better deal than this.'

In itself, Collingwood's inclusion of Kink proved astute – he took five marks and kicked three goals. At one stage during the second quarter, Collingwood led by 45 points. Richmond, however, had not been so cavalier as Collingwood in dispensing with their superstars: the Tigers had named injured captain Royce Hart as 19th man, despite the knee trouble that had reduced him to half a season – and, some feared, to half the player he'd been, even if that was still twice the player as most. At half-time, Hart was sent to centre half-forward. At full-time, Richmond were seven-point winners, on their way to a grand final and the premiership, leaving Collingwood bereft, as was becoming traditional, and Melbourne subeditors agonising over whether to headline their stories 'Hart Transplant' or 'Hart Break'.

---

7   Geoff Southby's infamous removal from the 1973 grand final during the second quarter via the fist of Richmond's Neil Balme may not have been decisive – Richmond were the better team – but it is a reasonable assumption that Balme had calculated that his day's work would be easier without the era's finest full-back getting in his way.

8   Rene Kink, who resembled an action figure which had acquired human scale and sentience, earned the ambiguous distinction of playing in six grand finals, including the 1977 replay, without winning one – five with Collingwood, one with Essendon. A hairdresser by trade, Kink was typecast as Tank O'Donohue in Bruce Beresford's 1980 film of David Williamson's The Club.

Back in Tasmania, Hudson and his repaired right knee made an astonishing recovery. In 1975 and 1976, Hudson captain-coached Glenorchy in the Tasmanian Football League, finishing as premiers and runners-up respectively. In 1977, he made a full-season comeback at Hawthorn, and led the VFL's goalkicking for the fourth time, with 110. He returned to Glenorchy the following season for two years of terrorising the defenders of the TFL, scoring a merely absurd 153 goals in 1978, and a ridiculous 179 in 1979. In both years, Hudson not only topped the TFL's goalkicking, but won its Brownlow equivalent, the William Leitch Medal.

Hudson's 1973 helicopter hurtle was the kind of thing that should, were football a fairytale, have turned a season. That it failed to furnish Hawthorn the matinee ending they desired was no fault of Hudson's: eight goals off one leg when overweight, barely ambulant and having hardly held a football in two years has to be reckoned a decent return on the gamble. Even immobile, Hudson was unstoppable.

29

The Battle of Windy Hill
Essendon 15.15.105 Richmond 16.19.115
Windy Hill
ROUND 7, 1974

No sport mythologises its extracurricular brutality like Australian football. It is a furtive, officially suppressed love. After every such eruption, League authorities and football media unite in a chorus of sanctimonious condemnation: bad for the game, set an example, etc. But love it unmistakably is. If you watch the crowd behind the barriers whenever fists start flying, you will behold delighted ranks of cheering, laughing faces.

When pundits and fans reminisce about the game's prelapsarian glory days, before Australian football was cleaned up, scrutinised by ever-multiplying umpires and cameras, they are not really mourning better football, or better players, for both have been improved and accelerated by evolving technology, nutrition, science and tactics. Were a time machine to make possible a contest between (for example) the 1950s Melbourne side which won five flags in six years and (to pick just one) the forlorn Carlton rabble of the late 2010s, that golden Demons generation would be lucky to lose by fewer than 20 goals, and to leave the field alive. What the wistful nostalgics really miss is the violence.

Richmond's visit to Essendon this election day afternoon,[1] then, endures as one of the most fondly indulged folk memories in Australian football. The Battle of Windy Hill transcended even the fearsome standards of mid-1970s melees due to two factors. One, the fact that it

---

1   In the 1974 general election, the Labor government of Gough Whitlam was returned, preferred to the Liberal/Country coalition led by Billy Snedden. Snedden, who had played for Western Australia's state amateur football team in the early 1950s, was a fan of Melbourne – a conservative lawyer supporting Melbourne, imagine. He served as club president from 1980 to 1985, and later as a director of the VFL.

happened at half-time, depriving field umpire Mike Henry of the option of calling a ball-up and inviting players to choose between the game and the fight. Two, the presence of pertinacious Perthite Mal Brown, enjoying surely the most eventful single-season career in VFL/AFL history.

If one was unacquainted with the detail of Brown's resume, it might seem surprising that he had not come to Victoria earlier. Though Collingwood had taken an early interest, Brown was 27 when Richmond recruited him in 1974, for a fee of $35,000. In nine seasons for East Perth in the WANFL,[2] Brown had played 166 games, won three club best and fairests, one Sandover Medal and damn near another, captain-coached the Royals to a premiership and been named All-Australian captain. He had also acquired a warranted renown for leaving opponents as black and blue as East Perth's guernseys. The first that most Victorian fans saw of Brown was the semi-final of the 1972 Championship of Australia tournament,[3] in which he picked a fight with most of Carlton's midfield, felling Trevor Keogh with one especially unabashed right jab.

This loosest and most destructive of cannons had adjusted readily to the VFL – either that, or opponents preferred to keep out of his way. Brown was a steady contributor as the Tigers continued their premiership form of the season before, and attracted approving notices from a Melbourne press which would have been within its rights to be suspicious, much as inhabitants of a frontier town might initially have offered a wide berth to the brooding stranger in the black hat. Against St Kilda, wrote Peter McFarline in *The Age*, Brown had '[resisted] the obvious urge to tangle with Kevin Neale,[4] marked well, kicked three goals and used his great football brain to set up about five others for teammates'.

Brown had a quieter day at Windy Hill, blanketed by Essendon full-back Geoff Pryor,[5] but few would remember or care, partly because

---

2   The Western Australian National Football League, or WANFL, dropped the 'National' to create the pleasing acronym WAFL in 1980, the name by which it remains known, following a couple of misbegotten rebrandings as the Western Australian State Football League and Westar Rules.

3   The Championship of Australia, pitting the premiers of state leagues against each other at season's end, had sporadically been a thing in the decades around the turn of the 20th century. It was revived in 1968 and continued until 1975. It was won only once by a non-Victorian club – in 1972, North Adelaide beat Carlton in the grand final by a point. Of the modern tournaments, Richmond won the most, with three, while Sturt lost four grand finals, all by convincing margins.

4   Kevin 'Cowboy' Neale kicked five of St Kilda's ten goals in the 1966 grand final, in which the Saints won their only premiership, at time of writing, by a point.

5   Geoff Pryor's 137-game career with Essendon was interrupted by his job with the Department of Trade, which posted him overseas in 1971–72; he retired from football upon being appointed Australia's trade commissioner in Milan. He was also founding president of the VFL Players' Association, forerunner of the AFLPA.

Richmond won anyway, but mostly because it was Brown who, once the smoke cleared, the dust settled and the blood dried, was widely blamed for starting the fight. Shortly before half-time, Brown tangled with Essendon's Graeme Jenkin – the same Graeme 'Jerker' Jenkin who, when playing for Collingwood, was scaled by Carlton's Alex Jesaulenko to immortal effect in the 1970 grand final; he clearly had a gift for the supporting actor role. After the siren sounded and players began heading towards the dressing-rooms, Essendon runner Laurie Ashley said something to Brown which Brown found disagreeable – which, on form, might have been any statement more hostile than 'Top of the afternoon, sir, I hope you're enjoying the match'.

Scenes similar to what ensued often prompt the exclamation that 'it's on for young and old'. This observation is more accurate than usual when describing the Battle of Windy Hill. The fact that unpleasantries ignited after half-time had been signalled meant that there were more than just players on the field: volunteering for the fight, or being conscripted, were trainers, runners, coaches, officials, umpires, 19th men (Essendon's John Cassin, clad in a dressing gown, was a notably enthusiastic participant), police officers, at least one on horseback and another in a different kind of uniform – Constable Barry Grinter, playing ruck for Essendon – and a bewildered six-year-old in a striped woollen vest; this was a young Richmond fan named James Ferguson, who had become separated from his family in the crowd and was being assisted in his search by one of the cops when it all kicked off. The officer gently ushered the kid away from the havoc, a gesture of touching incongruity in the circumstances.

A few of the crowd climbed the fence and joined in. Others preferred to contribute as artillery rather than infantry. Richmond ruckman Brian 'The Whale' Roberts was caught in the face by a beer can hurled from behind the pickets, and later required surgery on a broken nose, though doubt persists as to whether this damage was done by the projectile or by the fist of Essendon's Ron Andrews;[6] Richmond team manager Graeme

---

6   Ron Andrews was a 19-year-old playing his 14th game at the Battle of Windy Hill. The subsequent visit to the tribunal was far from his last – Andrews would be suspended for 24 matches of a 151-game career. The soubriquet 'Rotten Ronnie' notwithstanding, he was no mere knuckler and wrecker, and at his peak was one of the VFL's finest centre half-backs. In 1984 he went six rounds with Mark 'Jacko' Jackson before a crowd of several thousand at Perth Entertainment Centre – replicating, in more regulated circumstances, their many clashes on the football field. Jackson won on points.

Richmond[7] was injured by a similar missile. Also among the more serious casualties was the Bombers' fitness instructor, Jim Bradley, whose jaw was fractured. As hostilities subsided, Mal Brown, not noticeably the worse for having been trodden on by a police horse, was escorted from the field by a phalanx of police; he offered the crowd a cheery wave, a frayed bandage trailing from a triumphant right fist.

Contemplating the four quarters of football around the half-time donnybrook may be Australian football's equivalent of asking Mary Todd Lincoln, 'Other than that, how was the play?' But it wasn't a bad game, rugged yet skilful, rarely more than a couple of kicks in it. For Richmond, Ian Stewart was in characteristically commanding touch, with five goals from half-forward; Kevin Sheedy, as always, was in the middle of everything, inside the law and out, contributing three goals, unsentimentally helping to skewer the side he'd supported as a child, when he'd had to leave games at Windy Hill during the last quarter to start his paper round. For Essendon, Ron Andrews and Geoff Pryor were colossal in defence, and 18-year-old debutant Max Crow, a homesick farmboy from Underbool, kicked four goals.[8] It may even have been an important match in the context of Richmond's season: the kind of thing that, if you survive it, makes it feel like nothing is beyond you, including backing up a premiership, as the Tigers did.

But nobody really cared about any of that, then or now. Though no reports were made by the umpires on the day – they were busier trying to contain the fight than chronicle it – the newspapers shifted swiftly into think-of-the-children mode, and the League duly followed. By the end of the week, the VFL's investigation officer, Jack Chessell, was on the case. Chessell, a veteran football administrator, had worked for the League as a contracted gumshoe in 1972, looking into the infamous king-hit on Collingwood's John Greening by St Kilda's Jim O'Dea.[9]

---

7   Graeme Richmond, prevented by nominative determinism from working for any other club, held various offices at Richmond between 1962 and 1986. He also played a significant role in Melbourne's post-punk underground, as publican at St Kilda dive the Seaview Hotel, home of the much-mythologised Crystal Ballroom, where Richmond provided a venue, rehearsal space, postal address and crashpad to The Birthday Party, The Models, Hunters & Collectors, Whirlywirld and The Moodists, among others. Overseas acts of that ilk also frequented the Crystal Ballroom. It is altogether possible that Richmond attended the Tigers' 75-point thrashing by St Kilda at Waverley in Round 20, 1983, with his ears still ringing from the previous evening's show by Dead Kennedys.

8   Max Crow played 136 games for Essendon, 40 for St Kilda and 12 for Footscray. His daughter, Kim Brennan, won medals at the London and Rio de Janeiro Olympics, rowing in the single and double sculls.

9   John Greening, a dazzlingly gifted winger, was targeted by Jim O'Dea in the opening minutes of 1972's Round 14 game between Collingwood and St Kilda. He was unconscious for 24 hours, in

A week and a half later, Chessell returned a seven-page report on the Windy Hill affray, recommending charges against four players, two officials and one runner. At a marathon tribunal hearing lasting past 1 a.m., Ron Andrews got six weeks for assaulting Brian Roberts – Roberts, maintaining the no-squealers ethos, gamely attempted to blame his spectacular facial bruises on a kick from a police horse. It was Andrews' second tribunal appearance that week: he'd also been booked the week after the Battle of Windy Hill, for striking North Melbourne's Sam Kekovich, but that one hadn't stuck.

Essendon runner Laurie Ashley got six weeks for conduct unbecoming, and Essendon fitness instructor Jim Bradley six weeks for attacking Mal Brown. Seventeen-year-old Richmond rookie Stephen Parsons, who'd been playing just his third game, got four for striking Bradley – though the tribunal took his point that he thought the Essendon trainer was an unruly member of the public – and Brown one for ditto. John Cassin was cleared of assaulting Brown. As deliberations wore on, Brown helped himself to the VFL House telephones, and caught up with friends and family back in Western Australia.

There was plenty of blame to go around, but tribunal chairman John Winneke[10] laid most of it at the feet of Essendon's runner, informing him that he had 'the dubious distinction, Mr Ashley, of starting off what can only be described as an unseemly brawl'. The trigger, Winneke seemed satisfied, had been Ashley calling Brown a 'filthy' player; it is not recorded whether Ashley retorted to Winneke that Brown had been called worse, not always without justification.

The case against Richmond team manager Graeme Richmond, also for assaulting Bradley, was heard at a later and even longer hearing – taxis were not summoned until past 2 a.m. He was suspended for six months and fined $2000. A further ordeal awaited: police brought assault charges against Graeme Richmond and Stephen Parsons. The pair stood trial in September. Both were acquitted, the magistrate unable to sort right from wrong beyond reasonable doubt. One witness at the trial, a member of

---

intensive care nearly a fortnight, and there were fears for his life. He didn't play again for nearly two years, and his comeback ran to just nine games across three seasons. O'Dea was suspended for ten weeks.

10 John Winneke played 50 games for Hawthorn in the early 1960s, including the 1961 premiership, before retiring at 24 to concentrate on his legal career: he later became a judge of the Supreme Court of Victoria. A few days before the Battle of Windy Hill verdicts were handed down, his father, Sir Henry Winneke, a former chief justice of the Supreme Court of Victoria, was sworn in as governor of Victoria.

the Windy Hill crowd, testified that the indecorum had been touched off by Mal Brown taking three swings at Laurie Ashley's head; this witness was named in newspapers as Lindsay James Tanner, a law student from Moonee Ponds. Tanner was later an MP, minister for finance and deregulation – and chairman of Essendon Football Club.

Mal Brown kicked 25 goals in 14 appearances for Richmond, contributing to the Tigers' 1974 premiership – but not on grand final day. In Richmond's Round 20 match against Collingwood at Victoria Park – a 27-point win in which Brown scored two goals – Brown threw the ball at field umpire John Sutcliffe, earning a four-week suspension that ended his season and, it turned out, his VFL career. He went back west, where he coached at Claremont, South Fremantle – with whom he won the WAFL premiership in 1980 – and Perth, before serving on the WAFL Commission. A brief 1992 coaching comeback with South Fremantle ended in fitting style, Brown charged with misconduct for taking a swing at an East Fremantle player, leading with his right as he clutched his clipboard in his left.

Brown's son, Campbell, later cut a dash with Hawthorn and Gold Coast, but he inherited his father's Hyde as well as his Jekyll, reported 14 times and suspended for 29 weeks of a 205-game career, which ended when the Suns sacked him following an altercation during an end-of-season trip to the United States, which left teammate Steven May with a broken jaw.[11]

In Round 14 of 1975, there was a Second Battle of Windy Hill, an extraordinary affair in which Carlton and Essendon, in between skirmishes and set-tos that saw eight players reported, and summoned comparisons, aghast and/or titillated, with the Bloodbath of 1945, found time to score 42 goals between them. Savage though it was, it did not dislodge the First Battle of Windy Hill from its place in every fan's affections. If, one day, some sort of Sealed Knot society ever convenes to spend weekends entertaining tourists with re-enactments of cherished Australian football dust-ups, replica 1974 Richmond and Essendon guernseys will be among the most regularly worn costumes, and the competition for Mal Brown's number 18 will be rugged.

Mal Brown relished the stoush, today and all days, and he understood that everyone else savoured it as well, however piously they protested

---

11   Campbell Brown captained Australia at the 2016 kabaddi World Cup in Ahmedabad, leading a team which included Adam Schneider, ex Sydney and St Kilda, and Stephen Milne, ex St Kilda. Australia failed to set the tournament ablaze, winning just one match, against Argentina.

otherwise. Asked a couple of years after Windy Hill to justify himself, he replied: 'People, basically, like blood. It's a proven fact. You go to Spain, you see them stab to death bulls, et cetera, and here we like the gladiator sport, and I believe that people enjoy a bit of brutality, and the same people who sit there and say "Isn't it terrible", they'll be the ones who really like it, and that's why they go along every week to see something happen.'

Asked about it again a few decades later, and baited to agree that Windy Hill had been 'a dark day in football history', Brown corrected Mike Sheahan instantly. 'It was a marvellous day,' Brown beamed. 'I pissed myself laughing.'

30

Malcolm Blight's Torpedo
Carlton 11.10.76 North Melbourne 11.15.81
Princes Park
ROUND 10, 1976

It seems incredible that, except from extraordinary distances and/ or difficult angles, footballers ever miss set shots for goal. Kicking a football accurately is a key component of their job, for which they train exhaustively, and are remunerated handsomely. Yet they miss, frequently – indeed they miss, not infrequently, set shots that most people in the stands would back themselves, or indeed a half-blind great-grandparent, to make.

For all that an Australian Rules ball is a strange and annoying shape, prone to inconvenient caprices of flight and bounce, the issue is far more with the head than the foot. When we darkly mutter that we'd have little trouble kicking a ball between two sticks 6.4 metres apart, from somewhere inside the 50 – honestly, what are we paying this cross-eyed, bow-legged hack – what we mean is that we're capable of enacting the necessary physical mechanics. What we're not considering, as most of us have no idea what it feels like, is the difference made by a live crowd of tens of thousands, and a television audience of millions more, watching and (depending on allegiance) offering prayers or confecting curses. This pressure is amplified exponentially, one imagines – one can only imagine – when the set shot in question is after the final siren, and will decide the result.

Malcolm Blight's decisive goal at Princes Park on this June afternoon is the most storied after-the-siren kick in Australian football. There are a number of reasons for this. Most obviously, there's distance. When Blight outmarked Carlton's Mark Maclure as time expired, he was at least 70 metres from goal. Then there were the conditions, soggy, muddy and lousy; the ball must have felt like a pumpkin harvested on a wet morning. And there was the build-up, a sequence of events that the most delusional schoolboy Walter Mitty, acting out his most risible fantasies alone in the back yard, would have slapped his own face for dreaming.

When Carlton reached what would be their final score of 10.11.76, North were 8.14.62, with about 20 minutes on the clock in the concluding quarter. It is nigh certain that there are North Melbourne fans who have spent the decades since bewailing the weary pragmatism that recognised a lost cause, and impelled them to make an early start on their journey home from Princes Park. Carlton had been ahead all day, their small but swift midfield – the nascent 'mosquito fleet', at this stage including Trevor Keogh, Rod Austin and Rod Ashman[1] – making North look like baffled pachyderms attempting to swat away pestilent insects. Ashman had scored three goals, Keogh was nearing 30 kicks.

At half-time, with Carlton leading by 27 points, North's coach, Ron Barassi, had applied some old-school motivational psychology. He singled out Malcolm Blight, the South Australian champion[2] who was in his third season with the Kangaroos, and whose combination of absurd talent and mournful moustache conferred upon him the aura of a sad wizard. Barassi informed Blight that he was playing 'like a goose'. Even Barassi cannot have imagined the spectacular production of golden eggs that would be prompted by his scorn.

At three-quarter time, North Melbourne had clipped the deficit to 15 points – a tractable margin if you're playing a bad team on your home deck on a good day, but North faced the opposite propositions. Early in the last, North kicked a couple of goals – one of them by Blight – but so did Carlton. At 23 minutes, Carlton's Danny Halloran found himself in enough space in front of goal to (surely) finish it, and with enough time for Barassi to begin seething at the irony that the kid was wearing the same number 31 that had once adorned his own back. Halloran hit the post. It was Carlton's last score of the day.

---

1   Rod Ashman's 236-game career with the Blues was interrupted during 1979 by a stand-off as Carlton refused him a transfer to North Melbourne. As the fates dictated, his first game back, in Round 18 of that year was against North Melbourne. He collected 39 disposals and kicked two goals. In the later stages of his career, he was one of a small coterie of players of the time who wore leather cycling helmets to insulate against concussion.

2   Malcolm Blight was recruited from Woodville, where he'd won the Magarey Medal in 1972. He became the first to complete the Magarey/Brownlow double in 1978, a feat since equalled by John Platten and Nathan Buckley. He is the only player to have kicked 100 goals in a season in both the VFL/AFL and the SANFL.

North's next shot at goal was from Blight, from wide in the pocket as he tumbled, but nobody paid much attention to where it went: a free kick had already been paid to Keogh. Keogh's kick went to a contest, and was gathered by North's Shane Zantuck, who, after turning in a tight circle, took a snapshot at goal; the kick was already drifting wide to the nearside when it was hustled through for a behind by Carlton's Bruce Doull, just in front of a beige billboard advertising K-Tel's Brush-o-Matic, the discerning Australian's choice of lint remover. Doull kicked precisely to Austin, then Austin to Jack O'Connell, then O'Connell to Geoff Southby, not yet halfway through a stellar 268-game career with the Blues, but already recognised as the least distractible of footballers.

It may be that Southby believed that this pedantic clock management was an ignoble recourse, unbefitting his legion of warrior princes. It may be that he just thought that the game was up, and that opportunities for florid self-expression fell rarely to stolid defenders such as himself, so he might as well have some fun. Instead of kicking short and safe, Southby smacked a soaring handball, 20 metres or more, to Keogh, who found himself swiftly pinned, and hurried; he kicked towards Carlton's half-forward line, but to a stoppage, which North won. North's Stephen Icke collected the ball, took a couple of bounces to reach the obvious decision, and hoofed it hopefully upfield from behind the centre circle. It hit Malcolm Blight on the chest at centre half-forward, as he shrugged off Mark Maclure.

Blight knew there wasn't much time. He scampered backwards along his line. The kick, from 50 metres, straight in front, went a long way up, and came down almost vertically, landing in the gap between the goal umpire and the fence. Neither Blight nor any other North player celebrated as both flags were raised. They were still seven points down, and bracing for the siren.

The bounce cued one of those scrambles that can make Australian football players look like they're undertaking some obscure initiation rite involving the retrieval of soap from a skidpan of grease while wearing rollerskates and blindfolds. A high kick from Carlton's Phillip Pinnell was spilled by his teammate Leigh McConnon, who staged for a free kick to occlude his embarrassment; the umpire waved play on. Graeme Melrose gathered it for North and spread the ball to Peter Chisnall on the right half-forward flank. Chisnall's kick descended on North's forward pocket, where Carlton's Rod Austin[3] anticipated an easy chest mark. But when he made to gather the ball into his guernsey, it wasn't there: Blight had sidled up on Austin's blind side, and marked in front of him. Austin gestured towards the umpire with the exasperation of a pickpocket's victim attempting to interest constables in the rapscallion absconding with his wallet.

Blight was tucked hard into the boundary line, 25 metres from the goals, on the wrong side for a right-footer. The only thing working in his favour was that peculiar liberation that comes of having nothing much to lose. Blight opted for the checkside banana kick, dropping the ball with a reversed torpedo punt grip to catch the side of his boot. Even the most skilled practitioners of this prestidigitation often beclown themselves attempting it; Blight had never tried it in a match before. It landed in the same spot as his previous goal, almost clipping the rear brim of the goal umpire's hat. North Melbourne were now only a point behind, and though the goal wasn't so much celebrated by North's players as vaguely acknowledged, a flicker of hope was perceptible.

The next bounce was delayed while umpires shooed the runners off the field. Carlton won the ball out of the centre, and Trevor Keogh got it forward, but his kick was marked by North's John Byrne. Byrne's kick was marked by Melrose, between two Carlton players each expecting the other to make the contest, but Melrose's kick found only Pinnell, in open space at Carlton's half-back flank. Pinnell took the time he decently could, and then kicked long. Peter McKay flew high, as McKay often did, but not high enough to spoil Peter Keenan.[4] But Keenan's kick was inexplicable – short and to a contest, from which the ball tumbled back towards the end Carlton were kicking to.

Icke won it again, and his long handball got it back to Keenan, who laid it off to Gary Cowton, who belted it back forward. Frank Gumbleton emerged from the ensuing scramble for North but was tackled instantly;

---

3   Rod Austin, an outstanding backman over 220 games, played in just one premiership – 1979's – for a great Carlton team; injury kept him out of the 1981 and 1982 grand finals. In a game against Hawthorn at Princes Park in 1977, Austin joined the meagre fraternity of defenders who could claim to have held Peter Hudson goalless.

4   Peter 'Crackers' Keenan was playing his first season for North Melbourne, after 101 games with Melbourne. Keenan played in North's losing 1976 grand final side and in North's 1977 premiership team, but missed the 1978 grand final after being suspended for cuffing Hawthorn's equally disputatious Don Scott in the semi-final. Keenan wept as the tribunal passed sentence, and North lost to Hawthorn in the decider by 18 points; there are those, Keenan not least among them, who believe that his presence might have made the difference. There are also those who believe that Hawthorn's Leigh Matthews should have been reported in the semi-final as well, for the atrocious coathanger he threw at Graeme Melrose, in full view of the umpire.

his fumble was seized by North's Mark Dawson, who sprinted a few steps to steady himself, looked up, and kicked. At the other end, it was Blight versus Maclure again. This time, they met the ball side-on. At the last possible moment, Blight nudged Maclure off-balance, and for the third time in less than four minutes found himself skipping backwards to set himself for a kick at goal.

When the siren went, Blight had just reached what would be the starting point of his run-up. He was six or seven metres back from the corner of the centre square. He bowed, holding the ball over his head, a gesture of exhaustion and resolve. Keith Greig approached him, hands on hips. A brief conversation was had – and if one is going to listen to advice from anyone at such a moment, it might as well be a dual Brownlow medallist and your club captain, but what was there to say? A behind to draw, a goal to win, but a miracle and/or a gale-force tailwind required to even make the distance. As Blight started his run-up, North's Barry Cable[5] began walking towards the grandstand, not watching, already absorbing defeat.

No consensus has ever solidified about the precise distance travelled by the mighty torpedo punt Blight launched from his right boot; many of the several million people who claim to have been there insist that it went 100 metres or more. It was certainly kicked from well outside where a 50-metre line would have been from 1986 onwards. The ball was higher than the goalposts when it soared between them, and landed in the crowd just in front of the steps leading up to the Robert Heatley Stand. It was Blight's 16th goal of the season, but those North supporters who'd kept the faith and stayed until the end reacted like it was his 100th. A couple of mounted police officers made a brief feint towards restoring order, but settled for escorting the umpires from the field. Blight exited the arena on the shoulders of his teammates, carried off by those he'd carried home.

Blight's enjoyment of his triumph fell well short of any fair definition of hubris: he did not acquire a commemorative tattoo, nor commission a statue of himself (he did attend the unveiling of such a monument at the Adelaide Oval in 2015, describing himself as 'surprised'). Nevertheless, Blight was to be visited by nemesis. Almost exactly a year after his

---

5   Barry Cable won three Sandover Medals in two stints with Perth, as well as three consecutive Simpson Medals for being the best player in a WANFL grand final. One of the greatest rovers of the 1970s, Cable played in North's 1975 and 1977 premiership sides, and led East Perth to a WANFL premiership as captain-coach in 1978. He coached North Melbourne for four seasons in the early 1980s.

extraordinary exhibition at Princes Park, North hosted Hawthorn at Arden Street. Once again, Blight had a set shot for goal after the final siren. The conditions were similar: muddy. So were the stakes: a behind to draw, a goal to win.

There were a few minor differences. This time, Blight was much closer to goal, 20 metres out, if that, and dead in front. The weather was worse, to the extent that barely 9000 people had braved the tempest. And North could already have settled for a draw, earned by the behind Blight had scored as full-time sounded, but he'd been pushed in the back by David O'Halloran as he took his shot, and offered a free kick by field umpire Neville Nash. Blight accepted, and so his point was duly deducted before he began his run-in.

It was – obviously – the right decision. If Blight kicked a goal, North would win; a behind, and they'd be no worse off than they were. The kick lurched off the side of Blight's boot, yawningly wide of the right-hand behind post, out of bounds on the full – a feat which, from that range, might have been more difficult than scoring.

31

The Runaway Elephant
North Melbourne 19.10.124 Collingwood 17.13.115
Arden Street
ROUND 5, 1978

Because we know what happened shortly prior to this game, we can surmise that at some point in the days or weeks leading up to it, somebody in some sort of charge of things at North Melbourne said to his colleagues something of the order of the following.

'Gentlemen. In Round 5, we are due to host Collingwood at Arden Street. Collingwood, as you know, are reliably the biggest draw in the VFL. Also, this will be a replay of last year's grand final. Indeed, of last year's two grand finals – you will recall the draw, necessitating the replay the week subsequent, which we, of course, won. We head into this encounter with four wins from the first four games, and looking pretty handy to back up last year's flag, which would make three in four years. We are unquestionably the pre-eminent club of our era.'

Here, he might have paused, whoever he was, for some appreciative murmuring from the assembled, before proceeding.

'If I may continue. Malcolm Blight has already banked 14 goals, and even at this early stage seems a handy bet for the Brownlow and/or to finish the season as the year's leading goalkicker.[1] Also appearing will be dual Brownlow medallist Keith Greig, our splendid pair of folk hero ruckmen Peter "Crackers" Keenan and Mick "The Galloping Gasometer" Nolan, and two Schimmelbusches – Wayne, who requires little introduction, and

---

1   Malcolm Blight won 1978's Brownlow medal, and led North's goalkicking with 77, but this would be vastly outstripped by the 118 of Footscray's Kelvin Templeton. Blight led the VFL's goalkicking in 1982 with 94 (103 including finals), the year after the Coleman Medal for the feat had been formally introduced.

his younger brother Darryl, who looks quite a find. To recap: star-studded reigning premiers versus team with the biggest following in the League, in a grand final replay – in fact, if you will, a grand final replay replay. Yes, I know what you're all thinking: not really enough to guarantee a crowd, is it? So, I propose: an elephant.'

The Arden Street elephant has lumbered through footballing folklore ever since, to the extent that when North Melbourne returned to Arden Street for a JLT Community Series match against Hawthorn in 2017, the half-time diversions included a wander of the field by a couple of luckless interns in an elephant costume, establishing a benchmark for the most interesting thing ever to have occurred, in or out of game time, in any pre-season or night competition. But the innovative opening ceremony of North Melbourne versus Collingwood in Round 5 of 1978 was nearly a catastrophe. Had a few synapses sparked more frantically inside the skull of one very large and extremely confused animal, Arden Street's accoutrements might now include an overcompensatingly sombre memorial to the casualties of the most ridiculous disaster in the history of Australian sport.[2]

The North Melbourne of the 1970s are rightly regarded as pathfinders for the professionalism that, in the '80s, '90s and beyond, overwhelmed the amateurism of the VFL's first eight decades. The chairmanship of North by Allen Aylett[3] between 1971 and 1976, and his subsequent stint as VFL president, amount to one of the most transformative administrative careers in the League's history. It was Aylett who cleared the path from the VFL as it was to the AFL it became – who changed the game, for good and ill, from sport to showbiz. Among Aylett's more baneful innovations was the appointment, at North Melbourne in 1971, of the League's first marketing manager, Barry Cheatley, who'd played 81 games for North between 1959 and 1964, and had a name which sounded like it had been invented by some cloddish satirist in order to make fun of marketing managers.

Cheatley was a pioneer of the notion that a football game was insufficient enticement for football fans – a perplexingly durable belief

---

2   Arden Street would make another bid for this title in Round 4 of 1983, during the first quarter of North's match against Richmond. A couple of rapscallions clambering on the roof of a pie kiosk disconnected a hose to a gas canister as they descended, starting a swiftly accelerating blaze. Play was suspended as fans clambered over the fence and onto the field, where some took advantage of the opportunity for a kickabout.

3   Allen Aylett played 220 games for North Melbourne between 1952 and 1964, mostly as a rover, scoring 311 goals. He also played cricket for Victoria.

that people who might have been on the fence about going to the match would be tipped towards attendance by the promise of some minor pop star honking their new single to a tinny backing track over a low hum of people muttering 'Who the fuck is this dickhead?' through mouthfuls of Four'NTwenty. On Cheatley's watch, games at Arden Street were fanfared or punctuated by attractions including, but by no means limited to, the warblings of John Farnham, and spruiking for boxing matches.[4]

A palate too often tickled grows jaded, however, and by 1978 North Melbourne fans were the League's lotus-eaters, their senses addled by overexposure to sensual excess. It would take something big – literally – to rouse Arden Street regulars from their languor, and it occurred to Cheatley that one North member, Jack Allan, was an impresario whose circus was in town. With the always important question 'What could possibly go wrong?' rashly disdained, an elephant was engaged by way of curtain-raiser for the Collingwood game.

There are those timid souls who, if embarking upon such obvious folly, would at least have ensured that only appropriately trained personnel were allowed anywhere near the animal. But North Melbourne had not buccaneered their way to where they were through any hidebound observance of common sense. The elephant was guided onto the Arden Street turf by a lone handler, and ridden by an eight-year-old North Melbourne fan, one Sally Wood, plucked from the Kangaroos' cheer squad.

A circus elephant is trained not to startle at crowds. The brains behind this operation had not, however, considered that circus elephants are trained not to startle at crowds which fit inside circus tents. Arden Street was at capacity and beyond, crammed to the gunwales with 31,424 people, a roll-up previously exceeded only once in the ground's history.[5] A great many – possibly a majority – of those packed into the stands were Collingwood barrackers, never a cohort celebrated for their contemplative quiet. The elephant, after a brief, ruminative meander, abruptly decided it

---

4   At North Melbourne's Round 1 game against Carlton in 1971, creaking Cuban slugger Luis Rodriguez was driven on a lap of the ground by way of promoting the following Wednesday evening's bout at Arden Street between himself and Tony Mundine, the 19-year-old Australian middleweight champion. Rodriguez, widely assumed to have been enlisted to make up the numbers, knocked out Mundine inside a minute. Mundine's son, Anthony, had a successful rugby league career, before turning to boxing and winning several world titles.

5   This was in Round 19, 1949, when an estimated 35,000 saw North drub table-topping Carlton by 56 points, largely thanks to eight goals from Jock Spencer. Carlton enjoyed a measure of vengeance, defeating North in the subsequent semi-final, before getting trounced by Essendon in the grand final.

had had enough. Turning left down the Gasometer wing,[6] it accelerated, despite the efforts of its handler and a volunteer in a North Melbourne guernsey, each hanging from one grey ear, into a gait which, while not a fully-fledged stampede, was certainly more than a brisk, amiable trot.

The elephant's attempted getaway didn't last long – the length of two billboards advertising the Marlboro Football Awards[7] and Hard Yakka jeans, barely enough time for 31,424 people to remark that they hadn't seen anything like it since the last time Mick Nolan tried to run with the ball. The creature pulled up, suddenly and mercifully, in front of an open gate leading onto a terrace densely stuffed with people who'd have had nowhere to flee. On the whim of a baffled pachyderm, calamity was averted, lives spared, and the game went ahead.

It did so in a style which suggested that all concerned appreciated that they'd been presented with a tough act to follow. The match combined the intensity of the drawn 1977 grand final with the giddy, free-scoring abandon of the replay.[8] Collingwood led most of the day, but rarely by much, and North were in front when it mattered. Both sides attempted to unbalance the other with positional selections teetering on that line between audacity and insanity. North named at full-back Phil Baker, who'd kicked nine goals across the two 1977 grand finals, and then shifted him to full-forward, to be replaced by a first-year recruit from East Perth called Ross Glendinning.[9] Collingwood named Kevin Worthington in defence, and played him at half-forward.

The first half was a tale of answering onslaughts – seven goals to three in Collingwood's favour in the opening quarter, answered by eight goals to four by North in the second. The third quarter was a relative lull of three goals each. With one quarter to play, Collingwood held a six-point lead, but North had the wind, and two forwards rising to the occasion. When the siren sounded, Baker had five goals, John Burns seven, and North a nine-point victory.

---

6   The gasometer on nearby Macaulay Road, which loomed over Arden Street for decades, has been replaced by luxury apartments – one of which was sold, in 2015, by the real-estate business of Denis Pagan, who played in the gasometer's shadows between 1967 and 1974, and coached North's two 1990s premiership sides.

7   Tobacco advertising on radio and television was banned in 1976, hence the industry's interest in fence hoardings likely to be lavishly panned by cameras. Outdoor advertising for cigarettes was banned in 1996, and sponsorship by tobacco companies in 2000.

8   North Melbourne and Collingwood drew 9.22 to 10.16 in the grand final. North won the replay 21.25 to 19.10, the teams scoring more than twice the number of goals they had the week previously.

9   Ross Glendinning won the 1983 Brownlow Medal, and after leaving North Melbourne was named West Coast's captain when the Eagles entered the League in 1987.

For North, it was a step towards a fifth consecutive grand final (which they would lose, to Hawthorn). For Collingwood, it was a near miss in an unfulfilled season which would end in a 12-point preliminary final loss to North – a game also remarkable for devil-may-care selections on North's part, dropping Phil Baker for fears that damp conditions underfoot would impede his marking (he managed six goals when he returned for the grand final) and deploying Keith Greig, of all people, to tag Phil Carman, effectively sending a Ferrari to ram a Lamborghini.

For League football, however, Round 5 of 1978 was a step across the threshold between athletic contest and entertainment, and towards the extraneous fatuities that bedevil the game now, all rooted as they are in the theory that football is not enough to get people to watch football. It is unknowable whether a period of reflection vis-à-vis the wisdom of such fripperies might have resulted, had a tormented elephant ploughed tusks-first into today's crowd. It is certainly not a cause which would have been worth any toll of injuries, even if one believes that the path to Angry Anderson and Meat Loaf besmirching grand finals[10] was indeed trampled by Arden Street's runaway Dumbo.

In 2014, Brisbane announced that they were considering securing the services of an actual goddamn lion to enhance their pre-match formalities. Brisbane eventually thought better of it, but that they thought of it at all is sufficient to confirm that nobody ever learns anything.

---

10 Angry Anderson and Meat Loaf did not perform together, but the possibility of such a duet cannot be ruled out as postmodern irony approaches its event horizon. Anderson, late of Rose Tattoo, appeared at the 1991 grand final, driven onto Waverley Park in an AFL-branded baby-blue Batmobile facsimile, bemusingly accompanied by retired marathon runner Robert de Castella, before singing his solo hit 'Bound for Glory' like it had done something to upset him. Meat Loaf's performance at the 2011 grand final has been much discussed, but as those of us who were present mutter wearily to each other whenever someone seeks to appropriate our trauma, you cannot really know what it was like if you weren't there.

32

Fabulous Phil Loses It
St Kilda 11.17.83 Essendon 12.8.80
Moorabbin Oval
ROUND 4, 1980

The great players baffle us. It's part of the reason we watch them, to wonder what it must be like to possess that poise, that grace, that balance, that speed, that courage. Most of us learn at a young age that we possess these qualities only in ordinary quantities; your first dropped uncontested mark in a junior match is the beginning of your understanding that you are not made of the stuff from which League footballers are hewn. Sport is really pretty kind in its cruelty: it lets you know early on whether you're up to it or not. Other fields of endeavour tempt and delude with hallucinations of imminent greatness almost until retirement age.

So we watch the great players, and we marvel, and we do so mostly cheerfully and philosophically, until confronted with something like what happened during the second quarter at Moorabbin in Round 4 of 1980, as Essendon laboured to keep up with a St Kilda team who were playing a distance outside themselves. The Saints, wooden-spooners in 1979, had seemed to be continuing that form in 1980, with two losses, and a draw with Richmond, from their first three games.

The Essendon that St Kilda were hosting today were not a superlative vintage, but the Bombers had made the finals the year before, and had hopes of going further in 1980 than the 81-point pummelling they'd received from Fitzroy in 1979's elimination final, Garry Wilson insuppressible with 42 possessions. A key underpinning of Essendon's ambitions was the wiry 29-year-old wearing number 8, a recent arrival at Windy Hill. Playing his fourth game for his third League club, after eventful stints at Collingwood and Melbourne, was one of the most naturally capable footballers of his, or anyone's, generation: Phil Carman, who, in equal tribute to his abilities and deficiencies, was known both sincerely and ironically as 'Fabulous'.

Seen on television, the thing that happened presented as one of those recurring motifs of 1970s and '80s football – one of the cameras following the play whipping suddenly away, alerted by a hubbub in the crowd, towards the immediate aftermath of some off-the-ball incident. As was often the case, the viewer didn't see what had just occurred, but as was equally usually the case, it did not require advanced detective skills to piece events together. In this instance, St Kilda's Garry Sidebottom[1] was down, and clutching his head. Looming over him, Phil Carman. Between them, two remonstrating umpires.

This is where admiration of a footballer of a certain type can acquire a faintly resentful edge. As we mutter aw, bloody hell, not again, what we are thinking is this: why has this man been blessed with this talent when he appears so determined to waste it? Why were these gifts not bestowed upon someone more grateful – perhaps more humble – who would have turned them into 300 games, a few flags and a couple of Brownlow Medals? Why does someone who seems to find the difficult part – playing – so easy, struggle so desperately with the basics, like attending training and not hitting people?

As the umpires enacted the charade of looking at the number on Carman's guernsey before inking it into their notepads – even allowing for Carman's changes of club, it must have been as familiar to them as their own addresses – infuriated fans regarded Fabulous Phil much as the decent working schlub might regard the lottery winner who rakes his millions into a heap, douses it in paraffin, and sets it ablaze.

And then it got worse. Boundary umpire Graham Carbery seemed especially exercised by whatever Carman had done to Sidebottom. As the St Kilda ruckman climbed groggily to his feet, Carbery became even more demonstrative, bumping his chest repeatedly against Carman's, his Art Garfunkel bouffant almost tangling with Carman's Captain Kidd moustache. Had Carbery appointed himself the justly outraged

---

1   Garry Sidebottom left Essendon at the end of 1980 and transferred to Geelong, where he played seven games and is remembered principally for missing the team bus to the 1981 preliminary final, after failing to appear at the designated rendezvous near Lara: he had not been told he was in the squad. Peter Johnston was hastily deputised, despite having lunched on junk food washed down with a thickshake, and having smoked half a pack of cigarettes. Johnston didn't get a touch, and Geelong lost by seven points.

representative of all who wished they could play like Carman could, who dreamt of enjoying the career Carman might have had, if not for nonsenses like this? (Certainly, running boundary is nobody's first choice.) Carman took exception, as Carman so often did, and jerked his head forwards, hitting Carbery on the bridge of his nose.

Australian football traditionally extends players a measure of latitude when it comes to whacking their opponents; it's a rough game, and tempers are bound to unravel occasionally. But it is generally understood that any attack upon umpires is an outrage verging on sacrilege; even inadvertent, harmless contacts have resulted in suspensions.[2] Before Carbery composed himself sufficiently to inform Carman that he was going in the book for headbutting him, no League player had been suspended for assaulting an umpire, or anything remotely like it, since South Melbourne's Ted Whitfield had earned a season-long ban for taking a swipe at a goal umpire amid the bedlam of the Bloodbath in 1945.

Today should have been St Kilda's day. The Saints stoutly held off the fast-finishing Bombers to hang on to three points of what had, at one stage, been a 32-point final-quarter margin. It was their first victory under new captain-coach Alex Jesaulenko; they'd won by the width of an off-target last-second shot for goal by Tim Watson. Not for the first or last time in the career of Phil Carman, however, Phil Carman was the only thing anyone wanted to talk about.

Carman arrived at VFL House the following Monday night to answer three charges. One of striking Sidebottom, one of headbutting Carbery, and another of striking Carbery – the latter arising from an exasperated gesture by Carman which, whether or not it caught Carbery in the face, prompted a reaction from the umpire that suggested it had.[3] Carman attempted to depict the headbutt as an accident which had occurred during an animated discussion of whether or not Carbery could really have seen the incident involving Carman and Sidebottom. After a two-and-half-hour hearing, the tribunal took 16 minutes to reach a decision: four weeks for striking Sidebottom, 16 for headbutting Carbery. The charge of striking Carbery was not sustained, the tribunal unable to decide beyond doubt whether Carman's backhander had connected.

---

2 In 1985, during a reserves match against Sydney at the Lake Oval, Collingwood's John Bourke kicked field umpire Phil Waight, who had just reported him for kicking Sydney player Pat Foy. Bourke got eight weeks for kicking his opponent, and ten years for kicking the umpire.

3 In an interview with SEN in 2017, Carman acknowledged that he should have got another six weeks for this contact.

Inventively, Carman applied a few weeks later to the Supreme Court of Victoria under the 1978 *Administrative Law Act*, which governs the right of certain tribunals to affect a person's right to do their job. Mr Justice Starke[4] was unimpressed, further declaring that Carman's suspension 'would, I think, be accepted by any reasonable member of the community as being a very lenient one indeed'. Even more inventively, Essendon considered appealing directly to Queen Elizabeth II, who was visiting Australia to open the new High Court building in Canberra. It is uncertain how seriously this plan was ever pursued. But it would have been consistent with Carman's oft-tested gift for coming back from apparently hopeless circumstances if, due to some mishearing or mix-up, she'd accidentally knighted him.

Carman was edging towards his 30th birthday when he was, effectively, rubbed out for the rest of 1980. There was speculation that it might have been the depressingly appropriate conclusion to one of the most bewildering careers in League history, but it wasn't the end for Fabulous Phil and the VFL, not quite. He returned to Essendon in 1981, playing six solid games before an Achilles tear necessitated surgery. He saw out the season in the reserves, and finished his time at Essendon sidelined by another suspension: two weeks for striking an opponent in the reserves' elimination final.

Again, the valedictory laments for a squandered talent were solemnly composed and dutifully published – but, again, someone was willing to take their tilt at capping this fountain of mercury. Barry Cable, inheritor of Ron Barassi's job as coach of North Melbourne, signed Carman to a single-season deal for 1982. 'One More Chance', said *The Sun*'s headline, readable as both a stern admonishment and a hands-thrown-in-the-air sigh.

Carman played well for North – especially well, it was difficult to avoid noticing, against his former clubs. In Round 15 of 1982, Carman was the difference against Collingwood, scoring four goals in a 20-point win. More annoyingly for the League's lengthy list of failed and traumatised Carman-tamers, he kicked three goals in a 13-point win as North ended Essendon's season in the elimination final. The following

---

4   Sir John Erskine Starke had in 1966 pronounced the last capital sentence carried out in Australia – upon persistent thief Ronald Ryan, for shooting dead warder George Hodson during an escape from Pentridge prison. Starke, a convinced abolitionist, had no choice but to pass what was then a mandatory sentence; Ryan's hanging, on 3 February 1967, affected him profoundly.

week, Carman and North were soundly shellacked in the semi-final by Hawthorn, the Hawks helped by five goals from a ginger-haired 18-year-old debutant who would earn comparisons to Carman in terms of talent and temperament: Dermott Brereton.[5] It was Carman's last League match. He made a decision both he and North Melbourne would regret, and became captain-coach of Eastlake in Canberra.

When Carman's tale is told, it is usually as cautionary fable: the man who could have had it all, had he not thrown it all away. The material is certainly abundant, although Carman's misfortune occasionally had other authors. He missed two years of his apprenticeship in the SANFL due to a clearance dispute between his first club, Norwood, and Collingwood. In Carman's first season at Collingwood, in 1975, he finished three votes short of the Brownlow Medal, despite missing eight matches after breaking his foot while representing Victoria: he played seven fewer games than the Brownlow winner, Footscray ruckman Gary Dempsey.

But in 1977, Carman nigh certainly cost the Magpies an already long-desired premiership. Early in that year's semi-final, in which Carman kicked four goals in a two-point win over Hawthorn, he put down Michael Tuck with an entirely gratuitous cuff across the head. Carman was suspended for two weeks: the grand final and, as it turned out, the grand final replay. Tom Hafey, Collingwood's coach, always believed Carman would have tipped such a fine balance. While Carman has never disputed Hafey's assessment, he is entitled to wonder if Collingwood would have got there without him.[6] In 1979, Collingwood fell five points short of victory in the grand final against Carlton; by then Carman was not only mouldering at a struggling Melbourne, but about to be sacked due to his inability or unwillingness to submit to the regime of coach Carl Ditterich, a man who might have been expected to better understand a combustible maverick.

Phil Carman spent eight seasons in the VFL. He played 100 games, missed 30 through injury, and another 30 due to suspension. Aside from the best and fairest he won at Collingwood in his first season, he collected no major honours. His post-League twilight was a similar mix of nearly,

---

5   It would take Dermott Brereton a couple more years to dye and tousle his mane into the magnificent blond confection which endures as a benchmark for 1980s VFL mullets.

6   Collingwood's near-seizing of the 1977 premiership seems all the more remarkable when it is recalled that they finished 1976, under previous coach Murray Weideman, wooden-spooners. Bigger single-season improvements have only occurred since the competition expanded: Brisbane from 16th (and last) to third in 1998–1999, Richmond from 13th to premiers in 2016–2017.

not quite, and oh-dear-God-not-again. At Eastlake in 1983, Carman was suspended for ten weeks for striking field umpire Andrew Toy – once again, suspension cost Carman a grand final appearance, and (perhaps) his club a premiership. In 1984, Carman missed out again, suspended for striking an opponent (another charge of manhandling an umpire was dismissed), and so did his team, beaten by Ainslie for the second year running.[7] There were some seasons in the bush – and a suspension for pushing a goal umpire – and then a curtain call at his hometown club, Edenhope. To the surprise of many, Carman proved an effective coach at Sturt, in the SANFL – from a winless shambles in his first season, 1995, to beaten grand finalists in 1998. Sturt sacked Carman in 2001 after a falling-out between coach and board; the club won a flag in 2002 with a team Carman had substantially built.

Carman, and other self-saboteurs of his infuriating ilk, are often regarded as, if not exactly failures, then figures worthier of reproach than celebration. At which point it's worth wondering exactly what it is we want from football players – and what most of us would pay to have played 100 games of the sort Phil Carman did, what we would trade for a highlights reel that included, for example, those first two games back from injury in 1975, six goals against Essendon followed by 11 against St Kilda, Carman's trademark white boots dancing between opponents reduced to props.[8] Measured in fans lifted from seats, and fond memories implanted, Carman's career looks an outstanding success.

And if Phil Carman isn't the reason that Graham Carbery should be remembered, he is the reason that Graham Carbery is remembered, and Carbery deserves to be. He was a gay activist and advocate, serving as spokesman for the Homosexual Law Reform Coalition, at a time when that was a tough, brave thing to be – to say nothing of being an out gay man working in football. Two years before his contretemps with Carman, Carbery founded the Australian Lesbian & Gay Archives; when the fact of his sexuality became more widely known in the aftermath of the Carman incident, the abuse he received was further poisoned with a homophobic

---

7   Eastlake lost the 1983 and 1984 ACTAFL grand finals to Ainslie by margins which, in fairness, Carman at his best might have struggled to overcome on his own. The 1983 ACTAFL flag was the fourth won in six years by Ainslie under the captain-coaching of former St Kilda full-forward Kevin 'Cowboy' Neale. Ainslie's coach in 1984 was former Collingwood and Richmond player Rod Oborne, Neale having left to coach Central Districts in Adelaide.

8   The white boots, an affectation previously unheard of, had been pressed upon Carman by Ted Whitten, in his capacity as sales representative for Adidas. Carman's initial reluctance was overcome by a cheque for $200.

tinge, but he continued to run boundary. In the mid-1990s, he wrote a history of the Sydney Gay & Lesbian Mardi Gras. He refused to leverage Carman's headbutt into celebrity, and attendant Toyota advertisements, grand final walkabouts and *Footy Show* cameos; with the exception of a phone interview with Carman's biographer, Matt Watson, he never spoke of it publicly.

Graham Carbery died in 2017, aged 70. Carman had spoken of a hope that the pair would meet again in a more convivial setting, but it never happened.

33

The Players Become Pop Stars
St Kilda 12.4.76 Essendon 12.21.93
Moorabbin Oval
ROUND 17, 1981

Essendon made hard work of this – 33 scoring shots to 16, for a winning margin of just 17 points, as if they'd gallantly handicapped themselves by committing to score no more goals than their hosts. Having eased to a 19-point lead by the main break, Essendon were struck by jitters in the second half. It took an imperious mark and goal by Paul Vander Haar[1] to settle what should have been a routine win – this was fourth versus tenth, legitimate contenders who'd won their last ten games versus perennial cellar-dwellers who'd won four all year.

There were 23,126 people at the game, which means there are 23,126 stories of what people did that morning, between getting up and making their way to Moorabbin. But it is possible, verging on outright likely, that some of those present revved themselves up for the day by dropping the needle on one of the strangest records ever released in Australia, to which two of this afternoon's protagonists had contributed. The album was called *Footy Favourites*.

Footy Favourites featured one player from each of the VFL's 12 clubs, singing a song each. It was not an altogether original concept. The previous year, the New South Wales Rugby Football League and Tooth's Hotels had combined to sponsor the first *Footy Favourites*, a collection of popular hits interpreted by members of each of the 12 teams which constituted the NSWRFL (although, to bring the number up to 13,

---

1   The combination of Paul Vander Haar's surname and his spectacular aerial abilities earned him the inevitable soubriquet 'The Flying Dutchman'. His contest with Hawthorn's similarly soaring and equally blond Peter Knights at Windy Hill in Round 11 of 1978 is an all-time great marking duel.

thereby offering pleasing symmetry with the numbers of a rugby league team, Western Suburbs fielded duet partners). The results, while every bit as catastrophic as might have been anticipated, proved insufficient to deter a VFL response.

Credited with/blamed for the idea on the sleeve of the first *Footy Favourites* was Gene Pierson, who'd been a minor pop star in the late 1960s and early '70s, then a promoter and manager.[2] The link to the VFL was Jeff Joseph, who had at various points handled the affairs of The Seekers, The Mixtures and Zoot, but by 1981 was managing St Kilda's Trevor Barker.

Barker was always going to struggle to avoid an attempt to escort him on the journey from *The Winners* to *Countdown*. Barker looked like a rock star – depending on the length of his blond mane, like The Sweet's Brian Connolly, or Tom Petty. He played football like a rock star – flamboyant, expressive, at ease with applause, distinguished from workaday mortals by sartorial extravagance, in his case the long black sleeves he preferred.

Barker had played his first couple of seasons in the 25 guernsey, but by 1981 it was impossible to imagine him wearing any other number but 1 (which, like all St Kilda numbers of this period, was rendered in a voguish disco typeface). He'd even had a starring role in the video for one of the biggest-selling singles in Australian history – when Mike Brady hit the line evoking flying angels in the first chorus of 'Up There Cazaly', that was Barker soaring above South Melbourne captain Ricky Quade at the Lake Oval in 1977.

However, on the evidence of his version of Johnny Nash's 'I Can See Clearly Now' on the VFL version of *Footy Favourites*, Barker sang about as capably as Brian Connolly or Tom Petty might have held down the centre half-forward spot. It was perhaps for this reason that any ideas of pitching Barker as a solo crooner had been abandoned, and accomplices solicited to fill an album. Among them was another of Jeff Joseph's clients, also playing today at Moorabbin, Essendon's Tim Watson. Only just 20, Watson was already in his fifth season – he had been, at 15 years and 305 days, the fourth-youngest debutant in League history – and blossoming into the champion who would underpin the Bombers' eminence of the 1980s.

---

2   Gene Pierson booked AC/DC for their first ever show, paying the band $200 to play New Year's Eve 1973 at Chequers in Sydney. AC/DC were still fronted by Dave Evans – Bon Scott would not join until late in 1974. The first set included Chuck Berry, Rolling Stones and Beatles covers, along with the soon-to-be-nearly-as-well-known 'Rock'n'Roll Singer' and 'Can I Sit Next to You Girl'.

Watson's contribution to *Footy Favourites* was 'Ruby, Don't Take Your Love to Town', a Mel Tillis potboiler which had been a hit for Johnny Darrell and (more notably) for Kenny Rogers. (Everyone has had a pop at it at some stage, though, including Waylon Jennings, Roger Miller, George Jones, Bobby Bare and, in possibly the only reading weirder than Watson's, Leonard Nimoy.) It seemed a presumptuous choice by Watson – a first-person monologue by an embittered, crippled Korean War veteran wistfully pondering the murder of his vexingly gadabout wife.

Many years later, Watson shed light on the creative process behind *Footy Favourites* in a radio interview. He said he'd picked 'Ruby' because he thought, as a country song, it would be easy to sing – a common error of those who mistake the conversational warmth of the great country crooners for a lack of technical ability. He recalled the players involved in *Footy Favourites* being paid $500 each, and hustled into a South Melbourne studio in groups of four, for after-midnight sessions during the week, at which they were loosened up with whisky and what Watson described as 'oregano cigarettes'. Watson recorded alongside South Melbourne's Barry Round, who became so incapable while recording his appalling version of Elton John's appalling 'Little Jeannie' that he could not even be roused by Footscray's reigning Brownlow medallist Kelvin Templeton, delivering a spoken-word performance of the standard 'Who's Sorry Now' with the approximate ardour of someone reading out their own ransom note at gunpoint.

It is difficult to isolate a definitive nadir on *Footy Favourites*, so unfalteringly abominable are the performances. Melbourne's willowy winger Robert Flower, who chose The Village People's 'Macho Man', possibly evades opprobrium on the grounds of self-parody, witting or otherwise – one of the most graceful players of his era, the considerable joy to be derived from watching Flower was always diluted by the fear that a decent hip-and-shoulder would snap him in two. Carlton's Mark Maclure did to John Lennon's 'Imagine' what many a burly enforcer had tried to do to Robert Flower, but at least 'Imagine', unlike Flower, deserved the treatment.

The low point on the album – which, by definition, might be the low point of recorded sound – is furnished either by Geelong winger Michael Turner with his version of Peter Allen's 'I Go to Rio', or by David Cloke, then of Richmond, later of Collingwood, with his reading of Wayne Carson Thompson's 'The Letter'. While Turner is just about a worse singer than Cloke, 'I Go to Rio' is one of those songs so routinely butchered in karaoke abattoirs that one more tone-deaf squawk-through makes little odds.[3] Cloke, however, chose to tackle a genuine masterpiece – 'The Letter' was a US chart-topper in 1967 for The Box Tops, featuring on vocals a teenage Alex Chilton, later of Big Star – and Cloke tackled it much as he often tackled opponents, leaving 'The Letter' a mangled, limping ruin.

Suspicions that *Footy Favourites* was an exercise in phoned-in opportunism, rather than a pure-hearted articulation of the contents of its contributors' souls, were not ameliorated by an inquisitive contrast of the track listing of the VFL version with its NSWRFL predecessor: nine of the songs on the former had been covered on the latter. Comparing them further, it is hard to avoid noticing other similarities, and equally difficult to rise above suspicions that the evil geniuses behind the enterprise just decided they might as well double their money by wheeling baffled players of different codes in front of exactly the same backing tracks – although, in fairness, certain of these were pretty rocking, as might have been expected, given the involvement of Peter Cupples and John French.[4]

Cupples had been the singer in Stylus, an Australian soul outfit who'd become the first all-white group signed by Motown. French had engineered Skyhooks' 'Living in the 70s' and 'Ego Is Not a Dirty Word' – and, by way of demonstrating his ease with all points sublime to ridiculous, would go on to assemble a resume including Not Drowning Waving's elegiac 'The Cold & the Crackle' and Joe Dolce's idiotic 'Shaddap You Face'. Their arrangements of Carole King's 'Hard Rock Café' and The Police's 'Don't Stand So Close to Me' deserved better than, respectively, the performances of Laurie Serafini and Michael Moncrieff.

Serafini, the keystone of Fitzroy's defence, sang 'Hard Rock Café' like a tourist soliciting treatment for an awkward holiday ailment with the aid of the 'at the doctors' section of his phrasebook. Moncrieff, Hawthorn's full-forward, sounded like he'd not only never heard 'Don't Stand So Close to Me' before, but any pop music whatsoever.[5] North Melbourne's

---

3   This judgement is made with a heavy heart. Michael Turner was the author's favourite player of the period, and should you be tempted to seek out his frightful version of Allen's daft maraca-shaking singalong, you owe it to Turner to turn next to his 1980 Goal of the Year against Richmond: a three-bounce sprint, extravagant baulk and strike from nearly 50 metres.

4   Efforts were made by the author to contact both for further elucidation. Understandably, neither responded.

5   Michael Moncrieff's name would be a more exalted one had he not had the misfortune to hold down Hawthorn's full-forward position in between Peter Hudson and Jason Dunstall. He kicked 629 goals in 224 games for the Hawks.

Wayne Schimmelbusch (Ray Brown & The Whispers' '20 Miles') could perhaps be excused – even admired – for stepping up as his club's captain, in the manner of an officer hurling himself upon a grenade to spare his men.[6] Which left Collingwood's Ray Shaw (Frederic Weatherly's 'Danny Boy') to qualify for the very highest praise that might be honestly bestowed upon any selection from *Footy Favourites*, i.e. that it was merely fucking awful.

The two stars of *Footy Favourites* who appeared at Moorabbin this afternoon both submitted convincing reminders of what they were actually good at – despite, as was often the case, Moorabbin being affected by a peculiar microclimate which appeared to prevail only in its vicinity. Much of St Kilda's home ground was more suitable for bog-snorkelling[7] than football, almost as if some devious schemer associated with the club had deliberately overwatered the surface to slow up more skilful opponents.[8] Nevertheless, Barker was able to ascend from Moorabbin's mire to a characteristically spectacular mark in front of the members' stand in the third quarter, and Watson harvested from the swamp a best-on-ground 31 disposals.

Trevor Barker was not the last Australian football player to participate in the making of a terrible record.[9] But he remains the one with the most convincing claim to the title of rock star. Barker was as loyal to St Kilda, the team whose cheer squad he'd joined as a boy, as a glamorous singer refusing to abandon his band of old friends for a more lucrative solo career, much as Zoot had been ditched by Rick Springfield. Despite many offers from more successful sides, which during Barker's time was any of them, he stayed a Saint the entirety of his 230-game career, 165 of which St Kilda lost, and for at least half of which Barker took 22 cents of every dollar the chronically cash-strapped club owed

---

6   Wayne Schimmelbusch was himself immortalised in song – specifically, 'The Ballad of Wayne Schimmelbusch', credited to The Frozen Stiff, which appears to have been a collaboration between the actor Frankie Davidson and the singer and television presenter Ross D. Wylie. The phrase 'not good; in fact, bad' does it some justice.

7   The Bog Snorkelling World Championship is held annually at the Waen Rhydd peat bog, near Llanwrtyd Wells, in Wales. Unaccountably, it was never won by a 1970s or '80s St Kilda player.

8   They had. Danny Frawley, who played 240 games for St Kilda between 1984 and 1995, was also retained as a groundskeeper at Moorabbin. He later admitted that he and a colleague – a certain Tony Lockett – would routinely hose the field to ensure a discouragingly viscous playing surface.

9   Debate over which was the absolute worst could while away an Indian-Pacific train ride, but it is difficult to decline the credentials of 'We Love, We Live Football'. This outrage was released circa 1988, a leaden New Kids on the Block pastiche which featured players including John Platten, Gerard Healy, Paul Salmon, Dale Weightman and Justin Madden rapping, or at least pretending to. In the video, Warwick Capper moonwalked. Everybody involved should have been arrested.

him.[10] When one of the two St Kilda best-and-fairest awards he won came with a car, Barker returned it.

And Barker died young, though not in a manner that piques the boneheaded admiration earned by rock'n'roll burnouts: he was claimed by cancer in 1996, aged 39. Thousands filled Moorabbin Town Hall, and the footpaths outside, for his funeral. As is the case with all such tragedies, the overwhelming aspect was the future denied: in this specific instance, a nigh certain return to St Kilda as coach (after retiring as a player, Barker took Sandringham to two VFA premierships). The corollary, if no consolation, is a glorious youth, dazzling frozen in memory.

---

10 St Kilda's best-and-fairest prize is now known as the Trevor Barker Award. Barker holds the record for games played without ever appearing in a final. Geoff Cunningham, another fine St Kilda player of the same era, is runner-up in this category, with 224.

34

Rioli and the Krakouers
Richmond 18.14.122 North Melbourne 15.14.104
Melbourne Cricket Ground
ROUND 1, 1982

An irritating quirk of scheduling prevents this match from being remembered as possibly the most significant in the history of the involvement of Australia's Indigenous people in Australia's indigenous game. Making debuts for North Melbourne were two brothers from Mount Barker, Western Australia: Jim and Phil Krakouer, who for a few seasons had been accruing electrifying notices in the WAFL, and had helped Claremont to the previous year's premiership. Appearing for Richmond was another veteran of that 1981 WAFL grand final – Maurice Rioli, from Melville Island, north of the Northern Territory, who'd played for the losing team, South Fremantle, but had nevertheless backed up the best-on-ground Simpson Medal he'd won in the 1980 WAFL grand final, this time in a tie with Claremont's Gary Shaw.

Rioli and the Krakouers would become founders of distinguished football dynasties, catalysts of an overdue appreciation of Aboriginal players – and pathfinders towards a belated understanding of how poorly Aboriginal players had long been treated, by fans, opponents and even teammates. In 2005, two of the three would be selected in the AFL's Indigenous Team of the Century; Phil Krakouer can only just have missed out.

But Round 1 of 1982 wasn't quite Rioli's VFL debut. By way of fanfaring the season, the League yanked a game out of Round 2, to launch 1982 a week ahead of Round 1. The lucky fixture was Fitzroy versus Richmond, originally scheduled for the Junction Oval, but moved to Waverley in search of a bigger crowd. The disruption did not bother

Richmond in general, or Rioli in particular. Nor did the fact that the Tigers had a new coach – Francis Bourke, who had retired as a player at the end of the previous season after 300 games and five premierships with Richmond – and were missing ruckman Mark Lee, and full-forward Michael Roach, who had led Richmond's goalkicking the last three years running.[1] Rioli gathered a team-best 24 disposals as the Tigers eased to a 41-point win over the Lions; the $240,000 he was being paid over three years already looked a bargain. In *The Age*, Geoff Slattery compared Rioli to Alex Jesaulenko – akin to reviewing some emergent pompadoured yelper's first single by invoking Elvis Presley.[2]

For Richmond, signing Rioli and appointing Bourke – Jack Dyer's heir as pugnacious personification of the club – were efforts to recover an ebbing golden era. The Tigers had been premiers in 1980, stringing together an imperious finals run culminating in an 81-point conquest of Collingwood. In 1981, a premiership hangover had seen them stumble short of the finals, and coach Tony Jewell sacked. Rioli had been welcomed with the burdensome tribute of the number 17 that Dyer had once worn.[3]

North Melbourne were also straining to keep a premiership window ajar. They, too, had missed 1981's finals, but retained some of the great side which had played five consecutive grand finals for three flags under Ron Barassi: Malcolm Blight, Keith Greig, Arnold Briedis, David Dench.[4] They had been further bolstered a couple of seasons back by former Footscray ruckman and 1975 Brownlow medallist Gary Dempsey, and had just become the latest last-chance saloon to swing open its doors to volatile gunslinger 'Fabulous' Phil Carman. (Carman would not make his Kangaroos debut until Round 5, however.)

---

1   Into this breach stepped Brian Taylor, playing his sixth senior game, who kicked eight goals against Fitzroy. He finished with 71 for the season, while Roach's 1982 return dwindled to 35 from 86 the year previously. A way of playing both was never discovered by Richmond, who, in another addition to the club's glorious history of misadventures in list management, cleared Taylor to Collingwood, where he won the Coleman Medal in 1986, scoring 100 goals for the season – 10 of them against Richmond in Round 21.
2   Elvis Presley never visited Australia – although one of his cars did. In 1968, his 1960 Cadillac Series 75 Fleetwood limousine was taken on a national tour. The vehicle was custom-trimmed with gold plate, and fitted with a television, record-player, shoe-polishers and other vital accoutrements. A newspaper account of its visit to Canberra noted that two of the pearl buttons on the upholstery had been swiped during its sojourn in Melbourne.
3   From 2016, it was worn by Maurice Rioli's great-nephew, Daniel Rioli.
4   David Dench, captain of North Melbourne's 1977 premiership side, four-time club best-and-fairest winner, was gaoled for four months in 2008 for defrauding Victoria University with bogus invoices for maintenance work.

Another of North's prime mid-1970s vintage, Barry Cable,[5] had taken over from Barassi the previous year as coach. Cable had left Arden Street after North's 1977 flag to become captain-coach at East Perth, but had been forced to retire from playing in 1979 after severely injuring his right leg in a tractor accident on his farm. Cable, a Noongar man from Narrogin, was well attuned to the untapped reservoirs of Indigenous talent nourishing the football fields of Western Australia – and everyone in Victoria had heard tall tales of the Krakouer brothers, reputed to display, when in possession of the ball, a near telepathic intuition for where each other was about to be.

Geelong were on the hunt, deploying as recruiting sergeant Graham 'Polly' Farmer, more than a decade retired, but still the best-known Indigenous footballer in the country. But Barry Cable had been Jim Krakouer's boyhood hero, and North Melbourne had the deeper pockets: the Krakouers signed for three years for $750,000 – a tick over $2.5 million in mid-2010s money. By way of added enticement, North threw in a silver Holden Statesman, so Jim could drive his family across the continent in comfort. Phillip, laden with less baggage, in every sense of the word, flew.

When the ball bounced today, everyone in Melbourne already knew that Maurice Rioli was something special; another Indigenous recruit to the Tigers, Phil Egan, had also had a solid start against Fitzroy, and was in the team again. Nearly 40,000 heads craned forward to see if the Krakouers were worth the money they were earning, and the hype they'd generated.

For the first three quarters, anybody wearing blue and white would have answered yes, and yes, in between gusts of incredulous, delirious laughter. At the last change, North led by 21 points, and the Krakouers had trussed Richmond's midfield and defence in hogties of handballs and cats' cradles of short kicks, significantly to the benefit of Malcolm Blight, who'd kicked seven goals. In the final term, however, Richmond seemed suddenly galvanised by a collective unwillingness to serve as honour guard for the Krakouers' arrival in the big time: the Tigers kicked eight goals to two in the fourth, to win by 18 points. Rioli finished with three goals, and a decent claim to best-on-ground status, a title for which

---

5   In the Indigenous Team of the Century which included Maurice Rioli and Jim Krakouer, Cable was named as playing coach, starting as a follower. It wouldn't have lessened the compliment to Cable if he'd just been named coach, after which some shuffling of positions – Peter Matera into the centre, Rioli to rover – would have opened a deserved spot for Phil Krakouer on the wing.

his rivals were among the best attacking midfielders of the era: Kevin Bartlett, Dale Weightman, Geoff Raines.[6]

Wherever the fault for North's collapse lay, it was not with the Krakouers. Phil finished with a team-high 21 disposals, Jim with four goals, despite occasionally hanging onto the ball half a beat too long, as if not completely adjusted to the pace of the Victorian game. It did not take either brother long to find the extra gear they needed. In the Krakouers' Arden Street debuts a week later, against the fledgling Sydney Swans, they racked up 52 disposals and seven goals between them, one from what became a signature move, Phil gathering a loose ball along the boundary, then handballing blind, backwards over one shoulder, into space into which Jim swooped, collecting it on the bounce and scoring in one improbably elegant movement. Jim returned the favour to Phil, setting him up for a goal with a deft swat of a spinning ball out of midair, which could not have found its target more precisely and delicately had it been presented on a butler-borne velvet cushion. In *The Age*, Geoff Slattery noted, astutely, that the potence of the Krakouer combination was in the differences between the brothers, rather than the similarities: Jim, at 23 the older by a year, was more spectacular and explosive; Phil, collected and industrious.

Jim would be reported 16 times in his VFL career, for 25 weeks' worth of suspensions, many of those transgressions defences of his milder younger brother, and/or reactions to racist insult; though little discussed or reported at the time, such abuse was vicious and prolific, from the stands and from opponents. It was tempting to read the Krakouers' contrasting on-field personas as indicative of their off-field characters. Jim had been in prison twice as a teenager, once for rape, once for causing death by dangerous driving; a football club operating beneath the furious media scrutiny of later decades might have been reluctant to touch him. Phil had little reputation for being other than affable and equable.

Only 14,097 people saw the Krakouers' evisceration of the Swans at Arden Street. Among the many not there was King Carl XVI Gustaf of

---

6   Corners of the internet – and Geoff Raines himself – still smoulder about an alleged conspiracy concocted by umpires to deprive Raines of the 1980 Brownlow Medal. Raines was a sizzling favourite, backed in from 40/1 to 6/1 in the week before the count, but emerged with not a single vote, despite being best and fairest of the premiership team, and a flashy ball-gathering midfielder, always a plausible Brownlow CV. Raines has cast blame in the direction of umpire Peter Cameron, with whom he did not get on. The 1980 Brownlow Medal was won by Footscray's Kelvin Templeton. Richmond's Mark Lee, David Cloke, Kevin Bartlett, Francis Bourke, Jim Jess and Michael Roach all polled well, which cannot have improved Raines' mood.

Sweden – who, in the course of his state visit to Australia, was instead taken to Waverley to see Essendon knock over reigning premiers Carlton. The Blues recovered to win the 1982 flag, beating Richmond in the grand final – in which Maurice Rioli became the first player from a losing team to win the Norm Smith Medal, adding to his 1980 and 1981 Simpson Medals to complete an astounding two-state hat-trick of best-on-ground-in-a-grand-final accolades.

If the lives and careers of Maurice Rioli and Jim and Phil Krakouer are transposed to three hypothetical non-Indigenous footballers, they are extraordinary enough. Rioli played as both gamekeeper and poacher, a ruthless tackler who was himself almost impossible to pin down after he'd won the ball from yet another flustered opponent. After leaving football, he served nearly a decade as a Labor member of the Northern Territory's Legislative Assembly, then went home to the Tiwi Islands to work for the council. He was granted a state funeral upon his death from a heart attack on Christmas Day 2010, aged 53. Three of Rioli's nephews played League football – Dean at Essendon, Cyril at Hawthorn, Willie at West Coast, and so did one great-nephew, Daniel, at Richmond. The Rioli surname has acquired the properties of adjective, denoting preternatural smoothness, outrageous inventiveness and apparently limitless courage.

Jim Krakouer played 134 games for North Melbourne. His departure from the club in 1990 was as bitter as his arrival had been sweetened. Caught between the desire of a new coach – the Krakouers' former teammate, Wayne Schimmelbusch – to impose his authority, and the club's dismal financial outlook, which required a drastic pruning of its salary bill, Jim was exiled to St Kilda. In his first game in red, black and white, he had 36 possessions as St Kilda destroyed Footscray, but that was as good as it got; he played just 12 more games. In January 1994, he was arrested in Perth for his role in an amphetamine trafficking racket. He was sentenced to 16 years, and served nine.

Phil Krakouer played 141 games for North Melbourne. His final season at Arden Street, 1989, was scotched by a knee injury which hastened an end to his time as a Kangaroo. Though it was generally assumed, not least by the Krakouers, that he would follow his brother to Moorabbin, Footscray – despite Phil's pleas – drafted him in 1991. He stayed for seven games, in which only fleeting glimpses of his trademark insouciant dazzle were discernible. His 1986 Goal of the Year for North Melbourne endures as an advertisement for his gifts: a single-handed scoop of a loose ball on the boundary, a pirouette past Essendon's Frank Dunell that left the defender tackling daylight, and striking from the boundary, maybe 40 metres out, with that strange signature action, which looked more like Krakouer was bouncing the ball off his left foot than dropping the ball onto it.

There were further Krakouers, heirs to a tradition of incendiary talent and flammable temperament. Andrew Krakouer, Jim and Phil's younger brother, played a few games for North Melbourne. Another Andrew Krakouer, Jim's son, played for Richmond and Collingwood, either side of a 16-month prison stretch for assault with intent to commit grievous bodily harm. (Andrew's brother, Tyrone Krakouer, was gaoled over the same incident.) Nathan Krakouer, nephew of Jim and Phil, played for Port Adelaide, left them for Gold Coast, and retired after one season with the Suns, citing issues with alcohol, drugs and depression. A comeback with Port in 2015, after a few seasons out, yielded a few eye-catching displays, but ended in opprobrium, Port's interest in renewing his contract not stoked by an incident in which, at the end of a night out, he smashed a taxi windscreen.

Whoever they were, wherever they came from, they'd have been remarkable footballers. But when Maurice Rioli, Phil Egan and Jim and Phil Krakouer ran onto the MCG on the last weekend of March 1982, they would have been automatic inclusions in any all-time VFL Indigenous team even if they hadn't got a kick between them – there having been barely sufficient previous Indigenous VFL players to fill every position on an Australian football field. Within 30 years, nearly a tenth of AFL squads would be comprised of Indigenous players, who'd followed the path which began to be cleared in Round 1, 1982. Over those decades, for that reason, football would find itself, not always capably or comfortably, a primary crucible of Australia's discussion of Indigenous issues.

The influx of Indigenous talent that began in the early 1980s was an incalculable blessing upon the League, but at least as important was what it asked, not merely of the game, but of the country that watched it: what more had we missed? Who were the other Krakouers, Riolis and Egans – and Barry Cables and Polly Farmers and Syd Jacksons and Doug Nichollses, to say nothing of Indigenous Australians with abilities in other fields – who we'd never heard of? The answer to the question of why we didn't know was something Australia would continue to struggle saying out loud.

35

The Swans Land in Sydney
Sydney 20.17.137 Melbourne 16.12.108
Sydney Cricket Ground
ROUND 1, 1982

The subtle approach had clearly been ruled out. The first home game of Sydney's new team would be against Melbourne, though it was uncertain how many of the SCG's seats would be filled by this blatant entreaty to Australia's most venerable municipal rivalry. In common with antagonisms between first and second cities the world over, the Sydney–Melbourne vendetta had always been more keenly maintained by the smaller conurbation.

Similarly, South Melbourne's relocation northwards had been a much bigger deal in Melbourne than in Sydney, and not just because Sydney was more of a rugby league city. It was also that Sydney was never a rugby league city in the way that Melbourne was an Australian Rules city. In Sydney, going months, even years, without straying into a conversation about the local football code was as easy as it was difficult to experience the same obliviousness for a day in Melbourne. Just 15,764 people chose to spend this damp Sunday afternoon at the SCG – but, pleasingly for the VFL and/or illustratively of Sydney's relative indifference to sport compared with Melbourne's mania, this was still bigger than the biggest crowd – 14,186 at Parramatta versus Manly – that attended a rugby league game in Sydney the same weekend.

It was also difficult not to suspect that the VFL was doing its best to get the transplanted Swans away to a winning start. The Friday before the game, the Swans' new coach, Ricky Quade, must have been startled, if not encouraged, to receive a telegram from the League telling him that anything less than victory would be unacceptable. Any Melbourne fans given to lining their beanies with tinfoil might have wondered if similar admonishments had been imparted to the umpires, not that such chicanery would have struck many as necessary. Melbourne's 1981 had been among the most comprehensively ignoble seasons in VFL history. Despite the return as coach of Ron Barassi, and despite 76 goals from a cantankerous, anvil-headed, newly arrived full-forward called Mark Jackson, the Demons had won one game all year, and that by a point against their chief challengers for the wooden spoon, Footscray, in Round 3.

Every other week of 1981, the Demons had been treated as a percentage-boosting practice match by their opponents, the lowest of many low points a 129-point hosing by North Melbourne. Even by the standards of the greatest footballing mind of all, Barassi had rarely been more right than when he'd passed judgement on the first training session he oversaw upon his return to the club. 'Jesus Christ,' he told chairman of selectors Barry Richardson, 'they are bloody hopeless.'

Though the opposition looked the least of the Swans' worries, they were not short of other concerns. One was what they were now actually called. Purchasers of *The Football Record* for Round 1, 1982, may have been perplexed to read of 'Sunday's match between South Melbourne and Melbourne'. Sydney's *Sun-Herald*, previewing the match, referred even more bafflingly – or just plain derisively – to 'the Sydney Swans, the Melbourne football team'. Back in Melbourne, *The Age* described them as 'South Melbourne football club – playing as the Sydney Swans'.

The mixed messaging on nomenclature echoed the conflict and muddle in which the venture north had gestated. What the VFL saw as an act of evangelism which might convert the obstinately heathen New South Welsh to the Australian game was seen by the overlords of the team involved as a desperate flight from drought-parched pastures. In 1981, the South Melbourne board, stricken by vapours following a contemplation of the club accounts, which showed a loss of $180,000 for 1980, asked the VFL for permission to play 11 games of the 1982 season in Sydney, hoping to evade the circling vultures.

The League was enthusiastic, Swans fans less so. A pressure group, Keep South at South, led by a roofing contractor called John Keogh, got up petitions, held meetings and launched legal actions – and, on 22 September 1981, at an extraordinary meeting of members at a crammed Caulfield Town Hall, overthrew the board which had promulgated the Sydney move. This triumph occurred despite a comically obvious attempt by pro-Sydney forces to stack the numbers with last-ditch purchases of memberships. *The Age* reported that 740 membership applications had been received from employees of several Sydney-based enterprises, including Tooth & Co breweries, Visy packaging, O'Brien caterers, and various outposts of Rupert Murdoch's media empire. *The Age* quoted a tea lady at Visy, Valerie Jerrard, as having been approached. 'She does not,' intoned the story gravely, 'barrack for South.'

This unloading of the board prompted, in turn, discontent among the team. There was a players' strike. Ricky Quade, already appointed Ian Stewart's successor as coach for 1982, said he'd quit if the club wasn't going to Sydney. The VFL refused to change its mind about the move. An announcement that John Rantall would instead coach the Swans should, in theory, have been a masterly unifying stroke – he was a club hero who'd played 260 games for South, either side of a premiership-seeking stint at North Melbourne[1] – but so febrile was the atmosphere at Albert Park that it only resulted in further uproar.

By mid-December, the new board had quit, in favour of new president: veteran racing caller Bill Collins. His efforts to forge a solution were reported in tones, both sombre and hopeful, that might have reminded visitors from overseas of the coverage, a few years previously, of Jimmy Carter urging Anwar El Sadat and Menachem Begin towards compromise at Camp David. Peace broke out shortly before Christmas. Rantall resigned without coaching a game, clearing the path back for Quade.

Money had triumphed over sentiment, as money often does, but those behind the Swans' move nevertheless strove to present it as a romantic proposition – sort of the A-Team amalgamated with the Dirty Dozen. As if in keeping with the proposition of a guerrilla mission behind enemy lines, the Swans flew into Sydney on the morning of their first match, having never before set foot on the SCG; it was possibly the game's first instance of home ground disadvantage.

In 1982 the SCG 'oval' was actually more or less circular, necessitating an improvised adaptation of tactics. Nor did the ground have much in

---

1   John Rantall was one of several beneficiaries of the ten-year rule – a VFL initiative which, between August 1972 and May 1973, before all concerned thought better of it, allowed a player with a decade's service at a given club to accept a better offer elsewhere. North Melbourne voted against the rule being introduced, but took to it with particular alacrity, signing Barry Davis from Essendon, Doug Wade from Geelong and Rantall from South Melbourne. In 1972, the Roos were wooden-spooners, in 1975 premiers. Rantall, his mission accomplished, returned to South.

the way of facilities. There being no designated enclosures for coaches, each team's staff was allocated five seats at opposite ends of the Ladies' Pavilion. Barassi coached Melbourne sitting next to Mike Willesee, the broadcaster, Swans barracker and future Swans co-owner.

Sydney – or South Melbourne – had held together pretty well despite the summer's convulsions. Of the 20 who had been selected for the Swans' last game at Albert Park, a 33-point loss to North Melbourne, 13 lined up against Melbourne for the first game at the SCG. At Melbourne, the off-season had been understandably bloody – the Demons brought just eight survivors of the 53-point pantsing by Hawthorn with which they'd ended their miserable 1981. Among Melbourne's new faces were a clutch of debutants – Michael O'Sullivan, Adrian Battiston, Alan Johnson – and a couple of typically astute Barassi recruits: Stephen Icke, who'd played for Barassi in North Melbourne's 1977 premiership, and North's undervalued centre Brian Wilson.[2] They slotted in alongside a cohort of the mavericks, eccentrics and outright weirdos from whose infuriating company Barassi seemed to derive perverse enjoyment as he dragged them from club to club: Brent Crosswell, Peter 'Crackers' Keenan, Shane Zantuck. When they were all lined up alongside Robert Flower, Gerard Healy[3] and Mark Jackson, Melbourne did not look too shabby, on paper. On the turf of the SCG they would prove less convincing.

Sydney and/or South Melbourne announced themselves with ballyhoo that looked almost calculated to annoy the traditional fans the club had deserted. Mike Brady, red and white rosette adorning his lapel, sang a remodelled 'Up There Cazaly'; entitled 'Up There for Sydney', it audaciously if not outright heretically claimed the great South Melbourne ruckman for this resented reincarnation of his team. Some 25,000 red and white balloons were unleashed, before the Swans burst a modest run-through reading 'Sydney Swans Up There For Sydney' on one side, and 'Wards Transport Group' – the trucking company which had paid $1,035,000 to sponsor the Swans for three seasons – on the other.

A pinch of celebrity pixie dust was scattered among the crowd, in the forms of George Negus, Derryn Hinch, Jackie Weaver, Jimmy Hannan

---

2   Brian Wilson won the 1982 Brownlow Medal, aged 20 and already at his third club, having played
     for Footscray prior to joining North. He played 154 games for Melbourne, before joining St Kilda in
     1991. In a demonstration of the rarely fallible law governing the performances of players in front of
     their former fans, in his only game for the Saints against the Demons, he kicked six goals in a nine-
     point win.
3   Gerard Healy joined Sydney in 1986, and won the Brownlow Medal in 1988.

and Peter Russell Clarke. Also present were men who had, or had once had, ambitions of running the country: Bob Hawke, soon-to-be leader of the opposition, upon whom Sydney had bestowed their number-one ticket,[4] dapper in a white suit, and former leader of the opposition Sir Billy Snedden, now president of Melbourne (the football club, not the city, though occupants of the role are doubtless given to thinking it much the same thing).[5] Representing everything Melbourne enjoys hating about Sydney was the twinkling socialite Lady Mary Fairfax; the morning papers had reported that a post-match wing-ding was to be staged in the Swans' honour at Fairwater, the Double Bay pile at which the Fairfaxes threw their legendarily fabulous parties.[6] The Demons had been invited, as well; gossip was that Mark Jackson had promised to put his false teeth back in for the occasion.

Sydney still looked like South Melbourne: the red Vs on white guernseys would not morph into the red yoke with the Opera House cut-out until 1987. But they didn't play like South Melbourne – at least, not the South Melbourne of 1981. These Swans were swift and purposeful, and led by nine points at the quarter – winger Colin Hounsell scored South's first goal as Sydney. Then it was 28 points at the half, then 41 at the last break – at which Ron Barassi removed his volatile spearhead Mark Jackson from the game. Well marshalled by Swans full-back Rod Carter, serenely unfazed by his opponent's pugilistic theatrics, Jackson had been kept to two kicks.[7]

---

4   Bob Hawke led Labor to federal election victory roughly a year later. His fondness for the Swans is of uncertain provenance – he was born in South Australia, educated in Perth, and represented the northern Melbourne seat of Wills – but appears to have been sincere: one eyewitness account has him in the visitors' dressing-room at Victoria Park after Sydney beat up Collingwood in the first match of 1987, congratulating Warwick Capper on a nine-goal haul. After Hawke resigned from parliament in 1992, Wills was represented by Phil Cleary, former premiership player and coach with Coburg in the VFA, who won the seat as an independent.

5   Sir Billy Snedden was leader of the opposition from 1972 to 1975, later Speaker of the House. Notices of his death in 1987, aged 60, were less interested in his distinguished career in Australia's service than they were in the fact that he perished in the arms of a woman who was subsequently revealed to be a former girlfriend of his son. 'I'm sure the old man died happy,' a forgiving Drew Snedden told delighted newspapers some years later. 'Anyone would be proud to die on the job.'

6   Lady Fairfax was the third wife of media tycoon Sir Warwick Fairfax. When Sir Warwick died in 1987, the family business was taken over, and swiftly taken under, by his son. Warwick Jr now runs a leadership consultancy in the United States. His bio on its website says: 'When Warwick was head of the family media business, he personally experienced the challenges of leadership' – a euphemism which would be admired by any coach who has had to tackle the 'winless wooden-spoon season' chapter of their memoir. Lady Fairfax died in 2017, aged 95.

7   Rod 'Tilt' Carter played 293 games – 76 for Fitzroy, 217 for South Melbourne/Sydney. A rigorously old-school defender of the type who believed that venturing past the half-back line was likely to invite plagues of frogs, he kicked just one goal in his career – in his 215th game, against Melbourne at the SCG in 1986, as the Swans demolished the Demons by 124 points. The margin had already blown out past three figures when Carter snapped on the run from 40 metres. Had Carter not

But Melbourne were not quite their former feeble selves either. In his column in *The Sun-Herald* on the morning of the match, Melbourne assistant coach Adrian 'Gags' Gallagher[8] was confident, declaring: 'We've been experimenting throughout the summer, [and] we've weeded out players not suited to our play-on skills.' The Demons' debutants looked sharp – Battiston finished with 25 disposals, Johnson with three goals, O'Sullivan with two. In the last quarter, the Demons took enough out of the Swans' lead to prompt minor conniptions among the grandees in the grandstand, getting to within 25 points; Bill Collins later said he'd been less nervous calling at Newmarket. Sydney's line was held principally by Mark Browning, best afield, and by captain and reigning Brownlow medallist Barry Round. In the dressing-room afterwards, the mood was relief, rather than exultation; before the match, coach Quade had been physically ill with anxiety.

At Lady Fairfax's post-match soiree, guests were treated to oysters and champagne, served from around a metre-high swan carved from ice, and subjected to the squawkings of a jazz band; for dessert, there was blackforest cake and brandied marshmallows. It was a while, however, before the Swans could avail themselves of this cornucopia: Lady Fairfax's bouncers initially refused the footballers admission. It may have been that Fairwater's staff were more accustomed to a different class of guest – previous visitors had included Rudolph Nureyev, Pierre Trudeau, Rex Harrison, Liberace and Imelda Marcos. It would be preferable to believe that the doormen instinctively perceived the necessity of a metaphor for the difficulties the interlopers would experience, in eliciting the unabashed embrace of the standoffish city they had descended upon.

---

succumbed to this impetuous, self-indulgent folly, he would hold, by miles, the record for most games played without troubling a goal umpire. Instead, it remains with Collingwood's Ted Potter, who played a mere 182 games for no goals.

8   Adrian Gallagher, a triple premiership rover with Carlton, was co-owner with Barassi of the Mountain View pub in Richmond. Among the artefacts it would come to house under their proprietorship were a model of the MCG, hung from a ceiling, and the snapped-off piece of a behind post with which Leigh Matthews collided later in 1982.

36

Kevin Bartlett's 400th
Richmond 11.13.79 Collingwood 13.11.89
Melbourne Cricket Ground
ROUND 19, 1983

For much of 1983, this game had been Richmond's only real reason, aside from the compulsory nature of the schedule, to keep going. The Tigers were having one of those seasons – specifically, one of those seasons in which a hitherto formidable side, whether through complacency, hubris or age, disintegrates with confounding rapidity. It befalls all hegemons eventually, however invincible they once seemed, and as went Babylon, Rome, the Ottomans and the Hapsburgs, so had gone Richmond.

In 1980, Richmond had been premiers, bulldozing Collingwood in the grand final by a then-record margin of 81 points.[1] In 1981, they'd stumbled, finishing seventh, but in 1982 they'd recovered to be minor premiers, and grand finalists against Carlton, only losing their grip on the flag during a goalless third quarter memorably interrupted by a streaker, clad only in a Blues scarf, pestering a terrified Bruce Doull.[2]

The Tigers had found 1983 tougher going. Richmond lost their first five games, and floundered thereafter, kept off bottom place for most of the season only by St Kilda, at least until the week before they welcomed Collingwood to the MCG, in which the Tigers surprised everybody,

---

1   Since exceeded by Hawthorn against Essendon in 1983 (83 points), by Hawthorn against Melbourne in 1988 (96 points), and by Geelong against Port Adelaide in 2007 (119 points).

2   This was Helen d'Amico, subsequently discovered by an enraptured media to be a 17-year-old American-born stripper. Her intervention, just after Carlton recovered an 11-point half-time deficit, seemed to discombobulate Richmond more, despite (or perhaps – who knows? – because of) her manifest lack of interest in them. In the decades of drought which ensued before Richmond won their next flag in 2017, some Richmond fans, morbidly obsessive even by the standards of Richmond fans, tried to make The Curse Of Helen d'Amico a thing. D'Amico broke a long silence by appearing on *The Footy Show* shortly before the 2017 grand final, and conducting a ceremonial lifting of the curse by burning what was claimed to be the Carlton scarf she'd worn 35 years previously.

not least themselves, by clobbering eventual grand finalists Essendon at Windy Hill by 74 points.[3]

Many at Richmond blamed Collingwood for their club's decline, and not without reason. After the 1982 season, Collingwood had enticed two of Richmond's brightest stars, Geoff Raines and David Cloke, to Victoria Park; in that 1980 grand final mauling, as Collingwood clearly recalled, Cloke had kicked six goals, and Raines gathered 36 possessions. An audacious retaliation by Richmond, in the form of a huge offer to Collingwood's forward pocket prestidigitator Peter Daicos,[4] had tempted, but not seduced.

So Richmond wanted to beat Collingwood this afternoon anyway, to demonstrate to Cloke and Raines (though the latter was out injured) the error of their desertions; an earlier effort, in Round 8 at Waverley, had fallen eight goals short. More pressingly, however, Richmond wanted to fittingly commemorate the unprecedented accomplishment of one of their players. Today, Kevin Bartlett would become the first VFL player to run out for his 400th game.

For most of the game's history, this had seemed a feat akin to walking on Mars. In 1980, John Rantall – formerly of South Melbourne and North Melbourne, capping his career with a curtain call at Fitzroy – nudged the all-time mark to 336. Bartlett eclipsed that in the same year's qualifying final, kicking six goals against Carlton as he went, and just kept playing, nearly three further seasons, about half again the average League career.

On the day he played his 400th game, Bartlett was 36 years old – far too young to be caricatured, as he routinely was, as some wizened Methuselah. Bartlett's aura of a visitor from a previous epoch – he was, in fact, a technician with Telecom – was enhanced by his appearance. Though self-evidently possessed of a remarkably robust constitution, Bartlett was a scrawny, wispy figure with a face from a sepia portrait of a missing explorer, and an absurd combover which flailed wildly in his wake when he ran; were the yellow and black guernsey swapped for a tweed suit and a walking stick, he'd have looked like an irritable codger chasing the

3   Among the oddnesses of this game was a five-goal cameo by Dan Foley, who played just 13 games for Richmond over three seasons. He reappeared in the public consciousness in 2016, as a contestant on *The Block*, a television programme which combined early-21st-century Australia's two most tedious preoccupations: home renovations and reality TV shows.

4   Peter Daicos kicked 549 goals for Collingwood, many of them from angles which surely precluded the sighting of daylight between the posts and/or appeared to take outrageous liberties with what humanity thought it understood of the laws of physics. His name is still invoked whenever a player attempts an especially ambitious needle-threader from the pocket boundary.

paperboy who'd thrown the morning's *Herald* onto the roof. But the facts were what they were: when Bartlett made his debut, against St Kilda in Round 3 of 1965, The Beatles were top of the Australian singles chart with 'Ticket to Ride', Sir Robert Menzies was prime minister and Bartlett was paid in pounds, shillings and pence. At least two of his teammates today, 20-year-olds Phil Egan and Greg Conlan, had not started school.

When Charlie Pannam became the first player to play 100 VFL games in 1902, it's not clear that even Charlie Pannam noticed. Kevin Bartlett's 400th received greater acknowledgement than most Australian Olympic medals, and any Australian Nobel Prize. In the days before the game, he was presented with the key to the city of Melbourne by the lord mayor, Bill Gardiner. The prime minister, Bob Hawke, sent a congratulatory message. Mike Brady, in keeping with his post–'Up There Cazaly' role as League Bard, was reported to be composing a celebratory ballad, entitled 'Hungry', after Bartlett's Lou Richards–endowed nickname.

Richmond's cheer squad let it be known that the run-through for Bartlett's 400th would be of dimensions normally reserved for grand finals: 20 metres long, ten metres high, the product of 500 person-hours and $400 worth of black and gold crepe paper. In acknowledgement of Bartlett's guernsey number as well as the banner's heft, 29 people would hold it up rather than the usual dozen or so. Bartlett, whose preternatural sureness of foot was the underpinning of his game, as he skipped through packs and tiptoed around tackles looking like a hologram projected onto the mayhem behind him, tripped over on his way through it.

At least until the ball was bounced, Collingwood's players understood, to their credit, that today was not about them. They lined up opposite Richmond to clap Bartlett onto the field, and the Magpies' cheer squad toted 'KB' banners in black and white; Collingwood's players had also signed a card. But Collingwood still had a season to play for: they had arrived at the MCG one win and a fistful of percentage adrift of the final five (which was where they would end the season, hope finally extinguished by Fitzroy in the second-last match). On the field awaiting the opening siren, Bartlett's direct opponent, Collingwood half-back Ray Byrne, drew from his sock a toothless comb and presented it to Bartlett. Bartlett, unamused as the unreconciled balding usually are by such jokes, flung away a relic with a subsequent auction value which can only be wondered at.

If Bartlett still had any doubts about the interest in his accomplishment, he only had to look around him. Nearly 82,000 people had come to watch a late-season game between also-ran teams; only the grand final would draw a bigger crowd all year.[5] It may have been this concentration on one man that allowed 39 others a measure of freedom: for both teams, the first quarter was their highest-scoring of the match, Collingwood leading 5.0 to 4.4 at the first break.

Collingwood, corralling every available asset into their push for the finals, brought Graham Teasdale back into the ruck after more than a year out having a knee rebuilt. Before the 1982 season, Collingwood paid $190,000 for his transfer from South Melbourne, where Teasdale had played 121 games and beaten Kevin Bartlett to the 1977 Brownlow Medal – which Teasdale accepted in the worst suit ever worn in Australia, a brown velvet abomination which conferred the air of a pornographer's pallbearer. Teasdale had managed just 13 games before injury ended his first season in black and white, and he still wasn't right today, winning two disposals against Richmond. He was taken out of the game by Collingwood coach John Cahill at half-time, and never played League football again.

The second and third quarters were tighter. Richmond led by five points at the half, seven at the last change. Bartlett wasn't playing badly – he would finish the game, to the minor gratification of detractors who suspected him of being not so much hungry as greedy, with 16 kicks and no handballs. But the crowd, or at least its Richmond-partisan and neutral portions, had not seen what they most wanted to see – Bartlett's trademark arms-aloft celebration of yet another cunningly sharked goal. Nor would they: for the first time in 27 matches, Bartlett was held goalless. Richmond lost by 10 points.

Defeat did not bring an end to the observances of Bartlett's milestone. After the match, Bartlett hosted 200 guests at his house in Glen Waverley. The next day he was at Punt Road, at the end of a queue of 2000 people hoping for a handshake, a signature and a photograph – at least 400 people paid $2 each for the latter privilege. Among other attractions at the gala Richmond staged was a long-kicking competition, to which all 12 VFL teams sent a champion; it was won by Richmond's Jim Jess, with a torpedo punt measured at 69.2 metres. On the Monday, Richmond held a $100-a-head banquet in Bartlett's honour, and an auction of artefacts: the 400th game jumper went for $1750, the boots for $625.

---

5   In further evidence of the peculiar priorities of Melburnian football fans, the previous week's first-versus-second clash between North Melbourne and Hawthorn enticed just 17,720 to Arden Street.

Bartlett played three more times for Richmond, retiring at the end of 1983. His final tally of 403 games looked like one of those records that would stand forever, especially as the game grew faster, and its players bigger and stronger. But improved training and nutrition, better medical treatment and generally increased professionalism actually meant that long careers became less extraordinary. Bartlett was overhauled by Hawthorn's Michael Tuck in 1990, and Tuck by North Melbourne's Brent Harvey in 2016. Another member of the 400 club, Essendon's Dustin Fletcher, retired upon reaching the figure in 2015. At the end of 2017, there were more 300-gamers playing – nine – than the VFL had produced between its foundation in 1897, and becoming the AFL in 1990.

There have been few more inevitable coronations as coach than Bartlett's at Richmond in 1988. In keeping with the rule which usually governs great players taking charge of the clubs whose colours they'd worn, it went badly, though Bartlett is entitled to his subsequent insistence that the club's finances and internal politics were not conducive to success. In four seasons under Bartlett, the Tigers won 27 games, and – in 1989 – one wooden spoon.

Bartlett was sacked in 1991. Being sacked by Richmond at around this time was like being stung by a bee – painful, certainly, but hardly something you should take personally, impulsive defenestration of coaches being what Richmond did. The club had bounced Tony Jewell, who'd won the 1980 flag, and Francis Bourke, who'd led the Tigers to the 1982 grand final. But Bartlett did not return to Punt Road for 16 years, even when accorded 'Immortal' status by the club in 2000. It can have been little consolation to Bartlett that his replacement, Allan Jeans – who'd not only won four flags, but one of them with St Kilda, a confounding of history akin to conquering Europe as generalissimo of Andorra – could wring just five wins out of Richmond in 1992.

It is no slight on Bartlett's broaching of the 400-game barrier to wonder if he'd be remembered more appropriately if he'd swept his hair back into place for the last time a season or two earlier. The 400 is the thing everyone knows about him, a statistical curiosity that threatens to occlude everything else he accomplished. He played in five premierships. His career tally of 778 goals is exceeded in Richmond's history only by specialist full-forwards Jack Titus and Matthew Richardson, and only Titus, Richardson and Michael Roach, another full-forward, have scored more for Richmond in one season than the 84 that Bartlett kicked from a half-forward flank in 1980.

He won pretty much every individual award but the Brownlow. Indeed, so certain were some at Richmond that 1974 was Bartlett's year – of the dozen media awards on offer, Bartlett had won 11 – that the eventual garlanding of North Melbourne's Keith Greig prompted ungentlemanly outbursts from the Richmond delegation, a minor scuffle between officials from the two clubs – and, in due course, apologetic letters: to *The Age* from Richmond president Ian Wilson, and to Keith Greig from Richmond secretary Alan Schwab. ('In the excitement of the occasion,' explained Schwab, 'we over-reacted to defeat.')[6]

And Kevin Bartlett changed the game – or, at least, had the game changed because of him. It is to Bartlett, and his knack for dropping the ball just before a tackle, thus drawing a free kick for holding the man, that we owe the modern holding-the-ball rule – and also, therefore, the ritual massed roar of football's second syllable that attends any attempt by one of our team's opponents to hang onto the thing for a millisecond beyond initial contact.

---

6   Keith Greig's 1974 Brownlow Medal was his second in a row. The dudgeon of the Richmond officials – Bartlett himself took no part in the booing – was especially odd given that Bartlett wasn't even runner-up, but finished third. In second place was Melbourne's Gary Hardeman – an astonishing result for a defender in a wooden-spoon team who won three games all year (as of 2016, Hardeman, who was named centre half-back in Melbourne's Team of the Century, was a driver with SkyBus, between Melbourne airport and the CBD). Richmond, who in 1974 regarded themselves as virtuous protectors of old-school footballing values, and North Melbourne as moneyed parvenus, exacted revenge on grand final day, the Tigers beating the Kangaroos by 41 points.

37

Woof!
Richmond 14.13.97 Carlton 23.13.151
Melbourne Cricket Ground
ROUND 4, 1984

Val Perovic kicked the ball 21 times during this game. Which means that, 21 times during this game, the MCG vibrated to a noise like a shy sonic boom, created by a hefty proportion of the 45,810 people present barking, in unison, an exclamation of 'Woof!'

Australian football has little tradition of orchestrated fan participation: mass chants rarely spread beyond the cheer squads behind the goals, and with the exception of the lowing of 'Coooo-lllllling-woood' as the Magpie faithful sense victory, it is unusual to hear anything like the belligerent choirs that soundtrack European soccer matches. There is a logistical – and laudable – explanation for this, which is that Australian football also has little tradition, at least in the modern era, of violence between rival fans, which obviates the need to separate them, which means that cohesive singalongs are difficult to conduct. It is also the case that the average soccer game, though it may feature moments of great grace and skill, will also labour through becalmed longueurs: singing becomes something to do while there's not much to watch. Australian football can be ugly, or inept, but it is rarely altogether uneventful.

Perovic was by now used to this half-bellow, half-whoop which accompanied his every kick, much as a talk-show host comes to expect his punchlines to be answered by a rimshot and cymbal crash from the house band's drummer. The Woof had been following Perovic around, gathering momentum, for a couple of seasons, since being introduced by a group of schoolboys who watched games at Princes Park from in front of the old press box; Perovic later recalled noticing it for the first time in Round 7 of 1982, when Carlton hosted Geelong.

It started as 'Boof!' – Perovic also admitted harbouring vague concern that it might have been a different word that rhymed with 'Boof!', perhaps a conclusion leapt to on the basis of his Village People-ish moustache. When the football press began speculating about the gestation and meaning of the sound, they were set right by a letter from one of the originators, a Frank Andreula, who explained that it was intended as sincere homage to Perovic, an imitation of the impact of his boot upon the ball. As it grew in participation and therefore volume, the exclamation mutated, its evolution accelerated by Lou Richards in his column in *The Sun*: Richards misheard it, and reported it, as 'Woof!'. By 1984, the Woof had acquired the status of ritual, one of those things everybody did, even if hardly anybody knew why.

Perovic had arrived at Carlton in peculiar circumstances. He began his League career at St Kilda in 1973, initially a winger, but developing into a sterling centre half-back. Raised in Ballarat since the age of four, when his parents arrived in Australia from Croatia, he'd never moved entirely to town. Towards the end of 1979, new St Kilda president Lindsay Fox[1] demanded that country-based Saints relocate to Melbourne. Perovic took public issue with the edict, and found himself deemed surplus to requirements.

Perovic was offered what looked a dream move – from St Kilda, who'd just added another wooden spoon to their overstuffed cutlery drawer of ignominy, to Carlton, who'd just hung another flag from their much-garlanded pole. It must have felt like being a castaway mutineer from a rusty garbage barge who has his longboat picked up by the *Queen Elizabeth II*. But Carlton contrived to respond to their 1979 triumph by descending into rancorous chaos. After a vote by club members ousted long-serving president George Harris,[2] captain-coach Alex Jesaulenko resigned, and went to St Kilda.

---

1   Lindsay Fox played 20 games for St Kilda between 1959 and 1961. A few years before making his debut, he purchased a Ford F500 truck for £400. This vehicle was the foundation of what would become the imaginatively named Linfox, Australia's largest private trucking company, and make Fox one of Australia's richest people. He served as St Kilda president until 1985.

2   George Harris was Carlton president for 12 years in two stints. A dentist by trade, he spent much of World War II as a prisoner in Changi – along with his brother and father, all of them Australian soldiers captured by Japan when Singapore fell. Harris also played a minor role in the crisis that led to the downfall of Gough Whitlam as prime minister in 1975: in 1974, Harris approached deputy prime minister and treasurer Jim Cairns offering to secure loans for the government at a commission of 2.5%. Cairns signed a letter of agreement, then later told parliament he hadn't, prompting his sacking by Whitlam.

Carlton turned out to be good enough to withstand both the loss of Jesaulenko and internal political ructions. In 1980, the Blues finished the home-and-away rounds in second place, thanks partially to the addition of Perovic to a famously miserly defence, which already included such dogged obstacles as Geoff Southby and Bruce Doull; for the first of three times in his Carlton career, Perovic topped the club's Brownlow votes. St Kilda, meanwhile, were spared yet another wooden spoon only by the width of a draw with North Melbourne in the final home-and-away game – secured with a last-minute goal by the apparently immortal Barry Breen, whose point at a similar stage of the 1966 grand final had won the Saints their only premiership.[3]

Carlton flamed out of the 1980 finals with consecutive losses, but rebounded to win the 1981 and 1982 flags, Perovic effective in both grand finals. In 1983, Carlton were overrun by Essendon in the second half of the elimination final. In 1984, as the 'Woof!' grew ever louder, the Blues recovered their poise. They started the season with a 137-point pulverising of 1983's minor premier, North Melbourne, the biggest win in Carlton's history. (They would exceed this the following year, running up a 140-point margin against St Kilda in Round 2 of 1985, though Perovic was absent, injured, from this opportunity to remind his old club of the favour they had done him.) Justin Madden[4] and Wayne Johnston kicked five goals each against North, and at full-forward Carlton looked to have unearthed a diamond – imported Claremont spearhead Warren Ralph,[5] who booted nine on debut. Carlton finished the 1984 home-and-away rounds third – a distant third, admittedly, behind contemporary superpowers Essendon and Hawthorn – yet toted some hope into September.

---

3 Fitzroy were 1980's wooden-spooners, though they would have clambered above St Kilda had they found one more goal in their last match, which they lost to Carlton by four points, 21.20 to 20.22. This was typical of Fitzroy's season, in which they actually outscored minor premiers Geelong – and every other team in the League bar Richmond, Carlton and Collingwood, two of whom would contest the 1980 grand final. Unfortunately, the Lions also conceded more points than anyone else.

4 Justin Madden played 332 League games – 45 for Essendon, 287 for Carlton. He was elected to Victoria's state parliament in 1999, and held several ministerial portfolios. Another Carlton figure of more or less the same period, Peter 'Percy' Jones – a fine player, a less successful coach – stood for state parliament in 1985 as a Liberal candidate and lost. His slogan – 'Point Percy at parliament' – may have been more hindrance than help.

5 Warren Ralph kicked 55 goals in 1984, leading the club's goalkicking in what turned out to be his only full season for Carlton; injury in 1985 and an inability to convince incoming coach Robert Walls in 1986 saw him heading back to Western Australia. He also spent a year playing for Glenelg in the SANFL, during which time he won $882,849 when his numbers came up in the state lottery.

Perhaps it was Carlton's straight-sets exit from the 1984 finals, against Hawthorn, then Collingwood, that prompted Perovic to do what he did next. Perhaps it was the melancholy fact of becoming known principally for a crowd-sourced sound effect that prompted him to seek notoriety in another field of endeavour, two days after Carlton's season was ended at Waverley by seven typically exquisite goals from the boot of Peter Daicos. We may never know, and on balance it's unlikely that Perovic remembers. A brass plaque behind the bar at the Duke of Wellington hotel on Flinders Street recorded: 'On this spot, on the seventeenth of September in the year 1984, Mr Val Perovic, player of the Carlton football club, drank 37 375ml cans of Victoria Bitter in two hours. Witnessed by the hotel patrons, teammates and his very nervous dog.'

The licensee of the Duke of Wellington at the time was Brian 'The Whale' Roberts. The pub, Melbourne's oldest, was decorated with football memorabilia and known by the slogan 'Have an ale with the Whale'. Roberts was a mountainous and gregarious ruckman who had starred in Richmond's 1973 and 1974 premiership sides, before being traded to South Melbourne, along with Francis Jackson, Graham Teasdale, and $40,000 which Richmond didn't really have, for John Pitura – a calamitous transaction even amid the excruciating history of Richmond's eternal willingness to swap stout livestock for magic beans. Pitura played 40 indifferent games for the Tigers, while Teasdale won the Brownlow Medal with the Swans in 1977, Roberts got close to one in 1975, and Jackson played a solid 100 games in defence.

Roberts died in 2016, aged 70, possibly taking with him the truth about the degree to which he might have encouraged Perovic's prodigious swilling. Roberts was fond of spectacle: at least one photograph exists of him riding a horse through his pub while cradling a cattle-dog, for some reason. Equally maddeningly unknowable – for the crucial figure has sworn eternal silence on the matter – is whether news of Perovic's feat somehow reached a sturdy Tasmanian middle-order batsman who was then a matter of weeks from making his Test debut for Australia.

Perhaps David Boon – for it was he – vowed, upon hearing the tidings from the Duke of Wellington, to one day match or exceed Perovic's feat. In 1989, en route to that year's Ashes in England, Boon reputedly sank 52 375ml cans of VB on the day-long flight from Kingsford-Smith to

Heathrow.[6] It seems an extraordinary dereliction that the CSIRO have never done the rigorous research – adjusting for body mass, time, altitude and the volumes which may have been soaked up by the sumptuous moustaches of both contenders – required to determine which was the more exacting accomplishment.

The Woof endured beyond Perovic's retirement in 1985. In the 1990s, it was bestowed by Carlton fans upon Ang Christou, and passed briefly in the 2000s to Chris Bryan. In between times it awaits, patient and silent as the sword in the stone, its next worthy champion.

---

6   Legend has it that David Boon's broaching of the half-century, somewhere over Europe, was
     observed with a congratulatory announcement from the cockpit, and applause from other
     passengers. Australia trounced England 4–0 in the ensuing series, and Boon scored 442 runs at
     55.25 – significantly above his overall Test average of 43.65.

38

Jacko and the Wiz
Geelong 16.17.113 Sydney 14.8.92
Kardinia Park
ROUND 19, 1984

Only 10,897 people saw this match. It was Geelong's second-smallest home crowd of the season, underwhelmed narrowly by the meagre gathering of spiteful deviants who'd bestirred themselves a few weeks previously to watch St Kilda submit to a generally anticipated battering. (These cackling grinches were almost unpleasantly surprised, as the Saints, despite giving up eight goals to one in the first quarter, were finally inspired to within 13 points by a five-goal masterclass from Silvio Foschini.[1])

In fairness to all unconcerned, the day the Swans came to Geelong was a lousy one, weather-wise. And Sydney were struggling to attract punters at their newish home at the SCG, never mind inspiring a travelling legion to spring for interstate flights. This match shaped as a late-season non-event, between a home team who might make the finals but weren't going to win the premiership – and who wouldn't, it turned out, make the finals – and visitors whose chances of seeing September were something the most desperately overenthusiastic commentator would struggle to spruik.

But the 10,897 compelled to attend – by loyalty, habit or inability to think of anything better to do – did see something remarkable, if only in retrospect. This was the only on-field meeting of the two great intuitive showmen of the 1980s VFL: Geelong's Mark Jackson, and Sydney's Warwick Capper.

---

1   Silvio Foschini's lasting contribution to League history was the legal action that got him to St Kilda. Originally signed to South Melbourne, Foschini was unenthused about joining the Swans' move to Sydney. He claimed, successfully, that the clearance rules then in force were a restraint of trade. It was a key step on the road to the modern draft system.

Both Jackson and Capper were full-forwards, a role which, back when positions were less fluid, and players less adaptable, always attracted preeners, braggarts and grandstanders. It is impossible to imagine any full-forward joining a rock group and volunteering to play bass. (Both Jackson and Capper would also make records, of the kind on which people who do play bass prefer to be omitted from the credits.)

And, for all the clownery perpetrated by Jackson and Capper, on and off the field, during and after their football careers, they were both good full-forwards, even by the standards of an age in which the yardsticks were Tony Lockett and Jason Dunstall. Jackson, a roof-tiler by trade, played 82 times with three (at best, ordinary) teams, and kicked 308 goals; in 1984 he led Geelong's goalkicking with 74, and was beaten to the Coleman Medal only by Bernie Quinlan, Tony Lockett and Leigh Matthews, all of whom played more games that year than he did. His goals-per-game average of 3.76 was the same as Brian Taylor's, and a stretch ahead of that of any modern AFL forward. From his first appearance for Melbourne in 1981, Jackson scored goals in 79 consecutive games – a record from debut which, given the game's evolution away from spearhead-centred tactics, may stand forever. He was held goalless only once, against Richmond in Round 21, 1985, when he was just back from an eight-week suspension. Unfit and out of sorts, he had one kick at goal, which he scuffed into the man on the mark.

Jackson's first VFL club had been Richmond, but he hadn't been able to get a game for the Tigers. He went to South Fremantle, coached by kindred spirit Mal Brown. Jackson's 53 goals in 1979 helped South to second place at the end of the home-and-away rounds, but the night before the semi-final, he was voted out of the club by his teammates, and exchanged blows with Brown in the car park as he left. (South won the semi-final, but not the grand final.)

Jackson returned to Richmond, and spent 1980 in the reserves, kept out of the Tigers' premiership side by Michael Roach, David Cloke, Francis Bourke and Kevin Bartlett. The 131 goals he kicked for the seconds interested Melbourne, where Jackson had two fine seasons – 76 goals in 1981, the same in 1982. On game days, he treated crowds to what was, for the most part, joyous pantomime: twirling footballs on his fingers, climbing goalposts, performing donkey-kicks, and shaping up to opponents, and opposition supporters, with a self-mockingly pugnacious dance, his own interpretation of the Ali Shuffle.

It got, on occasion, out of hand in public: against Essendon at Windy Hill in Round 9 of 1982, Jackson picked up a beer can which had been thrown at him from the cheap seats, and threw it back. In private, Jackson and Melbourne were not getting on. Jackson – among other complaints – was weirdly incensed that Gerard Healy scored eight goals in the last game of 1982 to pip him as the Demons' leading goalkicker; in the dressing-room afterwards, Jackson had to be persuaded by Brent Crosswell not to settle the account physically.

In 1983, Jackson moved to St Kilda, now coached by Tony Jewell, who'd been at Richmond when Jackson was piling up huge tallies in the reserves. So Jackson's previous game against Sydney before he met them in Geelong colours in 1984 was in Round 5 of 1983, when St Kilda visited the SCG, a few weeks before Capper debuted for the Swans. Sydney won this profligate shootout between the season's two worst teams, 24.16.160 to 21.11.137, but Jackson stole the show, beating three opponents (Rod Carter, David Winbanks, Max Kruse), kicking ten goals and celebrating each by blowing kisses to befuddled home fans.

Jackson kicked 41 goals in ten appearances for the Saints; he was equal second (with Hawthorn's Michael Moncrieff) among 1983's VFL goalkickers when St Kilda sacked him, citing disciplinary reasons, including practical jokes which Jackson found funnier than the victims did, among them placing a brick beneath the brake pedal of Trevor Barker's car, and a lit cigarette in the pocket of Lindsay Fox. (Jackson still ended the season as St Kilda's leading goalkicker, a statistic which said as much bad about St Kilda as it did good about Jackson.) Reporters who visited Jackson at his parents' Nunawading home following his dismissal found a mournful figure, right arm in a sling due to an injury sustained the previous weekend. 'I still want to play League footy,' Jackson insisted. 'I don't want clubs to think that because I've been to three League clubs I am a dill. I am not a dill.'

This plaintive if doubtfully intentional echo of one of Richard M. Nixon's more debatable assertions found a sympathetic ear at Geelong, where coach Tom Hafey reckoned that Jackson would add much-needed bite to the Cats' toothless attack: in 1983, they'd scored fewer points than any other team. Hafey doubtless also imagined that his disciplinarian ethos would civilise Jackson. Hafey might usefully have pondered that Ron Barassi, no less, had once thought the same.

Jackson's inaugural outing for the Cats, in Round 1 of 1984, summarised his contradictions: he booted nine goals against Fitzroy, and got reported for belting the Lions' captain, Garry Wilson. In the same match, another tempestuous Cats recruit playing his first match for Geelong kicked three goals, and also got reported for belting Garry Wilson: his name was Gary Ablett. (Ablett got three weeks; Jackson escaped with a warning, after offering the tribunal a fascinating defence: 'If I'd intentionally gone to hit him across the head, his head would have dropped off.') Though Jackson would set a new single-season record for tribunal appearances (four) as early as Round 12, by the time Sydney came to town in Round 19, he'd only missed three games all year – one of them Geelong's visit to Sydney in Round 9, due to a two-week suspension for biffing Essendon's Merv Neagle – and had kicked 62 goals. The only names ahead of Jackson on 1984's leading goalkicker list were proper full-forward aristocracy: Bernie Quinlan, Tony Lockett, Paul Salmon.

At the other end of Kardinia Park this miserable Saturday afternoon was Warwick Capper, a precocious 21-year-old from Oakleigh, recruited a couple of seasons back, when the Swans were still South Melbourne. He was playing his 13th League game. The hair, already longish, would get longer. The shorts, already shortish, would get shorter. Capper, like Jackson, would launch his sideline as a professional buffoon concurrently with his career as a footballer – and Capper, like Jackson, would be remembered more for his off-field nonsense than his on-field accomplishments. It would be a shame in Capper's case, as well.

Warwick Capper would play 124 games for 388 goals, including 103 in 1987, one of two years he was runner-up for the Coleman Medal. Aside from his prowess as a goalkicker, Capper was as fine an aerialist as the game has produced, his blond mane and balletic athleticism making his ascent of packs resemble the exuberant camp of David Lee Roth pirouetting across a Van Halen video. Capper won Mark of the Year in 1987 with a horizontal levitation over Hawthorn's Chris Langford, like a freefalling skydiver somehow heading upwards – the only consolation to be had for the Swans from a 99-point mauling by the Hawks in the qualifying final. These acrobatics were all executed in an era in which grizzled defenders were still getting away with cuffing forwards about the head in marking contests, and were much more likely to do so when the forward looked like Capper.

When Capper came to Kardinia Park, all that lay in the future, along with the largely undignified post-football endeavours.[2] In Round 19 of 1984, Capper was about to realise how good he really was. He'd had a couple of decent games – five goals against Fitzroy in Round 10, four against Footscray the week after that – but at Kardinia Park he kicked six, a spree only contained once he was corralled by Geelong's Mark Yeates, who was moved onto him during the second half. Capper's prodigious ability to irritate opponents was also blossoming: Geelong's Mark Bos had his number taken for unduly rough play, in that he 'deliberately and violently' knocked Capper to the ground. Bos wouldn't be the last.

Despite Capper's heroics, Geelong beat Sydney, but it was little thanks to their own star full-forward. Mark Jackson had a rotten afternoon, barely getting a kick, scoring just one goal. It was Gary Ablett who rescued the Cats, taking 12 marks, many of them sufficiently sensational that even Capper might have acknowledged that some were nearly as good as one of his.

The historical record lacks concrete evidence that Jackson and Capper shook hands after the siren. It would be pleasing to think that they did, and that each recognised something of themselves in the other. Other footballers had turned themselves into celebrities, but most had done it after they'd finished playing, and mostly within the confines of the football world – football press, football radio, football television. Jackson and Capper, whether proceeding according to calculated strategy, or acting on some elemental impulse, saw no reason why their extracurricular infamy should be so constrained.

Jackson released his debut single a few weeks before the 1985 season. Entitled 'I'm an Individual' and released under the cunning alias of Jacko, it was the composition of Bob Brown, whose previous best-known contribution to the canon of Australian song was the wistful ballad 'Give Me a Home Among the Gum Trees'. 'I'm an Individual' was a dreadful record, if not notably worse than other novelty rap hits of the era, but it was perfectly congruent with the flourishing Jacko brand: the lovable

---

2   Warwick Capper's post-football career could not be accurately described as a study in decorous restraint, though he never lacked enterprise. Among the roles Capper was known to have inhabited – or claimed to be undertaking in order to scare up some column inches from credulous or indulgent newspapers – were DJ, coffee van baron (dispensing 'Cappercinos'), hamburger impresario, stripper, escort, porn star, stop-and-go-sign operative, professional appearer at parties, host of homestays at his Capperishly decorated Gold Coast apartment, developer of an accountancy app and reality TV star. In 2011, Capper was the first contestant dismissed from the first season of *The Celebrity Apprentice Australia*.

larrikin, an arched eyebrow doing for his macho bellicosity what implied inverted commas did for his more outrageous statements. It did what Jacko wanted it – wanted everything – to do: got him noticed. The video, which consisted largely of Jackson barking in a blue singlet, was played on *Countdown*, introduced by nonplussed guest hosts Martin Kemp and Steve Martin of big-shirted English poseurs Spandau Ballet, and the single peaked at number 15 nationally; in Victoria it was deprived of top spot only by USA For Africa's emetic famine-relief singalong 'We Are the World'.[3]

Warwick Capper's debut single, 'I Only Take What's Mine', released a few months later, failed to trouble the compilers of Australia's pop charts, but did succeed, if altogether inadvertently, in capturing the vacuous hubris of this period in the history of the Sydney Swans. Not so much the song itself – a grim pastiche of 1980s radio rock, strangely possible to forget even while one was listening to it – but the video, which looked like the result of every football club in Victoria collaborating on a negative campaign ad about Capper and his team and the city to which the Swans had moved. Rival fans who did not wish to deliver a hearty kick at Capper's tightly-swaddled backside before they saw it certainly did afterwards. Decades later, Capper was fond of claiming that 'I Only Take What's Mine' sold in excess of 1.5 million copies. Which, if true, would make it comfortably the biggest-selling single in Australian history. (It is not true.)

The 'I Only Take What's Mine' clip depicted Capper exalting in an assortment of vapid playboy clichés: lounging poolside with a bevy of not overclad women, descending a mansion staircase wearing a white tuxedo, driving an assortment of svelte coupes. The shot of Capper flinging a dart at a board bearing a picture of Mark Jackson was admittedly witty, and the footage of Capper playing football self-evidently extraordinary, but the rest, in the event of supreme power in Australia being seized by revolutionary communists – an occurrence the video made just that little bit more likely – would have seen Capper among the first against the wall. At the end, as the song faded mercifully away, Capper flew into the sunset with the concubine chosen from his cornucopia of options – the lucky

---

3   Jacko's follow-up single, 'Me Brain Hurts', was actually somewhat less terrible, but the record-buying public decided that they'd got the idea, and gave it a swerve. There was another Jacko single in 1991, entitled 'You Can Do This', which confirmed that Jacko couldn't. In 2000, music publications carried aghast reports of a collaboration between Capper and Jackson, an alleged EP of techno tracks entitled 'Rippin' Undies', 'Aussie Aussie Aussie Oi Oi Oi', 'Man of Mind, Man of Power' and 'Disco Biscuit'. Evidence for its existence is elusive; it is possible that it represents the line that the internet will not cross.

woman played by his wife, Joanne – aboard a helicopter furnished, like the cars, by the record's executive producer, and the Swans' new owner, Dr Geoffrey Edelsten.

Edelsten was a doctor turned medical tycoon, known for operating a chain of private clinics decorated like Elton John's bathroom, for being married to a model very many years his junior, and for roaring between parties in a fleet of Lamborghinis and Rolls-Royces adorned with custom licence plates that even other owners of custom licence plates thought obnoxious, among them 'MACHO', 'SEXY' and 'SPUNKY'.[4] In 1985, Edelsten became the first private owner of a VFL club, paying $2.9 million for the licence to operate the Swans, who were labouring to sustain the interest which had attended their arrival in Sydney. Average home crowds at the SCG were only just in five figures; given the way Sydney were playing, that might not have been a bad thing.[5]

Edelsten was the point man for the takeover of the Swans by marketing company Powerplay, whose chairman, veteran promoter Bob Pritchard – a former pop star and marketing director of Kerry Packer's World Series Cricket – had planned the venture meticulously. The conclusions of his research did little for any reputation Sydneysiders might have treasured as a community of stolid stoics; one apparently popular idea was to present every woman arriving at the SCG with a carnation. More usefully, the injection of cash brought Tom Hafey to Sydney as coach, and star quality into the squad: Warwick Capper's path to goal would henceforth be cleared by Greg Williams and Bernard Toohey from Geelong, Merv Neagle from Essendon and Gerard Healy from Melbourne, among others.

The crowds came back: Sydney's average home attendance more than doubled in 1986, Edelsten's first full season in charge, and on at least one weekend the Swans nearly outdrew the entire NRL fixture. The Swans' new admirers either forgave or actively enjoyed the glitzy showbiz bullshit which Edelsten forked liberally into the SCG turf – including a regime of

---

4   In the narrative of Warwick Capper's career, Edelsten functions as the Socrates to Capper's Plato, the sage schooling his protégé in the ways of self-sustaining celebrity.

5   The 1980s were tough for many clubs – the threatened and actual mergers of the 1990s did not emerge from clear sky. Warwick Capper's debut for Sydney was against North Melbourne in Round 14 of 1983. Just 7,404 people could be bothered to turn up at Arden Street, for a total gate of $10,832, leaving the clubs, after expenses, with $45 each. That same year, the diehard holdouts of what was now officially the Melbourne branch of the Sydney Swans cheer squad, but who clearly saw themselves as the Provisional South Melbourne cheer squad, welcomed the Swans onto the MCG to play Melbourne with a run-through declaring 'Sydney is sinking – time to return to the Lake'. In protest, fans who'd travelled from Sydney cancelled a friendly football match with their South Melbourne counterparts, for fears, one Sydney official gravely intoned, of 'a bloodbath'.

ghastly half-time entertainments, and a troupe of cheerleaders called the Swanettes, who cavorted inanely after every Swans goal.

More importantly, the Swans ceased sucking: they finished the home-and-away season second in 1986, and third in 1987. (They crashed out of both finals series, however, twice losing narrowly in 1986, twice getting roundly tanned in 1987.) In so doing, Sydney furnished an allegory for the entire Edelsten experiment: an impressive, flashy start collapsing in circumstances of ridiculous – and, to the rest of the country, richly amusing – pandemonium. In July 1986, Edelsten was sacked as Swans chairman and replaced by Sydney's lord mayor, Doug Sutherland. Edelsten threatened a retaliatory takeover bid, but had more pressing concerns. In December 1986, Edelsten was expelled from the New South Wales branch of the Australian Medical Association over alleged misconduct. In 1987, he was declared bankrupt, in 1988 struck off the NSW medical register, and in 1990 sentenced to a year in gaol[6] after being convicted of, among other malfeasances, soliciting hitman Christopher Dale Flannery to fix up a quarrelsome former patient.[7]

The simultaneous plummet of the Swans' fortunes was perhaps less spectacular, but nevertheless vertiginous. Warwick Capper was, as he usually was – not always at his own insistence – the centre of attention. At the end of 1987, he was not yet 25, one of the most-recognised athletes in Australia, had just banked his first 100-goal season and was imminently out of contract: ideal circumstances in which to press one's advantage with one's employers, or seek better offers elsewhere. Brisbane offered to make him the best-paid player in the League. Capper rebuffed this largesse, saying that he couldn't see himself in the Bears' drab guernsey, and doubting their prospects generally. But the Swans faffed, and Capper embraced his always-obvious destiny as a Queenslander. Brisbane were

---

6   After his release from prison, Edelsten recovered his fortune, his car collection, his mysterious appeal to much younger blonde women, and the interest of the tabloid press, whom he was happy as ever to service with headlines. Edelsten's extraordinary life story, basically *Citizen Kane* rewritten by Jackie Collins, acquired an unlikely highbrow dimension in the 2010s, when overjoyed newspapers discovered that his Swans-era wife, Leanne, had for many years conducted an affair with Clive James. In 2015, Edelsten did slightly better than Capper had on *The Celebrity Apprentice Australia*, and also outpointed his own most recent wife, Gabi Grecko, who appeared in the same series.

7   Christopher Dale Flannery, known by the forbidding but doubtless professionally useful nickname 'Mr Rent-a-Kill', was active in the early 1980s. Nobody is too clear on the precise number of his victims, and Flannery has been unavailable for comment since 1985, when he went missing. Among the more picturesque theories of Flannery's fate is the one adumbrated by Melbourne underworld figure Mark 'Chopper' Read, who believes that Flannery was fed, by persons unspecified, into a woodchipper on a farm near Seymour. Chopper and Jacko would later combine to produce a two-handed spoken-word show, which toured nationally.

still technically based on the Gold Coast, a district for which the bronzed, peroxided (and, in later years, Botoxed) Capper was surely the beau ideal of its gauchely flamboyant model citizen.

Capper was not bad at Brisbane, but Brisbane were not good, and it was a poor use of what should have been his best years. He returned to Sydney in 1991 – not least, ironically, because Brisbane had become disarrayed by the travails of a rakish benefactor, in this instance Christopher Skase. Capper played one more okayish season with the Swans, struggling against a knee injury to kick 38 goals in 13 appearances, and was directed towards the door at the end of the season. There was never much likelihood of Capper resigning himself to obscurity aged 28. With no VFL clubs calling, he signed for Southport in the QAFL; newspaper snippets tittered about other employment as a bouncer, aerobics instructor or putative star of a martial-arts epic entitled *Tokyo Triangles* and an action movie called *The Big Smoke*; both films unaccountably faltered somewhere during production. He also appeared in court on charges of assaulting the apparent paramour of his now ex-wife; he was acquitted.

It was fitting, and inevitable, that Mark Jackson and Warwick Capper would meet again, this time in cahoots. Decades after their retirements, the pair would perform together, peddling combatively nostalgic reveries of the twilight of the VFL's Wild West era, a Butch and Sundance who somehow survived the shootout. (The discussion of which of Jackson and Capper would be Butch, and which Sundance, would not occupy any deliberative body long.) They even took a tilt at politics. In 2009, Capper announced his intention to contest the Queensland state seat of Beaudesert, upon which Pauline Hanson[8] had set her sights. However, Capper's name failed to appear on the ballot paper. Capper blamed men's magazine *Zoo Weekly*, which was sponsoring his campaign – and *Zoo Weekly* blamed Capper's campaign manager, Mark Jackson. The possibility that the whole thing was some sort of shabby publicity stunt must, regrettably, be countenanced.

Of the two men who met this Saturday at Kardinia Park in 1984, Jackson probably enjoyed the more distinguished post-football career.

---

8   Pauline Hanson, founder of the One Nation party – since 1997, Australia's haven of choice for ethnocentric dingbats and xenophobic yahoos – has never formally declared an AFL allegiance. In 2015, she did tweet a photo of herself – sitting, notably, alone – at that season's Dreamtime at the 'G game. Her choice of hashtags – both #gotiges and #DonTheSash – suggested a desire to have money each way. One can only hope that she enjoyed the exhibition of Indigenous ceremony that preceded the game, and the fine 17-possession performance for Richmond of Bachar Houli, who a couple of years later would become the AFL's first Muslim premiership player.

He leveraged a role shouting in a battery commercial into modest fame on American television, joining the cast of a short-lived late-1980s *Mad Max* pastiche called *The Highwayman*, and accruing sufficient recognition that, in the glorious 1995 'Bart vs Australia' episode of *The Simpsons*, the writers were able to assume that a cartoon rendering of Jackson in Energizer-hawking mode would still raise a chuckle. Rather heartbreakingly, Jackson admitted, years later, that a major reason why he couldn't make it last in America was that he was, at the time, illiterate.

There are, really, two sorts of fame. There's the fame endowed by being exceptionally good at something, and there's the fame one can accrue merely by being willing to make enough of a spectacle and/ or nuisance of oneself. Capper and Jackson both had one, and then the other. There was rarely much doubt about which they prized more. A recurring motif of Jackson's lively interviews would be his pique at the insufficient credit he received for his exploits as a footballer. In 2003, the Swans held a ceremony to announce the Sydney/South Melbourne Team of the Century; Capper, upon not hearing his name, pushed over a table and flounced.

39

Leigh Matthews Crosses the Line
Hawthorn 17.15.117 Geelong 13.10.88
Princes Park
ROUND 12, 1985

It is an audaciously revisionist reading of events, but it's arguable that Mark Jackson didn't start it, or at least not the worst of it. Late in the last quarter, the game almost certainly beyond Geelong, five goals adrift, the Cats' Terry Bright kicked long towards his forward line. The ball fell to a contest between Jackson and Hawthorn's Chris Langford. Jackson, who'd kicked four goals, outmanoeuvred Langford and took the mark – or would have, had Hawthorn's Gary Ayres, arriving a step late, not launched a fist at the ball which, intentionally or otherwise, landed across Jackson's head.

The smart move for Jackson would have been to wait for the umpire to award the mark – and, hopefully, a 15-metre penalty for Ayres' (at best) clumsy intervention. The consequent certain goal from point-blank range might not have been enough to inspire a Geelong comeback, but for a team who arrived at Princes Park only out of the final five on percentage, and with Carlton and Collingwood, the teams above and below them, getting beaten by Footscray at the Western Oval and by North Melbourne at Victoria Park respectively, every little bit would help.[1] Instead, upon regaining his feet, Jackson made for Ayres, and punched him in the face. It didn't put Ayres down; a follow-up swipe might have, had Hawthorn's Rod Lester-Smith not wrestled Jackson away.

As is often the case, the instigator escaped punishment, and the retaliator copped it; the umpires who surrounded Jackson were not

---

1   Geelong finished sixth in 1985, a game and a half out of the finals.

enquiring after his health as he clutched his distinctive sloping forehead in either genuine or hastily feigned agony. As Ayres backed up to take the free kick which was now his, another scuffle began, Jackson again in the middle of it, eventually dispersed when the umpires shepherded Jackson back to his position in the goal square, where he paced and seethed before the jeering Hawthorn fans gathered behind a red Winfield hoarding, like a captive bear goaded by delinquent schoolchildren.

As Ayres kicked upfield, Jackson lumbered out of his pen and started on Langford. In the scrapping where the ball landed, Leigh Matthews slid hip-first into the head of Michael Kol, who got up as slowly as one might after being knocked down by a runaway dump truck, or indeed being hit hip-first in the head by Leigh Matthews; dazed, Kol handballed badly to Steve Hocking, whom Matthews tackled and dispossessed. A subsequent punt forward by Ken Judge trickled over the boundary near Hawthorn's right forward pocket. It is difficult to imagine anything that the umpires can have wanted less than a pause in play. Into the vacuum, and into Chris Langford, stepped Mark Jackson. There didn't look much in the dust-up, but it was sufficient for umpire Ian Robinson to reach for his notepad once more. Jackson retreated again to the goal square, and simmered.

Everything that had happened so far, while unedifying, had also been pretty unremarkable, certainly by the boisterous standards of 1980s football. It had been a niggly, irritable game, especially on the part of Geelong, two of whose players had been reported before three-quarter time – Neville Bruns for clouting Michael Tuck, Bernard Toohey for biffing Dermott Brereton. Jackson had now gone in the book for striking Langford and Ayres, and Ayres for striking Jackson. Shortly after play resumed, they were joined by Gary Ablett on a time-wasting charge, after he petulantly kicked the ball away following the award of a free kick to Hawthorn. It would be a busier than usual Monday night at the tribunal, but all concerned had seen worse; most concerned had done worse.

And then, a couple of minutes later, it happened. With Hawthorn's Peter Curran waiting to take a free kick on the Hawks' left wing, players flooded back towards the goal Geelong were defending. Among them were Leigh Matthews and Neville Bruns – Matthews ambling, Bruns jogging. Matthews noticed Bruns just before the pair drew level, and swung his right arm into Bruns' head. As Bruns collapsed into a roll, clutching the jaw that Matthews' fist had broken in two places, Matthews ran from the scene, stumbling over his victim's flailing legs as he went.

Umpire Robinson, concentrating on Curran, was facing in the opposite direction, and didn't see Matthews' assault on Bruns. Geelong's Steve Hocking did. Playing his 11th game for the Cats, Hocking[2] had been given the daunting job of tagging Matthews by Geelong coach Tom Hafey, with the proviso that when Matthews went forward, Hocking should remain in defence. Hocking's obedience of this instruction had given Matthews space; it also, as Bruns fell, gave Hocking a run-up.

The Code of Hammurabi and the Book of Leviticus both endorse the principle of 'an eye for an eye'. Whether Hocking had gleaned his ideas about retributive justice from either or both these ancient texts, or from his own contemplations of the subject, he was clearly of the belief that a nose for a jaw was a fair trade. As Matthews was helped up by trainers, his face smeared with blood and gristle, another general rumpus erupted. Mark Jackson, not helpfully, ran the length of the ground to remonstrate further with a dazed Matthews. Terry Bright also appeared to believe that, brutally punished though Matthews had been, it wasn't enough. It had become a gruesome, sickly spectacle: wherever the line is that divides cartoonish, pantomime, boys-will-be-boys knockabout from outright barbarity, Geelong and Hawthorn had led each other across it.

The following morning, the two coaches, Geelong's Tom Hafey and Hawthorn's Allan Jeans, were interviewed by Peter McKenna for the 'Coaches Corner' segment of Channel Seven's *World of Sport*. Hafey wore one of the Adidas training shirts he'd made a sartorial trademark, this one light blue with dark blue stripes on the sleeves. Jeans wore a blue jumper over a blue shirt and blue tie. Were it not for the logos of Hawthorn and their sponsor, HFC Finance, Jeans would have looked like a cop giving evidence. The similarity had doubtless occurred to Jeans – who, nearing the end of his long parallel career in the Victoria Police, had reached the rank of senior sergeant. But the beige desk of *World of Sport*, for these few minutes, acquired the qualities of a courtroom dock, and Jeans was in it. Neither he nor Hafey looked like they'd have much trouble compiling an extensive list of places they would rather be.

Hafey allowed that he was 'disappointed' at the reports of four of his players – Hocking's evener-up on Matthews had also been missed by the umpires – but expressed sympathy for Jackson. 'A man can probably only

---

2   Steve Hocking played 199 games for Geelong before retiring in 1994, and later served in various administrative roles at Geelong, and as the AFL's head of football operations. His younger brother, Garry, made his Geelong debut in 1987.

take so much,' Hafey said, 'and that's as far as I'm prepared to go.' Jeans, for his part, gave a short speech, both waffly and testy. 'I believe there's a certain element in the VFL,' he concluded, '[that] because I've adopted certain tactics and refused to do these things, that they've been under a false misapprehension if they had developed these tactics. Now, I'd say it is an untrue misapprehension to believe in that, alright? Now, that's all I'm going to say about it.' Jeans' delivery was icily vehement, notwithstanding the fact that what he'd said made no sense at all.

A puzzled McKenna persisted, asking Jeans if he'd spoken about the Bruns incident to 'the player concerned', Leigh Matthews having apparently been elevated overnight to the pantheon of folk devils whose names must not be mentioned. Jeans, who may have learned something from the generations of Melburnian ne'er-do-wells he'd interrogated, responded with a masterly exposition of evasion tinged with menace.

'You want to go back and dig skeletons out of the cupboard,' Jeans intoned grimly, 'I can say to you that certain incidents happened recently. If you want to go back, it's just as embarrassing for your club – I can recite incidents against the club that you played for, the same as against Geelong, if you want to go back into these incidents. Now, I think you have a certain responsibility to the game, the same as I do. I said I don't condone the thing, and left it at that. Now you want to continue with it. Just leave it at that, at this particular stage.'

If it had been a courtroom drama, this was the moment at which the prosecutor would have responded with a devastating yes-or-no question which forced a confession from the defendant, but *World of Sport* was not a courtroom drama. What happened instead was that McKenna, glancing at a director making wind-it-up gestures, awkwardly thanked Jeans and Hafey, Barry Crocker's song 'Come On the Cats'[3] blasted from the studio speakers, and Jack Dyer – who might well have thought that the violence which was so scandalising everyone would have been regarded, in his day, as little more than an especially hearty handshake – bumbled into

---

3   Barry Crocker initially became famous as the title character in *The Adventures of Barry McKenzie* and *Barry McKenzie Holds His Own* – two early 1970s films based on a proto-bogan character created by Barry Humphries. Crocker was also a much-beloved middle-of-the-road warbler, possibly best remembered for having sung the original theme tune for *Neighbours*. Born in Geelong, and a lifelong Cats fan who at one point trained with the club's under-19s, Crocker wrote and recorded 'Come On the Cats' in 1982, at the request of coach Billy Goggin. Despite a launch which saw Crocker taking a ceremonial lap of Kardinia Park in a Mercedes-Benz convertible before Geelong played Melbourne in Round 3 of that season, it failed to supplant 'We Are Geelong' in the affections of supporters.

shot to present the two miserably reluctant guests with sponsored gifts of surreal banality, in these febrile circumstances: a Bertocchi ham, Mrs Brite clothing detergents, and a tub of McMahon's honey.

The tribunal sat on the Monday evening. Ayres was cleared. Toohey and Ablett got a week each for their misdemeanours, while the charge against Bruns was set aside on the grounds that he was still in hospital – and, given the nature of his injury, literally incapable of speaking for himself. Jackson anticipated a long night – he made an early point of announcing that he'd prefer bacon, eggs and cornflakes for breakfast. He received the verdict with one leg slung over the arm of a chair, while fiddling with a bottle top. He got eight weeks, and jauntily informed the tribunal that he was going to burn the Christmas cards he'd bought them after they'd cleared him of another charge a fortnight previously. Jackson's father, George, who'd accompanied his son to the hearing, became involved in an affray with TV reporters in the car park outside, and was spoken to by police.

Nobody believed justice had been served: two players had been seriously injured, and the umpires had seen neither incident. The League thought of establishing some sort of inquiry, but received a legal opinion that it had no power to launch such investigations. The clamour for Something to be Done became deafening: on the front page of the edition of *The Age* that reported the tribunal verdicts, the gathering brouhaha was only just forced below the fold by the latest developments in the saga of a TWA airliner hijacked to Beirut by Hezbollah. Victoria's minister for police, Race Mathews,[4] assured a distraught public that the chief commissioner of police, Mick Miller, was on the case.

The League bigwigs thought they'd figured it out. A few weeks after the carnage at Princes Park, they summoned Leigh Matthews and Steve Hocking to face a special convening of the VFL Commission. The decision was made to impose upon Matthews the unprecedented punishment of revoking his registration as a player, on the grounds of

---

4   Race Mathews was principal private secretary to Gough Whitlam while Whitlam was leader of the opposition, and served as a federal MP before entering state politics. In 1986, he became embroiled in one of Australia's odder crimes. Mathews, also Victoria's minister for the arts, was the recipient of demands issued by a previously little-heralded group of agitators, Australian Cultural Terrorists, after they stole one of Picasso's 'The Weeping Woman' paintings from the National Gallery of Victoria. The letters, which addressed the minister as 'Rank Mathews' and described him as a 'pompous fathead' and a 'tiresome old bag of swamp gas', demanded increased arts funding, and threatened that 'The Weeping Woman' would be burned if this was not forthcoming. The painting was recovered, two weeks after going missing, from a locker at Spencer Street station. The thieves were never caught.

conduct unbecoming – with the rider that he could apply to reregister four matches later. Hocking, aided by the fact that the cameras had missed his assault on Matthews – and by the fact that two of Matthews' teammates, Peter Russo and Richard Loveridge, affected the customary amnesia when asked to give evidence – escaped penalty. 'I'm just glad the whole thing has reached its climax,' said Matthews. It had not.

Two days after Matthews was deregistered by the VFL, police charged him with grievous bodily harm and assault occasioning actual bodily harm – the first such charges laid for on-field violence. All of football, even Geelong, reacted with dismay at this intrusion by the real world. At the Melbourne magistrates' court a month later, Matthews pleaded guilty to assault occasioning actual bodily harm (the other charge was dropped). He was fined $1000.

Matthews' lawyer, Brian Bourke,[5] claimed that Matthews' behaviour had been out of character – an entreaty which might have prompted chuckles from a few of Matthews' opponents down the years, as they read accounts of proceedings while rubbing their scars. The magistrate, Brian Clothier, recognised the widespread bewilderment that had been occasioned by the charges, stating that, as he saw it, this was a crime which had three victims: Bruns, Matthews and football itself. Hawthorn's president, Ron Cook, took a less equable view, describing Matthews as 'the martyr of an action instigated for reasons unknown'.

The sanctimony was unbecoming, as sanctimony usually is. Leigh Matthews was a great footballer – one of the greatest – but there were reasons beyond pleasing sibilance why he'd acquired the nickname 'Lethal'. If he'd done what he'd done in any environment but a football field, he would have required all the gleaming character references from whichever acquiescent chaplains he could summon to avoid a prison sentence. But those who observed that many similar offences had been perpetrated during the game's history – not a few of them by Matthews, indeed – without a single guernsey collar getting felt by Melbourne's finest also had a point. In an eventual autobiography, Matthews professed, along with remorse, enduring bafflement – though he also muttered

---

5   Brian Bourke represented many footballers in various brushes with the law, including Wayne
     Carey and Gary Ablett Sr – though his most famous client was Ronald Ryan, who in 1967, despite
     Bourke's best efforts, became the last man hanged in Australia. Bourke, a South Melbourne/Sydney
     barracker, was the intermediary who persuaded Norm Smith to coach South between 1969 and
     1972.

darkly that Victoria's sports minister of the time, Neil Trezise, had played for Geelong.[6]

Matthews' conviction was overturned on appeal, the fine watered down to a good-behaviour bond. Matthews played out the 1985 season, his last, finishing a 332-game career in a grand final loss to Essendon, a match also distinguished, during the first quarter, by a wild all-in which, in any other setting, would also have resulted in stretches in the hoosegow for many of its protagonists.

Evidence of hypocrisy in the scourging of Leigh Matthews was not hard to find. It may have been, however, both more and less complicated than everyone thought – that there was simply something about what Matthews did to Bruns which gripped its witnesses at a level too visceral to fully comprehend. It was not so much that the act was cowardly, though it was that, but that it was so calm: Matthews attacked Bruns not during the rough-and-tumble of general play, or in reflexive response to pain, or amid the fury of a fight, but as if he was conducting some wholly quotidian – even absent-minded – task, like looking at his watch or scratching his head. Bruns – who, like many, had grown up idolising Matthews – always professed incomprehension of his assailant's motives.

Steve Hocking's vengeance upon Matthews, while scarcely less violent, was more fathomable; you didn't need to agree with what Hocking did to understand why he'd done it. Though never formally sanctioned, Hocking did not escape punishment: there were threatening letters, and menacing calls; for a time, he kept a whistle by his phone. Not everyone who got in touch was displeased with him, however. A farmer from Colac sent him an appreciative letter and a cheque for $20; Hocking returned the money.

---

6   Neil Trezise played 185 games for the Cats between 1949 and 1959, and was a member of the 1951 and 1952 premiership teams, later becoming club captain, and club president. He was a Victorian MP representing a Geelong seat for 28 years; his son, Ian, followed him into parliament. He died in 2006; his family declined a state funeral in favour of a ceremony at Kardinia Park.

40

The Jim Stynes Aberration
Hawthorn 11.14.80 Melbourne 10.18.78
Waverley Park
PRELIMINARY FINAL, 1987

It was only a few steps in the wrong direction.

With seconds to play, Hawthorn were four points down – and five points short, therefore, of a chance to defend their 1986 premiership against Carlton the following week. Kicking in from the goal square after a behind by Melbourne, Hawthorn's captain, Michael Tuck, required not one second of his 337 games of experience to surmise that there was only one way to go, and went straight down the middle.[1] His kick was immense, reaching the edge of the centre square, and was marked by Peter Schwab, the only one of the gathering pack to correctly calculate the trajectory of Tuck's colossal bomb. Schwab played on, and handballed quickly to Chris Langford, who'd started his run before Schwab took the grab. Langford's anticipation bought him a few metres, enough to look up and see Gary Buckenara leading.

Nobody will ever know whether Buckenara would have marked it: Melbourne defender Rod Grinter[2] mowed him down with a cross between a push in the back and a trip, falling across Buckenara's legs and sending

---

1 Michael Tuck retired in 1991, on 426 games, a tally exceeded at time of writing only by Brent Harvey. Tuck is also the only player to have won seven premierships, though 1987's was not among them – Hawthorn were handily beaten by Carlton in that year's grand final, on a day so unseasonably hot that, for the only time in his career, Tuck forswore long sleeves.

2 Rod Grinter, an elegant defender when concentrating on the ball, would later claim that this contact was accidental – that he'd stumbled and fallen into Buckenara. Judging by the replays, this is believable, but even this early in Grinter's career, his record invited scepticism. In 134 games for the Demons, Grinter was suspended for 31 matches – a total exceeded in the post-war era only by Dermott Brereton and Greg Williams, who played 211 and 250 matches respectively. His hit on Footscray's Terry Wallace in 1988, which broke Wallace's jaw and left him needing 80 stitches, and plates in his face, also hospitalised Grinter when the wound in his hand caused by Wallace's teeth became infected. Wallace later sued Grinter; the case was settled out of court. Incredibly, Wallace not only played the week after Grinter flattened him, but gathered 31 disposals against Fitzroy.

him sprawling. Umpire David Howlett paid the free kick, and sprinted in to show Grinter his mark, right on the 50-metre line. Then the siren sounded.

Buckenara found himself presented with one of those situations which, depending on one's disposition, is the stuff of dreams or fuel for nightmares. If he kicked it between the big sticks, Hawthorn would go to the grand final. If he missed, or failed to make the distance, Hawthorn would be done for the season. It was certainly the most important kick of Buckenara's career – indeed, given that no grand final had been settled with a kick after the siren, it was the highest-stakes single kick in the history of the game.[3] Buckenara's name had suddenly become one that would be remembered for decades. What he would learn in the next few seconds was how.

And then something happened which, while it improved Buckenara's chances, also took the moment away from him, relegating him to second billing at what should have been the defining moment of his career. He'd taken four steps of his run-up when the umpire stopped him, and signalled a 15-metre penalty.[4] Buckenara walked forward to the new mark, helped along by a few words of encouragement from his teammate Russell Greene. Buckenara kicked truly; he usually did. His fifth goal of the afternoon put Hawthorn into the 1987 grand final, put Melbourne's guernseys in mothballs for another year, and put a lanky 21-year-old from Dublin called Jim Stynes on his way to becoming the first Irishman to be buried with full state honours in Australia since Robert O'Hara Burke.[5]

---

3   This feat was equalled, sort of, by Geelong's Gary Ablett Sr in the 1994 preliminary final against North Melbourne, but he was shooting from point-blank range with the scores level, so any score would have done (he kicked a goal). Two weeks previously, Geelong's Billy Brownless had won the qualifying final with a goal after the siren against Footscray; Geelong were a point behind when he took his kick. By far the most glorious after-the-siren kick was the one that could not be taken. At the end of the 1967 Tasmanian State Premiership final, North Hobart were a point behind Wynyard, but North's David 'Dicky' Collins, who had just marked in front of goal, had a kick after the siren to either draw or win the game. Wynyard fans invaded the ground and pulled down the goalposts. The game was declared 'no result', and the 1967 premiership was never awarded.

4   The 15-metre penalty was abolished in favour of the 50-metre penalty the following year. Buckenara's was one of the last 15-metre penalties ever awarded, and certainly the most consequential.

5   Robert O'Hara Burke and his fellow explorer William John Wills died of starvation and exhaustion near Cooper Creek in June 1861. Burke and Wills were dispatched by the Exploration Committee of the Royal Society of Victoria, the secretary of which was John Macadam – he'd been an umpire at the first game of Australian football in 1858, between Scotch College (where he was a teacher) and Melbourne Grammar, and had the macadamia nut named in his honour by the great botanist Sir Ferdinand von Mueller. Burke and Wills were also incorporated into Lou Richards' lexicon of commentary hyperbole: a player could be said to have 'covered more ground than' or 'be in more strife than' the luckless adventurers.

It was not clear, when Buckenara kicked the winning goal, that he knew why the 15-metre penalty had been paid. Jim Stynes knew: exhausted at the end of just his 13th professional match of a sport he'd barely seen played a few years previously, and deafened to the blaring siren by the screams of the crowd, he'd gone to pick up Hawthorn's Robert DiPierdomenico, and run across Buckenara's mark. Maybe Buckenara would have scored anyway, but there was no telling that to Melbourne's long-suffering fans, who'd just seen their team shunted from their first grand final appearance since 1964.

The Demons had led all day. They'd been 22 points ahead at the last change, and had created several opportunities to ice it. Tony Campbell sliced at an open goal. Simon Eishold fluffed a set shot from a few metres out, if from a tricky angle. Graeme Yeats, snapping on the run, had gone close enough that some Melbourne fans were still hugging and cheering in triumphal ecstasy as the goal umpire waved a single, sobering flag.

But it was Stynes who'd made the terminal, and therefore memorable, blunder. In a swiftly famous photo snapped in the Demons' dressing-room afterwards, Melbourne's coach, John Northey, looked some distance from taking a detached and philosophical view as he confronted a shattered, hangdog Stynes.[6] It was doubtless no consolation to Stynes – little, to judge by his desolate expression at that moment, would have been – that he could say he'd made an impact in his first season.

Stynes was an early subject of what was called 'the Irish Experiment' – initially, a hunch of Ron Barassi that players of Gaelic football might be adaptable to the Australian game. The two codes had some similarities: a requirement to bounce the ball when running with it, movement of the ball by fist as well as boot, a disdain for any offside rule. They had enough in common, indeed, that it was widely supposed that Australian football had evolved from the Irish game, brought to Victoria by Irish convicts and prospectors, much as many Australian bush ballads are appropriations of Irish folk songs. However, evidence supporting this assumption is scant – and the first rules for Gaelic football were not written until 1884, when the Gaelic Athletic Association was founded in Hayes Hotel in Thurles, County Tipperary; by 1884, the VFA had already completed eight seasons.

---

6   The picture was shot by Wayne Ludbey, then with *The Age*, who was also one of the photographers who later snapped the image of Nicky Winmar confronting Collingwood barrackers at Victoria Park. Jim Stynes married Ludbey's sister, Sam.

Melbourne's first Irish recruit was Sean Wight, a Glasgow-born Kerryman. Wight made his debut under Barassi in 1985,[7] and was in and out of the team before hardening, in 1987, into one of the rocks upon which Melbourne's resurgence was founded. If Melbourne had clung on in the 1987 preliminary final, Wight's blanketing of Dermott Brereton, held to just one goal, would have been crucial.[8]

Jim Stynes arrived at Melbourne at the end of 1984, aged 18: he'd played in the Dublin team which had beaten Tipperary in that year's All-Ireland Minor (i.e., junior) Football Final. He had a lot to learn: the first he had seen of Australian football was a screening of *The Club* on Irish television. During the gameplay sequences of the movie, he couldn't understand why the crowd cheered when a player caught the ball, and why play stopped: Gaelic football does not recognise a mark with a free kick. After playing for Melbourne's under-19 team, for whom he was runner-up best and fairest, Stynes was farmed out to Prahran in the VFA to develop further: he was runner-up best and fairest there as well.[9]

Stynes' father – who, along with Stynes' mother, had flown out from Dublin for the preliminary final – had been able to offer his son some idea of what he was getting into. In 1967, Brian Stynes had been part of the Irish Civil Service team which had provided opposition for the first match played in Ireland by the Galahs – a team of VFL superstars who went to Ireland to play the Irish at their own game. The Galahs were captained by Ron Barassi – who, 17 years later, would bring Brian Stynes' then-one-year-old son Jim to Melbourne. (Oddly, Civil Service ran the Australians closer than either the 1967 All-Ireland champions Meath, or 1967 Connacht champions Mayo.[10])

---

7   The first Irishman to play for Melbourne was Paul Earley, who arrived in Australia shortly after Wight. He made his debut in the last match of 1984, and then returned to Ireland and the Gaelic football team of his home county, Roscommon. In 2013, Earley was the coach of the Irish team that walloped Australia's all-Indigenous team in that year's International Rules series.

8   In a cruel coincidence, Sean Wight died just less than a year before Jim Stynes, also of cancer, also in his mid-40s.

9   Jim Stynes' younger brother Brian played twice for Melbourne in 1992, and was part of the Port Melbourne team which lost the 1993 VFA grand final. In 1995, he won the All-Ireland football championship with Dublin. Another intriguing what-if of the early years of Irish recruitment is Niall Quinn, who attracted attention while touring Australia as a 16-year-old with a Dublin Colleges Gaelic football side in 1983. An enquiring letter to Quinn from Sydney was delayed by a postal strike. By the time Swans administrator Greg Miller turned up on Quinn's doorstep in Dublin, he had already signed to play soccer in England; Quinn later said that such was the largesse of the Swans' package, if he'd been offered it first, he'd have taken it. Quinn was condemned to suckle on the meagre consolation of a career with Arsenal, Manchester City and Sunderland, along with 92 caps for the Republic of Ireland.

10   The Galahs tour was the notion of Harry Beitzel, umpire turned media personality and entrepreneur. He mortgaged his house to underwrite the inaugural Galahs tour in 1967. The team,

Stynes made his AFL debut in Round 3 of 1987 – and, though nobody could have known it, founded a record in Round 18: from that game to Round 4 of 1998, in which he broke a hand against Carlton, Stynes turned out in 244 consecutive League matches, playing at times through serious injuries, including broken ribs, torn muscles and busted knees, to surpass Jack Titus's decades-old mark of 202 games in a row. It was a feat of endurance that would test the bronze statue of Stynes which now adorns the MCG's Avenue of Legends, never mind a creature of flesh and blood.[11]

Stynes understood instantly, however, that his first season was only going to be recalled for one thing. He now had to decide whether the same was going to be true of his entire Australian football career. On a post-season trip to Europe to get away from it all, he realised that there would be no escape: on a bus to Charles de Gaulle airport in Paris to catch a flight to London, he was accosted by an Australian backpacker who asked him: 'Aren't you the guy who ran across the mark?' He returned to Melbourne, traded guernsey number 37 for number 11, and built a football – and post-football – career which ensured that when his agonisingly premature obituaries were written, his gaffe against Hawthorn would be buried several paragraphs deep.

Jim Stynes played 264 games for Melbourne, and was among the best ruckmen of his era. He won the Brownlow Medal in 1991 – the first foreign-born player to do so – and pretty much every other honour available other than a premiership (Melbourne did scramble into the grand final from fifth place in 1988, but were contemptuously dismembered by a Hawthorn at the peak of their 1980s pomp, who stacked up a 96-point margin with such ease that it might be vaguely wondered if the other teams in the five, aware of the looming menace, had stepped aside and waved Melbourne

---

who travelled in green blazers with a gold kangaroo on the breast pocket, and beige slouch hats, included several members of Richmond's 1967 premiership side, among other VFL stars including Bob Skilton, Alex Jesaulenko, Hassa Mann, John Dugdale, John Nicholls and Ron Barassi. The 1967 tour visited Ireland and the United Kingdom, before finishing in New York with a spirited match against a Gaelic football team substantially comprised of Irish-American police officers: Dugdale – whose 1961 mark over St Kilda's Ray McHugh adorns the cover of *Carn* – and Barassi both had their noses broken, Mann his jaw. A second Galahs tour in 1968 included fixtures in Ireland, the United Kingdom and New York, and an exhibition game in Bucharest, of all places: the Galahs played in a stadium heavily populated by soldiers, presided over by a socialist realist artwork depicting a golden sun dawning upon Nicolae Ceausescu's proletarian idyll, and a sign proclaiming 'The Communist Party of Romania Lives!' In 1994, Beitzel was imprisoned for 18 months for swindling a couple of Pools winners out of $1.8 million. He died in 2017, aged 90.

11 Jim Stynes' record stands at time of writing. Adem Yze, also of Melbourne, gave it a shake, playing 226 consecutive games between 1997 and 2007, before being dropped from the side for one week.

through, as anxious penguins on an ice floe try nonchalantly to shuffle each other into water prowled by a hungry seal). After football, Stynes' work as a youth advocate and the founder of the Reach Foundation saw him named Victorian of the Year and awarded the Order of Australia. He became Melbourne's president in 2008, helping to rescue the club from its most recent episode of self-inflicted corporate chaos. He was also chosen as the face of a television advertising campaign for Australian bananas.[12]

When Stynes got sick, he responded with the airy forbearance which characterised him as a player, to the extent that his death in 2012, aged 45, still seemed a shock despite the widespread chronicling of his illness: Stynes had been unflinching in communicating his new reality, allowing cameras to record the scans, the surgery, the coffee enemas, the elixirs of his own urine. Statements of grief were issued from all points up to and including the prime minister, Julia Gillard. The quantity of things named in Stynes' honour, whether after his death or before his cancer was even detected – the medal for the best player in the Australia versus Ireland International Rules series, a bridge over the Yarra, a function room at the MCG, a government-funded scholarship, a song by My Friend the Chocolate Cake[13] – feels, in total, not so much an effort at commemoration as a collective hope of filling the vast void Stynes left.

If Jim Stynes had been born and raised within the shadows of the MCG's floodlight towers, grown up watching and playing Australian Rules, then spent his retirement fishing, he would still be a significant figure in football. He extended the expected repertoire of the ruckman – a fearsome tackler and deft distributor as well as a reliable winner of hit-outs. But because he came from where he came from, Stynes expanded the game's possibilities in another respect. He wasn't the first foreigner to play Australia's game at the top level, and not even the first Irishman – indeed, at least two Irish-born players, St Kilda's Joe O'Grady and Collingwood's

---

12 Jim Stynes' banana commercial was inoffensive, as these things go, involving him jogging through a banana warehouse, receiving a handballed bunch of bananas from a storeman, lifting some weights and reciting a slogan – 'Bananas are good enough for me' – which did not suggest many all-night brainstorming sessions on the part of the scriptwriters. There is a rich cornucopia of terrible TV commercials featuring Australian football players, curated by YouTube enthusiasts to the mortification of their stars, who must have hoped they would be swiftly forgotten. For sheer guileless on-camera ineptitude, it's hard to beat the Tip Top spot in which West Coast's Peter Sumich is out-acted by a loaf of bread. Few, however, arch the 21st-century eyebrow quite like the Myer/VFL ad cautioning against unofficial merchandise. A shot of two men pans upwards from the floor, comparing approved North Melbourne kit with bootlegged crap. The big reveal in the last shot is a contrast between an actual footballer – in this instance Phil Krakouer – and some random Asian-looking bloke.

13 'Jimmy Stynes' was an instrumental track on My Friend the Chocolate Cake's 1994 album, *Brood*.

Denis Lanigan, appeared in Round 1, 1897.[14] But Stynes' success, Stynes' personification of the rewards of determination, and Stynes' affable accessibility, made playing in the VFL/AFL seem a more open course, wherever one came from. Tadhg Kennelly, who came from County Kerry to play 197 games for Sydney,[15] once observed that his career could not have occurred without Stynes' example; and/but so did Fiji-born West Coast ruckman Nic Naitanui.

It is fitting that Stynes is principally remembered not for a few short steps, but for this giant leap.

---

14   Also appearing that first weekend were the Fiji-born Charlie Moore of Essendon, later the first League player to die on active service, in the Boer War, and Ivan Astruc of Fitzroy, born in Mauritius. Astruc played just six games. In 1888, *The Emerald Hill Record* reported a 'dark-coloured young man' of the same name appearing before the local beak on charges of offensive behaviour, his second such charge in a matter of months. He got off after explaining his intention to move to Perth, and was discharged on that basis, an Inspector Crampton declaring 'the police would be glad to get rid of him'. Astruc died in 1905, aged 28.

15   Tadhg Kennelly is the only player to have won both an AFL premiership (with Sydney in 2005) and an All-Ireland football championship (with Kerry in 2009). Kennelly is in this respect the pub quiz obverse of Ben Graham, the only player to appear in both an AFL grand final and an NFL Super Bowl, but on the losing team both times (Geelong in 1995, Arizona in 2009).

41

The Greatest Game of All
Hawthorn 21.18.144 Geelong 21.12.138
Melbourne Cricket Ground
GRAND FINAL, 1989

A beloved sporting cliché holds that a champion team will always beat a team of champions. The Hawthorn that emerged down the concrete-and-chicken-wire players' race onto the MCG surface this afternoon were both. Hawthorn acted like they owned the place, and if possession is nine-tenths of the law, they did. The Hawks were reigning premiers, had dropped just three games in 1989, and the core coterie of this mob of swaggering superstars – Gary Ayres, Dermott Brereton, Chris Mew, Robert DiPierdomenico, Michael Tuck – were about to contest their seventh consecutive grand final.

Hawthorn's cheer squad fashioned an opulent if deeply baffling run-through, suggestive of a brains trust who had been compelled to furnish so many grand final concepts that they'd scraped through the bottom of the barrel and into the hallucinogenic fungus lurking in the shade beneath. It appeared to depict an ample-breasted black woman in a gold gown and ceremonial headdress holding a cocktail aloft in a gilt-gloved hand as she slid down one bannister of a staircase, the posts at the end of which were fashioned into matching premiership cups marked ''88' and ''89'. The words next to this rum apparition barked, in capitalised orange print on a blue background: 'WELL HELLO HAWTHORN ... IT'S SO NICE TO HAVE YOU BACK WHERE YOU BELONG.'

Geelong's run-through was more modest, depicting a Cats player atop an awkwardly sketched russet horse, bearing aloft what was doubtless supposed to be a gold premiership trophy, but which might just as well have been a light bulb or a lemon-flavoured lollipop. The accompanying caption, in one of those olde worlde fonts often favoured by newspaper mastheads, read: 'The Charge of the Blight Brigade'. Aside from the opportunity for punsmithery offered by the name of Geelong's first-year coach, Malcolm Blight, there seemed something knowing, and somehow resigned, about the slogan. Geelong, much like Lord Cardigan's doomed, vainglorious Six Hundred, had acquired a reputation for stylish offensive swashbuckle, heedless of potentially catastrophic consequence. When it worked, Geelong were awesome, but more than once during 1989, most Geelong supporters would have muttered something akin to General Pierre François Bosquet's reaction to the carnage in the Balaclava valley on the morning of 25 October 1854: 'C'est magnifique, mais ce n'est pas any sort of way to play football; c'est de la folie.'

Geelong were certainly good enough to be here. The Cats had finished the home-and-away rounds in third place, and after an aberration in the qualifying final against Essendon, in which they'd looked unusually flat-footed and faint-hearted, they'd recovered to dismiss Melbourne in the semi-final and settle the account with Essendon, by 94 points, in the preliminary final. But they lacked, as individuals and as an institution, experience of a grand final. The Cats' average age was 25, so some hadn't been alive the last time Geelong had been in this place, on this day – back in 1967, when Geelong had lost to Richmond. One Geelong player, Mark Yeates, might have been thinking of his father, John Yeates, who'd kicked two goals when Geelong beat Hawthorn to hoist the 1963 flag – but as he jogged to his position at half-forward, Yeates had other things on his mind.

Geelong did, however, have Gary Ablett. The Abletts were a Drouin clan who'd become a Hawthorn family: two of Gary's older brothers, Geoff and Kevin,[1] had played for the Hawks, and their sister, Fay, was married to Hawthorn's captain, Michael Tuck. But Hawthorn had not been able to tame Gary, and Geelong hadn't tried to, indulging his lapses in discipline, his dilatory attitude to training, even his disinterest in learning the names of his teammates. After six seasons with the Cats, there were many rational judges willing to argue that Ablett was the best

---

1   Geoff Ablett played 202 games for Hawthorn between 1973 and 1982, including the 1976 and 1978 premierships, followed by brief spells at Richmond and St Kilda. He was famed for his speed, and was a four-time winner of the grand-final half-time sprint. Kevin Ablett played 31 games for Hawthorn, and a handful more for Richmond and Geelong. Kevin's son Luke Ablett was a member of Sydney's 2005 premiership side. Following retirement from football, he worked for Family Safety Victoria and became a campaigner for gender equality.

player ever to have worn Geelong's colours; some already believed he was the best to have worn anyone's.

Gary Ablett was one of the odder bundles of contradictions ever trussed in a single sleeveless guernsey. He was built like a cruiser, but moved like a catamaran, as if operating according to his own interpretation of the laws of gravity, and terrifically quick. He was a devout born-again Christian, and yet frequently in breach of the (one would think) implicit commandment about keeping your elbows in and your fists sheathed. He played with explosive exuberance, but rarely expressed much joy in his successes: his usual reaction to applause was a shrug. During rare, reluctant forays before cameras and microphones, there was a blankness about him: probably just shyness, but possibly, it sometimes seemed, a more profound disconnect, though from exactly what was hard to say. To his clear irritation, Ablett was very much the kind of person who excited copious effusions from the armchair school of psychological analysis.

Gary Ablett was the closest thing Australian football has produced to a Diego Maradona, a mage whose abilities sometimes reduced even his fellow professionals to astonished gasps and incredulous laughter, and whose flaws occasionally caused even his team's most ardent supporters to wish vaguely that he played for someone else, so they could just enjoy him without worrying about him, or relying on him. Geelong fans endowed him with the nickname 'God'; Ablett, who took seriously the entity already operating under that trademark, was mortified.[2]

Aside from the considerable, if volatile, asset of Gary Ablett, Geelong had a plan. The plan was not, strictly speaking, 'Go heartbreakingly close to last-gasp victory against all odds in an epic of positively Wagnerian *Sturm und Drang* which will be spoken of thereafter as possibly the greatest game ever played', though this was what transpired. Geelong's plan was what military strategists call a decapitation strike: a monstrous smiting of enemy leadership early in the conflict, to sow confusion and

---

2 Earlier in 1989, amid putrid conditions as Geelong out-fought Melbourne in the MCG mud
   in Round 12, Gary Ablett dropped Melbourne's Garry Lyon behind play; Lyon would require
   12 stitches in his face. No umpire saw the assault, and no camera caught it, but after a few days'
   anguished contemplation, Ablett shopped himself to the VFL, and was suspended for three
   weeks by a hastily convened tribunal. 'Three years ago now I gave my life to Jesus Christ,' Ablett
   explained. 'My relationship with God has become everything to me in my life. I deeply regret what
   I did to Garry by striking him, but I am not prepared to lie about it or compromise the truth in
   my relationship with God.' It is likely that many among Geelong's staff and supporters reacted by
   invoking the name of Jesus Christ, possibly in connection with a bicycle. Ablett further vouchsafed
   that 'I will learn enough to make sure it doesn't happen again'. (It did.)

wither morale among opposition forces as your troops advance. The target was Dermott Brereton. The weapon was Mark Yeates.

Brereton was not Hawthorn's captain. That role was occupied, as it had been since the retirement of Leigh Matthews, by Michael Tuck, who seemed to have been at Hawthorn since the Earth cooled: he was playing his 383rd game today and looked more than ever like he'd been hewn from a petrified stringybark. But it was Brereton who was adored by the Hawks faithful as the strutting, buccaneering personification of this ruthless, invincible team – and reviled by everyone else, not coincidentally, as a preening jackass. From his lustrous curly blond locks downwards, Brereton was to 1980s football approximately what Rik Mayall's Lord Flashheart character was to *Blackadder*: an obnoxiously cocksure caricature of supercilious macho egotism who positively thrived on the irritation and resentment of others. Even more annoyingly than that, Brereton was one of the best players of his time.

Any team preparing to face Hawthorn during these years would have had a conversation about how to stop Brereton. Malcolm Blight and Mark Yeates had merely allowed their discussion to proceed to a logical, if brutal, conclusion. Yeates required little persuasion; he and Brereton had history. Back in Round 6, Hawthorn had hosted Geelong at Princes Park. It was an extraordinary, preposterous match, at the time the third-most prolific exhibition of scoring in League history, an aggregate of 334 points split narrowly the Hawks' way, 26.15.171 to 25.13.163.[3] Early in the final quarter, Brereton picked Yeates out at a boundary throw-in, took a lusty run-up, and drove a knee into Yeates' testicles. As Yeates was stretchered off, a grinning Brereton walked alongside, conveying his greetings to Yeates' wife. Grudges have been legitimately borne over less.

Pre-bounce on grand final day, John Farnham sang 'Waltzing Matilda' and then, after the teams ran out, the national anthem, accompanied by the choir of the Victorian School for the Deaf and the Victorian Children's Choir, all gathered around a logo painted on the playing surface, touting Melbourne's – optimistic, it proved – bid to host the 1996 Olympic Games. Not one of the players sang along. The coin was tossed by Australia's cricket captain, Allan Border, recently returned from

---

3   The following week, unbelievably, Geelong played a part in exceeding even this, defeating St Kilda 35.18.228 to 16.13.109 for an aggregate score of 337, the equal-second-highest total in League history. The all-time benchmark is 345, compiled in Round 6, 1978, when St Kilda beat Melbourne at the MCG, 31.18.204 to 21.15.141.

a 4–0 drubbing of England in the Ashes; the team had done a lap of honour as part of the pre-match formalities, and a rank of Merv Hughes masks along one stretch of boundary fence would provide a surreal backdrop to some of what would follow. Geelong's captain, Damian Bourke, called heads, and heads it was: the Cats would kick to the scoreboard end.[4]

At the opening siren, field umpire Peter Carey[5] held the ball aloft in his left hand, and blew the whistle affixed to his right. He took four steps towards the red and white Channel Seven logo which served as a centre circle, and 94,796 people made that noise you only really hear at the start of grand finals. Years later, Dermott Brereton would liken being in the middle of it to standing in an empty swimming pool as its full volume of water was poured in from all sides.

It wasn't a good bounce. The ball lurched to Carey's right, towards the goal Hawthorn were attacking. It didn't do either ruckman any favours. Damian Bourke had to abort his run-up as the ball threatened to float over his head, while Hawthorn's Greg Dear was suddenly presented with several yards of MCG turf to cover.

Approaching from one wing, Geelong's Neville Bruns and Hawthorn's Robert DiPierdomenico adjusted abruptly to their left. From the opposite side, Geelong's Mark Bairstow[6] and Hawthorn's Michael Tuck tacked right. Chasing the flight of the ball were Geelong's Garry Hocking and Hawthorn's John Platten. Waiting in its unintended drop zone were Geelong's recently decorated Brownlow medallist Paul Couch, and Hawthorn's Anthony Condon. Also in the centre square were two unmarked rovers, Geelong's Andrew Bews, and Hawthorn's Darrin Pritchard. For Mark Yeates, the scarlet Sherrin's skewiff trajectory made no difference – nothing would. He launched himself off Geelong's left half-forward flank, sprinting diagonally across the centre square. The ball was falling, a contest gathering, a few metres in front of him, to his left, but Yeates didn't look up, or around.

---

4   Damian Bourke joined the 1989 grand final casualty list early on, taking no part after quarter time. In the 2010s, he made two unsuccessful attempts to become the first man to complete the grand final/Mount Everest double, with a view to planting a Geelong flag on the summit. On both occasions Bourke was lucky to escape with his life after being nearly buried by avalanches.

5   Peter Carey earned a measure of clip-show immortality in Round 15, 1999. While umpiring his 299th match, between Fremantle and St Kilda at Subiaco, he inexplicably intercepted a pass from the Dockers' Adrian Fletcher to Brad Wira, marking it neatly on his chest. It remains the only thing an umpire has ever done that a crowd has found even funnier than falling over while running backwards.

6   Mark Bairstow became a successful racehorse trainer in his home state of Western Australia. His jockeys ride in blue and white hooped silks.

Dear made it to the fall of the ball just too late to compete. Bourke won the hit-out with a backhanded lob as he turned and braced for Dear's arrival. Bourke's smack forward couldn't possibly have been intended for Bews, but he couldn't have placed it more perfectly if he'd had all the time and space in time and space. Bews was first to calculate where the ball was heading, and scrambled to cover the straight line on the ground beneath its arc through the air: it landed in his arms as he reached the edge of the centre square.

Yeates hadn't changed course. He was still gathering speed. At more or less the instant Bourke's half-blind tap reached Bews, Yeates got to where he'd been going in such a hurry. Dermott Bereton had run into the centre square directly from centre half-forward, following the ball. He deviated slightly to his right as he noticed Yeates looming from his left, the Geelong player now covering the swiftly shortening distance between them with huge, urgent strides. Meanwhile, Andrew Bews, his options dwindling as Hawthorn's midfield converged, considered or dummied a handball. It fooled the incoming Chris Mew, but Mew got a handful of Bews' left arm as he stumbled, and the ball came loose.

In the centre square, Yeates' right foot hit the turf just ahead of Brereton's left. Yeates had his right shoulder up, right elbow in. Brereton drew up his left arm like a knight brandishing a shield; he was about to wish he had one. The impact, when it came, lifted both men off the ground. Geelong's Michael Schulze, unwittingly entangled in the collision, broke Yeates' fall, but not Brereton's. Brereton landed right foot, right arm, right knee, left arm, left knee. Almost immediately, he got some of the way back to his feet, and found himself facing an oncoming Yeates, who looked caught between surprise at this instant resurrection, and curiosity as to whether Brereton fancied a further helping.

Further downfield, Bews was once again first to see where the ball had gone, and where it was going. He scooped it back up just ahead of his much taller teammate Barry Stoneham. Stoneham put his heft at Bews' disposal, throwing out an arm to shepherd off DiPierdomenico. Bews evaded Mew's diving tackle, wheeled right, looked up, and kicked across his body with his left foot. Gary Ablett, leading in front of Hawthorn's Scott Maginness, marked it on his chest with a dainty leap that looked more an act of levitation than a jump. Ablett landed running, marginally inside the 50-metre line. Without breaking stride, he trotted the length of his goalkicking run-up, executing a 180-degree pirouette near the end, to face the goal. He spun the ball in his hands, and exhaled.

Brereton was crouched next to Schulze, supporting himself on his right hand, facing the ground. As Ablett ran in and kicked the game's first goal from just on the 50-metre line, Brereton collapsed and rolled onto his back, his right arm clutching the left side of his ribcage, his right foot stamping the turf in evident agony, his face a tortured rictus. Before he disappeared beneath a scrum of trainers, runners and doctors, his prone, brown-and-gold-swaddled form resembled an immense swatted wasp, unaccountably adorned with a blonde mullet. It was 34 seconds since the ball had been bounced.

Geelong's seizure of the initiative seemed complete. The opening siren's echo had barely abated, the Cats were a goal in front, Ablett was in good touch, and Brereton was hurt, by all appearances badly. But then something happened for which Geelong had not planned: Brereton got up. Not on his own – it took three trainers to lift him to his feet, and keep him there as he tottered, gasping like he couldn't breathe in or out, before erupting yellow vomit. On the sideline, Hawthorn's Greg Madigan shuffled anxiously, waiting for Brereton to be helped off, so that he could replace him in time for the restart.

Madigan, 19, might have been thinking that the foundation of a fairytale was being laid: the little-heralded kid, playing his sixth game, replacing the wounded superstar and saving the day. Echoes, he might have pondered, of Brereton's own debut, stepping up for an injured Michael Moncrieff as a scraggy, ginger-mopped 18-year-old in a semi-final in 1982, and kicking five goals against North Melbourne. But Brereton, eyes scrunched shut and mouth wide open as he tried to scream away the pain, broke into a jog and headed towards the forward pocket, as his bemused rescuers peeled away. A few minutes later, Brereton backed into a contest in the forward line, marked over his head despite the uncompromising attentions of Steve Hocking, and kicked Hawthorn's second goal of the game. (Jason Dunstall had kicked the first, from a tumbling mark taken while fending off Geelong's Tim Darcy, as he did with even the strongest defenders, like he was holding a door open for someone.)

By quarter time Geelong must have felt like a hunter who'd shot a bear, but only annoyed it. The Cats added just one more goal to Ablett's early strike, through Billy Brownless after a splendid mark over Chris Langford, but Hawthorn had answered with 8.4 – two of those goals, ludicrously, from Brereton, who'd also held his own in a scuffle against the boundary fence with Steve Hocking and Spiro Malakellis. The Hawks' 40-point lead was 23 points bigger than the one they'd held at the same stage of the previous year's grand final, in which they'd gone on to squelch Melbourne by a margin nearing triple figures. But while Geelong may have had some idea of how severely injured Brereton was – one would not have required a medical degree to correctly diagnose broken ribs – they didn't know that Brereton wasn't the only serious casualty they'd inflicted.

In one Geelong attack, Paul Couch had lumped the ball hopefully down the wing and found only Robert DiPierdomenico. But as DiPierdomenico shuffled to take the intercept mark, Gary Ablett, a decent run-up behind, saw a chance to do to DiPierdomenico what Yeates had done to Brereton. It was a signature Ablett move, the threat of which had terrorised many defenders into getting out of his way, but DiPierdomenico, who had not acquired his own fearsome reputation by giving ground at such moments, kept his eyes on the descending Sherrin. Ablett hit him like a wrecking ball toppling a statue. DiPierdomenico knew instantly that his ribs were busted, but something else was wrong: he felt like he was inflating, and everything he tried to shout to his teammates emerged in a strangled contralto.

The second quarter was better for Geelong, but not much better. Though Hawthorn could do nothing about Ablett, who kicked goals absurd even for Ablett – checkside from the pocket, sharking and snapping in one movement from a throw-in – Geelong couldn't do anything about Hawthorn. Geelong kicked five goals in the second quarter, but Hawthorn kicked four, including another by Brereton, on the run, shrugging aside three tacklers in the goal square. At half-time Geelong had clipped only three points from the deficit. Hawthorn were 37 points ahead, but were running out of players.

John Platten was concussed, by the persistent attentions of Geelong's Garry Hocking, to the extent of being genuinely uncertain where he was.[7] Gary Ayres, the heart of Hawthorn's defence, a dauntless repeller of boarders who'd won the Norm Smith Medal from the back pocket in the 1986 and 1988 grand final victories, had a torn thigh muscle, and was

---

7   In 2017, John Platten joined a legal action against the AFL launched by John Barnes (Essendon, Geelong) and Shaun Smith (Melbourne, North Melbourne), seeking compensation for concussion-related injuries. Platten, by some estimations, was concussed 36 times during his career.

at best semi-mobile. Michael Tuck had split the webbing on his left hand. DiPierdomenico couldn't breathe, and Brereton was pissing red, one kidney ruptured. Allan Jeans, Hawthorn's coach – who'd been compelled to sit out the 1988 premiership season while recovering from a brain haemorrhage – revved up his brutalised players with a quaint parable about a boy, possibly himself, who'd saved diligently to buy shoes, but at the moment of decision was tempted astray by a cheaper pair, which swiftly disintegrated. 'Pay the price,' Jeans exhorted.

The third quarter was more of the same, an exquisite exhibition of attacking football in both directions, punctuated by moments from which the eyes of children should have been decorously shielded. In the clinches and wrestles, players shovelled sand from the MCG's bald patches into each other's eyes. DiPierdomenico became – incredibly – one of only two players to have his number taken, for throwing an elbow which left Garry Hocking spitting teeth, coughing blood and playing on despite wounds which would take six stitches to close. The teams kicked six goals each: at the last break, Geelong had only reduced the lead by another point. Hawthorn still held a considerable advantage, but were running low on men and ammunition; Geelong were younger, hungrier, angrier and clearly not prepared to surrender. Military history enthusiasts among the Hawks' players, staff or supporters would have been willing the team to a last stand that was more Rorke's Drift than the Alamo.

In a frantic, furious last quarter, Geelong very nearly came over the walls. The Cats kicked eight goals, three from Ablett, their focus not diverted by the intervention of a streaker, semi-clad as Batgirl. Hawthorn could only wring three more goals out of themselves in reply. Ablett's ninth goal, from a set shot on a tight angle, brought Geelong to within 11 points. A behind by Hawthorn's Peter Curran got the Hawks to what would be their final score of 21.18.144, 12 points ahead. Geelong's David Cameron – the only other player who'd been reported, in his case for roughing up Dean Anderson – booted his second goal to get the Cats within a kick. It left 38 seconds on the clock for Geelong to tie it up – to get the ball to Ablett, and hope – and look forward to a replay the following Saturday, against a Hawthorn so grievously depleted that they might have to draft members to make up the numbers. But from the bounce, Hawthorn forced another bounce, then another, and that was it.

The bill for what Hawthorn had spent was not long in arriving. Robert DiPierdomenico was hustled from the field and into an ambulance before the medals could be presented; he'd spend a week at St Vincent's recovering from a punctured lung (and, once able to answer for his whack on Garry Hocking, would get five matches). Garry's brother Steve also spent a night in hospital, with a ruptured testicle. Many other players had cause to be grateful for the upcoming summer off.

It may have dawned more swiftly upon Geelong that they'd been part of something extraordinary. Gary Ablett had equalled Gordon Coventry's 61-year-old record for goals in a grand final, and joined Maurice Rioli in a two-man coterie of players who'd won the Norm Smith Medal playing for a beaten team. (Collingwood's Nathan Buckley and West Coast's Chris Judd would later earn the same distinction.) When Geelong got home that night, thousands of blue-and-white-bedecked barrackers waited at the town hall, their appreciation undiminished by defeat.

It would become commonplace to eulogise the 1989 grand final as not merely the greatest grand final ever played, but the greatest game ever played. It is a makeable case, but not an unanswerable one. It was a glorious game of football, but many great games have been forgotten. It had the advantage of being a grand final, and grand finals are by definition dramatic, deciding as they do which of two groups of men will be beatified as immortal champions, and which will become the object of – depending on the margin – rage or pity. But being a grand final is no guarantee of lodgement in the collective memory: it is difficult to imagine that generations yet unborn will clamour for great-grandparental recollections of Hawthorn's lugubrious dismantling of Fremantle in 2013, for example.

There was, of course, the unbridled gladiatorial violence of 1989, and the enjoyment of officially unsanctioned biffo by fans and players alike is as transparent as the pretence of media and officialdom to be appalled by it. But violence is not unusual in grand finals, especially not the grand finals of the time: during the Hawthorn/Essendon rivalry of the 1980s, the bench-clearing melee seemed as fixed a part of grand final ritual as the national anthem.

The 1989 grand final endures because it was great drama, and like all great drama was carried by great characters – some of whose stature has since burgeoned, for one reason or another, further burnishing the reputation of this game. Brereton, DiPierdomenico and Ablett especially were personae who could only have flourished as they did in a less policed, less ruly, less businesslike age. It was an illustration of what was lost – and what was gained – so stark as to verge on cartoonish that a footballing universe whose domineering presence was Gary Ablett Sr was succeeded by one whose pre-eminent role model was Gary Ablett Jr. Ablett Jr was completely and unmistakably a professional, in every sense of the term. His father seemed, even then, and much the more so in retrospect, like an escapee from the yarns of Henry Lawson – the sort of peculiar, irascible warlock you hear of in fairytales and bush ballads, not see on a football field, or indeed anywhere in real life.[8]

But the real reason for the unceasing reverent elegies for this game is that it denoted, uncannily precisely, the end of an era. The 1989 grand final was the last game played under the aegis of the Victorian Football League. From 1990, the VFL would be superseded by the Australian Football League, formal acknowledgement of the game's evolution from a semi-amateur tribal passion play among the suburbs of Melbourne to a professional national competition. For those who cleaved to an old-school view of Australian Rules, the 1989 grand final was the last game of football – and as far as could be imagined from the least.

---

8   Dermott Brereton and Robert DiPierdomenico found their aptitude for showmanship readily convertible to post-football careers in media, Brereton emerging as an engaging analyst, DiPierdomenico as an ebullient wag and raconteur. Ablett was never any more comfortable in the spotlight than a goat is on a skateboard, and following his retirement at the end of 1996, embraced the opportunity to vanish from it, re-emerging into view only in circumstances involuntary and/or bizarre – most infamously when he was convicted of several charges relating to the fatal overdose of a 20-year-old fan, Alisha Horan, in his room at Melbourne's Park Hyatt in 2000. Ablett also made a few half-hearted attempts at evangelism: an eccentric op-ed under his name, entitled 'What Kind of World Do We Want to Live In?', was published for reasons surpassing understanding by *The Herald Sun* in 2010. So far as it was possible to tell, it was some sort of argument against the conclusions of Charles Darwin, commingled with a generic why-oh-why philippic about the decadence of the modern world.

42

The Highest Score
Brisbane 11.9.75 Geelong 37.17.239
Carrara Stadium
ROUND 7, 1992

Every time a record is set, it poses a question: is that it? Have we reached the limit of what is possible?

In athletics, it's a question of the capacities of human physiology. Nobody is ever going to run 100 metres in three seconds, or clear 20 metres at the high jump, or wang a discus out of an Olympic stadium into the car park, and into the annals of unlikely insurance claims by luckless motorists. So the ultimate record for all such events is somewhere between these absurd hypotheticals, and where we are now – and closer to the latter than the former.

In team sports, such as the various codes of football, time is the crucial factor. However brittle the opposition, getting a ball to a goal still consumes an amount of the clock, so there is only so much damage one can do to even the most feeble opponents, before the final whistle/siren – or a game-ending pitch invasion by irate fans brandishing uprooted stadium seats – delivers them from their misery. In some team sports, the scale of such batterings is also limited by local manners – in American football, the transgression censoriously known as 'piling it on' would be regarded as not cricket, if anybody involved knew or cared what cricket was, and no advantage in the league table is gained by running up what would be regarded as a cricket score, if anybody involved ditto.

Australian football lends itself to the thoroughgoing flogging for three reasons. One, it's a fast-moving, free-scoring game. Two, the practice of separating teams with equal points on the ladder by calculating points scored versus points conceded as a percentage is incentive to dish out a proper hammering if the opportunity presents itself. Three, it is the national sport of a people traditionally unsqueamish about pressing an advantage on the sports field, far past the point at which many folk would say something to the effect of 'Come on, chaps, let's not rub it in'. Recall the Socceroos' qualifying campaign for the 2002 World Cup, during which, across three infamous days in Coffs Harbour, they plastered Tonga 22–0 and pasted American Samoa 31–0, or Ricky Ponting batting again at the First Test in Brisbane during the 2006–07 'revenge' Ashes, despite holding a first innings lead of 445.

Brisbane had no reason to feel especially foredoomed as they welcomed Geelong to Carrara. The Bears had drawn with West Coast the week before, had enjoyed a bye the week before that, and had beaten Fitzroy the week before that. They knew that Geelong were themselves fresh from a bye, and prior to that had also beaten West Coast and trounced Richmond – but also that the Cats would be deploying a makeshift midfield, with Paul Couch, Garry Hocking and Neville Bruns all sidelined by injury. If ever conditions seemed auspicious for the assembly of the highest score in League history, it wasn't today.

Things started coming unglued for Brisbane on the Friday before this Sunday afternoon fixture. After training, four certain starters reported themselves injured: reigning best and fairest Michael McLean, Darryl White,[1] Marcus Ashcroft[2] and former Fitzroy ruckman Matt Rendell, all players any side would miss. Emergencies Matthew Ahmat and Nigel Palfreyman, both inexperienced teenagers, were summoned, along with reserves players Simon Luhrs and Craig Potter. Brisbane now faced $6000 in fines for starting two players not named by the Thursday night deadline, but doubtless reassured themselves that things could hardly meander any further awry.

Then, the day before the game, stalwart defender John Gastev, on his way to being the Bears' best and fairest for 1992, bailed out, his troublesome hip playing up. And then, Brisbane having made it onto the ground without any section of the squad being obliterated by a harpsichord falling from an overflying cargo plane, or any similar unlikely calamity,

---

1   Darryl White is not a member of the coterie of players who have scored a goal with their first kick in the AFL, but he is the only player whose first goal in the AFL has been acclaimed that season's Goal of the Year (he also polled three Brownlow votes on debut, in the same game in 1992). White was later a member of Brisbane's triple premiership side of the early 2000s, and named at full-back in the Indigenous Team of the Century.

2   Marcus Ashcroft was the first Queenslander to play 300 AFL games. He was also a triple premiership player with Brisbane.

ruckman Roger Merrett, who had come from Essendon in 1988 to captain the Bears through what would be remembered as the 'Bad News' years,[3] did a knee at the opening bounce. He'd miss the rest of the game, and the next six weeks.

All of which was unfortunate; none of which quite explained what ensued. At quarter time it didn't look that bad, or at least no worse than might have been expected from a good team playing a not very good team who'd lost five first-choice players in the previous 48 hours: Geelong led 7.4 to 2.2. There was one ominous portent: Gary Ablett already had three goals. Anxious Brisbane players, and fretful Bears fans, may have been pondering the previous day's near-equalling of the single-game goals record by Hawthorn's Jason Dunstall, who'd kicked 17.5 against Richmond, and worrying that Ablett had seen it as a gauntlet hurled at his feet.

A historian who only had the scores to go on might wonder if Brisbane came out for the second quarter. It would have made little difference if they hadn't. Geelong kicked nine more goals, abetted by Brisbane defenders who could only have been more accommodating if they'd lain their guernseys over any muddy patches. Andrew Wills sauntered unhindered through midfield to score one. Billy Brownless led into space which would have permitted the establishment of a medium-sized cattle station to set up another. Paul Brown scored from a handball chain started on the half-back line by Gary Ablett, wandering far from his post in search of further amusement. At half-time, Geelong had their century up, while Brisbane hadn't added to their two goals. If the scores had been reversed, the visitors could have blamed the heat: the crowd of just 7645 looked to be wearing maybe half that many shirts. Brisbane, the home team, had played most of the first half like they'd not only never seen the ground before, but like they'd never seen the game before.

The second half was played under lights, as a humid gloom encroached. For Brisbane, this was a mixed blessing. On one hand, it seemed to enable the Bears to at last find the goals, as they kicked five in the third quarter. On the other, it meant that such fans as remained in the ground, due to morbid curiosity or alcoholic incapacity, had a clear

---

3   Brisbane acquired the 'Bad News Bears' soubriquet during their lean and occasionally farcical early years via the 1976 baseball comedy starring Walter Matthau and Tatum O'Neal. Brisbane were also occasionally, if no less derisively, addressed as the 'Carrara Koalas', in reference to the motif which adorned the Bears' early branding, to the anguish of pedants troubled by the fact that the koala is not a bear.

view of Geelong scoring another seven, including three more by Ablett, who was kicking roughly every other goal with his non-preferred left foot, as if to issue himself with the challenge that Brisbane's backline were declining to. At three-quarter time Geelong led by 102 points, 23.14 to 7.8. Geelong's players may have been surprised, therefore, to find themselves huddling around an irate coach: Malcolm Blight rocketed his Cats for abandoning team principles and playing for themselves.

The message was received. In the final quarter, Geelong exuded a faintly crazed quality, like marauding soldiers, high on the rush of conquest, giddily looting a captured palace. They kicked 12 further goals, Ablett adding two more, including one with his left boot from beyond 50 metres. Geelong started the quarter 86 points behind the all-time high score – 36.22.238, posted by Fitzroy against Melbourne in 1979 – but reeled this quarry in, at first improbably, then inexorably, and finally inevitably, for the second-highest fourth-quarter score of all time, and the third-highest score in any quarter.[4] Andrew Bews equalled Fitzroy's record with a goal after another uncontested mark. Billy Brownless, marking ahead of Brisbane's Richard Champion,[5] a hardline holdout of the 1980s mullet, put Geelong ahead on the siren with a hooked behind.

'Be kind and make it brief,' Brisbane coach Robert Walls asked the media afterwards. 'You can understand how I feel.' But it could have been worse for Brisbane. They had John Hutton, who kicked eight of their 11 goals, to thank for the fact that they didn't concede both the highest score and the biggest winning margin. The other Bear able to limp off with chin up was former Cat Shane Hamilton, who collected a game-high 35 disposals. The 164 points between the two sides was only – well, 'only' – the sixth-most monumental annihilation of all time.

The deluge by which all such baths are measured remained the 190 points by which Fitzroy engulfed Melbourne in that Round 17 of 1979 – in which Walls had played for Fitzroy, contributing three of the Lions'

---

4   The record in both categories is the 17.4 South Melbourne scored in the last quarter against St Kilda in Round 12 of 1919, en route to a 171-point victory. Harold Robertson kicked 14 goals for South, seven during the final-quarter blitz. He was the brother of the champion sprinter and South Melbourne player Austin 'Ocker' Robertson.

5   Richard Champion became a television and radio presenter, motivational speaking impresario, and so forth. Among other accomplishments, he was a contestant on TV talent quest *It Takes Two*, in which celebrities performed duets opposite actual singers until the general public decided they had been sufficiently delighted. In the show's first season, Champion and assigned partner Wendy Matthews, late of Models and Absent Friends, survived seven episodes before their rendition of Huey Lewis & The News' 'The Power of Love' earned them the shepherd's crook. In season three, Russell Robertson, still playing at Melbourne, outstripped this accomplishment: in cahoots with Kate Ceberano, he was runner-up to Julia Morris and David Hobson.

36 goals. In Round 19 of 2011, Geelong got to within a goal of eclipsing both records, also against Melbourne: the Cats scored 233 points and won by 186, the Demons eventually rallying, relative to the somnolent indifference they had exhibited up to that stage, to hold Geelong to a single behind in the last two and a half minutes.

The record established by Geelong against Brisbane on this cruel afternoon in 1992 may stand forever. Salary caps and the draft have made the League more balanced. Defences have got better organised. As football has become more generally professional, the complete collapse of unit cohesion necessary to allow one team to score 30 or more goals has become extremely unusual. In the entire 21st century to date, the 200-point mark has been cleared only twice, both by Geelong: 35.12.222 against Richmond in 2007, and 37.11.233 in that rout of Melbourne in 2011, both contests between rampant premiers-in-waiting and dispirited rabbles so completely hapless as to prompt speculation vis-à-vis how much more embarrassing it could really have been if Geelong had played against 22 members of the crowd, selected by lottery.

43

Nicky Winmar Makes His Point
Collingwood 15.14.104 St Kilda 18.18.126
Victoria Park
ROUND 4, 1993

Clive MacKinnon, the photographer from *The Sun* who captured what was, before today, the most famous still image of Australian football, nearly missed the shot. High in the Members' Pavilion of the MCG on grand final day in 1970, perceiving a lull in the action late in the second quarter, *The Age*'s photographer Dennis Bull offered MacKinnon and *The Herald*'s photographer Bruce Howard his bag of Minties. It was a comradely gesture that might have had calamitous consequences, had MacKinnon not looked up prior to unwrapping his lolly and yelped, 'Look out, the ball's coming back!' All three men raised their lenses in time to snap Carlton's Alex Jesaulenko climbing Collingwood's Graeme Jenkin. MacKinnon's shot was the pick, capturing Jesaulenko at the peak of his ascent, hair and sideburns swept backwards by the winds of this rarefied altitude, splayed hands forming a cradle for the incoming ball, concentration miraculously unimpaired by vertigo.

MacKinnon's photograph is a masterpiece, and it would have been a shame if he hadn't got it: it is a quintessential summary of the graces of Australia's game. But if MacKinnon's attention had been any further diverted by Bull's Minties, we would still have seen Jesaulenko's mark, caught as it was by Channel Seven's cameras, and perfectly soundtracked by commentator Mike Williamson's immortal exclamation: 'Jesaulenko, you beauty!'[1]

---

1   Alex Jesaulenko rose to VFL superstardom from a supremely unlikely background. He was born a few weeks before the end of World War II in Salzburg, to a Ukrainian father who had served as a German police officer and a Russian mother who had already had one son called Alexander: the

If *The Sunday Age*'s Wayne Ludbey and *The Sunday Herald Sun*'s John Feder hadn't been keeping an eye – and a lens – on St Kilda's Nicky Winmar at the end of this spiteful match at Victoria Park, it is hard to know where to begin calculating what we would never have had. Winmar would still have done what he did – nothing about his demeanour suggested that he was playing to a camera – but his gesture would have lodged only in the recollections of the Collingwood barrackers towards whom it was made, who were unlikely to have been keen, all things considered, to tell the country about it.

St Kilda had played well. Not only had the Saints beaten Collingwood, who'd won their first three games of 1993, they'd beaten Collingwood in the legendarily antagonistic cauldron of Victoria Park, where St Kilda hadn't won since 1976 – a season in which Collingwood had been wooden-spooners – and they'd done it without their principal offensive weapon, Tony Lockett, suspended again, and largely without their midfield motor Robert Harvey, injured during the second quarter.[2] Two St Kilda players had been especially brilliant. One, Gilbert McAdam, a nippy forward, finished with five goals. The other, Nicky Winmar, an irrepressible winger as tough as he was fast – and he was plenty fast – had dispatched 20 kicks, scored one goal and laid seven tackles, continuing a run of early-season form already making bookmakers nervous about taking bets on the Brownlow.

Both men were Aboriginal: McAdam from Alice Springs via Central Districts in the SANFL, with whom he'd won the 1989 Magarey Medal, and Winmar from Pingelly via South Fremantle in the WAFL. McAdam had joined the Saints in 1991, Winmar in 1987. McAdam hadn't played at Victoria Park before, and though Winmar had warned him what to expect, he was still taken aback, as any decent person would have been, by the reception from Collingwood's cheer squad when the pair walked onto the ground at half-time in the reserves' game to size up the surface. 'Petrol-sniffers, abos, coons – they were calling us everything,' recalled

---

child had been removed from her and taken to the Lebrechtsdorf-Potulitz concentration camp in Nazi-occupied Poland, and was presumed dead. (He survived the war, however, and was eventually reunited with his mother, and introduced to his famous half-brother and namesake, in 1994.) In 1949, the family – then called Esaulenko – emigrated to Australia, where, after a stretch at the Bonegilla migrant camp near Wodonga, they set up home in Canberra. Alex Jesaulenko played 256 games and in four premierships for Carlton, and 23 games for St Kilda. He also coached both teams, and is almost certainly the last premiership captain-coach (Carlton, 1979) in VFL/AFL history.

2   Robert Harvey won consecutive Brownlow medals in 1997 and 1998, and set a club record of 383 games for St Kilda.

McAdam later. In the middle of the ground, he said to Winmar: 'Bro, we've got to do something today. We've got to make a statement. We'll show this mob, we'll make them quiet.'

On McAdam's own terms, they recorded a partial success. That they had shown this mob was beyond doubt. St Kilda had the win, iced with a point-blank goal after the siren by centre half-forward Stewart Loewe to make the margin 22 points, and (it would later be learned) McAdam had the three Brownlow votes, Winmar two, despite having his mercurial mobility limited by a back injury. But their heroics had not made Victoria Park quiet. The abuse of McAdam and Winmar, persistent throughout the game, swelled to an even uglier crescendo at the finish.

When the siren sounded, Winmar was well within hearing of the Collingwood cheer squad. His initial celebration of victory was orthodox: arms aloft, a tight turn in a gleeful circle. But then something caught his ear, or his imagination. Winmar turned to the purple-faced chorus in black and white stripes, lifted his guernsey with his right hand to expose half a torso of skin, and pointed to it with the extended middle digit of his left hand. 'I'm black, and I'm proud to be black,' he hollered at the aggrieved throng, before blowing them a kiss and jogging off in search of McAdam. Winmar made a point of being the last St Kilda player to leave the field; he was spat on as he jogged up the race into the dressing-rooms. By then, Gilbert McAdam's father, Charlie, down from Alice Springs to watch the match, had long since left the ground in tears, unable to listen to any more of what was being bellowed at his son.[3]

Of the two photographers who caught Winmar's salute to the Magpies fans, Wayne Ludbey had slightly the better shot – he'd been closer, and captured a full-length image of Winmar with his features arrayed in a steely grimace of jut-jawed, purse-lipped, fiery-eyed defiance. This would be the image people thought of later when they thought of it. John Feder had Winmar from the knees up, his mouth slightly open in an awkward smile around his white mouthguard. It was still a great photograph, but it radiated a somewhat pleading aspect. In Feder's picture, Winmar looked like he was asking for respect. In Ludbey's, he was insisting on it.

---

3   Gilbert McAdam played 53 games for St Kilda, and another 58 for Brisbane. After retiring from football, he became one of the inaugural hosts of National Indigenous Television's *Marngrook Footy Show*, before going home to Alice Springs in 2018 to host a radio sports show for the Central Australia Aboriginal Media Association.

The Sunday Age ran Wayne Ludbey's picture on page one, below the fold. *The Sunday Herald Sun* also put John Feder's on the front. But both photographers had to push hard at editors who couldn't – or wouldn't – quite see the significance of the moment. *The Age*'s accompanying report acknowledged that Winmar was reacting to racist taunting. *The Herald Sun* preferred to write it up as a less loaded gesture of triumph, though this seemed akin to captioning the clenched-fist black power salute by Tommie Smith and John Carlos from the podium at the 1968 Olympics – a gesture to which Winmar's would eventually be compared – as some sort of advertisement for gloves.[4] *The Herald Sun*'s copy noted merely that Winmar had 'copped plenty of flak', declining to note the precise nature of said flak, and concluded that Winmar's message had been 'We won with determination', which was one way of putting it. While the arguments consumed the newsrooms, Winmar spent the night at the Egypt-themed Richmond home of former *Countdown* presenter – and steadfast St Kilda fan – Ian 'Molly' Meldrum, who often hosted the Saints' post-match soirees.[5]

Reactions to the Winmar photo over the following days – and years – confirmed that the only people who didn't grasp its subtext and significance were those who were determined not to. *The Herald Sun* was notably shy about following it up: *The Age* better appreciated what it had. On the Monday following the game, Garry Linnell used his column in *The Age* to suggest that racial abuse on the football field be made a reportable offence. On the Tuesday, *The Age* reiterated this suggestion in its leader

4   The third man on the podium in Mexico City in 1968 was silver medallist Peter Norman of
      Australia, who had finished between Tommie Smith and John Carlos in the final of the men's
      200 metres – Norman's time of 20.06 seconds remains an Australian record. As Smith and Carlos
      raised their fists, Norman wore in support the badge of the Olympic Project for Human Rights – a
      protest movement, rather than an official Olympic organisation. Smith and Carlos were pallbearers
      at Norman's funeral in 2006. In 2012, Australia's parliament apologised to Norman for his non-
      selection for the 1972 Munich Games, an exclusion long suspected to be related to his actions in
      1968, though the Australian Olympic Committee disputed this. (Norman, in fairness, admitted that
      he was an unlikely selection after finishing third in the 1972 Australian national championships.)
      The AOC awarded Norman its Order of Merit in 2018.
5   Ian 'Molly' Meldrum adored St Kilda like he adored pop music, with an indiscriminate
      enthusiasm – St Kilda being, for most of Meldrum's life, the footballing equivalent of, say,
      Countdown favourites Uncanny X-Men, i.e. clearly keen, just no bloody good. In 1963, Meldrum,
      then a 20-year-old member of St Kilda's cheer squad, interceded in the Saints' final home-and-
      away match of the season. St Kilda began the day in fifth place, needing a percentage-boosting win
      against North Melbourne to reach the finals. In the fourth quarter, Meldrum, sporting a long scarf
      and a straw boater in Saints colours, climbed the Junction Oval pickets and ran out to St Kilda
      ruckman Alan Morrow and urged him to step it up, before being escorted from the arena by a
      police officer. St Kilda kicked nine more goals, doubling their three-quarter-time score to win by 84
      points and scrape into the four. (The Saints lost the semi-final to Melbourne.) The first of Meldrum's
      trademark Stetsons was a gift from St Kilda president Lindsay Fox.

column – opposite a brutal but perfect cartoon by Peter Nicholson, showing Winmar's gesture being mirrored by a braying, spluttering, beanie-blinded troglodyte behind the fence, lifting his shirt to reveal his protuberant white beer gut.

The next edition of *The Sunday Age* dedicated its entire letters section to the discussion – all of them, including a couple from Collingwood supporters, pro-Winmar (it is far from impossible that *The Age*'s editors also found themselves furnished with a wide selection of anti-Winmar missives, some possibly even punctuated, which they declined to print; there is much to be said for the days before social media issued a megaphone to every blockhead with a grudge). In Sydney, Australia's minister for immigration and ethnic affairs, Nick Bolkus, made approving reference to Winmar's gesture in a speech at a United Nations conference on racism: 1993 was the UN's International Year for the World's Indigenous Peoples, and would also be the year in which Australia's parliament passed the *Native Title Act*.

Collingwood's attempts at crisis management, meanwhile, were akin to a householder trying to evict a spider from his sink by unleashing upon his bathroom a bear, a flock of bats, and more spiders. Club president Allan McAlister, known for camera-shyness in the same way that Victoria Park was known as a genteel salon of cucumber sandwiches and languidly exchanged Latin quips, presented himself to Channel Nine's *Sports Sunday* and suggested that Aboriginal players need have no fears: 'As long as they conduct themselves like white people, well, off the field – everybody will admire and respect them.' Rather than – as might have been proper – recusing himself to a remote hermitage and an eternity of abject, penitent, silent shame, McAlister followed that up with: 'As long as they conduct themselves like human beings, they will be alright. That's the key.'

McAlister swiftly apologised – as did Collingwood captain Tony Shaw, who hadn't played in the game against St Kilda, but who had, in an interview ignored a few years previously, but now disinterred, said: 'I'd make a racist comment every week if I thought it would help win the game.'[6] McAlister also embarked on a goodwill tour of Aboriginal

---

6 Tony Shaw played 313 games for Collingwood between 1978 and 1994, and was the Norm Smith Medal–winning captain of the 1990 team that ended the Magpies' widely enjoyed 32-year premiership drought. In 1992, a survey of AFL footballers by *The Sunday Age* named Shaw the second-most disliked player in the competition, behind West Coast's Karl Langdon.

communities in the Northern Territory. It was a well-meaning, if tone-deaf excursion: some argued that McAlister was reinforcing an idea of Aboriginal Australia as exotic, outback, rather than dealing with the problem at his own club. (It was also vociferously noted by Magpies fans – correctly, if not with the most pure-hearted of motives – that Collingwood was hardly alone in needing to sort itself out on this front.)

While this hullabaloo accelerated, St Kilda instructed Nicky Winmar and Gilbert McAdam not to speak to the media, possibly a measure to protect the players, possibly an attempt to keep the Saints focused on a promising season – but lent a lustre of the surreal by the fact that Winmar and St Kilda were at loggerheads. Winmar wanted more money, which St Kilda did not want to pay him; he sat out the next two games before a truce was reached. He stayed at the Saints another five seasons, becoming the first Indigenous player to reach 200 League games, and finished his career with a season at Western Bulldogs in 1999. Winmar had been, at times, as much a headache for his own clubs as for his many bewitched opponents, but he'd have been famous even without the moment which made him famous.

Nicky Winmar did not arrive at Victoria Park in 1993 with any ambitions of becoming a symbol or a spokesman, and he developed little appetite for either. He led an itinerant post-football life in the West Australian bush from which he'd sprung, sometimes happy to give interviews on the anniversary of the photo, sometimes cutting up mobile phone SIM cards so people couldn't call him. As the fates had it, he ended up a figurehead of sorts for another community long marginalised within football. In 2016, Winmar helped promote the AFL's first Pride game, between Sydney and St Kilda, draped in a rainbow-coloured scarf alongside his gay son, Tynan.

Winmar's 1993 gesture proved obstinately resonant. It was copied by a new generation of Indigenous players – Shaun Burgoyne, Paddy Ryder, Andrew Walker, Lindsay Thomas – for an advertisement to promote Indigenous Round in 2013. It inspired a song, 'The Colour of Your Jumper', which was performed by Archie Roach at the Dreamtime at the 'G game that same year (Indigenous Round and Dreamtime at the 'G both being ripples from the rock Winmar dropped at Victoria Park). The Melbourne Museum paid $100,000 for the number 7 guernsey that Winmar had lifted to reveal himself. In 2018, a bronze statue of Winmar striking his famous pose was raised outside the new Perth Stadium, a location appropriate to where Winmar came from, if a strange distance from where he made his stand.

The year of the Winmar photo turned out to be one of those years when sport spins a yarn with a moral to it. The 1993 premiership – the premiership, that is, of the International Year for the World's Indigenous Peoples, as well as a year in which football's treatment of its Aboriginal players was scrutinised as never before – was won by Essendon. On grand final day, Michael Long[7] took charge against Carlton, kicking two goals and gathering 33 possessions to become the first Indigenous winner of the Norm Smith Medal. Earlier that week, Long's Indigenous teammate Gavin Wanganeen[8] had won the Brownlow Medal. Nicky Winmar had written the headline; the story appeared obediently beneath it.

---

7   In November 2004, Michael Long undertook a walk from his home in Melbourne to Canberra, to meet Prime Minister John Howard to discuss Indigenous issues. The Long Walk is now the name of both an Indigenous advocacy charity, and a ceremony preceding the Dreamtime at the 'G match during Indigenous Round.

8   Gavin Wanganeen's 1993 Brownlow Medal, though entirely deserved, was nevertheless shrouded in controversy. Wanganeen won by a point from Carlton's Greg Williams – who polled no votes for his efforts against Melbourne in Round 10, when he had 44 disposals and was best afield by a margin that Blind Freddy, had he been among the umpires, could not have missed. Williams had already won the 1986 Brownlow Medal with Sydney, tying with Hawthorn's Robert DiPierdomenico – a result which, given that it necessitated Williams and DiPierdomenico both getting through a season unsuspended, might have been regarded by more superstitious peoples as a portent on a par with the birth of a five-headed goat. Williams would enjoy some consolation for the 1993 snub by winning a second Brownlow in 1994, but never relinquished his claim on the third he believed he had been unfairly denied. In 2006, he appeared vindicated. One of the umpires in the infamous 1993 game, Murray Bird, said that he'd made a case for Williams, but had been overruled by his senior partner, John Russo, who had not appreciated Williams' input vis-à-vis his interpretations of the game's laws during the match in question. ('Fuck him,' was Bird's recollection of Russo's reaction – a claim Russo denied.) Williams instructed solicitors to examine his options, to little avail.

44

Anzac Day
Collingwood 17.9.111 Essendon 16.15.111
Melbourne Cricket Ground
ROUND 4, 1995

Before 1915, 25 April was just another date.

In 1914, 25 April was Round 1 of just another VFL season. It was also, possibly – we know it was 'one night the latter part of April'[1] – the same date that a gang of excitable young Bosnian Serbs passed around their table in the Zlatna Moruna café in downtown Belgrade a newspaper clipping announcing that Archduke Franz Ferdinand, heir to the Austro-Hungarian throne, would be visiting Sarajevo a couple of months hence.

On 25 April 1914 Essendon drew with Geelong, 8.13 each at Corio Oval. At Victoria Park, Collingwood drew with Carlton, 8.8 to 6.20. A year to the day later, one of Collingwood's better players against Carlton, defender Alan Cordner, climbed out of a boat approaching the dent of Turkish shoreline not yet known as Anzac Cove.

By the end of 25 April 1915, Cordner – a relation of the Cordner dynasty who would play mostly for Melbourne – was listed missing. He was declared dead a year later. His body was never found; nor was the gold pocket watch Collingwood had presented to him prior to his embarkation. He was one of six current or former VFL players known to

---

1   This is according to the recollections of Borijove Jevtic, one of the conspirators who plotted the killing of Franz Ferdinand. Other accounts vary, and are less convenient to the elegant butterfly-wing narrative being established here, but: it is as likely as not that on 25 April 1914 a group of young men in Belgrade were contemplating the murder which would make 25 April 1915 a venerated date in Australian history, and – eventually – the Anzac Day game a highlight of the AFL calendar. It's not even impossible that a descendant of one of the Archduke's assassins has played in the fixture, or one day will.

have been killed at Gallipoli on the first day of battle.[2] Jimmy Gordon, who kicked two goals for Essendon at Corio in Round 1 of 1914, would be wounded five times on active service, before being killed in action in France in September 1918, weeks before the war's end.

You can read too much into coincidences; indeed, almost any amount you read into coincidences is too much. And if one is determined to read something into Collingwood and Essendon playing a draw on Anzac Day 80 years on from 25 April 1915 – and 81 years since they played a draw on the same date, admittedly against other clubs – it's hard to know what, though there's something symmetrical about a game commemorating World War I being fought to a stalemate. Any such bewilderment seems as congruent to the occasion as the result: the story of Anzac Day has been, in no small part, the story of Australia's ongoing attempt to figure out what Anzac Day actually means. Since 1995, one of the focuses of that discussion has been an annual football game, between the Bombers and the Magpies.

Just as Australia and New Zealand co-opted Gallipoli after 1915, to the extent that the thousands of British, Irish, French, Indian (and Turkish) troops buried on the peninsula lie substantially unremembered, so Essendon and Collingwood claimed Anzac Day after 1995 so completely that the memory of earlier games on that date has faded. The first were played in 1960 – a volte-face from 1959, when 25 April was still regarded as so sacrosanct that, because Anzac Day fell on a Saturday that year, there was a two-week gap between Round 1 and Round 2. But late in 1959, the Returned Servicemen's League in Victoria polled its members about the future of Anzac Day observance – whether to maintain the shuttered, austere status quo, or permit a measure of frivolity. By a hefty margin, the RSL's members were in favour of lightening up a little – and the RSL perceived an opportunity for fundraising. In April 1960, just in time for the new season, Victoria's parliament decided to allow sport and other entertainment on the sacred date so long as it did not clash with marches and services.

The VFL was initially wary; the fixture for 1960 had already been drawn up. A few days before the season opened, the League had

---

2   Among them was Lieutenant Rupert Balfe, who'd played a handful of games for University. A medical student, Balfe was also a friend of Robert Menzies, future prime minister, who mourned Balfe in verse in *The Brunswick & Coburg Leader* in July 1915. Menzies' valedictory poem read, in part: 'The blood of chivalry/Pulsed quicker in his veins/He could not stay!' Menzies, however, did stay – and, while declining to enlist in the Australian Imperial Force himself, enthusiastically supported conscription for overseas service.

a rethink. It was announced that Fitzroy versus Carlton at Brunswick Street and St Kilda versus Melbourne at the Junction Oval would be played on Anzac Day – which, in 1960, was a Monday, which made rescheduling easier. Fearers of a vindictive God were given cause for concern by a storm which struck on the Wednesday before, and drenched Melbourne for 72 hours. The front page of Saturday's edition of *The Age* bore photographs of a tram ploughing gamely through waist-deep water on Mount Alexander Road in Flemington, and an FJ Holden being driven along a footpath flooded higher than the car's front bumper. All four VFL matches scheduled for the Saturday were called off. On the Monday, the two Anzac Day games went ahead, drawing a combined crowd of 65,815: £1341, 19 shillings and tuppence was raised for RSL funds. There were mutterings that the VFL had declined to also play the four abandoned Saturday matches on Anzac Day for fear of obliging themselves to further charity. Victoria's premier, Henry Bolte,[3] frothed that the League had conjured 'a proper mess'.

A precedent of football on Anzac Day was nevertheless instituted, and emulated most years thereafter. These games were popular. In 1977, 92,436 people packed the MCG on Anzac Day to see Collingwood, revitalised by first-year coach Tom Hafey, beat Richmond, who'd let Hafey go despite four premierships in 11 years – against stiff competition, possibly the most sensationally self-abnegating decision ever made by the Punt Road brains trust. In 1986, the VFL pushed its luck and used Anzac Day to stage its first double-header; only 40,000 odd were enticed to the MCG by Melbourne versus Sydney followed by North Melbourne versus Geelong. This experiment was not repeated, but Anzac Day football continued. In 1994, the year before Essendon and Collingwood staked their claim on the date, St Kilda played Richmond on 25 April at Waverley.

The Essendon versus Collingwood Anzac Day blockbuster was the notion of Essendon coach Kevin Sheedy. By 1995, Sheedy was about halfway into a near three-decade shift at Windy Hill, and he remembered playing for Richmond in that teeming MCG back in 1977. A few years before that, Sheedy was a soldier, performing two years of national service

---

3   Sir Henry Bolte was premier of Victoria from 1955 to 1972, a term that overlapped substantially with Sir Robert Menzies' epic second stretch as prime minister. While both were Liberal Party leaders, Bolte was a bruiser and brawler with none of Menzies' patrician hauteur. Though Collingwood or Richmond might have seemed more congruent choices, Bolte was a keen supporter of Melbourne, and for many years either or both the number-one ticketholder and club patron.

between 1969 and 1971, although his football career was not interrupted, as a few were, by a tour of duty in Vietnam.[4]

Sheedy pitched his plan for an annual dedicated Anzac Day clash, between two of Victoria's best-supported clubs, to Collingwood and to the RSL. Sheedy had, as usual, sized up his prospects astutely: the Victorian RSL's long-serving president, the choleric conservative Bruce Ruxton, was fond of claiming that his parents had taught him to say 'Collingwood' before 'mother' or 'father'. Collingwood required little persuasion that they were uniquely qualified for the majesty of the occasion.

Sheedy had tapped into something bigger, however. From the 1980s onwards, Anzac Day had become steadily more popular. As the passing years thinned out the veterans of the World Wars from the Anzac Day parades, more people were turning out to see them. Peter Weir's 1981 film *Gallipoli*[5] had burnished the Anzac legend afresh, work continued by the 1985 Channel Nine miniseries *Anzacs*. It is also possible that the 1988 bicentennial transferred some of the angst which had once occluded Anzac Day to Australia Day, which was now seen by many as a commemoration of the more ambiguous invasion. In 1990, on the 75th anniversary of the Gallipoli landings, Prime Minister Bob Hawke accompanied 58 veterans, aged 91 to 103, back to Anzac Cove. They were met, this time with hugs and handshakes, by Turkish veterans of the Dardanelles campaign – a profoundly moving spectacle which further affirmed the idea, debatable though it was, of Gallipoli as the altar upon which a blood sacrifice had consecrated a nation.

By 1995, on the 80th anniversary, appetite for Gallipoli remembrance had clearly swelled still further. The MCG's gates were closed at 1.30 p.m., 40 minutes before the bounce. Outside, 20,000 people were turned away, rather more than had ventured to Princes Park to see Melbourne versus

---

4   Around a dozen VFL players served in Vietnam. Sheedy's future club Essendon were especially unfortunate in this respect, a contingent of six summoned from the Bombers' ranks – one of whom, Keith Gent, was badly wounded near Saigon in January 1968. Glenn James, later the VFL's first Indigenous umpire, who officiated the 1982 and 1984 grand finals, went to Vietnam as a conscript. James played for 17 Construction Squadron in one of the football competitions contested by Australian units in Vietnam between 1967 and 1971. Ironically for an umpire who would become known for being so quick on the draw with his notepad that he acquired the nickname 'Jesse', James was affectionately accused, years later, by Geelong's Wayne Closter – captain at the time of 2nd Advanced Ordnance Depot – of having swung an elbow at him during one especially tense grand final at Vung Tau. Closter played 191 times for Geelong. In 2007, in recognition of the games lost to his service overseas, the AFL formally elevated him to the 200-game club.

5   The screenplay of *Gallipoli* was written by David Williamson, playwright of *The Club*. Williamson has a cameo in the film, as a ruckman in the scene depicting Anzacs playing football in the shadows of the pyramids.

Footscray two days previously. The more determined elements of this thwarted throng were dispersed by mounted police. Many retreated to the Fitzroy Gardens to listen to the game on radios, just about within earshot of the collective roar of 94,825 more fortunate or punctual people – the second-biggest home-and-away crowd in League history.[6]

The game was portended by the familiar, faithful rituals of flag, bugle, silence and Ode of Remembrance. In following years, as the Anzac Day game was bedded in, and as the wars of the 21st century furnished uniformed guests wearing more recently acquired decorations,[7] these trimmings would proliferate. By 2000, an Anzac Medal was being awarded to the Anzac Day player held to have best exemplified the Anzac spirit, and the teams were competing for a trophy made in part from ironbark salvaged from a Villers-Bretonneux ammunition wagon and scrap metal recovered from Gallipoli's trenches. The guernseys evolved into Anzac-themed specials: Essendon's scarlet sash comprised of red poppies, Collingwood's stripes repurposed as rolls of honour.

Eventually, Anzac Day football burst beyond the confines of 25 April, as every match held around the date began launching with solemn martial ceremony; Richmond and Melbourne even tried to make Anzac Day Eve a thing. By 2018, an especially determined Melburnian football-goer could have stood in contemplative hush with their beanie over their patriotically engorged heart for five accumulated minutes over that weekend's round.

In 1995, nobody hanging from the MCG's rafters or clinging to its gunwales could have been sure what kind of game they were likely to see. Neither Collingwood nor Essendon had enjoyed great seasons in 1994. So far in 1995, Collingwood had played three good teams (Carlton, West Coast, Geelong) and lost three times, while Essendon had played three poor teams (Fitzroy, Fremantle, Melbourne) for three wins.

Happily for those correspondents who'd hoped to roll out some overwrought analogies between sport and warfare, the opening exchanges

---

6 The biggest home-and-away crowd in League history is the 99,256 who rammed the MCG to see the top-of-the-table clash between Melbourne and Collingwood on the Queen's Birthday Monday in Round 10, 1958 – actually a couple of thousand more than attended that year's grand final between the same clubs.

7 In 2012, Fremantle awarded their number-one ticket to Corporal Ben Roberts-Smith, the most decorated Australian soldier of modern times. Roberts-Smith won the Victoria Cross and Medal for Gallantry while serving in Afghanistan with the Special Air Service. On receiving his VC, Roberts-Smith said: 'It's just like being on a football team; you don't let your mates down, you go as hard as you can until the game's won.' The Dockers' previous number-one ticketholders, mildly amusing Fremantle rock group Eskimo Joe, were hopefully philosophical about being bumped, in the circumstances.

were precisely the kind of frenzy which occur on any battlefield in the furious swashbuckling that occurs before defences can be assembled, or front lines established: in the first quarter, the Magpies and Bombers scored six goals each. Either Collingwood were better than they'd looked so far this season, or Essendon worse. The play settled afterwards, but the scoreboard did not: at half-time Essendon led by 16 points, at three-quarter time Collingwood were 14 in front.

The Magpies had one big idea: funnelling everything to Saverio Rocca[8] at full-forward. Abetted by the midfield dominance of Nathan Buckley, and by the bullocking and bullying of Dermott Brereton, the former Hawthorn champion playing his second game for the club he'd supported as a boy, Rocca finished with nine goals. The Bombers had more options: there were six multiple goal-scorers for Essendon, including Che Cockatoo-Collins, Mark Mercuri, Dustin Fletcher and James Hird. It was Hird, weaving through bodies in a forward pocket like a motorcycle between trucks, who snapped on the run to put Essendon a goal ahead with a couple of minutes to go. It was Rocca who equalised for Collingwood, scoring from a kick earned with another spectacular exposition in an afternoon-long seminar in the art of the pack mark. At the death, Buckley might have won it for the Magpies when he swooped on a loose ball in the centre and found open ground ahead. With the siren imminent and any score good enough, a long punt towards the posts and a lucky roll might have delivered victory, but Buckley went short, looking for Rocca, who was double-teamed by Bombers defenders and couldn't reel in the mark.

The draw was a fitting result for a tremendous game of football, which would come to be advanced as key evidence supporting the case that the mid-1990s were as good as the game ever got – professionalised to the extent that the skills were honed to levels previously unreached, but not so much that telling research had been done into how to stop opponents from playing. To further indulge the rococo comparisons that this Anzac Day game invited, this was perhaps football's final epoch of dashing cavalries in embroidered tunics and feathered bonnets, before the fields were churned by drab but effective automatons which reduced many contests to unsightly slogs.

8   Saverio Rocca, after scoring 748 goals in 257 games for Collingwood and North Melbourne, enjoyed a successful second act in the NFL, as a punter for the Philadelphia Eagles and the Washington Redskins. In the 2008/09 NFL season, while playing for the Eagles, Rocca faced former Geelong captain Ben Graham, then punter with the Arizona Cardinals, in the NFC championship game, roughly the NFL's equivalent of a preliminary final.

Anzac Day 1995 proved significant for another reason. After hostilities were concluded, Essendon's Melville Islander superstar Michael Long complained of having been racially abused by Collingwood's Damian Monkhorst amid the tumult of the final quarter. It was two years since Nicky Winmar had made his memorable stand against racist insult from crowds. This was the equivalent moment for such behaviour among players, Indigenous footballers having forever copped such garbage from both sides of the fence, and forever been expected to accept it. Long decided he'd heard, and had, enough. He demanded an apology.

Collingwood activated the wagon-circling mode they'd rehearsed after the Winmar incident, president Allan McAlister insisting that 'Damian Monkhorst is a fine, upstanding young Australian and there is no racism whatsoever in Collingwood', and furthermore – and a bit weirdly – 'we are doing all we can for the Aboriginal people of Australia'. The AFL deputised its investigations officer, Martin Amad, to sort it out. As would become traditional in such matters, many people who one might have hoped would know better demonstrated that they didn't. Long – and other Indigenous players who supported him by speaking of similar experiences – were dismissed as sooks and/or snitches.

After one abortive attempt at mediation between Long and Monkhorst, Long got his apology – the two men later became friends – and more besides. Within two months, after consulting with Indigenous players and players from overseas backgrounds, the AFL announced the first racial vilification policy in Australian sport. League CEO Ross Oakley explained the new rule – Rule 30 – in the Round 13 edition of *The Football Record*, the cover of which featured a handshake between one dark-skinned and one light-skinned mitt, and the caption 'Racism: The Game's Up'. Oakley took a demonstrative swipe at football's equivalent of retired colonels chuntering indignantly into their brandies at such newfangled concepts as basic civility. It was, Oakley wrote, 'totally unacceptable for former or current players to put forward the attitude of what is said on the field stays on the field'. In coming years, in awkward admissions and abashed confessions from former players, something of the extent of what had been said on the field would become apparent.

45

The Merger Match
Melbourne 15.11.101 Hawthorn 15.12.102
Melbourne Cricket Ground
ROUND 22, 1996

We over-mythologise the one-point game. Not entirely without reason – a one-point win is by definition exciting, to a degree that overcomes any resentment of the fact that we've paid for a whole seat, but are only using the edge. But they're not unusual – one point is high among the most common margins across VFL/AFL history. And they're arguably – aside from the obviously crucial indicator of the score – not even decisive. If you've seen one team beat another by four or five goals or more, you've seen the best team win. The team that wins by the lone behind is (surely) merely the luckier of the contestants: a single whimsical bounce of the ball at any stage of a game so close could tip the balance in either direction.

But if ever a match demanded affirmation of the role of chaos and fortune in determining destiny, it was this one – a game which could have been the last that either team played, at least against each other.

It had always been assumed that there would be casualties of the VFL's evolution into the AFL, and the expansion of the competition from the suburbs of Melbourne to the entirety of Australia. The League's suzerains believed that the city could and/or should not support more than half of the AFL's teams, and that rationalising was inevitable, if not desirable: $6 million had been made available to reward clubs willing to swig the hemlock. 'Emotion aside,' wrote AFL CEO Ross Oakley in *The Age*, 'in the long run, Victoria cannot financially sustain our current number of clubs.' Oakley would learn that airily declaring 'emotion aside', where football fans were concerned, was like saying 'razor-sharp teeth and jaws that can snap a human leg aside' when a crocodile gets into your tent.

Melbourne, to a degree that they could well have taken personally, had been the subject of much merger speculation. From the mid-1980s, various hybrids had been explored, advocated or the subject of demented fantasies. An amalgamation of Melbourne and North Melbourne had been discussed, the team to play with North's royal blue and white stripes on the front of their guernseys, Melbourne's navy blue with red collar on the back. It had been posited that Melbourne and Richmond were an apposite mix, given the proximity of the MCG to Punt Road, but agreement could not be reached on whose name and colours would be kept. Some, including Collingwood president Allan McAlister, who may just have been amusing himself, suggested merging Melbourne, Richmond and North, presumably to be represented by a tiger-striped kangaroo with devil's horns.

A Melbourne–Fitzroy deal was proposed, as was a Melbourne–St Kilda hook-up. (The latter, yoking together the Demons and the Saints, would have provided the designer of the new club's emblem with an interesting conundrum.) But as 1996 proceeded towards an almost suspiciously apposite climax of the two teams in question meeting in the season's final home-and-away game, it was the Melbourne–Hawthorn fusion which gathered traction. The club's hierarchies seemed amenable, and the AFL was positively agog.

The logic was brutal, as logic usually is. It would be a marriage of convenience, as such arrangements often are, between young talent and old money. Hawthorn were a good team lacking resources, Melbourne a mediocre club with plenty. United, they'd have financial stability off the field, and a fine side on it: a forward line of Paul Salmon, Jason Dunstall and Garry Lyon, a midfield of Shane Crawford,[1] Darrin Pritchard and Jeff Farmer, a backline anchored by Mark Graham, Chris Langford and Alastair Clarkson, a follower combination of Jim Stynes, Todd Viney and John Platten. A host of distinguished Demons vouchsafed their endorsement, including Ron Barassi, Don Cordner and Frank Adams. Hawthorn's board was in favour, and the team's captain, Jason Dunstall, seemed acquiescent, saying: 'It comes down to the bottom line, and if you haven't got the dollars, you're not going to survive.'

---

[1] Shane Crawford won the Brownlow Medal in 1999. He forged a post-football career as a television presenter, including an irregular spot on *The Footy Show* in which he attempted to break world records. He established new marks for (among others) eggs cracked with head in 60 seconds (90), live golden orb spiders tolerated on body for 30 seconds (153) and fastest 100 metres in a pantomime horse costume (12.045 seconds, in tandem with Stawell Gift winner Adrian Mott).

Many, however, were unenthused, and animated by the passion of those who scent blasphemy. When Hawthorn's board announced its decision to members at Glenferrie on 15 August, voices were raised, argy-bargy perpetrated. The resistance, arrayed as Operation Payback, was led by the formidable figure of former dual Hawthorn premiership captain Don Scott, lending Hawthorn's board an understanding of the terrors that had once clutched the guts of Hawthorn's opponents when Scott was on the warpath.[2] Scott, abetted by businessman and Hawks fan Ian Dicker, appeared no more inclined to compromise in this cause than he had in the ruck; he had, he told the meeting, already raised $150,000 of a projected target of $1.7 million to preserve Hawthorn's independence.

In *The Age* of 29 August, the page containing details of the AFL package intended to encourage the merger also bore advertisements from those determined to halt it. 'Save the Hawks!' implored one, before announcing an Operation Payback rally at Glenferrie. 'Demons Forever!' urged the other, promoting an organisation called The Demon Alternative. This was a group convened by former Melbourne player and Victorian MP Brian Dixon, among others; with the bankroll of mining magnate Joseph Gutnick, who had pledged $3 million, they hoped to stave off unification from their end.[3]

Nevertheless, by the time the teams met in what had become known as the Merger Match, negotiations had proceeded far enough that it was known what the new team would be called – the Melbourne Hawks – and what they would wear: an unwieldy agglomeration of the clubs' strips, a golden bird representing Hawthorn gatecrashing the Demons' venerable navy blue with scarlet yoke. (In retrospect, it looks eerily like a prototype guernsey for the Adelaide Crows.) Thought had even been given to what

---

2   Don Scott, having done so much to save Hawthorn, later claimed to take little interest in the club's fortunes. A contrary figure even as a player, Scott combined a ferocious on-field persona with off-field interests in equestrian pursuits and fashion, often arriving at one of his not infrequent 1970s tribunal appearances dressed like a Rolling Stone, and carrying a handbag.

3   Joseph Gutnick was an ordained rabbi as well as the founder of Great Central Mines, which prospered from West Australian diamonds and gold in the late 1980s. His emergence as Melbourne's saviour, adorned with red and blue yarmulke, was unlikely at a couple of levels. One, as *The Age* noted at the time, was that the Melbourne establishment, of which the Melbourne Football Club was a pillar, was not historically famous for its hospitality to Jews. The other, as Gutnick confirmed to perplexed reporters, was that if Melbourne ever did play in a grand final again, his obligation to observe the Sabbath would prevent him attending. When the Demons got there in 2000, he sought a dispensation from the President of the Rabbinical Council of Victoria, permitting him to attend as long as he walked to the game, therefore correctly abjuring technology. The fact that said eminence was Gutnick's father, Chaim, did not sway the answer: no. Gutnick served as Melbourne's president from 1996 to 2001, and never saw them play on a Friday night or Saturday afternoon. He declared bankruptcy in 2016.

they'd bellow off-key in dressing-rooms in the event of victory: the mooted Melbourne Hawks song was a mashup of the two clubs' established themes, entitled 'Gold, Red & Blue'. Proponents of the union might have claimed prescient symmetry in the fact that the original melodies of Hawthorn and Melbourne's songs, respectively 'The Yankee Doodle Boy' and 'You're a Grand Old Flag' were both composed by George M. Cohan, if the combination hadn't sucked quite so badly. Meetings were scheduled for mid-September, at which Hawthorn and Melbourne members would vote yay or nay.

Of the two playing rosters, it was Melbourne's who had reason to regard the prospect with greater trepidation. A Melbourne Hawks assembled from the teams who played this match would surely have been more Hawks than Melbourne. Though Melbourne had finished well ahead of Hawthorn in 1995 – ninth, while Hawthorn were spared the wooden spoon only by the terminally limping Fitzroy – the positions had switched in 1996. At the bounce, Hawthorn could still fall into the finals with a win, in the (likely) event that Richmond, their rivals for eighth place, got done by North Melbourne at the same venue the following day. Melbourne were being kept off the bottom of the ladder only by Footscray, and by Fitzroy, now firmly tucked into the bed nearest the door. The Demons were playing, as the cliché of dead fixtures has it, for pride – but pride, today, seemed an especially valuable commodity.

For Hawthorn, Operation Payback started the day with a rally at Glenferrie, which also served as a homecoming for Dermott Brereton, somewhat estranged from the club since being delisted at the end of 1993, and wandering to Sydney and Collingwood.[4] Brereton's eyes welled as his name was chanted. Among the banners waved was one which read 'First Fitzroy/Now us/We won't merge/Kiss our arse' – which compensated in clarity for what it lacked in rhyme or meter.

There were 63,196 at the MCG, not bad for ninth versus 13th at season's end, and certainly an improvement on the 20,527 who had been tempted to Waverley by the same fixture back in Round 8 – but perhaps nevertheless an indicatively meagre one for two distinguished clubs almost literally playing for their lives. And Melbourne and Hawthorn

---

4   Dermott Brereton played seven games for Sydney in 1994, 15 for Collingwood in 1995. At Sydney he was suspended for more games than he wasn't – seven weeks for stomping on the head of Hawthorn player Rayden Tallis during a pre-season game, another seven for breaking the jaw of Richmond's Tony Free in what turned out to be his last game for the Swans. His subsequent year at Collingwood wasn't bad, though – 30 goals in those 15 appearances, as a foil to Sav Rocca's 93-goal season.

indeed played like extinction awaited the defeated. Even leaving aside the febrile mood surrounding the match, and the portent invested in it, it was one of the games of the season, if not the decade.

As the siren sounded to launch hostilities, Melbourne's Todd Viney and Hawthorn's Shane Crawford were already exchanging jabs and elbows. Within seconds of the bounce, two Demons were down – Jim Stynes steamrolled by Paul Salmon in the ruck, Paul Hopgood felled by the forearm of John Platten. Though both were bloodied, both recovered, and the intensity thus established did not ebb thereafter. Hawthorn got the game's first goal through Jason Dunstall, an occurrence on which few bookmakers would have offered odds. But Melbourne made it clear that if they were going out, whether of the season or of existence, they intended to do so swinging. At quarter time, Melbourne were 11 points up, their supporters wondering why they'd spent most of the year watching such rubbish: these Demons were unrecognisable as the team who'd surrendered a 73-point margin to West Coast the previous weekend.

Hawthorn answered the challenge in the second quarter, recovering to take a 19-point half-time lead, and it looked like the dominant theme of the game might be a full-forward shootout. At the main break, Jason Dunstall had seven goals for Hawthorn, including six in the second quarter, David Neitz four for Melbourne.[5] The third quarter saw Melbourne regain the lead, three mighty set-shot goals by Jeff Farmer[6] helping the Demons 12 points ahead at one point. But Dunstall was, as Dunstall usually was, insuperable. He kicked his eighth towards the end of the quarter, and looked to have set up his ninth with a demonstration of Dunstall distilled: leading in response to a two-bounce bolt down the wing by Darren Kappler, he planted himself on his chosen launching spot with an abruptness that left his opponent – Luke Norman – suddenly stranded a yard ahead of the drop zone, facing the wrong way.

Dunstall marked over his head, falling backwards to his left as Norman tumbled hopelessly atop him. However many times opponents had seen Dunstall do it, they seemed powerless to stop him doing it, and Dunstall lined up for what would be his ninth of the game – and his hundredth of the season. So cold a sharpshooter was Dunstall that it

---

5   Incredibly, given Melbourne's long and rich history, it took until Round 20 of 2007 for David Neitz to become the club's first 300-game player. He is also Melbourne's all-time leading goalkicker, with 631.

6   Jeff Farmer played 118 games for Melbourne, and 131 for Fremantle; the latter part of his career in particular was blighted by disciplinary issues and brushes with the law, including arrests and/or convictions for domestic violence, assault, and criminal damage.

is unlikely that he was bothered by the MCG's aisles filling with Hawks fans anticipating a celebratory pitch invasion; he had been mobbed in such circumstances on five previous occasions. It has to be assumed that Dunstall missed for other reasons, but miss he did, hooking to the left. At three-quarter time, Hawthorn were back in front, but only by two points.

The fourth quarter was furious, even measured against the first three; it is not impossible that the trainers and medics covered more ground than some players, so often did clashes leave someone slow getting up. The lead, and blows, were freely traded. Dunstall found himself with another set shot for his ninth/hundredth, a free kick after the hand of Andrew Lamprill clutched desperately at his ankles as he ploughed through a pack of defenders in a manoeuvre evocative of the car-destroys-caravan scene in *Mad Max*. Dunstall didn't miss this time. As the previously thwarted revellers poured over the fences in jubilation, Hawthorn had a seven-point lead. There were red and blue scarves and beanies visible in the rejoicing throng as well; as far as anyone knew, they'd all be barracking for the same team next season. It took eight minutes to clear the ground.

Dunstall's tenth put Hawthorn 13 points clear, but Melbourne would not roll over. David Neitz hauled in a towering pack grab and kicked his fifth goal. He scored his sixth after sliding on his knees into a deft chest mark. It came down, as one-point games do, to acts of resolve, caprices of luck. The final score of Hawthorn 15.12 to Melbourne 15.11 was reached with nearly four minutes to play; between then and the final siren was a desperate stalemate of tackles, wrestles, spoils and smothers, mostly on the right of Melbourne's half-forward line, none better or braver than Daniel Chick's staunching of a potentially decisive Melbourne attack, on the very tip of Jeff Farmer's boot.[7]

Players of both clubs had been instructed not to comment on the possibility that they'd be teammates in 1997, but it was difficult to interpret the performance of both sides as anything but a determination that if their colours were coming down for the last time, they would be lowered with honour. A telling illustration of the prevailing sentiment on the field was Hawthorn's Chris Langford, who'd been knocked cold at the start of the final quarter by a Darren O'Brien shirtfront, removing

---

7   Daniel Chick left for West Coast in 2003, where he was part of the Eagles' 2006 premiership team – that year's grand final also a one-point game in which victory hinged on one of his smothers, in this instance one which set up a handball to Adam Hunter for what turned out to be the winning goal. In 2002, Chick had his left ring finger amputated at the second knuckle to spare himself any further dislocations of the troublesome digit.

his number 24 guernsey as Hawthorn left the ground and waving it to the faithful, a flag uncaptured. Among the Melbourne fans clapping their team off, signs read, simply, 'No Merger'.

It was a great result for Hawthorn – Richmond were beaten by North the following day, and the Hawks went to the finals, though they didn't last long. It was considerable consolation for Melbourne, whose players had taken until the last game of 1996 to realise that they were actually a pretty decent team; four years later, six of them would play in a grand final, albeit on the losing side. And it was a total treat for any football fan. But it could scarcely have gone worse for those advocating turning the two clubs into one, in much the same way that the overseer of a rocket laboratory seeking to dismiss an irritating employee would be flummoxed if said underling came up with a workable cold fusion machine on the anticipated day of their sacking.

It is unknowable if things would have been different if this game had been a bust. But the Hawthorn resistance were especially fired up. When Hawthorn's members met at Camberwell Civic Centre on 16 September, Don Scott stood before them, eyes ablaze, and flourished the putative guernsey of the new team. Scott ripped the hawk motif from it to reveal his truth, that this new team would be to all intents and purposes Melbourne, with Hawthorn, the club for which he'd played 302 games, reduced to a cosmetic appendage. The crowd were so rowdy that even triple premiership coach Allan Jeans was booed for his pro-merger sympathies. Another triple premiership coach, John Kennedy, also believed to be pro-merger, left early after being accosted and abused by the anti-merger former Victorian minister for ethnic affairs, Walter Jona.[8] The proposal was rejected, 5241 votes to 2841.

Melbourne's members met at Dallas Brooks Hall – the original venue, Melbourne Park, was being used that night by the Dalai Lama.[9] After an equally unruly assembly, and despite a last-minute conversion to the 'no' cause by Ron Barassi, Melbourne voted yes, 4679 to 4229, though it was proxies wrangled by the board that carried it, rather than those present. But with no partner, there was no merger, and the two clubs moved on

8   Walter Jona died in 2007. John Kennedy attended his funeral, as did Peter Hudson, Peter Knights and other Hawthorn grandees. As chairman of the Parliamentary Road Safety Committee, Jona had seen to it that Victoria became, in 1970, the first jurisdiction in the world to make seatbelts compulsory.

9   The Dalai Lama's AFL allegiances are maddeningly opaque, but the Tibetan leader does own a Sherrin and a Collingwood guernsey, both presented to him by Collingwood's Heritier Lumumba, during a visit to Australia in 2011.

independently, each under new presidents: Ian Dicker at Hawthorn, Joseph Gutnick at Melbourne. Hawthorn would build towards becoming the dominant team of the early 21st century. Melbourne wouldn't.

But that Hawthorn hegemony would be established under the coaching of Alastair Clarkson, who'd been among Melbourne's best players in Round 22, 1996, with 29 possessions and a goal. Helping him out as assistant coaches at various stages of the Hawks' early-21st-century supremacy would be three other players who turned out for the Demons today – Todd Viney, David Neitz and Adam Yze. The merger kind of happened anyway.

46

Fitzroy's Farewell
Fremantle 24.13.157 Fitzroy 10.11.71
Subiaco Oval
ROUND 22, 1996

This was always going to be a melancholy occasion. However, the fates and the fixture conspired to make Fitzroy's final game as dismal an affair as it could imaginably have been – beaten by 15 goals, 3000 kilometres from home, more than a century of history ending against a mob of blow-ins who'd only joined the AFL the season previously. Among 22,000 witnesses were a bare few hundred devotees possessed of the financial wherewithal and sentimental attachment necessary to have underwritten the trip across the Nullarbor. A few carried a banner reading 'Born 1883, Murdered 1996'.

The victim was, in truth, already dead when delivered to Subiaco. The week before, Fitzroy had run onto the MCG for the last time, and limped off it 151 points adrift of Richmond, the second-worst beating Fitzroy had ever endured,[1] witnessed by nearly 49,000 people taking their chance to bid the Lions adieu; more frequent attendances of that size in preceding seasons might have spared the club its looming oblivion. (As the teams left the field, Tigers fans, long Hatfields to the Lions' McCoys, joined spontaneously, empathetically and magnificently in on Fitzroy's club song, the triumphant melody of 'La Marseillaise' recast in this instance from battle cry to requiem.[2])

---

1   Fitzroy's worst loss was sustained in Round 6, 1991, when they were beaten by 157 points by Hawthorn at North Hobart Oval. The Hawks heaped up their highest ever score, 36.15.231. Jason Dunstall kicked six goals and was still outscored by two teammates, Ben Allan and Darren Jarman, with seven each.
2   With a few tweaks to the lyrics, 'La Marseillaise' made the journey to Brisbane with Fitzroy. Written in 1792 by French army officer Claude Joseph Rouget de Lisle, already famous for having the most French name in France, the stirring melody which now serves as his country's national anthem was composed in an effort to rouse his comrades to hold the line against Prussian and Austrian invaders seeking to throttle the revolution in its cradle. It was always the perfect song for Fitzroy, a defiant

The game before that, while technically not as severe a mauling, had been even more woebegone: an 87-point loss at Princes Park to the Brisbane Bears, by whom Fitzroy were scheduled to be absorbed. Just under 6500 people turned up to see, as they saw it, the parasite consume the host.

It had been an awful season for Fitzroy. The jackals which had long been sniffing had now followed the Lions from the Junction Oval to Victoria Park to Princes Park to the Western Oval, as Fitzroy sought to outrun their creditors, and the inevitable. The Roys had won one game, at home – well, 'home' – against Fremantle in Round 8, in front of barely 5000 sullen masochists.

Money grew tighter, despite the plucky endeavours of tin-rattling, raffle-holding, rally-convening supporters.[3] Results got worse, good players became harder to keep, coaches got fired (Bernie Quinlan, 1995) or quit (Mick Nunan, 1996). Sponsors grew more sceptical, though Fitzroy maintained some standards: in 1984, they turned down a $100,000 guernsey sponsorship offer from the Daily Planet massage parlour of Elsternwick.[4] Surreally, the final straw had been the calling in of a loan from the government of Nauru.[5]

---

glorying in the struggle, rather than the result. It maybe doesn't suit Brisbane quite so well, but its imposition did at least mean the extirpation of the two Bears-era Brisbane songs, both of which were dreadful. The first, 'Dare to Beat the Bear', was hacked by Mike Brady from the well-worn 'Up There Cazaly' template, while the second, to the admittedly rousing tune of 'The Battle Hymn of the Republic', was honking bullshit depicting the Bears as sentinels of Queenslandic nationalism. No other club song in League history – not even Port Adelaide's – has more obviously incited, or deserved, a massed salute of 'wanker' gestures from home fans.

3   One revenue-raising ruse was the sale of 96 bricks from the demolished Haydn Bunton Stand at Brunswick Street: these relics fetched $1000 each. A speaker at one Festival Hall rally in 1986 was Bert Newton, who grew up in Holden Street, Fitzroy, and agonised about 'what sort of life we'll live in Australia without Fitzroy'.

4   The proprietor of the Daily Planet was John Trimbole, nephew of Robert 'Aussie Bob' Trimbole, the infamous marijuana baron. John Trimbole eventually fulfilled his dream of sponsoring a sports team, founding – and driving for – Daily Planet Racing in the Australian Touring Car Championship and V8 Supercars. Whenever asked, John Trimbole claimed not to know his uncle all that well; apparently tired of the question, he renamed himself John Trimble. The Daily Planet closed in 2018.

5   During the 1980s, Nauru was by some estimations the world's richest country per capita – a fortune hewn substantially from the fossilised gull crap which coated its surface, and was prized as fertiliser. At the peak of its birdshit boom, Nauru provided all services to its citizens free, not bothering to collect taxes; government-built houses rented for $4.87 a month. Cases were reported, possibly by metaphor-hunting journalists invoking the too-good-to-check clause, of locals using banknotes as toilet paper, and of a police chief importing a yellow Lamborghini – a debatably sagacious purchase in a country with 19 kilometres of paved road and a 40 kilometres per hour speed limit – and finding he was too fat to get behind the wheel. The guano ran out, and so did the cash, not least due to hubristic investments. Aside from lending money to Fitzroy, which can't have seemed much more sensible, even then, than betting the national economy on trap four in the fifth race at Dapto, Nauru built the tallest building in Melbourne – the imaginatively named Nauru House – launched a national airline hardly anyone used, and funded a West End musical based on the life of Leonardo da Vinci, which even the kind of people who go to see musicals didn't go to see. Nauru was eventually reduced to

Various mergers and/or relocations had been suggested during Fitzroy's years of atrophy, which could have sent them to Canberra, Tasmania, the Gold Coast or Sydney, or seen them become a component of the Fitzroy Bulldogs or Melbourne Lions or one of several other proposed or rumoured or imagined consolidations. The most recent had been North Fitzroy Kangaroos, a union of North Melbourne and Fitzroy, reported as imminent by Melbourne newspapers in mid-May of 1996: 'It's a Deal', declared *The Herald Sun* in the bold type reserved by newspapers for headlines they're pretty sure won't embarrass them. It wasn't. Other clubs feared the creation of an indomitable leviathan with deep pockets and an equally capacious playing list, and it wasn't like North needed the help: they'd been at or near the top of the ladder all year, and were heading for the 1996 premiership.

On 4 July 1996 the papers still thought the North Fitzroy idea was a goer, but reported that Footscray, who'd staved off a merger with Fitzroy seven years previously, were inserting a spanner in the works, taking legal action to stop Fitzroy breaching their co-tenancy of the Western Oval. That afternoon, the AFL's clubs voted 14 to one against the North–Fitzroy merger. When Brisbane revived their merger proposal, it seemed irresistible: it would clear Fitzroy's debts, which were running past $4 million, and strengthen the AFL's shakiest frontier team, still struggling for purchase on the local imagination after a decade of existence.[6]

Also mitigating in favour of a Brisbane–Fitzroy amalgamation was the fact that such a union would upset only one bunch of fans, rather than two, as Brisbane didn't really have any – even in a year in which they would finish the home-and-away rounds third and reach the preliminary final, the Bears remained box-office typhoid, with an average home attendance of barely 18,000. And, though it mightn't have been the primary consideration, here was an opportunity to banish Brisbane's horrible cerise and lemon guernseys, and nonsensical 'Bears' nickname.[7]

---

earning a living as a holding centre for asylum seekers unwanted by Australia.

6   By 1996, Brisbane Bears founder Christopher Skase was five years into self-imposed exile on Majorca, a destination chosen for its agreeable climate, and for Spain's even more agreeable lack of an extradition treaty with Australia. Skase rivalled Alan Bond as Australia's principal personification of the vacuous materialism of the 1980s boom, and of the reckoning which followed it. (Bond enjoyed a brief tenure as president of Richmond in 1987, or at least enjoyed it more than Richmond did.) Skase was an obnoxiously large-living billionaire who launched the Bears in cahoots with much-beloved actor Paul Cronin, star of *The Sullivans*. Skase, fond of arriving at Bears games at Carrara by helicopter, did a runner in 1991 following the implosion of his Qintex business empire, a step ahead of the charges resulting. He never returned to Australia or faced justice, and died in 2001, aged 52.

7   A koala is not a goddamn bear. It just isn't.

Fitzroy, so the sell went, would not be wholly extinguished. The 'Lions' marque would endure, as would the colours, more or less – the scarlet beneath the blue yoke would be darkened to Fitzroy's prototypical maroon, the gold crest replaced with the imperious feline from Fitzroy's logo – as originally designed by George Coates, who played 128 games for Fitzroy in the 1940s and '50s, and whose son Michael played for the club in the 1980s. The new team would look far more like Fitzroy than Brisbane.

There were few reports of Bears fans chaining themselves to railings outside the Gabba in protest; there were few reports of Bears fans. Fitzroy supporters were less sanguine. Three games after the merger was announced, Fitzroy played Collingwood at Victoria Park. The Lions' cheer squad hoisted a run-through bearing the crass declaration 'Seduced by North, Raped by Brisbane, F***ed by the AFL'. One unrepentant perpetrator observed, shruggingly, that it wasn't like the AFL could fine a club which didn't have any money and was about to cease existing. 'We haven't had our say yet,' he told *The Age*, 'and that's our say.'

There was no halting of Fitzroy's death march, however, and the trudge to oblivion was a lonely one. Until the well-attended if abject farewell to the MCG in the season's second-last week, Fitzroy could barely persuade anyone to come and wave the club off: at none of their last three home games did the Lions attract a five-figure crowd. There had been some suggestion, especially since Fremantle's faint hopes of playing finals had evaporated, that it wouldn't hurt anyone to let Fitzroy die at home, but the AFL – happy, for obvious enough reasons, to let the Lions be knocked on the head in as remote a locale as possible – insisted that the fixture was the fixture. On the day of the game, *The Sunday Age* devoted the front page of its sports section to a doleful photograph of an airliner lifting off from Tullamarine. 'They're leaving on a jet plane. They won't be back again,' said the caption. 'Goodbye Fitzroy.' (*The Sunday Age* had already spent the inevitable 'Lions Weep Tonight' headline, as it covered the crisis back in June.)

The Subiaco surface was adorned with immense logos, almost the length of the centre square, reminding spectators that 1996 was the League's centenary season: given that Fitzroy were one of only three clubs, along with Carlton and Collingwood, to have played all of the previous 99, this seemed a cruel addition of insult to injury. Fremantle, to their credit – and without any contribution from the AFL – took pains to imbue Fitzroy's last rites with dignity. Ron Alexander, Fremantle's chairman of selectors, understood what was being lost: he'd played six seasons for Fitzroy between 1976 and 1981, two of them as captain.

The Dockers put on a minor production pre-match, and paraded a few former Fitzroy players, including Kevin Murray, Bernie Quinlan and, representing Fitzroy's greatest player, Haydn Bunton Sr, his son, Haydn Bunton Jr. At the finish – Fitzroy's final final siren – as some Lions players wept, the Dockers had arranged for such lamentations to be soundtracked by West Australian Opera Company soprano Sara Macliver, shrouded in black, trilling 'Auld Lang Syne' from the roof of the Town & Country Stand. The Fremantle crowd, few of whom had left, stood for a minute's silence; then Fitzroy, one of the oldest clubs in the AFL, were clapped off by an honour guard of the newest.

The four quarters of football in between were far from the best Fitzroy had played in their storied history, but far from the worst they'd played during their last wretched season. They outscored Fremantle in the last quarter, though trimming an 88-point deficit to 86 points is the scantest imaginable consolation, akin to the bailiffs giving back your trouser-press as they load the rest of your possessions onto the truck.

Fossicking for positives would have been pointless even if they'd been easier to find, but Fitzroy's John Barker, Jarrod Molloy and captain Brad Boyd had games as decent as games played in such hopeless circumstances can be, and Marty Warry, making his eighth – and, it would turn out, last – AFL appearance, kicked four goals.[8] For the Dockers, Craig Callaghan, Scott Chisolm and Gavin Mitchell were all good, but it's hard to imagine that even Craig Callaghan, Scott Chisolm and Gavin Mitchell cared: they knew they'd been flogging a dead lion.

It wasn't the fault of anybody wearing Fitzroy colours in Round 22 of 1996, but by this point Fitzroy had become the equivalent of one of those Motown outfits who keep touring long after everyone who sang on the original great records has retired, died or ambled into dissolute insanity, to be replaced by imitators in similar costumes. While everyone remembered and loved the hits – Bernie Quinlan, Mick Conlan, Paul Roos, Gary Pert, Garry Wilson, even Alan Gale, Haydn Bunton and Wilfred Smallhorn – the numbers still willing to buy a ticket for the show had dwindled to a grimly fanatical and somewhat maudlin hard core.

---

8   Most of Fitzroy's last team played on, at Brisbane or elsewhere. Martin Pike, Fitzroy's last best-and-fairest winner, eventually arrived at the Lions in time for their early-21st-century hegemony via an interregnum at North Melbourne, and ended up a four-time premiership player.

The desolation of these diehards was real, however, and perhaps insufficiently acknowledged – not because nobody cared, but because to care meant to empathise, and few football fans enjoy imagining how it would feel to witness the obliteration of the club which comprises a portion of their identity. As the Reaper bore down upon Fitzroy, the rage and grief of the faithful had no more articulate spokesperson than Barry Dickins, the determinedly dishevelled playwright who wrote the 'Sentimental Roymance' column for *The Melbourne Times*, and claimed to have coined the phrase 'Royboys' – the title of one of his plays – for the Lions' ultras. In a column for *The Age* after Fitzroy's merger with Brisbane was confirmed, he described the feeling as 'Frightened. Angry. Impotent. Full of soundless wrath and this incredibly profound emptiness and deafening loneliness.'[9]

It might have been different, some still insist, had Fitzroy's last decent team – that mid-1980s vintage of Quinlan, Conlan, Wilson, Roos and Pert – been able to end a premiership drought which had begun in 1944. Though it is almost always useless to judge decisions made at the time with knowledge acquired since, it is easy to see why some Royboys holdouts – football's kin of those Japanese infantrymen who waged World War II into the 1970s – refuse to concede that their cause was necessarily lost.[10] If Fitzroy had hung in a while longer, they mutter, ridden out the League's financially lean 1980s and '90s, they could have shared the bonanzas pending, against which Fitzroy's debts were pocket shrapnel. In 2015, the AFL sold six years of television rights for $2.508 billion: the '08' would have got Fitzroy out of hock, with enough left over to build an immense golden statue of Bernie Quinlan, and a mechanism which would revolve it to face the sun in perpetuity.

---

9   Fitzroy are also deployed as a literary prop in the Jack Irish crime novels of Peter Temple. Irish is a still-bereft Fitzroy fan, and a son and grandson of Fitzroy players, whose social circle consists of a pub full of wistful men much older than himself, who pass their days reminiscing about bygone games; the device denotes Irish instantly as an unmoored but nevertheless determined sort. In the television adaptation, Irish was played by Guy Pearce, a Cats fan who once claimed that he would sooner return his Emmy than see any given Geelong premiership struck off.

10 Lieutenant Hiroo Onoda of the Imperial Japanese Army was deployed to the Filipino island of Lubang in December 1944, months after Fitzroy had bested Richmond in that year's grand final, 9.12.66 to 7.9.51, to win their eighth (and, it turned out, last) premiership. Lieutenant Onoda was one of a doughty few Japanese soldiers who continued to wage World War II for decades beyond its cessation, infuriating the blameless locals at whom they took pot shots but pleasing journalists seeking an amusing analogy for anybody who maintains fealty to a cause long past the point at which everybody sensible has given up on it. Onoda finally laid down his rifle on 9 March 1974. It cannot be conclusively proved that his first words after surrendering were not: 'Have Fitzroy won another flag yet?'

47

Footscray aka ...
Western Bulldogs 11.10.76 Fremantle 10.20.80
Princes Park
ROUND 1, 1997

Not since 1925, when North Melbourne, Hawthorn and Footscray joined the VFL, had there been such a dramatic rewriting of the fixture. Three new teams appeared on the schedule for 2017, though none was an entirely new entity. One, Port Adelaide, were an imported version of a club from another league. They were playing at the MCG this same Easter Saturday, away to Collingwood.[1] Another, the Brisbane Lions, were an amalgamation of the Brisbane Bears and Fitzroy; they would be debuting the following afternoon against Adelaide at Football Park. The third were an old club with a new name: Western Bulldogs, previously Footscray.

If anyone had assumed that the change of name would fire up the supporter base, they were, at this early stage of the innovation, disappointed – fewer than 9000 people fronted. Attendance might have edged nearer five figures were it not for a startling hike in ticket prices. The AFL had set general admission at $12.50, but fans arriving at the ground were told it was $17.50, and once 2500 tickets had gone at that price, it would be $24.50. *The Age* reported dozens of Bulldogs supporters turning around and going home.

There were other reasons for the lacklustre roll-up. The Bulldogs had suffered a poor 1996, finishing second from bottom above a drain-

---

[1] Port Adelaide were soundly beaten by Collingwood at the MCG, as if Collingwood were rubbing in the fact that their previous deployment of black and white stripes and the magpie had compelled the arrivistes to change their colours and avatar. (Port Adelaide, though founded 22 years earlier than Collingwood, in 1870, took until 1902 to adopt black and white.) The author has heard a credible report of a group of Crows fans making a day trip to witness the Power's AFL debut, reasoning that a return airfare to Melbourne was a small price to pay to see Port get a hiding.

circling Fitzroy. There seemed little reason to expect improvement, some canny transfers notwithstanding – Matthew Dent from Fitzroy, and Paul Hudson and Simon Minton-Connell, both from Hawthorn and, respectively, the son and nephew of the great Peter Hudson.[2] And today's visitors were never likely to inspire overnight queues. Fremantle were starting only their third year in the AFL, their supporter base was nearly 3000 kilometres away, and arguably their biggest individual draw was the statistical curiosity of Dale Kickett, just the third man in League history to be playing for his fifth different club.[3]

Plus, the venue was unfamiliar, or unfamiliarish. The Bulldogs had left the Whitten (formerly Western) Oval, their home ground for more than a century. (A formal farewell match was played later in the season, which the Bulldogs lost to West Coast.) They were now co-tenants with Carlton at Princes Park – not the most arduous journey undertaken in the history of the Australian continent, but still the other side of the Maribyrnong River, which in Melbourne separated that which was west from that which was not. Princes Park was now officially known as Optus Oval. It said something about the old Footscray, perhaps, that whereas Princes Park had been renamed to please a corporate sponsor, the Western Oval had only given up its name in order to honour someone who loomed even more heftily in Footscray club mythology: Ted Whitten, who had entered immortality a couple of years previously.

All those disincentives to attend conceded, it would nevertheless be pleasant to imagine that the large-scale away-staying was actually, or also, a mass protest at the indignity which had been wrought upon one of the game's proudest identities. Footscray had fallen victim to one of the grimmer plagues of modern times: rebranding, that bizarrely persuasive cult which holds that if you change one letter of the word 'soup', you can convince people to wash themselves with it. Incoming club president David Smorgon, scion of an industrial dynasty, fretted that the Footscray label had become intractably entrenched in the popular consciousness as 'underprivileged' and 'third-rate'.

---

2   Paul Hudson and Simon Minton-Connell were good forwards who had the misfortune to play during the same era as several great ones. Many 21st-century clubs would have been delighted with Hudson's career figures of 479 goals from 245 games, or Minton-Connell's 305 from 112.

3   Dale Kickett played 181 games with Fitzroy, West Coast, St Kilda, Essendon and Fremantle. The other two players to share the five-club distinction are early 20th-century journeyman Les Abbott (39 games for Collingwood, Carlton, Richmond, Melbourne and South Melbourne) and 1920s palooka Les Hughson (73 games for Collingwood, Hawthorn, Carlton, St Kilda and Fitzroy). Dale Kickett is therefore the only player to represent five clubs without being called Les.

Rather than seeing Footscray's hardscrabble history for the fantastic sales pitch it could have been – few are the feel-good films about a sports team escaping a hard-bitten blue-collar identity by changing their name at the behest of marketing consultants – it was decided that Footscray would detach themselves from the roots that allegedly hobbled them by assuming the wilfully vague name Western Bulldogs. No consultation with members was made, nor referendum held. It was presented as merely a cosmetic tweak: technically, this was still Footscray Football Club, just now trading as Western Bulldogs. But there was no doubting what it meant: the striking from the League ladder of a name which had, since Footscray's foundation in 1877, represented a pugnacious, defiant pride in honest, rugged – if often ill-rewarded – toil. There was a contempt about it, as well; suggesting to Collingwood, Carlton or Richmond that they might change their name would seem as preposterous as demanding that they forsake football for croquet.[4] Western Bulldogs also sported a newish look – a snarling bulldog-head motif had been fatuously emblazoned upon the red and white band across the middle of their blue guernseys.[5]

The renaming of Footscray was not merely a crime against a noble heritage, but against all geographic common sense, the area of Melbourne represented by the Bulldogs being east of almost all of Australia's landmass. It was also unpopular with a cohort of Footscray barrackers who not merely disliked the change, but suspected it could be cover for a future relocation – perhaps, some feared, to the western suburbs of Sydney, even if planting a team there was surely something only a lunatic would ever attempt. This lobby, Footscray Forever, sought legal advice about reversing the name change, despite heavy hinting by the AFL about the fortunes which had already been spent on merchandise bearing the new marque. The revanchist agitation was eventually abandoned at the end of 1997 with a compromise under which the initials 'F.F.C.' began appearing on the back of Bulldogs guernseys in 1998.

---

4 An affront of this sort was at one point suggested about St Kilda. Circa 1986–87, talk of Southern Saints gained mercifully meagre traction: the club advertised for staff under the name, and football cards and season tickets were printed, before the idea died an unlamented death, as did a new club song. Written by Mike Brady and bellowed by Doug Parkinson, 'The Saints Fight Back' did pretty much for music what the St Kilda of this period did for football, i.e. made you wonder why you'd ever taken an interest.

5 These were not, however, the worst things ever worn by the Bulldogs. That accolade falls to the 1935 guernsey of fussy red and white vertical stripes on a blue background with a red and white V-neck, in which the players looked eerily like they were wearing a uniform made from the flag of Cuba. These were used for just one season, before being destroyed in a dry-cleaning mishap – one would prefer to believe deliberately.

Most importantly, however, the Bulldogs were on the field, which had not always seemed a certainty in recent years. At the end of 1989, Footscray had been $2 million in debt, and on the verge of being subsumed by Fitzroy. Newspapers reported the merger as a done deal; the League and the two club boards presented Fitzroy Bulldogs as a fait accompli. Footscray – and their name, it was surely supposed – were saved by a heroic fundraising effort by club barrackers, who rattled tins and shook buckets in pubs and malls and traffic jams, held rallies and raffles, and sold red, white and blue stickers and badges emblazoned with unflattering references to the League's CEO: 'Up yours Oakley' became the 'Give me liberty or give me death' of an extraordinary insurrection in Melbourne's west.

One supporter, Irene Chatfield, lodged an injunction against the amalgamation in Victoria's Supreme Court. In response, the VFL gave Footscray three weeks to raise $1.5 million. They cleared it comfortably, in the process winning ICI as a new major sponsor. Peter Gordon, the local solicitor who led the campaign and became club president once victory was secured, said half the donations came from outside Footscray; it turned out there were advantages to being everyone's second-favourite club (or, with due respect to St Kilda, everyone's second-favourite second-favourite club).[6]

Footscray had not only survived that scare, but flourished. The Dogs played finals in 1992, 1994 and 1995 – a record good enough that they could afford to regard their miserable 1996 as a blip, a transition season from coach Alan Joyce, whose third attempt to resign had been accepted after consecutive batterings by North Melbourne, Geelong and Sydney, to Joyce's former assistant, Terry Wallace. They had a new name and a new guernsey, new players to go with their new ground, a newish coach and a new season. What Western Bulldogs needed now was a win.

They nearly got one, though this was mostly due to the skittish goalkicking of their opponents: the Dockers scored 3.4 in the first quarter, 7.16 in the next three. Though the Bulldogs played the first quarter like they were all wearing each other's boots, scoring just one behind, Fremantle's impression of The Gang That Couldn't Shoot Straight not

---

6   According to Ross Oakley's memoir of his period as the VFL/AFL's CEO (1986–96), Collingwood president Allan McAlister offered to bung a couple of hundred thousand into Footscray's fighting fund if the Bulldogs would transfer star rover Tony McGuinness to the Magpies, a proposal which could only have been more fabulously Collingwood if McAlister had dangled Ted Whitten out of a window by one ankle while he made it.

merely allowed the Bulldogs to stay in touch but gifted them the lead. At three-quarter time the Bulldogs were 17 points ahead – and new recruits Hudson and Minton-Connell looked like they'd been born in red, white and blue. Hudson was among the Bulldogs' best, and Minton-Connell had three goals.

But it was a largely dreadful exhibition of football, and it remained dismal in the last quarter. It was the kind of game where the result is usually guided by whose will to live ebbs first – but which is sometimes decided by some freakish phantasmagoria, like an interminable series of tedious experiments with inert elements somehow resulting in an eyebrow-removing explosion. It was the latter which finally chose a winner. With the final siren about to answer the prayers for deliverance of all present, Fremantle's Winston Abraham[7] gathered possession just forward of the centre circle, slithered between attempted tackles by Brad Johnson[8] and Matthew Dent, and wellied it desperately from beyond 70 metres.

The pack gathering in front of the goals all underestimated the flight of Abraham's mighty punt. It landed behind them, bounced between the big sticks, and won it for the Dockers. As full-time was signalled, the desolate Dent descended into the standard footballer's crouch of chagrin, striking that pose which resembles Rodin's *The Thinker* remembering something regrettable about the Christmas party. Minton-Connell went further still, slumping to the turf with such abjection that he later appeared in the injury list as mildly concussed. The Bulldogs had lost their first game with their new name, in their new guernsey, at their new ground, but they'd at least learned that the new recruits were invested in the cause.

Despite the ill-wishes of embittered, self-appointed treasurers of the game's history, who continued to bewail the excision of the Footscray name, Western Bulldogs rapidly improved. The following week, they beat Sydney at Princes Park, the week after that Richmond at the MCG. (It was suggested at around this time that Richmond could follow the Bulldogs to Princes Park, to which Tigers CEO Jim Malone responded with the

---

7   This was the highlight of Winston Abraham's seasons at Fremantle. He moved to North Melbourne in 1998, where he played in the 1999 premiership team and won Mark of the Year in 1998 (he'd already won Goal of the Year in 1996). His career deserved better than to end with a 50-metre penalty and an opposition goal as he limped from the field with a ruined knee, but that was what happened against Essendon in Round 1 of 2001, when Abraham inexplicably tackled a stationary James Hird, who had marked and was waiting to take his kick.

8   Brad Johnson would become Footscray/Western Bulldogs' games record holder, with 364.

stirringly unequivocal retort that 'the Carlton Football Club is a historical enemy of the Richmond Football Club and will always remain so, and we are opposed to giving them any assistance'.) By Round 11, the Bulldogs were top of the ladder, and by the end of the home-and-away rounds still third.

Footscray's first season as Western Bulldogs ended as it began, with the collapse of a seemingly commanding position. A few minutes into the final quarter of the preliminary final against Adelaide, the Bulldogs were four goals clear, before a Crows comeback saw them fall two points short of vindicating their rebadge with a grand final appearance, in what would have been the all-time underdogs' derby against St Kilda. In the game's dying seconds, the Bulldogs' Chris Grant missed from inches, albeit in circumstances that would have made it a remarkable goal even for Chris Grant – on the run, in semi-control of a hastily gathered ball, on a tight angle.[9]

It was proof that some things cannot be covered up with wishy-washy pseudonyms and alterations to uniforms. Footscray's failure to slough off an institutional custom of picturesque heartbreak was emphasised at 1997's Brownlow Medal count, when Chris Grant joined North Melbourne's Corey McKernan in the unhappy fraternity of players who have polled the most (or equal most) votes, but been deprived of the prize by a suspension during the season.[10]

From joining the League in 1925, it took Footscray 29 years to win their first flag. It would take Western Bulldogs 19 years from the adoption of the new name to win the club's second. It is arguable therefore that the erasure of Footscray was justified, though it is unknowable what, if any, difference it made to the team's performances. But something was lost when Footscray was lost, and not just for the club's supporters.

---

9   There are Bulldogs fans still as convinced as the Bulldogs' players were at the time that a Tony Liberatore snapshot which would have given them a five-goal lead in the final quarter was incorrectly adjudged a behind. A photo taken by The Age's Ray Kennedy caught Liberatore leaping into the arms of teammates Paul Hudson and Brett Montgomery in cock-a-hoop celebration of the goal that was not. The image is evocative of actors taking a triumphal bow just as the chandelier falls down.

10 Chris Grant played 341 games for the Bulldogs. In a heartstring-twanging demonstration of the peculiar hold that traditionally luckless sides have over players who could accrue more money and prizes elsewhere, at the end of 1996 Grant rejected a huge offer from Port Adelaide, in part due to a pleading letter from a six-year-old Bulldogs fan, one Ryan Adams, enclosing 20 cents of his pocket money. In 2017, another Bulldogs fan wrote a heartfelt, childish scrawl to Jake Stringer, also on the verge of departure. Though this correspondent enclosed $20 – quite a hike even after adjustment for inflation – Stringer left for Essendon anyway. He was, perhaps, shattered with disillusion by the footnoted admission that the author was a 53-year-old man called David Bowers – who, in fairness, thanked Stringer for the joy he'd brought to himself and his three kids.

Even fans of other teams like a story they can buy into, and Footscray's was admirable; there is little about which we Australians congratulate ourselves more earnestly than a generous sympathy for the battler. Footscray's was a name that meant a great deal, as names of places always do. It is no coincidence that almost every sports team in the world declares itself as coming from somewhere, and therefore standing for something.

In 2012, Western Bulldogs quietly ditched the dog's-head emblem on their guernseys, and reverted to the plain red and white hoops on blue that Footscray had worn to the Junction Oval to play Fitzroy on their VFL debut in 1925. Nobody complained.

48

Tony Lockett's 1300th
Sydney 22.13.145 Collingwood 14.10.94
Sydney Cricket Ground
ROUND 10, 1999

If one tracks Sydney's home attendances through the first half of 1999, one notices something that would seem odd, if one was unaware of the subtext. For the first four games they played at the SCG this year, the Swans pulled crowds in the mid to high 20,000s – a little down on 1998's average, but reflective of the fact that they were drawn mostly against unfancied teams, and had got off to a slowish start themselves. Sydney lost their first three games, and by the time Collingwood came to town in Round 10, Sydney had just four wins from nine, and were looking an uncertain proposition.

But the Swans were, suddenly, box office again. The week before, Sydney had hosted West Coast, and drawn 36,787 people. Granted that the Eagles perched atop the table, and offered the considerable attraction of Ben Cousins in his pomp – Cousins obliged with 32 possessions and three Brownlow votes as West Coast won by 13 points – but West Coast were not a club with a large local following, Perth being even further from Sydney than Sydney appeared to be from serious contention for the 1999 flag.

Turnout for the Collingwood game eight days later was even bigger – 41,280, nearing the SCG's capacity, even though Collingwood were a shambles, with one win for the season, and destined for the wooden spoon. Even allowing for the Magpies' hefty diehard faction – and perhaps also for the possibility that there are those who feel that watching a weak Collingwood side getting duffed up is an afternoon agreeably spent – it might have seemed, in different circumstances, a mystifying blip.

It was not. It was the lure of witnessing history. Tony Lockett, Sydney's full-forward, was closing on the most awesome statistical summit in the game: the 1299 career goals amassed by Collingwood's Gordon Coventry between 1920 and 1937. For decades, it had looked insurmountable. Even the 1990s' stellar class of full-forwards had, thus far, fallen short. Gary Ablett Sr retired in 1997 with 1031 goals[1], Jason Dunstall in 1998 with 1254. Lockett rolled remorselessly on, like the tank he resembled: implacable, intimidating and devastating. The real reason for the crowd at the West Coast game was that Lockett by then had 1294 in the bank; equalling Coventry's record against the Eagles would have required only slightly better than his average game.[2] But Lockett was held to three by one of the few men ever capable of restricting him: West Coast's Ashley McIntosh, incumbent All-Australian full-back and, along with Carlton's Stephen Silvagni, the pre-eminent defensive damp blanket of the 1990s. So it was that Lockett's eclipsing of Coventry's mark against Coventry's club became a near certainty.

Sydney's cheer squad suffered no qualms about the possibility of jinxing the moment. One side of the run-through declared: 'There's only one Tony Lockett' – or at least, it tried to. The 'one' was either forgotten, or had fallen off, inadvertently if correctly emphasising what – and who – was the real attraction of today's game. The other side reminded '3 goals to go', as if there was the vaguest chance that anybody present was unaware of this. (*The Sydney Morning Herald* had charted Lockett's progress towards the record with a countdown graphic, updating the dwindling deficit each week.)

Lockett was always more a tradesman than a showman, a Stakhanov rather than a Nureyev, manufacturing his prodigious output as if mindful that no extra points were awarded for artistic impression. Some players, on a day like today – essentially a benefit match in one's own honour, complete with obligingly hopeless opposition – might have been tempted to milk it, to delay the gratification in order to stoke greater acclamation when the moment came. Lockett did not. He got it done before quarter time.

---

1   Gary Ablett Sr was for many years officially credited with 1030 goals. In 2019, he was awarded another, after a fan called Stephen Wade, watching a 1982 Ablett appearance for Hawthorn on YouTube, noticed that a goal long recorded as the work of Richard Loveridge was actually kicked by Ablett. And they say that obsessively watching footage of old, forgotten games is a waste of time.

2   Lockett's average of 4.84 goals per game is eclipsed among serious contenders only by two players whose careers were ended early by injury: John Coleman (5.48) and Peter Hudson (5.64). It is obviously and regrettably unknowable whether either would have maintained that strike rate over nearly 300 games.

For his first goal, Lockett ran around the mark from a set shot, taking advantage of a dozing Collingwood backline, and scored on the run from 30 metres or so: 1298. For his second, he marked a long kick in the goal square, as apparently bothered by the oncoming attentions of Collingwood's Damian Monkhorst and Mal Michael as the grazing elephant is by the bumbling fly. Coventry's record was equalled not with the point-blank set shot Lockett could have had, running in to deafening anticipatory applause, but with a desultory, irritable-looking play on, belting the ball into the rafters from about six inches out, with his left foot: 1299.

A few seconds before the first break, Collingwood's Scott Burns, tagging Sydney captain Paul Kelly, scuffed the ball out on the full, as the pair scrapped for possession. Kelly was awarded a free kick about 60 metres from goal. He looked up to see Lockett leading ahead of Mal Michael – who, like so many full-backs before, and a few more to come, seemed strangely startled that the most predictable thing in football had happened again. Such was the dilemma presented by Lockett, as quick as he was big. Play behind him, and even if you caught him you couldn't reach around him to spoil. Play in front, and it might be the last thing you ever did, Lockett being the sort who saw obstacles as things to be run through, rather than around. Lockett marked Kelly's typically perfect pass on his chest.

Lockett found himself almost exactly where he'd been standing when he ran off the mark for his first goal, earlier in the quarter, but any thoughts he had of deflating the grand occasion by playing swiftly on again were extinguished by the quarter-time siren; he'd have to take the set shot. As he prepared himself, the SCG's security guards spread out around the ground, with particular concentration on the boundary nearest Lockett. Their task had just been made even more futile by the break – however they had planned to disperse the invasion that would be cued by the record-breaking goal, they would not be able to appeal to anyone's conscience about interrupting the game.

Lockett was famously uncomfortable with attention. If a single moment summed up his attitude, it was an incident back in 1988, when a young Channel Ten reporter called Eddie McGuire pitched up hopefully at Melbourne's Mercy Hospital, where Lockett was being treated for a broken ankle; Lockett threw one of his crutches at him. Lockett was a country boy by raising and temperament, almost a real-life version of the title character of Barry Oakley's *A Salute to the Great McCarthy*,[3] and/or of some Bunyanesque ogre who'd learned his trade booting wheat sheaves over grain silos.[4] Since arriving in Sydney from St Kilda four years earlier, Lockett had revelled in the relative anonymity an AFL superstar enjoyed north of the Murray.[5] He must have contemplated, if only fleetingly, the six-goal lead the Swans already held, and considered kicking it wide.

But Lockett hadn't got to 1299 goals by missing from 30 metres on a slight angle. The ball wobbled off his boot like a lop-loaded helicopter, a horrible kick in every respect but its trajectory: 1300. Lockett's teammates reached him first, celebrating and protecting. Thousands of barrackers hurdled the fences to surround them in joyous ripples – among them, a 14-year-old Swans fan called Jarrad McVeigh.[6] The figure at the centre of this genial riot looked as unfazed as he always did, but this was not Lockett's first experience of such adulation: he had received the jubilant mobbing traditional on the kicking of one's 100th goal of the season on six occasions – three times with St Kilda, three times with Sydney.[7]

The first-quarter break ended up lasting ten minutes, as the euphoric throng were shooed back to their seats. Lockett kicked six more after quarter time as Sydney cantered to a 51-point win; having started the game

---

3 Barry Oakley's 1970 novel *A Salute to the Great McCarthy*, in which a promising country footballer migrates from the back of Bourke to play in the big city, was made into a film starring John Jarratt, Barry Humphries and Judy Morris. Intriguingly, the cover of the 1974 paperback features a still from the movie – a rear view of a glamorous blonde wearing a Swans guernsey bearing number 39, and as such has to be considered a subliminal influence on Warwick Capper. In further portentous coincidence, the town from which McCarthy hails is called Warwick.

4 The Riverina settlement of Mirrool holds an annual event at which contenders are invited to kick a football over the town's grain silos, some 32 metres high. The tradition appears to date to the late 1970s, and a pub bet by local coach Mark Newton; the ball was kept behind the bar of the Royal Hotel, where in 1989 it was noticed by Geelong's Billy Brownless, en route to a wedding in West Wyalong. (Brownless was from the vicinity, a son of Jerilderie.) Brownless accepted the dare, and made the kick. The modern Silo Kick Challenge was insituted in 1992; Brownless was the winner. It has been won eight times by local farmer (and Ariah Park-Mirrool ruck-rover) Rob Harper.

5 Up to a point. For all that Tony Lockett presented, on and off the field, all the approachability of a rumbling volcano with slopes prowled by crocodiles and surrounded by minefields and a moat, he was avidly sought by sponsors, at various points spruiking for Lowes, Puma, Nissan, Hungry Jack's (an establishment to which he may have known the way), Lone Star Steakhouse (ditto) and – after the thuggish mullet of his youth thinned out – Advanced Hair Studio, believed to have coughed up $100,000 annually for the privilege of re-thatching Lockett's scalp.

6 Jarrad McVeigh made his debut for Sydney five years later, and became a 300-game player and a premiership captain.

7 While at the Saints, Lockett made a habit of monstering the Swans, scoring 112 goals against them in 17 appearances. When he played for St Kilda at the SCG in 1993, a pig painted with Lockett's number 4 and a misspelling of his nickname, 'Plugger', was turned loose during the match – although the pranksters responsible, some of whom may well have been Sydney players, had not done their homework sufficiently to discern that Lockett would be absent injured. Sydney lost anyway.

with 1297 goals, he finished it with 1306. Afterwards, he was driven on a streamer-strewn lap of honour in a svelte scarlet vintage Cadillac Eldorado convertible – a suitably noble conveyance, though given its occupant, a growling M1 Abrams, its tracks greased with the guts of pulverised enemies, might have been more appropriate. Lockett shared the ride with Sydney official Terry Bartley, who earlier had taken receipt of the 1300-goal ball from security staff. (A letter from Lockett requesting the ball's return had been pre-prepared, to be pressed upon whomever in the crowd caught it; the recipient was one Graeme Diamond, who told reporters that he had sustained 'a few belts to the head' while establishing possession, thus learning how many of Lockett's opponents had felt down the years.) The SCG speakers broadcast 'One Tony Lockett', a musical homage, set to the 'Guantanamera' template, by former Models singer James Freud.[8]

Lockett was chaired from the ground by his teammates – not a trivial undertaking; he played at around 115 kilograms – and delivered to an interview with Jason Dunstall, now a reporter for Channel Seven. Lockett dropped his usual guard somewhat, revealing that he was uncertain about playing on much further. He'd slowed down 'a real lot', he said, which cannot have made Collingwood's shattered defenders feel better about themselves. 'If I'm going to be holding up the shift for a young bloke,' Lockett told Dunstall, 'I think I'd step aside and let the bloody young feller in for the future.' He was 33.

Lockett did retire at the end of 1999, signing off with five goals as Sydney were crushed by Essendon in a qualifying final: 1357. But after two years out, he returned to the Swans, prompting earnest conversations between AFL defenders and their insurers, as they contemplated lining up against a Swans forward line which now also included Barry Hall, another half-man, half-bulldozer who'd arrived at Sydney via St Kilda.[9]

Lockett looked pretty good; he'd lost some weight. But in his first game back, against reigning premiers Brisbane in Round 1, he – and

---

8   Upon its release shortly after Tony Lockett broke the goalkicking record, 'One Tony Lockett' spent
     a week at number 38, and prompted at least one chortling columnist to ask if perhaps Lockett could
     see his way clear to breaking this record, as well. This was unfair: the subsequent album *Today's
     Legends of AFL Football*, credited to James Freud & The Reserves, was kind of brilliant, an obvious
     sequel to Mike Brady's *The Songs of Football's Greatest Sons*, and almost as entrancingly weird as
     anything TISM ever did, featuring homages to, among others, Michael Voss ('Voss the Boss'), Garry
     Hocking ('Buddha'), Scott Wynd ('Wynd 'em Up'), and the self-explanatory 'Wanganeen', 'Jarman'
     and 'Rocca Brothers Rock'. Freud took his own life in 2010, aged 51.
9   Barry Hall would exceed Lockett for career games (289 to 281). But in a further illustration of
     the singularity of what Lockett accomplished, Hall finished with 746 goals – which, while a
     minor hillock of beans compared with Lockett's towering total, still makes Hall one of the 20 top
     goalkickers in League history.

everyone else – learned how important his heft had been. He was beaten by the same full-back against whom he'd kicked that 1300th goal, and eight others that same day; Mal Michael, now in Lions colours, held him to one. Lockett played just twice more for just two more goals: 1360.

It would be absurd to suggest that Tony Lockett underachieved. But the menace Lockett exuded was underpinned by a genuine capacity – perhaps, even, relish – for violence. In 281 games, he was reported 16 times, and suspended for a total of 23 weeks – an entire season, so perhaps another hundred-odd goals. The counter-argument is that maybe this rap sheet became another of Lockett's advantages, buying him half a yard in any contest as opponents calculated the likelihood of ending up like (to cite a few of many cautionary examples) Essendon's Brad Fox, half-strangled in the Moorabbin mud, or Melbourne's Shaun Smith, stretchered from the SCG unconscious, or Sydney's Peter Caven, his nose smashed.

It was the last of these that earned Lockett, then at St Kilda, his longest suspension – eight weeks, for leaping elbow-first into Caven as the Sydney defender marked with the flight of the ball, head obliviously lifted as Lockett charged him. In the same game, Lockett scored 11 of St Kilda's 16 goals as the Saints recovered a 51-point deficit to win it by a point with almost the last kick – a Lockett goal, inevitably – and attracted further opprobrium for making tactless gestures in the direction of Swans fans.

Ironically, one of the factors which tempted Lockett to become a teammate of Caven's in Sydney was the intensified scrutiny by Melbourne's media subsequent to this incident.[10] More ironically still, Sydney ended up having to apologise to Lockett, after Caven, his face still heavily bandaged, appeared on Andrew Denton's eponymous Channel Seven talk show, and was presented by the host with an effigy of Lockett and a selection of weapons; Caven decapitated the dummy with a baseball bat, hitting it very nearly as hard as Lockett had hit him. St Kilda's fury, in the circumstances – 'Outrageous,' stormed Saints president Andrew Plympton – was mildly hilarious, all things considered.

The ancient Greek poet Archilochus posited, in an observation recycled by Erasmus and Isaiah Berlin, that 'a fox knows many things,

10   Tony Lockett was supposed to move to Collingwood in 1995, but the board decided against it – the crucial vote, according to newspaper reports of the time, was that of former player Wayne Richardson, whose son Mark was occupying the Magpies' full-forward position. As is traditional, Richmond also had their chance, and blew it.

but a hedgehog one important thing'. Tony Lockett had little outwardly in common with a hedgehog – and possibly rather more with the tractor which might tread such a creature into the tarmac of some rural thoroughfare. But he shared the key quality of Archilochus's avatar of single-minded focus. Lockett knew one important thing – how to kick goals in Australian football – and he knew it better than anyone else who ever played.

The only contemporary or subsequent full-forwards to get anywhere near him – Matthew Lloyd, Lance Franklin, Matthew Richardson – got nowhere near him. Lloyd played 11 fewer games for 434 fewer goals. Franklin, when he drew level with Lockett's number of appearances, was nearly 500 adrift of Lockett's tally of goals. Richardson played one more game than Lockett, and kicked 560 goals fewer – a difference exceeding the entire careers of Chris Grant, Peter Daicos or Fraser Gehrig. It is possible to astonish oneself awhile with arithmetic of this sort: you can add Nick Riewoldt to Jonathan Brown and still fall short of Lockett, or Saverio Rocca to Tony Modra, or (if you want to go old-school) Bob Pratt to Jack Moriarty. Tony Lockett bagged more goals than the plausible-ish all-time forward line of Malcolm Blight, Alex Jesaulenko and Dermott Brereton managed between them.

Gordon Coventry had also known one important thing – the same important thing as Tony Lockett. George Coventry, Gordon's son, had been flown up to Sydney by the AFL to see Lockett break the old man's record – and the old man's club. 'Tony is a bit bigger than Dad,' he said, 'but both had a short, sharp lead, a good, strong mark and a straight kick.' George Coventry also passed onto reporters the portion of his father's wisdom that Tony Lockett had figured out for himself. 'Dad once said to me: you don't have to be a Stawell Gift winner to be a good full-forward. You just have to be quick out of your blocks and stay in front of your man.'

As simple, and as impossible, as that.

49

Whiskas Makes His Debut
Richmond 15.11.101 Geelong 9.12.66
Melbourne Cricket Ground
ROUND 12, 1999

The cover star of Round 12's edition of the publication by now known as *The AFL Record* was a fresh-faced, wispy-fringed West Coast player enjoying a spectacular fourth season in the League. 'Rising stars of '99', announced the cover line. 'Eagles' Ben Cousins leads the way.'[1]

Other features of the Round 12 *Record* included an interview with Richmond president Leon Daphne, a brief profile of promising Sydney Swans rookie Adam Goodes (which included a prescient comment from St Kilda coach Tim Watson: 'He's a terrific kid already, but he's going to be a real superstar of the game'[2]), an interview with Brisbane's Marcus Ashcroft on the occasion of his 150th consecutive game,[3] and a fascinating piece on the difficulties of combining an AFL career with a day job, and/or studies towards a post-football life.

This story, by Peter Ryan, noted that in 1998 the 583 men who played in the AFL made an average of $101,957 each – good coin, to be sure, but concentrated in a short period, and unlikely to underwrite a lifetime's fishing following retirement from the field. Many players worked towards future careers, or maintained present ones, though both were becoming

---

1   Not great timing, it turned out. Ben Cousins had one of his quietest games of an otherwise prolific season, as the Eagles caned Port Adelaide by 65 points; he got just 11 touches and one goal. Cousins nevertheless finished the season as by far West Coast's most productive player, with 515 disposals, fully 61 ahead of his nearest rival, Michael Braun.

2   This assessment of Adam Goodes was about the only thing Tim Watson got right during his ill-starred tenure at the Saints, during which they won 12 games out of 44. It may have been some consolation to Watson that St Kilda subsequently did even worse under Malcolm Blight in 2001; Blight was sacked after 15 matches, and three victories.

3   Marcus Ashcroft's consecutive appearances streak topped out at 170, 74 short of Jim Stynes' all-time record.

more difficult as the demands of the game grew. The article cited dual Adelaide premiership player Matthew Robran, a consultant with Ansett, and Geelong's Michael Mansfield, a stockbroker with ABN Amro, as having to scale back their collar-and-tie gigs. In what endures as both a retrospectively startling illustration of how late the AFL left behind its semi-amateur origins, and as the set-up for any number of punchlines, the article noted that the Melbourne Demons of the time had only four players categorised as professional footballers.

However, what made the Richmond versus Geelong edition of the Round 12, 1999, issue of the *Record* a true collector's item was the presence, on the page listing the teams, of a mistake. Not a typographical error, as such – more a dogmatic refusal to acknowledge a truth. At number 32 for Geelong, the *Record* listed a player called Garry Hocking. A player of that name had indeed worn that number for the Cats the week before, and would do so again the week following. But not today. Lining up in Geelong's midfield this Saturday evening, and with the deed poll to prove it, was Whiskas.

Hocking had been sold on the stunt by Chris Clarke, CEO of advertising agency Pure Creative. Watching a match at the MCG earlier in the season, Clarke had found himself wondering how far sports marketing could be pushed. A team called the Cats had what advertising people call a synergy with purveyors of cat food. Geelong were receptive to fundraising ideas, as organisations with debts of $7 million usually are. Garry Hocking was Geelong's most recognisable player, known by the nickname 'Buddha', and identifiable by an odd-shaped mop of unruly curls which made him look like he was wearing a headband when he wasn't. He was his team's highest possession-getter, and one of the last still playing of the near-great Geelong side who had lost four grand finals between 1989 and 1995.

The offer was $80,000 to Geelong, and $20,000 to Hocking, for the temporary legal name change and a few other abasements, including photos of Hocking – or, as he now was, Whiskas – gazing with reverent awe upon tins containing beef and chicken casserole, and tender chunks of chicken in jelly. (One such featured in a 2015 exhibition entitled 'A History of Geelong in 50 Objects', alongside arguably more venerable artefacts, including Edward 'Carji' Greeves' 1924 Brownlow Medal.)

The announcement of Hocking's moniker modification prompted glorious spluttering umbrage from the AFL, not an organisation hitherto noted for an ironclad reluctance to trade the game's dignity for sponsorship dollars. League CEO Wayne Jackson, fulminating on 3AW, said, 'We would not want, next week, to be confronted with somebody that wanted to call themselves General Motors or fish and chips or whatever you want to do, because I think it does have the potential to bring the game into disrepute.' Jackson further portended a bleak vision of a future Brownlow count, at which 'Whiskas got three votes, and Pal dog food got two, and Hungry Jack's got three'. The AFL., he vowed, and *The AFL Record*, would not lower itself to abet such tawdry shenanigans. Geelong, pressed for comment by breathless newspapers, took it less seriously. 'It's not a matter of life or death,' Geelong CEO Brian Cook told *The Age*.

Neither was the game in which Whiskas played. While Richmond and Geelong still had semi-plausible hopes of reaching the 1999 finals (though neither would), no sane observer rated either a meaningful flag chance. The week before, Geelong had been convincingly stuffed by Essendon, and Richmond had lost by two points away to Port Adelaide, in putrid conditions which had restricted the teams to seven goals between them. As the Tigers and the Cats arrived at the MCG, the fact that one of the players on the field had renamed himself after a pet food was the most interesting thing about the fixture. Geelong ran through a run-through emblazoned with a cartoon of Hocking, the warning 'The Cats Are Hungry' and the exhortation 'Go Whiskas!'.

As the game began, puzzled Richmond fans might have wondered if Hocking's – or, rather, Whiskas' – ruse had taken in their coach, Jeff Gieschen.[4] Given the job of silencing Geelong's veteran midfield engine was Duncan Kellaway, more accustomed to playing in defence, alongside his younger brother Andrew. Gieschen's gamble paid off. By half-time, Hocking's sponsors might have been doubting the wisdom of their investment: Whiskas had barely had a touch on the field, and for that reason had spent more than 15 minutes of game time off it, benched by Cats coach Gary Ayres. Whiskas' teammates had picked up some of the slack, however, and at the main break Geelong were just two goals adrift.

The Cats edged three points closer during the third quarter, but disintegrated in the last as Richmond ran away by 35 points. Matthew

---

4   Prior to taking the Richmond job, Jeff Gieschen had been an assistant coach at Geelong – and before that, coach of West Perth and a player with Footscray. He later spent 14 years as the AFL's National Umpiring Director. Among his innovations was the abolition of the umpires' white uniforms, in a bid to excise the epithet 'maggot' from the lexicon of barrackers' abuse. Football fans have not conspicuously struggled to think of other things to call them, however.

Richardson was almost precisely the difference between the teams, finishing with six goals for the Tigers. Whiskas had a dreadful game, just six kicks and four handballs, few of which went where intended; commentators calling the game were relieved to be infrequently confronted with the ethical dilemma Whiskas posed them. (They refused, in general, to play along.) Anyone who'd seen Hocking hoover up 30 disposals against Essendon the week before would have wondered if his arrangement with Whiskas had included dining on the stuff before the bounce.

Though their sponsoree's abject performance on the day scotched any hopes that Whiskas executives might have harboured of hearing their company's name called on Brownlow night, the deal worked out pretty well for them. Their $100,000 outlay brought them widespread coverage across all media, and not only in Australia – the jape was a late-1990s prototype of what would become known as a viral story, reported in outlets not usually much interested in Australian football, or indeed in cat food, including *The Guardian*, the BBC and CNN. Most of this was relayed in somewhat tittering tones, and probably rightly: there was little more to the story than Geelong, and Garry Hocking, reasoning that $100,000 was a decent return for a minor quantity of inconvenience and mockery.

But it is nevertheless possible to perceive the arrangement as an astute combination of satire and prophecy (these two disciplines, in an increasingly ridiculous 21st century especially, growing ever less distinguishable). For all the sanctimonious denunciations by AFL pharisees, Hocking's agreement with Whiskas was merely a *reductio ad absurdum* commentary upon the hollowing out of the game by commercial interests. One would not live long on the difference between naming a player after cat food, and painting the logo of a car manufacturer on the goal square.

Garry Hocking deserves more than a footnote in the chronicle of the game's struggle with commercial temptation. He was a garbage collector by trade, and for 274 games performed, with great skill, a similarly unglamorous yet vital role for Geelong – picking up the pieces, taking out the trash. (He missed six weeks of the 1992 season with an ankle injury incurred when he and teammate/colleague Paul Couch took time out of a bin round to play kick-to-kick with a few locals.) Had a few things happened not much differently, Hocking might have won a couple of premiership, and at least one Brownlow Medal. He was third in the 1991 count, runner-up by a single vote in 1993, third in 1994 and 1995, and fourth (but only two points from the lead) in 1996. (He would have been ineligible in two of those years, however, due to suspensions earned by his generally unyielding approach to the game.)

Such is football's fickle cruelty, however, even to those who are exceptionally good at it: what might have been the worst game Hocking ever played is the one best remembered.

50

The Perfect Season Ruined
Essendon 12.9.81 Western Bulldogs 14.8.92
Docklands Stadium
ROUND 21, 2000

A premiership is a premiership, and in 2000 Essendon were unusually – perhaps unprecedentedly – emphatic premiers. From their 94-point whipping of Port Adelaide in Round 1, the Bombers spent the entire home-and-away season atop the ladder, and finished it a full 20 points clear of second-placed Carlton.

Essendon's progression – or, rather, procession – through the finals could not have been more insouciant if they had ditched the scarlet-sashed black guernseys and done it dressed in tails, spats and top hats, toting parasols and twirling canes: the Bombers beat the Kangaroos by 125 points in the qualifying final,[1] the Blues by 45 in the preliminary, and the Demons by 60 in a grand final they could have won by more, but for uncharacteristically sloppy kicking for goal – Essendon were 10.16 at half-time – and for the fact that a 57-point-lead at three-quarter time in the last game of the season rarely encourages urgency.[2]

It would be pernickety to consider Essendon's 2000 any kind of failure – except to the irritatingly, infinitesimally slight degree that it was. Specifically, it was a failure to complete the perfect, undefeated season: a grail which has remained unsnatched throughout the VFL/AFL's history.

---

1 Essendon's score that day of 31.12.198 is the highest ever in a final, and the 125 points was the second-biggest ever post-season margin, behind the 133 points by which Essendon bounced Collingwood in the 1984 preliminary final. The nine-goal first quarter and ten-goal third quarter of Essendon's 2000 qualifying final in particular were sublime, the Kangaroos reduced to extras in a beautifully choreographed production.

2 Geelong led Port Adelaide by 90 points at the same stage of the 2007 grand final, but piled on another six goals in the final quarter to win by 119 points. In fairness to the gloating, showboating Cats, it had been 44 years.

Prior to 2000, the nearest any team had got were 1929's Collingwood, who cruised unconquered through the home-and-away season, and won the premiership, but not before falling sensationally to pieces in a semi-final against Richmond. As a bemused 'Old Boy' reported in *The Argus*, 'The Tigers swooped and sprang to such effect that the Collingwood play became weak and unconvincing. The harder Collingwood tried, the more relentless did the Richmond pressure become.' Jack Baggott, Jack Titus and Maurie Hunter kicked five each for Richmond as the Tigers won by 62 points. Normal service was resumed on grand final day, Collingwood beating Richmond by 29.

Essendon went to Docklands for 2000's second-last home-and-away game this Friday night with every expectation of leaving with their immaculate copybook unblotted. Essendon had beaten second-placed Carlton by five goals the week before at the MCG, in front of 91,571 people who assumed they were watching a grand final dress rehearsal, and when the Bombers had met the Bulldogs back in Round 6, they'd buried them 63 points deep. Tonight was first against sixth in a season in which those five places looked worth a normal year's ten; at the bounce, Essendon had 80 ladder points to the Bulldogs' 44. Bulldogs coach Terry Wallace speculated that his team would need to score 25 goals to beat Essendon – something the Bulldogs had managed once all season, against a listless Fremantle at Subiaco.

Essendon coach Kevin Sheedy would have welcomed such a shootout, as any coach able to deploy such weapons as Mark Mercuri, Scott Lucas and Matthew Lloyd[3] might. Sheedy would also, in his 20th season at Windy Hill, have recognised when he was being kidded by a rival. The week before Essendon swept Carlton imperiously aside, the Bulldogs had throttled the Blues, swarming Carlton's forward line with spare defenders. It was old-school Footscray football, as the Bulldogs goaded and hustled Carlton into conceding a free kick count of 26 to nine. The Bulldogs beat Carlton by three points, and only needed 11 goals to do it – six by Simon Garlick,[4] one by a spindly 18-year-old debutant from Warragul called Bob

---

3   Matthew Lloyd, mostly famous for kicking an impressive quantity of goals – 926 in 270 games – was also known for a pre-kick ritual of flinging a handful of grass into the air to judge the wind. In 2006, the AFL introduced a new rule to limit players to 30 seconds of preparatory buggering about before taking a shot; it was immediately colloquially christened the Lloyd Rule.
4   Simon Garlick later served as CEO of Western Bulldogs.

Murphy.[5] Sheedy and Essendon prepared for the Bulldogs to try repeating this choking dose.

The late withdrawal of Essendon captain James Hird, suffering back soreness, shifted the odds slightly, but no sober bookmaker was turning away bets on the Bulldogs; Essendon had not only won 20 times in 20 starts in 2000, but done so by an average margin of 52 points. Against Carlton, the Bulldogs had been able to make a weather-lashed Princes Park work for them; at Docklands, a playing surface like a putting green was protected by a roof. Essendon's depth was such that they were able to drop Paul Barnard, a player good enough that he'd kick four goals in the grand final. A younger Lou Richards might have seen this obvious mismatch as a cue for one of the extravagant forfeits he used to promise in his *Sun* columns – perhaps offering to burn down Victoria Park, for all the likelihood that he would be obliged to follow through on it.

The Bulldogs jumped the Bombers, scoring the first two goals through Nathan Brown[6] and Steven Kolyniuk. Essendon also found themselves a man down early, Damien Hardwick limping for the sidelines on a twisted ankle. If the Bombers were remotely fazed, they performed a convincing impression of a team who were not. At quarter time, they were five points behind. By half-time they'd levelled it at 7.3 each, thanks to an audacious Kevin Sheedy ploy: despite the forced removal of Hardwick from Essendon's defence, Dustin Fletcher was dispatched from full-back to full-forward, and responded with two goals, one of them a mighty roost from just outside the centre square.

When proceedings were halted by the half-time siren, and players stopped and took stock, their attention was caught by the spectacle of the Bulldogs' Brad Johnson, lying facedown on the left half-back flank, and not looking terrifically conscious. Conclusions were leapt to by his teammates, and by his captain: Scott Wynd was the first to express his displeasure to Essendon's John Barnes, who had been in Johnson's vicinity immediately prior to his descent to the turf. Matters escalated with abandon. Essendon's Gary Moorcroft ran from the interchange bench to accost the Bulldogs' Tony Liberatore, who eventually emerged from the

---

5   Bob Murphy played 312 games for the Bulldogs and became captain – though would be cruelly compelled to watch his club break their 62-year premiership drought in 2016 from the sidelines, having done a knee against Hawthorn in Round 3 of that season. Murphy also wrote a thoughtful column in *The Age*; the volume of his collected journalism, *Murphy's Lore*, and his memoir, *Leather Soul*, are among the best books about football by a footballer.

6   Nathan Brown forged a post-football career as a commentator with 3AW and elsewhere – and, in cahoots with his wife, Kristine Fabiyanic, as a scented candle impresario.

fracas with a torn guernsey and a split temple. Johnson got back to his feet; clearly ropeable, he took some restraining by the Bulldogs' trainers.

The pattern of the first half repeated in the second: the Bombers' free-flowing attack versus the Bulldogs' dour defence, Essendon asked to perform a quickstep through quicksand. In *The Age* the following Monday, Stephen Rielly called Terry Wallace's set-up 'the first game-long zone in the code's history', noting that 'this was nothing like our game, established upon the individual duel, had seen before. Two thirds of the Bulldogs lineup turned up to play with not the slightest intention of being responsible for an opponent.'

The Bulldogs' amorphous quagmire could not ooze everywhere or congeal everything, however – Essendon's Michael Long was proving especially uncontainable – and by the last break the Dons were 15 points clear. Their perfect home-and-away season looked just five quarters away. And, Essendon would have been thinking, the final four of those quarters would be against a woeful Collingwood, due to be spared the 2000 wooden spoon only by St Kilda, who were undertaking yet another season impressive only if interpreted as a serialised football-based interpretation of the works of Jean Genet and/or the Marx Brothers.

But in the last quarter, the scoreline compelled the Bulldogs to dismantle their defences, and flood their own forward line rather than Essendon's – the more so after Justin Blumfield put the Bombers 21 points ahead. Essendon, however, proved unable to execute the opposite manoeuvre. The Bulldogs kept finding room to run; incredibly, inexplicably, they reeled the Bombers in.

Chris Grant goaled for Western Bulldogs from close range. Then Trent Bartlett outmarked Sean Wellman in the goal square, but before he could take his kick, he was sent to the sideline under the blood rule, having been collected by Chris Heffernan as he'd gone to ground. Steven Kolyniuk took the kick and scored – and did so again a few minutes later, after out-leading Heffernan.

The circumstances which deprived Essendon of their lead, 90 seconds from the end, were a demonstration, salutary and farcical, of how tiny is the margin for error in the assembly of a perfect season. Amid a tussle against the boundary on the Bulldogs' half-forward line, Dustin Fletcher scuffed the ball out on the full. Steve Kolyniuk, clearly – and forgivably – believing he was having one of those quarters in which an individual player is endowed by some occult agency with powers verging on the supernatural, scooped up the ball, and sized up the range. The umpire decided it was Chris Grant's kick. It didn't matter. Whatever voodoo was coursing through Kolyniuk had rubbed off on the ball. Grant ran around the mark to widen the angle, and scored. The Bulldogs led by five.

They won the final centre clearance, Kolyniuk kicking to a mark on the 50-metre line by Rohan Smith, just as the siren confirmed the Bulldogs' bespoiling of Essendon's season – and the Bulldogs' hitherto uncertain place in the finals. Smith's teammates, and the red, white and blue contingent of the crowd, were so absorbed in celebrations that few noticed his kick extending the margin to 11 points. Brad Johnson ran the length of the field to say something to John Barnes; it was not, to judge by his body language, 'Hard luck, old son, all the best for the finals; do let's go for a cream tea sometime.'

The game cost Essendon more than the perfect season: after reviewing video of the half-time dust-up, the tribunal fined five Bombers a total of $12,500 (and nine Bulldogs $22,500). Barnes was suspended for a week for the bump on Johnson that had sparked the stoush, and Johnson received the same sentence for a retaliatory whack at Barnes. Essendon also lost Hardwick with his ricked ankle, though he would be back for the finals, and Dean Rioli with a shoulder injury; he would not. In their last home-and-away game, the Bombers showed some symptoms of arrested momentum, labouring to shrug Collingwood aside, but their promenade through the finals confirmed the Round 21 blip against the Bulldogs as aberrant – and yet an infuriating, unshiftable stain upon an otherwise flawless masterpiece.

If one wishes to pile quibbling atop pedantry, you could make the case that the perfect, perfect season requires an undefeated premiership, the Coleman Medal, the Brownlow Medal and the Norm Smith Medal. Matthew Lloyd won the Coleman for Essendon in 2000, with 94 goals in the home-and-away season (he kicked 109 for the year), and James Hird the Norm Smith on grand final day, but in the Brownlow the Bombers could do no better than Hird's equal seventh, eight points behind the winner, Melbourne's Shane Woewodin. The 1950 Bombers lost one match of an 18-round home-and-away season, won the flag and had the leading goalkicker – John Coleman – but not the Brownlow. Collingwood's 1929 team went closer to the complete sweep, unbeaten in 18 home-and-away games and losing just one final en route to the flag, fielding the League's leading goalkicker (Gordon Coventry) and that year's Brownlow winner

(Albert Collier). There was no Norm Smith Medal in 1929, Norm Smith being a few years from his debut, but Horrie 'Tubby' Edmonds, who kicked five of Collingwood's 11 goals in the grand final, would have been a likely recipient.

The opposite feat – the winless wooden spoon – has been accomplished several times, not all of them by St Kilda. The absolute worst season ever to have been flung together may have been Hawthorn's 1950, in which they lost all 18 games, by an average of 57 points. The dawn amid this darkness was the debut of Camberwell schoolteacher John Kennedy, who would be best and fairest in his first three seasons, and gradually rebuild the club in his own forbidding image, eventually coaching the Hawks to their first three flags.

A case might also be made for the 2013 Greater Western Sydney side, who lost 21 games in a longer season, but did win one, against Melbourne. Speculation that the suspensions-gutted, scandal-scarred Essendon of 2016 might be the first to go a 22-game season without winning lasted only as long as Round 2, also against Melbourne, who seemed to harbour some grudge against blank W columns. Essendon won two more matches that year, and only just finished last, 0.6 of a percentage point behind Brisbane. The last few weeks of 2016 must have been excruciating for those Bombers barrackers who'd punted their life savings on the basis that i) we must extract solace where we can, and ii) the pre-season odds on an Essendon wooden spoon, short though they were, were better than bank interest.

51

The Worst Guernsey Ever
Kangaroos 11.14.80 Collingwood 14.14.98
Docklands Stadium
ROUND 21, 2000

Football fans are hopelessly sentimental creatures, which is why they respond to tampering with their club's nomenclature or iconography with defensive horror, akin (or so they prefer to think) to a belligerent patriot clutching the regimental standard in one hand and bloodstained cutlass in the other, as barbarians surge o'er the battlements.

For several generations of VFL/AFL fans, club colours seemed an immutable fact of life – for many decades, they barely changed. A few clubs manifested indecision during the League's early years: Richmond played in vertical stripes and a horizontal cummerbund before submitting to the embrace of the gold sash, South Melbourne evolved to the V from a sash, via an experiment with all-red, and St Kilda toyed with yellow highlights. A couple of the incoming clubs of 1925 also took time to settle down, but North Melbourne finally arranged their royal blue and white into vertical stripes in 1933, and Hawthorn did the same with their brown and gold in 1950. For the next half-century, give or take some cosmetic fiddling, mostly around cuffs and collars, the League's uniforms remained, more or less, uniform.

This began to change from the mid-1990s, as the AFL's nationwide expansion introduced new clubs – who, crucially, had new colours, any alteration of which would be less likely to prompt aggrieved squawks of 'Sacrilege!' from the zealous. This encouraged the taking of further liberties, as did the evolution of guernseys from wool to synthetics capable of supporting more intricate designs. At around the same time, the so-called 'clash' guernsey began to become a thing.

Alternative kits had long been a feature of European soccer leagues, for obvious reasons – a match between Manchester United and Liverpool, or Internazionale and Atalanta, or Levante and Barcelona, if all insisted on wearing their home colours, would be confusing for players, officials and spectators alike. But the VFL/AFL had survived without clash guernseys, notwithstanding a couple of occasions in the 1910s and 1920s when Geelong wore all blue against Collingwood. If there was a compelling case for alternative guernseys, it was really only whenever, as today, Collingwood met North Melbourne, especially before colour television arrived in Australia in 1975 – but matches between the two clubs had taken place for 75 years without anyone going to the wrong huddle at quarter time or king-hitting a teammate.

The real reason for the introduction of clash and other alternative guernseys was, of course, to generate new streams of merchandise revenue, and to provide sponsors with opportunities. This reaped a bountiful harvest of eye-ache, and though further fresh hells doubtless await, it is daunting to try naming anything that has been, or imagining anything that could be, worse than what the Kangaroos suited up in for this match. It might not have been the most crass, garish and hideous outfit which has ever been worn onto an AFL field, but no serious discussion of that benchmark can ignore it.

The name under which the Kangaroos were playing was an indicator of their suggestibility for such wretched burlesque. In 1999, North Melbourne dispensed with their geographical identity, and began trading as 'the Kangaroos' – to broaden their appeal beyond their home patch, and/or roll the pitch for a relocation to Sydney, Canberra or the Gold Coast, or perhaps to seize a future as a wandering national team.[1] It did them no harm on the field. The Kangaroos won the 1999 premiership, easily accounting for a Carlton exhausted by their clamber into the grand final from sixth place; this unlikely ascent had included the Blues' one-point win over flag favourites Essendon in a preliminary final memorable for the final-quarter heroics of Anthony Koutoufides, who came out of the back pocket to score two goals from pack marks

---

1   From 1999, the Kangaroos played some home games in Sydney and Canberra. In the mid-2000s, the AFL offered to underwrite a move to the Gold Coast, but this was rejected by the club's board under incoming chairman James Brayshaw in late 2007. The North Melbourne name was restored at the beginning of 2008, prompting a 25 per cent surge in membership.

before returning to his lines to take several vital contested grabs in defence.[2]

Off the field, however, the no-longer-North-Melbourne Kangaroos were adrift from their moorings – and, as with all spiritually unanchored organisations and individuals, susceptible to the blandishments of predatory hucksters. A club surer of who they were and where they stood would not have abased themselves as the Kangaroos did this Sunday afternoon. Some of the 30,003 at Docklands might have been braced by puzzled notices in the newspapers for what they beheld as the Kangaroos took the field; to others it would have been a shock. Few, however, could have altogether suppressed a combination of gasp, giggle and, in extremis, dry heave.

The Kangaroos were wearing orange. Specifically, they were wearing a version of 2000's away guernsey – white with royal blue yoke, truncated royal blue stripes, and kangaroo motif – rendered in orange. With black shorts, and black socks. The reigning premiers could scarcely have looked sillier if adorned with revolving bow ties and jesters' hats. This risible ensemble had been donned, inevitably, at the behest of a sponsor: mobile telephone concern Orange.

The Kangaroos' orange jumper lives in infamy as the only thing that ever succeeded in making the Kangaroos' captain, Wayne Carey, look ridiculous on a football field.[3] Carey, playing his 226th game for the club today, was one of those players – one of those people – blessed and/or cursed with an ability to warp reality around them. The question

---

2   Stephen Kernahan, the former Carlton captain, declared this the greatest ever single-quarter performance by an individual player. Kernahan's bias notwithstanding, he has a case.

3   A number of largely self-inflicted mishaps would serve to render Wayne Carey serially undignified off the field, however. His eventual autobiography, *The Truth Hurts*, earned plaudits for its brutal honesty, but it had a great deal to be brutally honest about – drugs, alcohol, arrests and sundry boorish behaviour. Most notorious if not necessarily most serious was Carey's 2002 departure from North Melbourne amid the storm summoned by his affair with the wife of his vice-captain, Anthony Stevens. Carey made a comeback with Adelaide in 2003. Probably nothing in the history of Australian football has been more inevitable than Carey scoring the first goal of his first game against North Melbourne, a three-bounce run followed by a low kick straight into the Kangaroos cheer squad, laying the foundation of a nine-goal win for the Crows. (No belief in karma can possibly survive contact with football.) In an earlier era, of a less pervasive media and more decorous general culture, Carey's off-field conduct might not have become public knowledge: it is a distance more than likely that some stars of football's less rigorously scrutinised years fell short of sainthood in their personal lives. The combination of Carey's fame with the accelerating tabloidisation of an internet-spooked media made him the bridge to a new way of living for footballers, in which social media imprisoned all AFL players in the online panopticon, where they could be heckled and abused and humiliated across the internet all day, every day. In 2017, Travis Cloke, then of Western Bulldogs, previously of Collingwood, stood down for a few weeks, citing mental health issues exacerbated by online abuse, which he'd attracted by doing nothing worse than playing a few indifferent games.

of whether their elemental charisma is a byproduct of their immense talent, or whether their immense talent is magnified by their elemental charisma, is probably unanswerable. They're the ones who stand out even among the most distinguished of their peers, the ones to whom the eye – and the camera – is drawn. At an athletics meet, Usain Bolt. On a cricket field, Shane Warne. In a Formula One pit, Ayrton Senna or Michael Schumacher. They're the ones who cause a nervous, overeager uncertainty even in those good enough to compete alongside them, as if they can't quite believe they're permitted in this rarefied company. In the modern era of the AFL, where that vibration is amplified still further by saturation media coverage, one thinks of Gary Ablett Sr, Lance Franklin, Tony Lockett, James Hird, Ben Cousins. And perhaps, most of all, of Wayne Carey.

The argument over who is the greatest football player of all time is an unwinnable one, which means it's also an unlosable one, which is why people enjoy having it. This discussion usually – unless your interlocutor is being obtuse or recherché or just plain annoying and advocating for Jason Akermanis[4] or someone – revolves around maybe half a dozen names, and Wayne Carey's is always one of those. Certainly, if one was to compile an all-comers team drawn from the period after the VFL became the AFL in 1990, it's tough to think of who you'd write in before him.

The bare facts tell some of the story. The Wagga Wagga–born Carey was, under the rules that governed these things in the 1980s, originally zoned to Sydney. The Swans' recruiting officer of the time, Greg Miller, first saw Carey representing New South Wales, aged 12, at a carnival in Darwin. Five years later, Miller, now working for North, where he would become CEO, saw Carey again, playing in a representative school match in Adelaide, where Carey was then living – though still tied, in theory, to the Swans. At a chance meeting with Sydney CEO Ron Thomas at VFL House in 1987, Miller made his pitch – not so much for Carey as for a young full-forward of whom he also liked the look, a kid from Corowa called John Longmire.

---

4   Jason Akermanis was a freakishly talented footballer, a key reason that Brisbane won three premierships in 2001, 2002 and 2003, and a deserving winner of the 2001 Brownlow Medal, even in a year in which that necessitated polling more votes than Andrew McLeod, Michael Voss and Ben Cousins. He is deployed as a hyperbolic absurdity in this scenario principally as an excuse to mock his off-field antics, notably the infamous 2010 newspaper column in which he fretted about gay players in shared post-match showers, as if concerned about being sized up for recruitment – and, while coaching at North Albury in 2014, getting suspended for cyber-bullying umpires, expanding footballing oafery into realms undreamt of by his antecedents.

If the argument over who is the greatest football player of all time is an unwinnable one, the argument over which is the worst transfer deal ever agreed to by a League club isn't even an argument. Sydney let Longmire and Carey go to North for $70,000 – $60,000 for Longmire, $10,000 for Carey. The Swans did eventually get Longmire back, as a successful coach, though not before he'd played 200 games for North, scored 511 goals and won a premiership and a Coleman Medal. Carey never came home. He kicked seven goals the first time he played against the club that, as he later put it, had thrown him into the Longmire deal 'like a set of steak knives'. He would spend 13 seasons at North/Kangaroos, most of them as captain, for 244 games, 671 goals and two premierships. He would be four times named All-Australian captain, and anointed an AFL Hall of Famer. But there was a deal more to it than that.

Like no other player of his era, like few of any era, Carey was able to bend the game to his will. Denis Pagan, coach for most of Carey's career, realised there was little point attempting to govern what North's opponents found ungovernable, and generally let the big centre half-forward loose, banking that Carey would beat whoever was put on him, and however many of them. (Glen Jakovich, West Coast's superb centre half-back, owed much of his reputation to the fact that he was one of vanishingly few defenders who could make Carey look like he was working for it.) Carey could score with either foot, from almost anywhere. He was quick despite his size – 192 centimetres, nearly 100 kilograms – and terrifying because of it. He was an imperious pack mark, a handballer of generous range and meticulous accuracy, and a ferocious tackler. On a football field, there was nothing of which Carey was incapable.

This Sunday afternoon at Docklands was not an especially noteworthy one for Carey, in and of itself – one goal, 17 kicks, an average kind of performance on a day when average was good enough to rate him among his team's best. It didn't compare with any of Carey's masterpieces: the 1997 qualifying final, in which he'd beaten Geelong by himself, scoring seven of North's eleven goals and laying on two others; the 1999 qualifying final, when he'd kicked six goals in sucking mud against Port Adelaide; the eleven-goal bullying of Melbourne in Round 17 of 1996, as North ambled to a 113-point victory; or the Sunday afternoon in 1998 when he'd taken his team to Subiaco and he'd beaten Jakovich – playing, admittedly, with a rickety ankle – as North beat West Coast, Carey scoring five goals and scooping up three Brownlow votes as he got his team home by 14 points.

For portions of that last game, there'd been nobody in North's forward 50 but Carey – but who else did they need? 'No Carey, no North' had become a common compliment to him, and an implied slight to his side.

The Kangaroos had Carey today, but – despite playing Collingwood – could not count on widespread popular support. The only result to be hoped for by the aghast neutral observer beholding what the Kangaroos were wearing, or – surely – by the Kangaroos partisan nobly acknowledging that greater stakes were in play, was an upset win for the Magpies, who arrived at Docklands 11 ladder places beneath the hosts, having won once in the previous 15 weeks; such an outcome would surely damn the tangerine travesty to eternal obloquy. This judgement was duly furnished by benign fates, though not until late on, when Collingwood overran the Kangaroos in the final quarter, abetted by two goals from Nick Davis – not the last time he would have a decisive impact on a match at the death.[5] 'The premiers,' chuckled *The Sydney Morning Herald*, 'wore an orange strip but played like lemons.'

Even those who appeared to have least reason to complain about the Kangaroos' cantaloupe calamity – Collingwood, who in the circumstances should have felt impelled to worship it from that day forward as a potent totem – hated it. Collingwood coach Mick Malthouse[6] complained that several Collingwood players, confused by the Kangaroos' black shorts and black socks, had launched handballs towards the wrong recipients, though given how badly Collingwood had been playing since Round 5, it's unclear how certain Malthouse could have been about this.

Subsequent seasons supplied plentiful competition for the title of Worst AFL Guernsey Ever. In adjudicating this matter, some parameters must be established. It does not seem right to consider costumes worn during pre-season or night competitions, or other such nonsenses about

5 Nick Davis joined Sydney in 2003. In 2005's semi-final against Geelong at the SCG, he conjured a final quarter to rival that of Anthony Koutoufides against Essendon in 1999. Sydney, when the hitherto anonymous Davis stepped up, had kicked three goals all day, and were 23 points behind. Davis bagged the last four goals of the game, sealing victory with the final kick. A bad day for Geelong; a bonanza for Geelong's television repair shops.

6 Mick Malthouse joined Collingwood at the beginning of 2000, and stayed for eleven seasons, including the 2010 premiership year. His career ended at Carlton, who sacked him halfway through 2015, by which time he had coached 718 games across four clubs, eclipsing the record of 714 established by Jock McHale at Collingwood. A marginal but vituperative tendency insists that McHale should only be credited with 713, having been bedridden with pleurisy and influenza during the 1930 grand final, during which it fell to club treasurer Bob Rush to rouse the Magpies to victory over Geelong with a stirring half-time address. The full-blown foil-hat version of events insists that the AFL cooked the books so that Malthouse would beat McHale's mark against Collingwood in front of a huge MCG crowd – rather than a week earlier, when Carlton were playing St Kilda in front of 12,125 indifferent Kiwis in Wellington.

which no sane person cares, and during which normal decorum can be assumed suspended. This excuses from deliberations such disasters as Geelong's stupid pre-season T-shirts of 2010 onwards, and Hawthorn's 1995 pre-season guernsey, a baffling arrangement of brown and gold diamonds on a blue background, which looked like bathroom linoleum chosen while drunk in 1970s Moonee Ponds.

When one contemplates the catastrophes which have been worn in competitive matches, there are plenty which have offended at a basic aesthetic level. Port Adelaide have been prolific on this front, led astray by fealty to their asinine nickname, the Power.[7] Port teams have sported both realistic and stylised lightning bolts. The former made them resemble weather maps. The latter made them look like they had done insufficient research into previous employments of stylised lightning bolts as features of uniforms.

Port's crosstown rivals have risen to this challenge. Adelaide have made several riotously unconvincing attempts to render their crow mascot more akin to a fearsome avian marauder than the mildly querulous scavenger of reality. None of which were worse than Adelaide's 2013 clash guernsey, of white with blue, red and gold splotches down one side, which made the Crows look like they'd wandered between Jackson Pollock and a semi-completed canvas.

Fremantle, for a while in the late 1990s, essayed a 3D conceit that made one want to ask for special glasses that might enable one to not see it. West Coast, in the early years of the 21st century, wore to their away games fuzzy red, blue and gold with a descending eagle, which evoked the test pattern of the state broadcaster of the kind of country which has a public holiday in honour of the emperor's goat. Brisbane, in 2007 and 2008, wore blue and white with a gold lion and fading yellow trim at the bottom, which suggested that the lion was yet to be house-trained. Hawthorn, in 2015 and 2016, played away in shimmering gold chevrons, only silver helmets and laser rifles from being cast as footsoldiers in a terrible science-fiction movie directed by a Scientologist.

But while the above were merely unpleasant – in a couple of cases, actually disorienting – to look at, the Kangaroos' apricot aberration was

---

7   When Port Adelaide joined the AFL from the SANFL in 1997, they were unable to deploy under their time-served nickname of the Magpies, on the grounds that Collingwood were already using it. Despite the existence of an obvious and badass solution – capitalising on Port's maritime heritage and playing as the Pirates – they decided upon the Power, a branding signifying nothing. In 2014, as if in acknowledgement of their founding misjudgement, Port established a junior fan club called the Pirateers.

not merely bad, but worn for bad reasons. When one adds venality as a qualification in the hunt for the worst guernsey in League history, the field narrows dramatically. In Round 3 of 1997, Carlton accepted $250,000 from the manufacturers of M&Ms to play, for the first time in their storied history, in a colour other than navy blue – sky blue, specifically, but that was at least still blue, and only for one game (at least initially – a similar kit later got a run as the away guernsey). St Kilda toyed, between 2001 and 2003, with a yellow-dominated clash guernsey at the behest of Pura Milk, but while the guernsey was nowhere near as simply stylish as the Saints' familiar black, white and red panels, it was not, in and of itself, repellent, at least if you had a fetish for traffic hazard warnings.

Tempting though it is to argue for an edict forbidding any footling with the basic guernsey templates, there are occasional reasons to welcome such deviations. During the 2010s, League clubs began commemorating the AFL's Indigenous Round by wearing their colours reimagined as Aboriginal artworks, all of which looked magnificent. Other one-offs have at least been worn through noble motive, in support of various charitable causes. Essendon get a pass, therefore, for the guernsey which, for one match in 2010, converted their scarlet sash into a seatbelt to promote safer driving. (Essendon, along with Collingwood, were the last holdouts against clash guernseys – the impetus in this instance came from Bombers ruckman David Hille, who as a younger man had been the only buckled-up passenger in a car which had crashed, killing three unsecured friends.) Hawthorn's 2010 camouflage-print Kokoda Trail homage was gauche and ghastly – but, again, the cause was honourable.

The Kangaroos' amber enormity, both ugly and mercenary, therefore endures as the worst guernsey any team has worn. Such is the genius of marketing people for fixing what is not broken that it may well find itself challenged – but, like the team that wore it, it will take some beating.[8]

---

8   Just before the beginning of the 2019 season, and just as *Carn* was about to be sent to print, the Western Bulldogs unveiled the jumper they intended to wear in their Round 1 game against Sydney. The match was to be played at Docklands Stadium, renamed Marvel Stadium under the terms of a new sponsorship deal with the Walt Disney Corporation. The Bulldogs' gormless commemorative get-up, a homage to the Marvel Comics character Thor, was instantly widely judged a potential rival to the Kangaroos' peach perfidy of 2000 as Worst Guernsey Ever, and may therefore have invalidated the premise of this entire chapter.

52

Jason McCartney's Comeback
Kangaroos 13.14.92 Richmond 13.11.89
Docklands Stadium
ROUND 11, 2003

Football commentators, when swept away by especially heady transports of excitement, are fond of declaring that the spectacle they are narrating could not be invented – that you couldn't make this up, that you cannot script drama such as this, that you wouldn't read about it. They are wrong, on two counts.

First is that authorial imaginations capable of inventing, for example, entire alien civilisations, with their own native fauna and flora, systems of government and economics, traditions of law and culture, technology as yet unmatched by humankind, and so forth, would probably not be unduly exercised by choreographing a close-run thing between, say, Carlton and St Kilda on a Saturday afternoon at the Melbourne Cricket Ground.

The second is that one of the appeals of sport is that it furnishes the kind of storylines which a screenwriter could conjure, but would scarcely dare put in front of a discriminating producer or intelligent audience – for fear, respectively, of being laughed out of the pitch meeting or seeing the screen at one's premiere occluded by a besplattering of tomatoes. Jason McCartney's comeback, on this Friday night at Docklands, could have been conceptualised, scripted and filmed, but it would have taken the most shameless hacker-outer of mawkish matinee glop to do it, and the most sentimental of simpleton to enjoy it as a work of fiction.

At the end of 2002, Jason McCartney had an impressive career behind him, and was hoping for reasons to look forward. He was 28, and had played 181 games over 12 seasons, first at Collingwood, then at

Adelaide, the last five years at North Melbourne. McCartney was a solid footballer, rather than a spectacular one – he'd accrued just six Brownlow votes across his decade and change in the AFL – but he was reliable, and versatile, the kind of artisan who builds the platform on which the headliners perform. You can watch your team a lot without really seeing a player like McCartney, but you'd notice pretty quickly if he and his fellow grafters ceased showing up.

There had been some poor timing, bad luck, and lousy judgement. McCartney was drafted from Nhill by Collingwood just after they'd won the 1990 premiership. In Adelaide's 1997 premiership year, he was only able to get on the park in the first six rounds. Having been traded to North for Mark Stevens in 1998, he played against his old club in that year's grand final, but North were well beaten, as was McCartney, with just three kicks all afternoon. In 1999, North won the premiership, but McCartney, who hadn't missed a game all season, missed out on a medal: he'd been reported in the preliminary final for striking Brisbane's Clark Keating – a daft, pointless forearm across the head, late in a marking contest, in the last quarter with the game all but won – and suspended. He may have thought, at the time, that it was the worst thing that could happen to him.

The winter of 2002 had been a tough one for the Kangaroos, as they adjusted both to the fact and the manner of the departure of Wayne Carey, their club's captain and greatest ever player. It had been especially hard sledding for McCartney, who was often deputised to fill the unfillable hole Carey had left at centre half-forward. He didn't do badly – a couple of goals against Sydney, three against Carlton – but his form ebbed, then a hamstring went. At the end of 2002, he was out of contract, and there was a new coach incoming – former West Coast and North Melbourne player, and latterly Collingwood assistant coach, Dean Laidley, replacing Denis Pagan, who was bound for Carlton.

All things considered, McCartney was looking forward to his end-of-season fortnight away with unusual eagerness. The day after the best-and-fairest count, the team departed for six days in New Orleans, before the group split to do their own things. McCartney spent a few days in Sydney, and then left with his teammate Mick Martyn – a dual premiership full-back who was about to be delisted by North after 287 games[1] – for a place both had visited and enjoyed before: Bali. Though they were staying in

---

1 Mick Martyn would follow Denis Pagan to Carlton in 2003, and play 13 games, bringing his career total to 300.

the party district of Kuta, they were more intent on recovering from New Orleans than contributing further to their post-season hangovers.

Nevertheless, on the Saturday night of 12 October 2002, McCartney and Martyn were persuaded out by friends holidaying in the vicinity, including players and staff from other AFL clubs.[2] They had dinner at the Macaroni Club, then went on to drinks amid the gaudy neon shamrocks of Paddy's Bar, the idea being to finish the night at the open-air, thatched-roof Sari Club opposite. A few minutes after 11 p.m., a suicide bomber blew himself up inside Paddy's. A few seconds after that, as patrons of Paddy's who could still move scrambled, terrified, into Legian Street, a white Mitsubishi van parked outside the Sari exploded.

The Bali bombings killed 202 people, including 88 Australians, and injured hundreds more. McCartney was among those able to limp away from the scene under his own steam, but he was badly hurt: burned on 50 per cent of his body, and with a lump torn from his left calf by hot shrapnel. The less-injured Martyn flagged down a local on a motorcycle, put McCartney on the back, and sent them to their hotel, which retained an English-speaking doctor, who called for an ambulance.

At the overwhelmed Sanglah General Hospital in Denpasar, McCartney and other casualties were tended by staff more used to dealing with tourists maimed in moped mishaps. On the Monday morning, McCartney was among the critically injured evacuated to Darwin aboard a C-130 Hercules belonging to the Royal Australian Air Force. After further treatment, McCartney was taken to Melbourne on another RAAF flight, and by helicopter from Essendon airport to the Alfred Hospital, where he was placed in an induced coma for six days. Doctors put his chances of survival at four in five. Playing football again looked a longer shot.

Yet, 237 days later, there Jason McCartney was at Docklands, leading out the teammates who'd barely been able to recognise him when they'd visited him at the Alfred. Though North might have been on the verge of letting McCartney go before the bombing, they had done right by him since: they'd offered him a contract of $42,000 plus $2100 per senior appearance, should he make any, and found him a part-time job at the club. Encouraged, McCartney played in a practice match for Port Melbourne reserves as early as March, on the day of his 29th birthday,

---

2   One was Steven Febey, who had just retired at the end of a 258-game career with Melbourne. He was just outside Paddy's when the first bomb exploded. Though not seriously physically injured, he struggled afterwards with post-traumatic stress disorder.

and had since been solid for Port, then North's affiliate in the VFL, give or take a few games missed with workaday footballing injuries.

Whichever members of the Kangaroos' cheer squad composed the run-through for McCartney's comeback understood that plain speaking would say it better than poesy. 'Welcome back Jason McCartney,' it read. 'An inspiration to all.' McCartney, as he had all season, wore long sleeves to cover the pressure bandages protecting his body, gloves over his scarred and still-fragile hands, and skin-coloured sheaths swaddling his legs, a layer of armour which took an hour to put on. But he had the number 5 back on his back, and two other numbers, in black, above the sponsor's logo on his chest: 88, and 202.

McCartney started on the bench, and stayed there for the first quarter, an open but inconclusive term of which Richmond just had the best, 4.2 to 3.4. At quarter time, coach Dean Laidley told him to play full-forward, and play it old-school: park himself in the goal square and lead from there. For the second quarter, this was the end at which Richmond's cheer squad were ensconced; as McCartney jogged to his position, the yellow-and-black-clad ranks, from whom he could normally have expected a ringing earful, rose in a standing ovation.

Players returning from a long injury layoff often speak of the difficulty of getting back up to AFL speed – and those are players who have not, within the last year, narrowly survived a bomb blast which left them having to learn to walk again. Between accepting the applause of Richmond's cheer squad and the half-time siren, McCartney didn't get a touch. The Kangaroos went into the main break a point adrift, 8.5 to 8.6, and McCartney began the third quarter back on the bench. His team were down a rotation, though: Leigh Colbert was on his way to hospital with a damaged pancreas after colliding with teammate David King in a marking contest. Ten minutes into the third quarter, the margin still within a kick, McCartney went back to full-forward, where he stayed for the rest of the match.

Everybody in the ground – everybody, that is, but the most dementedly dogmatic of Richmond supporters – wanted only one ending to this game. A fourth-quarter clock ticking long into time on, Richmond in front, margin under six points. A last, long, hopeful punt upfield by a Kangaroos player. A pack forming in the forward 50, players jostling. A leap from behind the mob by North's number 5, a foothold in someone's hip, a knee perching on someone else's shoulder, and those silver-gloved hands at the end of arms wrapped in blue and white-hooped sleeves plucking the spinning gold Sherrin from the sky, and cradling it safely to ground as full-time sounded, cueing an after-the-siren kick, from just sufficient difference to render the anticipatory tension unbearable, but which would hold steady enough to seal the fairytale.

It didn't quite happen like that, but real life did not short-change by much. Early in the last quarter, David King kicked towards centre half-forward. McCartney saw it first and bolted from the square to meet it half a pace in front of his opponent, Richmond's Andrew Kellaway – who, to his professional credit, had all night looked uninterested in featuring as an extra in any romance, marking McCartney doggedly. This time, however, McCartney got away from Kellaway, swatted aside his attempts to spoil, and took the mark on his chest, as the two players tripped over each other, maybe 30 metres out, dead in front; Kellaway gave the turf an irritable tap of his right fist.

For someone who'd played mostly in defence, McCartney had a decent record in front of goal: 62 in his 181 previous games. He slotted his 63rd like he was warming up in front of an empty grandstand, rather than in view of tens of thousands at the ground, and hundreds of thousands watching at home, who wanted him to score like they had barely ever wanted anything. It was surely the first time that many Richmond fans had applauded a goal which put their opponents nine points ahead.

McCartney's goal did not win the game for his team, but he had a hand – more accurately, a wildly swung foot – in the one that did. With the Kangaroos back behind by three points, he beat Kellaway to a loose ball, and gathered it deftly from the ground in his right mitt. With his back to goal, he made to swivel and kick in one movement as Kellaway applied a tackle. Kellaway did just enough to stop McCartney making proper contact: the ball missed the instep that might have guided it between the big sticks and hit the tip of McCartney's boot as the two players fell, sending it tumbling and scuttling into the goal square. Of the players sprinting in pursuit of McCartney's inadvertent daisy cutter, the Kangaroos' Leigh Harding was quickest. Sensing, correctly, that McCartney's kick didn't have the momentum to clear the goal line by itself, he seized the ball and hoofed it into the upper decks. Kangaroos 13.14, Richmond 13.11, and though two minutes remained, the scores did not change.

McCartney had decided a few weeks beforehand that his first game back would be his last game ever. He announced his retirement to the crowd after the final siren, in a post-match interview with Channel Nine's Tony

Jones, broadcast over the stadium's public-address system. 'I've used up every inch of my determination,' he said, 'my fitness, and I suppose mental effort. It's fitting that I hang the boots up as of tonight and go out on a great note. I'm spent. It's been a tough time, but that's enough for me, mate. Once I got selected, I knew I didn't have much more in me. It's been a huge mental battle to get to where I am today. Look, my body's still healing and it needs a rest, and mentally, it's been hard carrying the hopes of a nation, I can tell you, so I'm going to enjoy a couple of beers tonight with my family and friends. I love these guys, they've been great to me – what a way to go out.'

McCartney's teammates chaired him off. Celebrations and media interest in the days following were of the intensity more usually associated with premierships, at one point attracting federal leader of the opposition and North barracker Simon Crean. He'd missed the match to address the Queensland Labor Party conference as part of a bid to ward off an imminent challenge to his leadership; he left $100 behind the bar before leaving the pub, as if in penitence for his disordered priorities.[3]

A little over a week later, McCartney undertook a more exacting accounting with what had befallen him. Among the calls he'd received after his comeback game was one from police in Bali. In a courtroom in Denpasar, McCartney and other survivors of 12 October testified against Amrozi bin Nurhasyim, the first of the Bali conspirators to face trial. Wearing a short-sleeved brown and red Balinese print shirt, McCartney spoke candidly about the damage done to his career and to his body, demonstrating by peeling off one of the bandages protecting his scarred skin.[4]

---

3   Simon Crean saw off this attempt to unhorse him, but not another later in the year – he resigned and was replaced as Labor leader by Mark Latham, who led the party to defeat in the 2004 federal election, and resigned as leader of the opposition himself in January 2005. Latham reinvented himself as a populist blowhard, sort of an Australian Donald Trump tribute act, fulminating from a variety of media pulpits at all manifestations of the chimera of political correctness – including those afflicting, as he saw it, the AFL, whose campaigning on social issues such as same-sex marriage irked him. In one of the less surprising occurrences of the 21st century, in 2017 Latham hosted Sam Newman as a guest on one of his tedious chat shows, programmes which largely comprised members of the most privileged demographic on Earth – heterosexual white male Australians – whining at each other about how tough life was for them. Latham's AFL allegiances are difficult to pinpoint. Photographs exist of him draped in a Port Adelaide scarf during the 2004 grand final – though it would obviously be extremely unusual for such a garment to adorn the red neck of someone so uncouth.

4   Amrozi bin Nurhasyim was convicted and sentenced to death, a bracing ethical test for the most adamantine opponent of capital punishment. He was executed by firing squad along with two fellow conspirators – his brother Huda bin Abdul Haq, and Imam Samudra – on 9 November 2008. In 2012, Jason McCartney testified in the trial of another member of the Bali cell, Umar Patek, who had been arrested by Pakistani police in Abbottabad in January 2011, a few months before the town acquired infamy as the final hiding place of Osama bin Laden. McCartney's testimony against Patek was assisted by a brief highlights reel of his career in Australian football, a game with which the judges were unfamiliar. Umar Patek got 20 years.

Anybody who succeeds at top-flight sport of any kind has put themselves through a physical and psychological ordeal that would – and does – defeat most. It is likely, as a consequence, that athletes end up calibrating pain as the rest of us do not, just as they can perform feats of calculated and improvised skill that the rest of us cannot. Football folklore abounds with tales of indestructible stoics declining to abandon the arena despite injuries which would see most people taking weeks off from the most milquetoast of chairbound office jobs: Richmond's Francis Bourke, barely able to see for blood from a cut eye, taking the mark and scoring the goal that sealed victory against North Melbourne in Round 21 of 1980; Hawthorn's Dermott Brereton and Robert DiPierdomenico, refusing to desert their posts during the 1989 grand final despite broken ribs and damaged organs; Fremantle's Nat Fyfe, one of the Dockers' best in the 2015 preliminary final, playing most of the match with a broken leg. It is casting no aspersions to observe that none of them had come through the half of what Jason McCartney had.

As McCartney was always punctilious in observing, however, he was but one among many casualties of Bali, an atrocity which killed or injured hundreds, bereaved thousands and bewildered a country unused to being a victim of terrorism, or of hatred of any sort. Though Australians had died in Islamist outrages before Bali, including the ten killed in the United States in the 9/11 attacks of 2001, Bali was the first time it felt like Australians had been specifically targeted. That a moment of redemption occurred on the field of Australia's national game was not much, measured against what was lost, but it was something.

McCartney, who'd been agonisingly close to three premierships, got there eventually. In 2016, he was list manager at Western Bulldogs when they won one of the least likely flags in League history, confounding all odds to break a 62-year drought. For the club he worked for, it was relief, and liberation. For McCartney, merely the second time he'd done the impossible.

53

In the Tank
Melbourne 12.10.82 Richmond 12.14.86
Melbourne Cricket Ground
ROUND 18, 2009

Many players have found themselves in the position occupied by Richmond's Jordan McMahon as the final siren sounded: ball in hand, screams of crowd in ears, set shot still to take, result of game entirely dependent on their ability to kick, under immense pressure, in a straight line. But McMahon may be unique in having enjoyed, as he began his run-up, the earnest best wishes of the opposition coaching staff. Short of compelling their players to wear flippers and straitjackets, Melbourne's high command seemed to have done their best to lose this match. If such was their intention, they were on the verge of being cruelly thwarted by the transcendental ineptitude of Richmond.

Few of the 37,438 who showed up on this Sunday afternoon would have expected much; indeed, the fact that any number exceeding the friends and families of the players bought tickets was a heartening or alarming demonstration of the devotion of football fans. Nearing season's end, Melbourne were bottom of the ladder with three wins. Richmond had managed four wins and a draw with North Melbourne, and seen coach Terry Wallace invited to resign. Neither side fielded a player with any serious interest in the Coleman or Brownlow medals.[1] With just four more rounds to endure after today's non-event, both sides were thinking about next season. One side, however, may have been overthinking it.

---

1   Won in 2009, respectively, by Carlton's Brendan Fevola and Geelong's Gary Ablett Jr. However much Ablett might have enjoyed that year's Brownlow count, Fevola enjoyed it more, to the extent that Carlton sacked him.

The AFL draft, borrowed from American sports, is rooted in an elegant logic. In the interests of keeping the competition competitive, each year's worst-performing team gets first pick of the incoming crop of players, the second-worst team gets second pick, and so on. The problem is that this provides a theoretical incentive for playing poorly. If your season looks a lost cause, there's a rugged wisdom to flushing it entirely, in the hope of bolstering your playing stocks for the next – especially when a rider to the AFL draft, instituted in 2006 and in 2009 yet to be recognised for the grievous temptation it was and scrapped, gave a club an additional 'priority' pick at or near the top if they finished a season with fewer than five wins.

Melbourne would not be the first club to be suspected of – to put it charitably – planning a season or two ahead. Ironically, the Demons had previously played the part of the team allegedly gifted a win. Their last match of 2007, against Carlton, acquired infamy as the 'Kreuzer Cup', the gossip being that Carlton were keen to avoid victory in order to secure the priority selection which would grant them first dibs on the year's likely top draft pick, Matthew Kreuzer.[2] A few months later, Carlton's then-assistant coach, Tony Liberatore, said that while he'd never heard an explicit directive to tank, 'I could feel it, if that makes sense. Nobody ever said, "We're not going to win today," but the feeling in the group was that it was a bit of a laugh.' In that final round of 2007, Carlton duly crumbled to their 11th consecutive loss.

Any such subterfuge must be subtly undertaken – even the harrowed Melbourne and Richmond fans of 2009 would have noticed if their players began kicking the ball to the opposition deliberately – but the potential rewards are undeniable, especially given that tanking is difficult to diagnose beyond doubt, and the appearance of it is easy to defend. What better time, after all, than the twilight of a busted season to give some rookies and reserves a run in the firsts, or see if that full-back might work out at centre half-forward?

Melbourne coach Dean Bailey did more or less the latter at the start of the last quarter against Richmond. At the bounce, with the Demons only three points in front, James Frawley, who'd spent most of his career in defence, stood at centre half-forward, as if he'd forgotten to change

---

2   Matthew Kreuzer proved solid for Carlton, but (with due acknowledgement that you can play this game all day) the same draft saw Trent Cotchin go to Richmond at two, Patrick Dangerfield to Adelaide at ten, Cyril Rioli to Hawthorn at 12, and Alex Rance to Richmond at 18.

ends after three-quarter time. Matthew Warnock, another defender, who'd kicked as many goals in his 37 games to date as Frawley had in his 35 – one – was stationed at full-forward. The club's best on-baller, Nathan Jones, and most effective tagger, Clint Bartram, were stuck in forward pockets. Forward Brad Miller, who'd never played in the ruck, played in the ruck. Ruckman Paul Johnson played at full-back.

If it was a genuine strategic experiment, it was an unusually bold one, akin to launching an invasion of an enemy country by sending the catering corps in the first wave. However, it nearly won the Demons the game anyway. Though Melbourne appeared to have offered their opponents every assistance short of bearing them about the field in palanquins, Richmond found ways of failing to take advantage, notwithstanding a best-on-ground performance by an admittedly unhindered Ben Cousins, reminding everyone why taking a chance on him had been, as repeating patterns in the expectation of different results goes, an act of only moderate insanity.[3] And if there was a memo, some Melbourne players had not received it, or were ignoring it – goals by Jack Grimes and Ricky Petterd late in the final term gave the Dees a two-point lead. (Later reports suggested something of a mutiny at three-quarter time, some players declaring that they intended to win despite the implicit preference of their coaches.)

And so it came down to the final seconds. A loose ball just inside the Tigers' forward 50, seized by Richmond's Matt White. A handball backwards to Richard Tambling.[4] A kick under pressure, just exceeding the necessary 15 metres, to Jordan McMahon, who marked dead centre, 45 metres from goal, about half that from the nearest Melbourne defender, right on the siren. He wiped both hands on his shorts, exhaled, jogged in and scored. In fairness to all concerned, the exultation of Richmond's

---

3   It is not known whether Ben Cousins, the 2005 Brownlow medallist, ever struck some bargain with a scarlet gentleman with horns and a tail at a rural crossroads, but it would explain a great deal. Cousins commanded football fields with poise rarely rivalled in the game's history, and seemed equally befuddled by all of life beyond the boundary line. His first club, West Coast, ran out of patience after 238 games and one too many drug-related misadventures, and sacked him in 2007. Richmond signed Cousins after he served a year-long ban imposed by the AFL for conduct unbecoming; Tigers coach Terry Wallace later claimed he was genuinely worried about what might become of Cousins if he didn't. Cousins played 32 games for Richmond before retiring, after which things did not improve, Cousins' interactions with police, judges and wardens becoming more frequent.

4   Richard Tambling, though he played 108 serviceable games for Richmond, is a name which can nevertheless prompt upending of furniture when Tigers fans recall their team's draft history. In 2004, Richmond took Brett Deledio with pick one – a choice posterity smiled upon – but Tambling at four, passing up Lance Franklin and Jordan Lewis, whom Hawthorn took at five and seven.

players and the desolation of Melbourne's were both clearly genuine. Some Demons were in, or close to, tears – but one of the things which always mitigates hardest against attempts from on high to throw sporting contests is that professional athletes dislike losing even more than the rest of us.

Muttering nevertheless persisted about Melbourne's 2009 season. It wasn't just the Richmond game. The week before, against Sydney, Melbourne had lost by 18 points in another game notable for some eccentric selections. In the final round – with the wooden spoon already safe, as it were, but a fifth win possible, if unlikely, against the table-topping St Kilda – Melbourne got a couple of goals ahead of the Saints, at which point James Frawley was taken off Nick Riewoldt, who finished the day with six goals as St Kilda idled to a 47-point victory. During this period, it is worth noting, Melbourne also turned over Fremantle by 63 points, and given the Demons' general woefulness, it would be stretching credulity to suggest that they orchestrated this triumph to put the AFL's bloodhounds off the scent.

They came sniffing eventually, however. The rumours about 2009 refused to dissipate. When Dean Bailey was sacked by Melbourne chairman Jim Stynes in 2011 following an abject 186-point surrender to Geelong, he didn't blow the whistle, exactly, but did kind of sigh wistfully into it. At his farewell press conference, asked if he'd ever tanked, or tried to, Bailey replied: 'I had no hesitation at all in the first two years in ensuring the club was well placed for draft picks ... I experimented to a level which meant that we got players into certain positions and we developed them in those positions, and I think they've benefited from it ... you can't expect a player to go out there and just not try. Players were trying, of course they were trying during that period. I was asked to do the best thing by the Melbourne Football Club, and I did it. I did the right thing by the Melbourne Football Club.'[5]

In 2012, Brock McLean, who'd played for Melbourne in 2009 (though not in the games under question), said baldly that the Demons had been tanking – and that this, indeed, was the reason he'd sought a trade to Carlton. 'Definitely,' McLean told Fox Footy's On the Couch, 'and I think you would have to be Blind Freddy not to figure that one out.' (Had Blind Freddy been available, Melbourne might have started him at centre

---

5   Dean Bailey died in 2014, aged 47, from lung cancer.

half-back.) Former Melbourne chairman Paul Gardner said he thought the Demons had been tanking in 2008 as well as 2009. (It is possible that this was a misjudged defence of the club he loved, as if mortified by the idea that they could have been playing so badly if not doing so deliberately.) Jim Stynes, in his (posthumous) autobiography, wrote: 'Melbourne never sat down our coach, Dean Bailey, and instructed him not to win games. But he, I and everybody at the club knew what an important bearing on the club's future that extra draft pick might have. People at the club found themselves shrouded in that reality. It went against the grain to find solace in failure, but that was the system in place.'

There were further unedifying revelations. Newspapers discovered that in 2009 there had been a conclave of Melbourne coaching staff in a tin shed, known within the club as 'the Vault', at the Junction Oval – a crisis meeting called after Melbourne beat Port Adelaide in Round 15, making three wins for the year, and imperilling the priority pick. 'Stay the course,' Melbourne's football manager Chris Connolly was reported to have urged fellow conspirators.

In early 2013, the AFL released a 1000-page investigation into the affair. They had interviewed 58 people, including some veterans of 'the Vault', and rummaged through Melbourne's hard drives. The AFL's curious findings were, in sum, that nobody had done anything wrong, but they were going to be punished anyway. The AFL cleared Melbourne's team of trying to lose matches, and Melbourne's coaches and executives of telling them to do so. They nevertheless decided that Dean Bailey and Chris Connolly had acted in a manner prejudicial to the AFL's interests. Bailey, by then assistant coach at Adelaide, was suspended for the first 16 rounds of 2013. Connolly, still at Melbourne, was suspended for a year (and, after a discreet interval, sacked). The club was fined $500,000.

Bemusing though this verdict was, karma had already exacted a far more humbling punishment. Whether they'd done it by hook or crook, Melbourne had entered the 2009 National Draft holding the first two picks. They chose Tom Scully from the Dandenong Stingrays, and Jack Trengove from Sturt. Scully played one good and one injury-depleted season for the Demons and then, the instant his contract expired, departed for a million dollars a year and stardom at Greater Western Sydney. Trengove was a fine player who deserved his elevation to Melbourne's captaincy at the age of just 20 – making him the youngest team leader in League history.

But after four solid seasons, he had four more in which he barely played, plagued by a persistent foot injury. He was delisted by Melbourne at the end of 2017, and left for Port Adelaide.

Richmond, thanks somewhat to Jordan McMahon's after-the-siren steadiness, finished 2009 second from bottom, so at the same draft they were the next club called after Melbourne. The Tigers' recruiters decided to plunge on a kid from Castlemaine via the Bendigo Pioneers – possibly a little rough around the edges, slight aura of having been raised by the wolves that other wolves cross the street to avoid, but maybe the makings of a decent midfielder. His name was Dustin Martin. Elsewhere in the same draft, in which karma had clearly decided it was really going to ram the point home, Melbourne took Jordan Gysberts at 11 and Luke Tapscott at 18. Gysberts played 19 games in three seasons before being traded to North Melbourne. Tapscott played 48 games in four seasons before being delisted. With pick 20, Fremantle took Nat Fyfe.

54

The Newcomers' Derby
Greater Western Sydney 13.16.94 Gold Coast 9.13.67
Manuka Oval
ROUND 7, 2012

Something had to give – although, judging by an attendance of 8603, it was not going to be 'a hoot, by the people of Canberra'. After six rounds of 2012, Greater Western Sydney and Gold Coast both arrived at Manuka winless – and, by all appearances, friendless. Gold Coast could claim a couple of creditable losses – by three goals to Essendon, seven points to Fremantle – and GWS could plead that it was their debut season. But the first encounter between the AFL's 21st-century newcomers nevertheless shaped as a pathetic struggle between two runts for the right to be eaten last.

It also seemed, at least at the time, like a compare-and-contrast lesson in how to establish and brand a new football club, and how not to. In Gold Coast's first season, the year before, they'd been beaten up as regularly as everyone expected, winning just three games, all against teams (Port Adelaide, Brisbane, Richmond) as likely to make the finals as they were to stage a well-reviewed production of *Die Fledermaus*. But Gold Coast at least looked the part – which is to say, they looked like their identity had been fashioned in as long as it takes to note that the Gold Coast is warm, so 'Suns' will do as a name, and that the sun is red and/or yellow, so there are the colours.

Gold Coast had observed the fundamental rules of creating the iconography of a sports club, a vastly more straightforward process than professionals insist on making it look. A team needs to be rooted in a particular place, and in its attendant regional mythology; these are readily exportable, which is why it's possible to meet devoted Manchester United supporters in Guangzhou and rabid Chicago Bulls fans in Bamako. A team then needs a nickname taken from a predatory and/or graceful animal, an honest trade, a swift and/or violent item of machinery, or just something generally perceived as powerful and/or badass – but it must be a plural, otherwise the team sounds less like a band of brothers, and more like a bank or an energy utility.

And a team needs colours which are striking, and simple. Aside from the silly 'GC' logo on the front of Gold Coast's guernsey, which looked to have been prised off the hood of some disreputable Chinese facsimile of a Japanese SUV – it should, instead, have been another of the beautiful old-fangled clefs that adorned the guernseys of Carlton and Fitzroy – the Gold Coast Suns had punctiliously ticked all requisite boxes.

Everything about GWS looked like it had not only been designed by a committee, but by a committee of the kind of people who enjoy sitting on committees. There was the meaningless, insufferably bureaucratic name Greater Western Sydney, more suggestive of a body which collects bins and issues parking fines than a football club. It was an inexcusable choice, especially for a team designed to represent the part of Australia which may have the country's most coherent sense of regional identity – Sydney's western suburbs. This was to say nothing of the jarring overlap between 'West Coast' and 'Western Bulldogs'. A bolder – yet more sensible – decision would have been to pick one of the western suburbs to name the team after, and let the region gather around it.[1]

There was the nickname, the Giants, an abnegation of imagination which could only have been worse had GWS been called the Things. It wasn't just that there were already American football (New York) and baseball (San Francisco) teams trading as the Giants, and that an NRL team (from the Gold Coast, ironically) had failed under the name, it was the spurning of the opportunity to adopt a properly congruent avatar; even other names considered for GWS (Wolves, Warriors) had little to do with western Sydney.

GWS could have been (for example) the Bushrangers, several of whom once stalked the Blue Mountains, within GWS's catchment area. Or GWS could have taken the name of one of the blue-collar trades by which the denizens of the Western Suburbs enjoy defiantly defining

---

1   Another idea for Sydney's second club remained on the drawing board – the Sydney Celtics, to be partially recruited from Ireland, and branded in homage to the Irish contribution to the game. It would be pleasing to think that this notion was formally abandoned when someone imagined the club song.

themselves. Or they could have embraced as their emblem some creature from Australia's menagerie of impressively dangerous fauna. The Giants could have been the Dingos, the Goannas, the Redbacks, the Emus, the Huntsmen, or any one of several varieties of snake.[2]

And then there were GWS's colours: charcoal and orange. Neither of these, the launch publicity boasted, had appeared in League uniforms before, and while the obvious retort that there might have been reasons for that was unfair – they didn't look at all bad together – the effect was blown by the imposition of a stylised letter G. As a whole, the Giants' jumper design made GWS's players look like they'd come to a fancy-dress party got up as cans of some variety of lawnmower petrol.

This was GWS's second home game at Canberra's Manuka Oval. Another component of the thinking behind the unwieldy Greater Western Sydney concept was that the citizens of the nation's capital, traditionally a solid Australian football town, and not known for a giddying surfeit of things to do at weekends, would also get around the Giants. In return for $26 million from the ACT government to fund four games in Canberra in each of GWS's first ten seasons, an apologetic 'Canberra' was added to the back of GWS's guernseys. (Another obvious move might have been to base the team in Canberra, and call them the Kookaburras or somesuch, but the capital's population of 400,000 had been weighed against the roughly 10 per cent of Australia's population who live in Sydney's west.)

GWS's first game in Canberra, two weeks previously, had gone badly – yet quite well, considering. Though they'd lost by seven goals to an indifferent Western Bulldogs side, that was still the closest the Giants had yet come to victory. But mitigating against optimistic delirium on the part of the Giants today was the return to the Suns of Gary Ablett Jr, Gold Coast's captain, talisman and general reason for being, who'd had a couple of weeks out injured.

---

2   Notwithstanding distinguishing quirks of Australian hawks, eagles, crows, magpies and swans, it is a shame that only one AFL team – North Melbourne – has adopted a distinctively Australian animal as emblem. A survey of minor and country leagues reveals how much fun is being missed by the professionals. Who would not relish cheering the Dingley Dingos, the Tyabb Yabbies, the Tullibigeal Grasshoppers, the Charles Sturt University Bushpigs, the Gladstone Mudcrabs, the Katherine Camels, the Buln Buln Lyrebirds, the Campania Wallabies, the Myponga-Sellicks Mudlarks, the Skipton Emus, the Warwick Redbacks or – though chanting it could become tiring – the Mangoplah-Cookardinia United-Eastlakes Goannas? A few teams in the USAFL, Australian football's American league, deserve recognition for their svelte incorporation of local wildlife: the Little Rock Coyotes, the Seattle Grizzlies, the Las Vegas Gamblers and (especially) the Fort Lauderdale Fighting Squids.

Ablett Jr was, beyond the sort of argument people only make when they're trying to start an argument, the greatest player of the early 21st century. He'd been drafted by Geelong as a father-son pick, and been unfazed by the fact that seeking a name for yourself in football when you were called Gary Ablett Jr was like pursuing a career in physics as Albert Einstein II. The attention attracted by the surname alone had proved too much for Ablett Jr's talented younger brother, Nathan, who left Geelong after 32 games, his last the 2007 grand final, in which he kicked three goals.[3]

In nine seasons at Kardinia Park, Ablett Jr had compiled a tenable case that the two greatest players of all time had the same name – although aside from an unusual, and unusually public, profession of Christianity, he appeared unlike his father in every respect. On the field, Ablett Jr was a diligent accumulator rather than an explosive disrupter, an engine, not a warhead. Off the field, he was a model professional with a reputation as gleaming as his shaven dome, as opposed to an erratic eccentric with a temperament as recalcitrant as his fraying hair. At Geelong, Ablett Jr had won two premierships, a Brownlow Medal, two club best and fairests, and three Leigh Matthews trophies – the award given, since 1982, to the League's most valuable player, as voted for by players.[4] For a new club seeking a marquee name to underpin their legitimacy and lure punters through the gates, Ablett had been the obvious choice: he'd signed to the Suns for $9 million over five years.

Against GWS at Manuka, Ablett did what Ablett almost always did: gathered 30-plus disposals, and functioned as the animating energy of his team. (Gold Coast were, in this respect, not so much Suns as a solar system, bodies held in obedient orbit by the gravitational pull of a much greater, life-giving power.) But in the early stages of the game, at least, more attention was caught by the biggest signing in the home team's colours.

Israel Folau was not the most storied Australian football player recruited by GWS. Former Brisbane triple premiership player Luke Power and former Port Adelaide stalwart Chad Cornes both had superior claims to that title, not least because Israel Folau wasn't really an Australian

---

3   Nathan Ablett emerged from retirement briefly in 2011, playing twice for Gold Coast. Mark Thompson, Geelong's coach during Nathan Ablett's regrettably brief career, always insisted that Nathan could have been as good as his brother – which is to say, as good as anyone ever.

4   Gary Ablett Jr would receive this confirmation of his peers' esteem twice more at Gold Coast, making him the first five-time winner. He had previously been the first three- and four-time winner.

football player. He was, rather, one of the tiny coterie who have played more than one code of football at the top level. Folau had been a rugby league superstar with the Melbourne Storm and the Brisbane Broncos, and had also represented Queensland and Australia. GWS, seeking a name that might resonate in the rugby league heartland they were seeking to subjugate, had offered him $4.2 million over three years, which was verging on Ablett money; other reports suggested even more. The example the Giants were seeking to follow had been set by Gold Coast: lining up for his 23rd game for the Suns today was Folau's former Broncos teammate, and fellow Australian rugby league international, Karmichael Hunt.[5]

Folau played 13 games for the Giants, and in most of them looked no less out of place than an inflatable wavy-arm tube figure on a funeral director's forecourt.[6] But he helped get his side off to their startling start today, drawing a free kick in the first minute for a shove in the back from Michael Coad, converted by an advantage call from the umpires into a goal for Devon Smith. GWS scored the next three, as well: Liam Sumner, Stephen Coniglio, Callan Ward. It took Ablett, bustling industriously through midfield to pick out Harley Bennell, to put a Suns goal on the board before the first break.[7]

The Suns' marginal advantage in experience, and major advantage in Ablett, dictated the second and third terms. Gold Coast kicked four in the closing minutes of the second quarter – Kyal Horsley, Josh Caddy twice, David Swallow – to lead by 13 at the main change, and fought off a GWS rally to be four points in front at three-quarter time. GWS looked the side less likely to launch a decisive final-quarter blitz, but that's what they did. While the Suns forgot where the goals were, the Giants found them five

---

5   Karmichael Hunt was playing his third code, having previously jumped from rugby league to rugby union. He played 44 games for Gold Coast, few worth the seven-figure salary the Suns were reportedly paying him.

6   Israel Folau would also take up rugby union after leaving the AFL. A few months after Australia's riotously overdue decision to legalise same-sex marriage in late 2017, Folau declared that those who availed themselves of this opportunity would be, to paraphrase him somewhat, honeymooning in Hell. The outrage Folau's nonsense elicited can have been nothing compared to the relief of GWS's PR department that he was no longer their problem. Splendidly, at the next game Folau's Waratahs played after the story broke, they not only collapsed from a 29–0 start against Crusaders in a fashion sufficiently dramatic to suggest divine intervention, but the Christchurch Stadium DJ serenaded them off with The Village People's 'Y.M.C.A.'.

7   Harley Bennell left the Suns under a cloud at the end of 2015. After being dropped for drinking alcohol after a match, photographs were published appearing to show Bennell in ill-advised proximity to rails of white powder, though the final straw was an intemperate exchange of opinions with a Surfers Paradise nightclub bouncer. Fremantle took a chance on him, though Bennell also tried the Dockers' patience.

times, four in a five-minute burst at the end: Adam Treloar,[8] Jonathan Giles, Jeremy Cameron, Jonathan Giles again. In the dressing-room afterwards, the Giants found themselves having to remember, for the first time, the words of their club song (a composition of The Cat Empire's Harry Angus, entitled 'There's a Big, Big Sound', it was a genuine ripper, a swaggering jazz noir that sounded like Calexico or DeVotchKa at their more upbeat).[9]

This game proved a preview of the fortunes that the AFL's two newest teams would experience in their early years: the Giants acquiring momentum as the Suns lost their way. It was the Giants who played finals first, in 2016 – falling a goal short of the grand final in a monumental preliminary final against eventual premiers Western Bulldogs. The Suns had little to show for their early labours but Gary Ablett Jr's second Brownlow Medal, in 2013. (In 2014, were it not for a shoulder injury sustained in a tackle by Collingwood's Brent Macaffer, Ablett would surely have had a third – he finished four points behind the winner, West Coast's Matt Priddis, despite missing the last seven weeks of the season.) Given the lack of success enjoyed by Gold Coast during their years as The Gary Ablett Experience, it's arguable that the best thing that happened to GWS was something that didn't happen: the widely anticipated arrival of their own parachuted superhero, Hawthorn's Lance Franklin, who instead went to the Swans.

Rather than building their team around a star player, the Giants built theirs around a star coach: Kevin Sheedy, lured out of retirement at fearful risk to his career win/loss ratio. Speaking to media afterwards, Sheedy suggested that seven matches to a first victory wasn't bad, given that it had taken him six at Essendon. 'I'm slowing up,' he added, with humility both false and mistaken: Essendon won their second game under his charge.[10]

---

8   During his time at GWS before transferring to Collingwood, Adam Treloar inspired what might have been the all-time zenith of improvised commentary punsmithery. Channel Seven's Basil Zempilas, reflecting on the state of an opponent who had come off a distant second-best in a confrontation with the blond midfielder, observed: 'He fought Treloar, and Treloar won.'

9   GWS's club song was unusual among the anthems of expansion teams in being other than bloody awful – largely because its composer was clearly mindful of the traditions of the songs of the established clubs, i.e. big, camp show tunes bearing somewhat self-mockingly braggadocious lyrics. The best-known versions of the original club songs were recorded circa 1972 by The Fable Singers, a choir assembled by the record label of the same name. Among their number were the film critic and television presenter Ivan Hutchinson, and Melbourne jazz legends Frank Traynor and Smacka Fitzgibbon. In early 2018, the AFL commissioned re-recordings, prompting a response from fans comparable to that which might be occasioned by the Louvre announcing its decision that the *Mona Lisa* would look better with a beard.

10 In fairness, he wasn't that far wrong. In 1981, Kevin Sheedy's first season as coach, Essendon lost five of their first six games – and then didn't lose again until the last round. The Bombers finished

GWS were not some zany band of plucky ragamuffins, however. They had been permitted significant salary-cap wiggle room, and several early helpings from the draft smorgasbord: the 2011 National Draft alone had seen the Giants take Jonathan Patton, Stephen Coniglio, Will Hoskin-Elliott and Toby Greene, among others, inside the first 20 picks. Gold Coast had been offered similar largesse: their 2010 haul included David Swallow, Harley Bennell, Josh Caddy, Dion Prestia and Tom Lynch.

Neither GWS nor Gold Coast had any excuse for being bad teams, but the putative fanbases of both proved pretty adept at finding excuses to avoid going to see them play: by 2018, both clubs had average home attendances of around 12,000–13,000. The teams intended to expand the reach of Australian football might instead have defined its limits.

---

fourth, and lost the elimination final to Fitzroy. In two seasons at GWS, Sheedy coached 44 games for three wins and 41 losses.

55

Adam Goodes Dances
Sydney 19.8.122 Carlton 9.8.62
Sydney Cricket Ground
ROUND 9, 2015

In almost every respect, this match was unremarkable: a sweatless belting by a home team, already certain finalists, of a visiting riffraff with one win for the season to date, and little reason to expect many more. (Carlton duly won 2015's wooden spoon – quite a feat, considering that this necessitated being worse than Brisbane, which in 2015 was like being wetter than water.) Sydney eased to a 63-point lead by three-quarter time, and lifted their boot off Carlton's neck a little in the final term, to win by an even ten goals. Lance Franklin kicked seven for the Swans, but such was the disarray of the Blues' defence that there was little of the usual joy to be had from watching him, as one might admire a five-for by a champion fast bowler rather less if the opposition batsmen had been blindfolded and sent to the crease equipped with golf clubs.

Nevertheless, this Friday night non-event became the most ardently discussed, dissected and disputed game of 2015. It was the sucking core of a wildly whirling vortex of inanity, a peerless illustration of the paradox which holds that the more that modern media – and modern social media – examines something, the less anyone learns. It did at least acquire some utility as a reliable litmus test for the dickheadery levels of one's fellow citizens, whose views on the subject could reveal a great deal about them very quickly, usually unwittingly. And it nearly finished the career of one of the game's greatest players.

With about six and half minutes to play in the second quarter, Adam Goodes – dual Brownlow medallist, four-time All-Australian, 444 goals from 357 games to that point, not the sort of player teams other than the

2015 Blues tended to leave standing around on his own in the forward 50 – marked, unbothered, about 30 metres from the sticks, dead in front. Goodes goaled, putting Sydney 47 points ahead, 9.3 to 1.4. By way of celebration, he danced towards a terrace largely populated by Carlton barrackers, slapping his hands against his elbows, and finishing with a mime of a spear-carrying action, and a joyous battle whoop.

There was one sensible response to what Goodes did, and it was: an Indigenous player has kicked a goal during Indigenous Round, so he's doing an Indigenous dance – good on him. (Among the Carlton fans towards whom Goodes gambolled, while there was booing and gesturing, there was also laughter, and some applause which might not have been sarcastic.) However, non-sensible responses were not merely abundant, but at times almost impressive in their fatuity.

Even before Round 9 of 2015, there was history between Adam Goodes and that cohort of white Australians perturbed by any image of a triumphant and/or assertive black man. During Indigenous Round in 2013, Sydney played Collingwood at the MCG on a Friday night. Goodes conducted a masterclass, kicking three goals, gathering 30 possessions and earning three Brownlow votes as the Swans plucked the Magpies by 47 points. With about 90 seconds left on the clock, Collingwood's Darren Jolly chased the ball over the boundary line as Goodes chased him.[1] As the pair drew up, outrun by the yellow Sherrin, Goodes' ear was caught by something over the fence. He turned around, called to a nearby steward, and pointed towards the source of whatever it was. As security escorted a girl draped in black and white from her seat, Goodes stalked across the field to the dressing-room, distraught, without waiting for the final siren, or the acknowledgements of his team's victory and his own best-on-ground performance.

It emerged that Goodes had been called an 'ape', and that the spectator who had insulted him was a 13-year-old girl. Goodes' response was punctiliously gracious: he declined to press charges, accepted the culprit's apologetic phone call, and urged that no blame be assigned to her, nor media pursue her. The responses of other AFL players, flickering across social media, were resoundingly sympathetic: Geelong's Joel Selwood, Richmond's Jack Riewoldt and West Coast's Nic Naitanui were

---

1   Darren Jolly played 237 games for Melbourne, Sydney and Collingwood, winning premierships at the latter two. He and his wife, Deanne, were contestants in two series of renovation-porn reality show *The Block*, winning season ten.

among those who tweeted support for Goodes.[2] Collingwood president Eddie McGuire visited the Swans' rooms after the match to apologise on behalf of his club.[3]

It was far from the first instance of racial abuse of an Indigenous player, and it would not, lamentably, be the last. But it seemed like there were – with due recognition that this is a much, much easier thing for white folks to suggest – some grounds for optimism. At the instant the incident occurred, stewards, police, fellow players and League authorities alike unhesitatingly took the word, and the side, of the aggrieved Indigenous footballer – not a response which could have been anticipated for most of the game's history. There was general agreement that further education all round was required, though it is always worth wondering how many times Indigenous players can be expected to patiently talk everyone through the basics of not behaving like a goose at the football.

There were those unminded to help, largely well-rewarded white columnists and broadcasters with little experience of being called anything they didn't deserve. And there were, as there always are, angry morons on the internet, though their opinions merited no further consideration than usual. And there was, again, Eddie McGuire, who on the Wednesday morning following the match was co-hosting his Triple M show with former Western Bulldogs player Luke Darcy when the subject of a promo for *King Kong*, shortly to open at Melbourne's Regent Theatre, came up. 'Get Adam Goodes down for it, do you reckon?' said McGuire. 'No, I wouldn't have thought so, absolutely not,' replied a horrified Darcy, as if earnestly wishing that McGuire's seat was fitted with an ejector mechanism. McGuire wittered further in this vein, an aberration he later ascribed to tiredness and painkillers. Goodes declined to accept his apology.

Those who had decided to dislike Adam Goodes as a consequence of this brouhaha did not have their mood improved by 2014. Goodes

---

2 In 2016, Nic Naitanui was the subject of a similar contretemps, when a (white) Perth primary school student elected to dress as the West Coast ruckman for his school's book week, despite the slenderness of Naitanui's literary canon. The hapless infant's mother not only crowned her son with a wig of dreadlocks and painted him brown, but shared a picture of this homage online. Naitanui responded that the kid's innocence 'hurts my heart', and noted: 'It's a shame racism coexists in an environment where our children should be nurtured not tortured because they are unaware of the painful historical significance blackface has had previously,' before expressing his wish to 'meet the little champion reader'. There really should be some mechanism by which players get paid extra for having to keep explaining this stuff.

3 Many have leveraged a position in Australian football into a position of wider importance, few with the dauntlessness demonstrated by Eddie McGuire in his brisk ascent from teenage sports reporter to ubiquitous radio and television broadcaster to president of Collingwood on his 34th birthday, and CEO of Channel Nine eight years later.

was garlanded Australian of the Year – for, among other things, his co-founding (with former Swans teammate Michael O'Loughlin) of the Go Foundation, an educational advocacy focusing on Indigenous youth. Goodes had a decent season on the field, as well, and it was no fault of his that Sydney were dismasted by Hawthorn in the 2014 grand final. But something was happening in the stands: Goodes was being booed.

Some defended this conduct, mostly that mystifying echelon of white people who presume to instruct black people in what does and does not constitute racism. They had, if one is extending greater generosity than their motivation merited, perhaps half a point. There are times when it is okay to boo a player, especially in the context of a match in which the player in question has perpetrated some malfeasance; it was fair enough, for instance, when Melbourne fans razzed Goodes during the 2007 game in which he took an unsavoury whack at Simon Godfrey. It's even sometimes okay to boo a player over a protracted period, when the player in question has chosen to play the pantomime villain. Jason Akermanis, one of those who (predictably) argued that Goodes was a big sook, or words to that effect, could only have assumed this role more obviously during his playing days if he'd turned out in a top hat, with a chuckling canine sidekick and curly waxed tips on the ends of his stupid moustache.

But this argument failed to acknowledge that when crowds persistently boo or otherwise insult a player, they are booing or otherwise insulting what that player represents. Adam Goodes consistently represented a refusal to pretend that rewarding a few dozen Aboriginal Australians for being good at football meant that everything else was okay. Such was the background racket when Carlton came to the SCG for Indigenous Round, 2015. Goodes and the Swans took the field wearing guernseys designed by Goodes' mother, Lisa Sansbury.[4] Somewhere on his mind were the Under-16 Indigenous footballers of the Flying Boomerangs, whom he'd met during the week, and who'd taught him a war dance.

As he walked off after the game, Goodes was asked by Matthew Richardson, reporting for Fox Footy, if his celebration had been directed at the Carlton fans. 'Not at all,' replied Goodes. 'Indigenous Round, proud to be Aboriginal, and representing.' Over ensuing days, a number of good

---

4   The practice of enlisting Aboriginal artists to adapt club guernseys for Indigenous Round began in the 2010s, and was AFL-wide by 2014. Some have been designed by current or former Indigenous players, including Port Adelaide's by Nathan Krakouer in 2017, Essendon's by Gavin Wanganeen in 2016, and Adelaide's by Andrew McLeod in 2014.

questions might have been asked about Goodes' caper – about its origins, its significance, the role of dance in Indigenous culture – but none were. Instead, the responses – certainly the loudest responses – clustered on that bracket of the spectrum between neurotic and idiotic. As calamitous mischance had it, Eddie McGuire was calling the game for Fox Footy. At half-time, he spluttered of Goodes' dance: 'We've never seen that before. And I don't think we ever want to see it again, to be perfectly honest, regardless of what it is.' He later dismissed Goodes' celebration as 'a made-up dance, this is not something that has been going on for years'.[5] Others unsettled included Leigh Matthews, who saw it as provocation, and commentator Dennis Cometti,[6] who upon further reflection was decent enough to admit, 'I don't think I fully understood what that was all about' – a sentiment which should be less rare than it is.

Goodes played the following week against Gold Coast, and the week after against North Melbourne. Sydney won both games, and Goodes played well in both. When Sydney came back from the bye, Goodes was a bit off against Richmond, but so were the Swans. He kicked three goals in dispensing with Port Adelaide at the SCG, was solid in a win over Brisbane at the Gabba, and certainly wasn't among the Swans' worst as they got mowed by Hawthorn at Stadium Australia, nor when spanked by West Coast at Subiaco. But at the away games, there was no mistaking it: Goodes was being singled out, his every touch eliciting a low drone of derision. In the final quarter against the Eagles, the game more or less lost, Goodes' Indigenous teammate, Lewis Jetta, kicked a futile goal, and celebrated with a mimic of Goodes' dance. There was none of the exuberance of the original, though: Jetta was sour, angry, defiant.[7]

It got to Goodes. He requested, and received, an indefinite leave of absence from the Swans. He would, at the very least, sit out the Round 18 match at home to Adelaide; there were rumours that he might not play

---

5   All of which was even weirder when one recalled Eddie McGuire's sincere contrition for his remarks in 2013 – he offered to quit his broadcasting roles and his position at Collingwood – and weirder still when one contemplated McGuire's otherwise stout record on Indigenous matters, including his chairmanship of the Michael Long Learning & Leadership Centre. McGuire offered to stand down from this as well, but Long refused his resignation.

6   Dennis Cometti played for West Perth in the late 1960s, and was briefly on the books of Footscray in 1971, though he never played a senior game. As a commentator, he was admired for a droll drawl, and baroque wordplay to which it did great service. The spectacle of Western Bulldogs' Tony Liberatore emerging from a tangle with an eye injury was narrated by Cometti with: 'He went into that last pack optimistically, and came out misty optically.'

7   Lewis Jetta was traded to West Coast at the end of the 2015 season, after which, as is the way of these things, his occasional celebrations of goals with Goodes-style dances attracted markedly less disfavour from the home fans.

again. This prompted the expectable inanities from the usual suspects. Once it became clear that Jason Akermanis, Andrew Bolt, Miranda Devine, Alan Jones and Sam Newman[8] were all on one side of an argument, that really should have been an end to it.

As Round 18 approached, there were more demonstrations of support for Goodes. Many AFL players, Swans and not, Indigenous and not, defended Goodes' dance as inoffensive and/or kind of cool. The AFL Players' Association issued a statement backing Goodes. Writing in *The Age*, Western Bulldogs captain Bob Murphy correctly observed that 'I can't talk on behalf of Adam or his people, nor would I want to' – if only such humility had been in more plentiful supply – '[but] every time I've heard the boos of this mob I've hung my head in despair, chin to chest. I suspect it's been the same for some players at every club in the AFL. There is no training or armour for those kinds of hits to the soul.' More sensationally, the upper house of the New South Wales parliament unanimously passed a resolution, moved by Greens member Jeremy Buckingham, condemning Eddie McGuire for 'being a continual boofhead'.[9]

If Round 9 was Indigenous Round, Round 18 became, for one year only, an unofficially declared Adam Goodes Round. At the SCG, supporters stood and applauded at the seven-minute mark of the third quarter, honouring Goodes' number, 37. Adelaide fans brought along an Indigenous flag, and directed all their booing at Kurt Tippett, who had departed the Crows for the Swans amid acrimony in 2012; he did not mend any fences by kicking three goals against his old club in the first quarter. Elsewhere, Richmond, playing Hawthorn, and Western Bulldogs, playing Essendon, got their Indigenous Round guernseys out of the cupboard; Bob Murphy wore number 37 for the coin toss. Port Adelaide, hosting St Kilda, invited past Indigenous stars of both clubs – Nicky Winmar, Byron Pickett, Gavin Wanganeen – to greet the teams as

---

8   Sam Newman was a superb ruckman over 300 games with Geelong, and later pursued a living in media, notably as a fixture on Channel Nine's *The Footy Show*, where he installed himself as resident misanthropic grouch and provocateur. A clearly intelligent and witty man, Newman found it easier, and doubtless more profitable, to trade in petty and puerile cruelties, often at the expense of women and Indigenous people – done, as these things often are, in the name of rebellion against the entirely imaginary apparatus of repression known to those who fear it as political correctness.

9   Jeremy Buckingham MLC explained that he had proposed this unusual resolution because he was himself a lifelong Collingwood barracker, and embarrassed by McGuire. Emboldened, in 2016, Buckingham tabled a resolution describing then-US presidential candidate Donald Trump as a 'revolting slug, unfit for public office'. This motion was also passed, though it was a shame that an opportunity was missed to attract global attention to another traditional Australian insult in danger of disappearing from the colloquial lexicon – 'galah', perhaps, or 'ratbag' or 'drongo', all equally applicable to America's 45th president.

they ran out. Other sports – the NRL, V8 Supercars – offered tributes to Goodes.

Some individual players, including Collingwood's Travis Varcoe and Melbourne's Heritier Lumumba and Nathan Jones, wore armbands or wristbands of red, black and gold. Around the League, Indigenous players who kicked goals celebrated in dance: Sydney's Lewis Jetta, Melbourne's Jeff Garlett, Fremantle's Michael Walters and Danyle Pearce. North Melbourne's Lindsay Thomas pulled aside his guernsey to reveal the Aboriginal flag tattooed on his chest. Heartened, Goodes returned the following week, as Sydney travelled to Geelong.

Geelong's hierarchy left no doubt about the reception they expected. Coach Chris Scott declared that anyone who booed Goodes would simply be outing themselves as a bigot. The teams were welcomed by a joint run-through bearing congratulations for Geelong captain Joel Selwood on his 200th game and Sydney's Luke Parker on his 100th, either side of a demand for 'Respect, Unity, Fairness'. Goodes' first touch, in a tussle with Jake Kolodjashnij, elicited only the clamour that might usually be expected, and his fine goal in the first quarter, slapping the ball from the hands of Geelong's Harry Taylor and scoring on the run, attracted no untoward jeering. By way of celebration, Goodes contented himself with high-fiving his teammates.

Adam Goodes played out Sydney's season, which ended in a semi-final loss to North Melbourne. His decision to retire would normally have attracted the game's most fulsome tributes – he had played 372 games, a figure exceeded by just seven other players, and by no other Indigenous footballer. One of those tributes would have been participation in the traditional pre–grand final lap of honour for departing greats, but Goodes – as great a player as there has been – felt unable to take for granted the civility of the crowd, and declined the invitation. He might well have been right: a few weeks later, the department store David Jones unveiled Goodes as a brand ambassador, and its Facebook page was deluged with imbecilic vitriol.

Throughout this dispiriting saga, Goodes kept his own counsel, his only interview of the period given to University of Sydney student newspaper *Honi Soit*. Michael O'Loughlin did, however, offer clarification about the dance done by Goodes at the SCG. Goodes, O'Loughlin explained, had been miming not the hurl of a spear, but the downward thrust of a heavy boomerang – and it was intended as no more or less than an Australian equivalent of the haka, a statement of pride in which all Australians could hopefully one day participate. Demonstrating both an insight and a gentle humour woefully lacking throughout the affair, O'Loughlin concluded: 'It was a very special moment in this country. The only problem is Adam can't dance to save himself, but I would give him ten out of ten for effort.'

56

The Supplements Surprise
Essendon 11.14.80 Melbourne 10.7.67
Melbourne Cricket Ground
ROUND 2, 2016

Essendon weren't supposed to win this game. In 2016, Essendon weren't supposed to win any games. In January, the Court of Arbitration for Sport rendered its final decision on the fate of Essendon players embroiled in what had become known as the Supplements Saga, a scandal which by that point had been rumbling for so long that the mention of it was sufficient to cause those of sensitive disposition to drop abruptly dead with boredom. The practical upshot of the CAS's ruling was that 34 current or former Bombers were suspended for the entire 2016 season.[1]

The players disbarred included 12 still on Essendon's books, including captain Jobe Watson, vice-captain Dyson Heppell and several others any team would miss one of, never mind all of. The 2016 wooden spoon, it was widely supposed, was pre-wrapped in red and black ribbons. In Round 1, what remained of Essendon travelled to Queensland and duly received a ten-goal thrashing from Gold Coast – not, during the Suns' inglorious tenure in the AFL, an embarrassment endured by many.

Essendon's opponents today, Melbourne, had a full list to choose from, but no certainty that this would do them any good: the 13th they'd finished in 2015 had been their best showing in some years. The Demons had recruited unsensationally, but the kid they'd picked up at number

---

1   The players were technically banned for two years for taking the prohibited peptide thymosin beta-4, but this was dated from the AFL's original not-guilty decision of March 2015 that the World Anti-Doping Agency had appealed against, and credit was given for some provisional suspensions already served. The ban affected five current players who'd moved on to other clubs: Angus Monfries and Paddy Ryder at Port Adelaide, Jake Carlisle at St Kilda, Jake Melksham at Melbourne, Stewart Crameri at Western Bulldogs.

four in the 2015 draft, Clayton Oliver, looked like a goer, busy on debut in Round 1 of 2016 against Greater Western Sydney, who Melbourne had beaten by two points at the MCG. Nevertheless, anyone wanting to back Essendon to beat Melbourne this Saturday afternoon would have found bookmakers glad of their custom, and concerned for their sanity.

The Bombers had recruited to patch their gaps, even if they'd had less fun with this than they could have. One frankly irresponsible observer[2] suggested that Essendon follow the example of *The A-Team*, *The Dirty Dozen* and *The Wild Bunch*, and load the squad with the ornery mavericks and eruptive renegades of less reconstructed eras, and see how the pampered, sculpted, bronzed and hairstyled modern footballer liked his chances against David Rhys-Jones, Mark Jackson, Phil Carman, Peter Keenan, Ronnie Andrews, Mal Brown, Lazar Vidovic, Barry Hall, Robbie 'Mad Dog' Muir and Carl Ditterich. Even aged 70 or thereabouts, Ditterich could surely have caused men half a century younger to ponder the wisdom of getting in his way, and the seats and merchandise would have sold themselves.

Essendon did embrace their outlaw status somewhat. Among other ring-ins, the Bombers acquired from Fremantle Ryan Crowley, an effective tagger who conveyed the air of having recently shot a man in Reno just to watch him die – but while Essendon needed stopping power, signing someone who'd previously been suspended for ingesting illegal substances seemed almost interestingly perverse (in 2015, Crowley had tested positive for methadone secreted in a painkiller). So did talking out of retirement dual Geelong premiership player Mathew Stokes, even if his arrest for cocaine possession had been a few years back (he was placed on a bond after pleading guilty in 2010). None of which made any less sense than – as was later alleged by Essendon team services manager John Elliott – enlisting the arbitrational expertise of 'colourful' Melbourne 'identity' Mick Gatto, wondrously described by Elliott as a 'well-known dispute resolution specialist', which was indeed one possible characterisation of Gatto's talents.[3]

Essendon also had a new coach, who'd arrived at Windy Hill knowing he would face a challenge, even if – prior to the CAS plucking

---

2   Specifically, the author of this book, in his column for *GQ Australia*.
3   Following this revelation, *The Footy Show* dispatched Sam Newman to interview Mick Gatto at the Villa Romana restaurant on Lygon Street in Carlton; other media also attended. The show was stolen, however, by Gatto associate Angelo 'Fat Ange' Venditti, guffawing, 'Don't open the boot,' as Gatto returned to his black and silver Rolls-Royce.

several key vertebrae from the backbone of his team – it hadn't seemed like this big a challenge. In Essendon's peculiar circumstances, John Worsfold had seemed to some a curious choice: it had been on his watch at West Coast that a few Eagles players developed a culture of bacchanal which made their 2006 premiership either an outrage or – given that the substances involved were the opposite of performance-enhancing – kind of a miracle, akin to The Rolling Stones circa 1971 straightening themselves out sufficiently to play in time through *Exile on Main Street*.[4] (Worsfold, for his part, radiating something of the weariness of a road-rattled rock'n'roll tour manager, later insisted he had done everything anyone reasonably could have to keep the Eagles in order.)

But the most significant presence at Windy Hill in 2016 was an absence: James Hird, one of Essendon's greatest players and, more recently, coach of a club that had not only employed him, or merely loved him, but actually worshipped him. Not infrequently, as Essendon had been beset, embattled and finally beleaguered by the Supplements Saga, it had less resembled a football club than the compound of some eccentric sect of zealots: Jamestown, a redoubt of mesmerised adherents of their shimmering idol, unable or unwilling to comprehend the disaster enveloping them. In their bewilderment, Hird's disciples were scarcely alone; it was an unusual scandal, in that while everyone understood that there was a scandal, and the people in charge at Essendon more or less admitted as much, nobody seemed too clear on what had actually happened, least of all the people in charge at Essendon.

The story began to break in February 2013, with a press conference at which Essendon's chairman, David Evans, announced that the club had been looking into a supplements programme which the Bombers had operated in 2012, Hird's second season as coach, overseen by sports scientist – at least, that's what it said on his resume – Stephen Dank.[5] What they had learned, said Evans, was 'slightly concerning'; this would prove approximately Australian football's equivalent of Louis XVI's

---

4   A report into the goings-on at West Coast during this period by retired Victorian Supreme Court judge William Gillard was commissioned by the AFL in 2008, but did not see daylight until 2017. It prompted suggestions – not least from Kevin Bartlett – that West Coast's 2006 premiership should have either an asterisk placed next to it or a line drawn through it, and that Ben Cousins' 2005 Brownlow Medal was also tarnished. Any ideas that the award therefore be passed along to that year's Brownlow runner-up were complicated, however, by the fact that the player in question, Cousins' fellow Eagle Daniel Kerr, had an even longer rap sheet.

5   Stephen Dank was banned for life by the AFL, and also by the NRL, due to his involvement in a similar programme at Cronulla-Sutherland. In 2016, he was slightly injured when six shots were fired at his home. In 2017, he was declared bankrupt.

diary entry for 14 July 1789, in which France's king, oblivious that he had taken his first step towards the guillotine, noted the date which would become known as Bastille Day with: 'Nothing.' A few months later, as the 2013 season started, Essendon issued a report, which included the phrase 'pharmacologically experimental environment never adequately controlled or tested'; this translated uncomfortably readily as: 'We gave the players lots of drugs, and we're not altogether sure, upon mature reflection, what they were.'

Resignations followed as further investigations were undertaken by the Australian Sports Anti-Doping Authority. Essendon's CEO, Ian Robson, quit, as did chairman David Evans. The sword of James Hird, however, gleamed unfallen-upon. Hird not only continued to coach Essendon, but to coach them vexingly well: the Bombers won their first six games of 2013. The AFL realised that, on form, they were going to be presented with a titanic pickle come September: the possibility of a disputably legitimate contender reaching the finals, even winning the flag. Despite a late-season slump that saw Essendon lose five of their last six games, they still finished seventh.

In the week before the final round, the AFL acted: Essendon were banned from the 2013 finals series, fined $2 million and stripped of draft picks; Hird was suspended for 12 months, but even this proved insufficient to diminish him in the glassy eyes of the faithful, and in December 2013, Essendon agreed to pay Hird a lump sum to tide him over during his compulsory sabbatical.

But Essendon didn't fall apart in 2014. While Hird warmed his solid-gold bench, Essendon were coached by his former assistant – one-time Essendon premiership captain and two-time Geelong premiership coach Mark 'Bomber' Thompson. Thompson had not been unbesmirched by the Supplements Saga: he'd been fined $30,000, but permitted to continue working.[6] Under Thompson, Essendon finished seventh in 2014, only losing an elimination final to two late goals from North Melbourne's Drew Petrie.

---

6   Mark 'Bomber' Thompson played in three Essendon premiership sides, one as captain: the 1993 'Baby Bombers', for whom Thompson served as the gnarled, battle-scarred sergeant urging a platoon of callow, knock-kneed youths, including Lance-Corporal James Hird, to conquer heights they might otherwise have believed beyond them. As coach of Geelong, he broke the Cats' 44-year premiership drought in 2007, and won another flag in 2009. The shenanigans at Essendon affected him profoundly, resulting in serial strangenesses both private and public. In 2018, he was charged with possession and trafficking after police investigating a drugs ring raided his home in Port Melbourne.

Essendon did, however, fall apart upon Hird's return in 2015, and he resigned after a run of ten losses from 11 games, the climactic indignity a 112-point undoing by Adelaide at Docklands. Hird pitched his departure as a gesture of heroic self-sacrifice to unshackle Essendon from the pillory in which they had now spent the thick end of three years, though some suggested that this was a thought that might usefully have occurred to him on one of the 925 previous days that had dawned since the story broke. Hird was given another million dollars by way of settlement of his contract, but 34 of his former or current players were in a less comfortable position: although they'd been cleared by the AFL, and ASADA did not appeal the decision, the World Anti-Doping Authority did. The hammer descended in Essendon's disfavour on 12 January 2016. As the season loomed, the Bombers, to employ the obvious metaphor, prepared for take-off with their wings, engines and armaments removed.

Essendon's startling victory over Melbourne two games in was difficult for neutrals to assess. It was an upset win, and everyone enjoys upset wins, so long as it is not their team who've been upset.[7] But the obstacles Essendon overcame had been self-deployed. Applauding Essendon as they beat Melbourne felt like cheering a victorious army who'd prepared for battle by poisoning their own officers – admiration for the soldiers' pluck abnegated by the memory of their foolishness.

But the Bombers played – there was no getting around it – well. They got in front early, with two first-quarter goals by Zach Merrett, and when Melbourne came back at them in the second quarter, they dug deep to recover their lead, and deeper still through the arm-wrestle of the third quarter, in which the sides managed two goals between them. In the last, goals from Clayton Oliver, Jack Watts and Jesse Hogan looked to have done it for the Demons, but Essendon would not be told. One of the most famous names in the club's history, Daniher – Joe Daniher, whose father and three uncles had played for Essendon – steadied the Bombers with a goal to level the scores. Kyle Langford put them in front, before Darcy Parish sealed it: 18 years old, playing his second game, he got on the end

---

7   The question of which is the greatest upset in League history has a number of possible answers, but it's hard to argue with the credentials of Fitzroy's game against Geelong in Round 10 of 1963. Fitzroy hadn't won all year, and were missing their captain-coach, and only genuine star, Kevin Murray. Geelong were on their way to the premiership, and included Polly Farmer and Bill Goggin. In the bog of Brunswick Street, Fitzroy splashed merrily past a mired Geelong, winning by six goals. Appropriately for such a miraculous resurrection, four of Fitzroy's goals were kicked by a player named Lazarus – Gary Lazarus, then aged 17. Fitzroy didn't win another game in 1963, or in 1964.

of a handball chain linking Bombers captain Brendon Goddard[8] to David Zaharakis, and scored on the run. Essendon fans reached for the scarves they must have doubted they would have reason to whirl all season.[9]

A run from there to the finals would have tested the capacities of the most imaginative composer of fairytales, and no such thing occurred; Essendon won just twice more in 2016, and took home the wooden spoon. But their season in purgatory was not entirely negative. Some youngish players (especially Joe Daniher and both Merrett brothers) rose splendidly to the challenge. Some newcomers (Darcy Parish, Anthony McDonald-Tipungwuti) relished the drop into the deep end. Even some of the suspended players found a way to view their enforced year off as an opportunity. Jobe Watson worked as a barista in a New York coffee shop, one of whose patrons he married. At the press conference announcing his return for 2017, Watson wore a cap emblazoned with the commendably enlightened statement 'Feminist', which struck few if any observers as the sort of thing Ronnie Andrews would have done. Watson also surrendered the Brownlow Medal he won in the tainted year of 2012.[10]

As for Hird, he presented his club, and the League, with another problem: managing the legacy of what both Essendon and the AFL correctly regarded as one of the game's most brilliant ornaments. Hird was more decorated than most Christmas trees – two premierships, one as captain, Brownlow and Norm Smith medallist, five-time All-Australian, five-time club best and fairest, twice even Essendon's leading goalkicker – and deservedly so. He had been an exquisite footballer – swift, clever and brave, radiating that impish joy of someone delighting in finding difficult things easy. It was like he needed the trademark long sleeves to accommodate his arsenal of tricks. If people, Hird perhaps not excluded, had assumed that someone who couldn't put a foot wrong on the field couldn't possibly stumble off it, it was an understandable error. Hird dazzled.

---

8   Brendon Goddard had been a member of the St Kilda team which had narrowly failed to win the flag in 2009 and 2010. In a career move akin to joining the crew of that handsome four-funnelled liner leaving Southampton in April 1912, he signed to Essendon to chase a premiership, just months before the supplements story broke.

9   The whirling of scarves by Essendon barrackers at moments of triumph is a homage to the exuberant if ungainly celebration of then-coach Kevin Sheedy after Essendon hung on to defeat reigning premiers West Coast at the MCG in Round 16, 1993. Upon the final siren, Sheedy dementedly flailed his jacket around his head like a man shooing swooping magpies while carrying his shopping.

10   The 2012 Brownlow Medal was re-awarded to Hawthorn's Sam Mitchell and Richmond's Trent Cotchin, who had tied for second place at the count. In 2015, Mitchell prompted a minor rumpus by taunting Essendon's players with a mimed injection gesture. Disappointingly for fans of inane sanctimony, he apologised before high horses could be mounted.

There was also the question of what consideration of his wellbeing Hird was owed; even, perhaps especially, when the downfall is self-orchestrated, few people react well to being deprived of their destiny in their early 40s. In 2016, there were sightings of Hird selling posh Colombian chocolate at Box Hill market, and much consequent mean-spirited sniggering, as if trying to establish a new business wasn't a reasonable thing for someone in Hird's position to be doing. In January 2017, an ambulance was summoned to Hird's Toorak home: he had overdosed on sleeping tablets. He spent five weeks in the Albert Road Clinic, media nearly as long camped on his lawn, genuinely dreading and/or ghoulishly anticipating football's Diana moment.

When Hird walked out of Windy Hill, it was widely assumed that he'd done so for the last time, that he would be airbrushed from history in the manner of some transgressing apparatchik of the Stalin epoch, a name never again to be spoken. He was welcomed back into the football fold, however, with bemusing rapidity. In 2017, Hird was asked to present the Norm Smith Medal after the grand final. In 2018, Fremantle offered him a job; he declined. Another aspect of Hird's career everyone seemed to have agreed to forget was his actual record as coach: just 41 wins from 84 games, reaching one final, in which Essendon had suffered a ten-goal trampling by Carlton, expulsion from one finals series, and at least some measure of responsibility for a team being reduced to a level at which a 13-point win over Melbourne could be judged one of the greatest upsets of a given season.

In football as in life, there is little limit upon our willingness to absolve those who amazed us, once. In football as in life, it's hard to know whether this is a noble inclination towards forgiveness, or an inability to admit to ourselves that we've been had.

57

The China Syndrome
Gold Coast 4.14.38 Port Adelaide 16.14.110
Jiangwan Stadium
ROUND 8, 2017

Port Adelaide kicked as many goals in the first quarter as Gold Coast did all afternoon: four, a number believed bad luck by the locals, and who could consider their suspicions confirmed if this was the first display of Australian football they witnessed. The Suns were horrible, and the Power did little more than was necessary to run up a percentage-boosting score. Had this game been played anywhere else, it would never have been spoken of or thought about again – although Port's Justin Westhoff would have been grateful for one addition to his highlights reel, a deft volleyed goal from the forward pocket boundary. Westhoff's post-match assessment of the manoeuvre, though admirably candid, rather tarnished its majesty. 'I think I just pulled it out of my backside,' he said, 'but I'll take it.'[1]

A more accurate summation of the match was provided by its first goal – the first goal ever kicked in an Australian football match played for AFL premiership points in China. It was an ugly scuff by Gold Coast's Michael Barlow, from a couple of inches out, through the legs of Port's Jared Polec, and it was as good as it got for the Suns, whose view of the heels of their opponents grew increasingly distant thereafter.

The game was so bad and boring that it was hard to know what part the conditions played in the general torpor. It was hot and clammy in

---

1   Early in his career, Justin Westhoff, undisputable champion of the 'Man from Ironbark' lookalike contest that flourished across the AFL during the early 21st century, was the subject of one of the game's unlikelier experiments in player psychology. When Westhoff arrived at Port Adelaide from the Barossa Valley hamlet of Tanunda, he was shy even for a country kid arriving in the big smoke. Port's coach, Mark Williams, sent him to work in a McDonald's for a week, so he'd have to talk to customers, and/or congratulate Port supporters on their wedding days.

Shanghai, and the city's air can be such that a visitor might wonder why the citizens bother smoking. The players might still have been feeling the effects of their journey – neither Gold Coast nor Adelaide had direct flights to Shanghai, and after factoring in the layovers, it wouldn't have been much less hassle to stage the fixture in Istanbul or Buenos Aires, either of which would have been less of an adjustment as far as the outdoor temperature was concerned. Gold Coast coach Rodney Eade estimated his squad's travel time at 21 hours each way.

This was not the first game of Australian football played amid the concrete deco of Jiangwan Stadium. In 2010, Melbourne and Brisbane had staged a pre-season exhibition match at the venue, a fine game despite its meaninglessness, won by the Demons after a six-goal final-quarter charge, including the last three by Liam Jurrah – the decisive one on the siren.[2] And it wasn't the first AFL fixture played for points outside Australia; in 2013, St Kilda and Sydney had met in Wellington, the beginning of an unrewarding three-year Anzac Day residency in New Zealand for the Saints, in which they were beaten sequentially by the Swans, the Lions and the Blues.

The Shanghai match was, however, the first unmistakable signal of a truly global ambition for the code, or at least of the truly global ambition of Port Adelaide honcho and television presenter David Koch, who had made the leap from the sofa of Channel Seven's *Sunrise* to Port Adelaide's chairmanship in 2012.[3] He announced the Shanghai voyage in late 2016. After dispensing an amount of anodyne waffle about 'the respect and friendship that Australia has for China', he declared his intent of 'building a future for the AFL, and a future for Port Adelaide, in China'.

Port had some history here. They had announced a China Engagement Strategy in 2014, the most obvious fruition of which was sponsorship of

2   Liam Jurrah, a Warlpiri man from the remote Northern Territory community of Yuendumu, played 36 games across four seasons for Melbourne, in which he kicked 81 goals. At his best, he was extraordinary, an agile aerialist – he took the 2010 Mark of the Year – and inventive onballer with a prodigious knack for manufacturing somethings out of nothings. Jurrah was unable, however, to keep out of handcuffs, court or prison. The game has seen few richer talents more flagrantly squandered.

3   David Koch was one of the presenters of Channel Seven's *Sunrise*, one of the bewitchingly inane morning programmes in which Australian television specialises. He was appointed chairman of Port Adelaide in 2012, when the Power were at a low ebb, struggling financially, having stumbled through a couple of grim seasons, and been traumatised by the death of one of their players, John McCarthy, who had fallen from the third floor of a Las Vegas hotel during an end-of-season trip. Under Koch, Port recovered on and off the field, though he was heavily criticised in 2017 for saying the Power 'blew it' by losing an elimination final, in extra time, to a kick after the siren by West Coast's Luke Shuey.

the club, announced the same year, by Shanghai Cred, the agribusiness and real-estate concern founded by Chinese mogul Gui Goujie.[4] The relationship went both ways: Port sponsored China's national team, the Red Demons, at 2014's iteration of the AFL International Cup in Melbourne. Rarely had a team wearing a Port Adelaide badge sustained such hideous batterings as the 19.5 to 0.1 loss against Canada and the 28.25 to 0.0 defeat by New Zealand, though China did give both Japan and Sweden a bit of game, and beat Finland – though the Icebreakers, as Finland's national team were known, may have been disoriented by more than one consecutive hour of sunlight.[5]

Port also sponsored the South China Football League, and sent development officers to China. In 2016 Port recruited the Red Demons' captain, Guangzhou-born Chen Shaoliang, to their academy; he debuted for Port's SANFL team in 2017. Early in 2017, Koch accompanied Chinese premier Li Keqiang and Australian prime minister Malcolm Turnbull to see Port beat Sydney at the SCG. Though Koch presented Li with a Port scarf, Li – mindful of his location, and of Turnbull's allegiance to the Swans – diplomatically wore both teams' colours.

This outreach had been encouraged by AFL authorities, similarly dazzled by the potential of a country with several cities whose metropolitan areas heaved with populations greater than that of Australia entire. Port wanted to play one match in China every year for at least the next decade. It looked, however, like it might be a tough sell. *The Global Times* – the English-language offshoot of the Chinese Communist Party's *People's Daily* – previewed the match with an article beginning 'In Chinese, "olive ball" means three foreign sports: rugby, American football and Australian football. None are popular to the majority of people in China.'

Port needed opposition for their inaugural visit, ideally a team they could beat, and who could be persuaded to abandon their own fans. Gold

---

4   In late 2016, Gui Goujie backed a successful bid by mining tycoon Gina Rinehart to buy S. Kidman & Co., Australia's largest private landowner; several previous attempts by Chinese interests to buy Kidman had been blocked by Australia's government. Rinehart attended the Jiangwan match, wearing a Port scarf.

5   China, rebranded as the Dragons, did better in the men's section of the 2017 Australian Football International Cup, finishing third behind Croatia and Germany in Division 2 of a competition revamped to forestall mismatches. Papua New Guinea were champions for the second tournament running, defeating New Zealand by a point in the grand final. Papua New Guinea also have the coolest name among international teams – the Mosquitoes – though Pakistan's Shaheens and Japan's Samurais run it close. France's Les Coqs are either extremely naive, or asking for trouble.

Coast fit both bills, in that they weren't very good, and that their home ground on matchday often resembled a tumbleweed nursery. Port paid the Suns $500,000 to move Port's scheduled Round 8 visit to Carrara even further north. Though the Shanghai game was very much a Port Adelaide project, this would technically be a Gold Coast home game, a quirk which was to have consequences, deeply irritating to Port Adelaide, profoundly hilarious to everybody else.

Port assumed that in bunging Gold Coast half a million to accompany them on their China conquest, they had acquired all the privileges of home ground hosts. But a crucial detail had not been discussed, and picturesque was Port's fury upon learning that Gold Coast intended to play in Shanghai in their home colours of scarlet and gold, which very much resembled those of the Chinese flag. Port were unamused by this obvious undercutting of their own claims on the affections of the People's Republic. 'We're the club leading the AFL into China, we have bought this game and paid good money for it,' fumed Koch. Gold Coast, he asserted, were 'playing silly buggers'. He threatened to disbar the Suns from participating in any future such excursions; the Suns should have asked if Koch could confirm this injunction in writing.

Other concerns were raised, environmental and cultural. Gold Coast coach Rodney Eade said he would not take any players who suffered asthma or other respiratory issues, to spare them Shanghai's polluted, humid atmosphere, which could descend into a hybrid of smog and soup (although, on the weekend of the game, Shanghai's air quality forecast was better than Melbourne's). Both teams sat pre-embarkation instruction in Chinese mores, including chopstick technique and general etiquette, although as ever with these things, it's difficult to understand how the experts handsomely paid to conduct such seminars stretch them beyond: 'Learn the local lingo for "please" and "thank you", don't act like a dickhead, and that'll take care of 98 per cent of it.'

There was also an amount of mithering about the propriety of players wearing the accursed number 4, which in China is associated with death. Port's Paddy Ryder, thus burdened, considered changing it, but didn't. The conscience of Gold Coast's Jack Martin was untroubled. Australian media mourned, hopefully in jest, that fans would be forbidden from snacking on Four'N Twenty pies. (In 2017 Port confirmed a partnership with Four'N Twenty which would ensure provision at future Shanghai games.[6]) Some outlets milked column inches from the idea that the game might be called off amid rising tensions between North Korea and the countries within range of the missiles with which the cranky hermit kingdom had been deafening fish in the Sea of Japan.

Jiangwan Stadium was built in the mid-1930s, one of the components of a dramatic urban development scheme – the Greater Shanghai Plan – completed before the city was captured by the Imperial Japanese Army in 1937, following a merciless battle since likened to 'Stalingrad on the Yangtze'. Repaired after the war, Jiangwan hosted athletics events, including the National Games of China. More recently, it had served as a driving range for golfers. Turning it into an AFL ground necessitated the erection of temporary grandstands to shorten the playing field, insulation of the concrete benching with 5500 cushions, and retention of 1500 security personnel – roughly one bouncer for every six attendees – to monitor crowd behaviour, including a ban on alcohol (corporate hospitality excluded).

Slightly over 10,000 people bought tickets – both a miserable roll-up even by the standards of Gold Coast home games, and (so all concerned insisted) a triumphant sellout, estimated to be about half fans from Australia, mostly Port by allegiance, visiting for the match, along with roughly 3000 curious Shanghainese, with the numbers made up by Australian expatriates. Enticements other than the game included stalls promoting Australian food, wine and tourism; David Koch had more or less admitted that it was basically a trade fair with a football game attached. 'Nobody,' he conceded beforehand, 'gives a toss about Port Adelaide in China, or [the] AFL, to be honest. They love brand Australia. The game will be Australia Day in Shanghai.' South Australia's premier, Jay Weatherill, a Port supporter of daring vociferousness in a state whose capital's loyalties were divided, flew in for the game.

The Suns and the Power took the field via a joint run-through declaring 'Open to the World, History in the Making', a bold combination of meaningless clichés. It is difficult to imagine that what ensued won any

6   The first Four'N Twenty pie was baked in 1947 by Bendigo pastrywright L.T. McClure. Four'N Twenty's association with Australian football was an enduringly canny marketing stunt: early television advertisements featured Jack Dyer, Lou Richards, Bob Skilton and Ted Whitten, among many others. Garment-rending and teeth-gnashing attended the sale of Four'N Twenty Pies by then-owner Peter's Ice Cream to American concern Simplot in 1995. In 2003, Simplot sold Four'N Twenty to Australian manufacturer Patties Food, a homecoming which prompted many a patriotic tear, and an ungainly stampede among subeditors trying to be first to the 'Bye Bye American Pie' headline.

Chinese converts; if the first game of Australian football had been like this, it wouldn't have caught on among Australians. By quarter time it was clear that the live coverage by state broadcaster China Central Television, anticipated to reach near grand final numbers of four to five million viewers, was going to look less like an advertisement for Australian football, and more like a propaganda film cautioning against the depravity of physique and spirit inculcated by capitalism, especially where Gold Coast were concerned. 'Some of the fumbles were inexplicable,' raged Rodney Eade afterwards. 'I thought there was something wrong with the ball.' The Brisbane *Courier-Mail*'s correspondent correctly assessed that 'it was a premiership match, but it turned out to be an exhibition'.

The Shanghai venture was a success for Port Adelaide, yielding four premiership points, and commercial partnerships worth, in the club's estimation, north of $6 million, with more to come. Whether it was a success for Australian football was a more open question. Despite the zeal of proponents of international expansion, it has never been satisfactorily established that selling Australia's game overseas is an imperative akin to colonising Mars to escape Earth's demolition by a hurtling asteroid. Nor has it been adequately considered how crucial the game's status as a local eccentricity is to its place in Australia's affections – whether it is less a product that should be exported, more a peculiar native creature requiring our protection.

Bibliography

The following is a necessarily incomplete list; a complete catalogue of resources would necessitate an accompanying volume. Below are the books, publications and websites which have ranked among the most helpful in the writing of *Carn*.

Books
Doug Ackerly, *Coleman: The Untold Story of an AFL Legend*, Doug Ackerly, Carlton, 2014.
Robert Allen, *Cazaly: The Legend*, Slattery Media Group, Melbourne, 2017.
Graeme Atkinson, *Everything You Ever Wanted to Know about Australian Rules Football but Couldn't Be Bothered Asking*, Five Mile Press, Canterbury, 1982.
Kevin Bartlett & Rhett Bartlett, *KB: A Life in Football*, Slattery Media Group, Docklands, 2011.
Kevin Blackburn, *The Sportsmen of Changi*, University of New South Wales Press, Sydney, 2012.
Kevin Blackburn, *War, Sport & the Anzac Tradition*, Palgrave Macmillan, Basingstoke, 2016.
Geoffrey Blainey, *A Game of Our Own: The Origins of Australian Football* (third edition), Black Inc., Melbourne, 2010.
Martin Blake, *Mighty Fighting Hawks: A Celebration of Hawthorn's Three Premierships in the Clarkson Era*, Penguin, Melbourne, 2015.
Chaz Bowyer, *Fighter Pilots of the RAF 1939–45*, Pen & Sword Books, Barnsley, 2007.
Mark Branagan & John Lefebvre, *Bloodstained Angels: The Rise and Fall of the Foreign Legion 1932–38*, Mark Branagan, Middle Park, 1995.
Ashley Browne (ed.), *Grand Finals: The Stories Behind the Premier Teams of the Victorian Football League. Volume 1, 1897–1938*, Slattery Media Group, Docklands, 2011.
Warwick Capper (with Howard Kotton), *Fool Forward*, BAS Publishing, Melbourne, 2005.
Wayne Carey (with Charles Happell), *The Truth Hurts*, Macmillan, Sydney, 2009.
Elliot Cartledge, *Footy's Glory Days: The Greatest Era of the Greatest Game*, Hardie Grant, Melbourne, 2013.
Elliot Cartledge, *Footy's Revolution: The Inside Story of the AFL*, Hardie Grant, Richmond, 2018.
Cecil Clark, *B.C. Provincial Police Stories*, Heritage House, Victoria (BC), 1999.
Manning Clark, *History of Australia*, Melbourne University Press, Melbourne, 1999.
Ben Collins, *The Red Fox: The Biography of Norm Smith*, Slattery Media Group, Docklands, 2008.
Peter Corris & John Dale (eds), *Best on Ground: Great Writers on the Greatest Game*, Viking, Camberwell, 2010.
James Coventry, *Time and Space: The Tactics that Shaped Australian Rules – and the Players*

and Coaches Who Mastered Them, HarperCollins, Sydney, 2015.

John Devaney, The Full Points Footy Encyclopedia of Australian Football Clubs, Full Points Publications, Lincoln, 2008.

Barry Dickins, You'll Only Go in for Your Mates, Allen & Unwin, North Sydney, 2001.

Chris Donald, Fitzroy: For the Love of the Jumper, Pennon Publishing, North Essendon, 2002.

Jack Dyer, Captain Blood, Stanley Paul, London, 1965.

Mark Fine, The Book of Footy Lists, Slattery Media Group, Docklands, 2011.

Ross Fitzgerald (ed.), Heartfelt Moments in Australian Rules Football, Connor Court Publishing, Redland Bay, 2016.

Ross Fitzgerald & Ken Spillman (eds), Australia's Game: Stories, Essays, Verse & Drama Inspired by the Australian Game of Football, Slattery Media Group, Richmond, 2013.

Martin Flanagan, 1970 & Other Stories of the Australian Game, Allen & Unwin, St Leonards, 1999.

Martin Flanagan, The Last Quarter, One Day Hill, Camberwell East, 2008.

Mick Gatto (with Tom Noble), I, Mick Gatto, Melbourne University Press, Carlton, 2009.

Sean Gorman, Brotherboys: The Story of Jim and Phillip Krakouer, Allen & Unwin, Crows Nest, 2005.

Gideon Haigh, Game for Anything: Writings on Cricket, Aurum Press, London, 2005.

Tony Hardy, Finding Jack Dyer: The Remarkable Story of 'Captain Blood', Legend of the Australian Football Hall of Fame, Slattery Media Group, Richmond, 2013.

Steve Hawke, Polly Farmer: A Biography, Fremantle Arts Centre Press, Richmond, 2014.

Nicole Hayes & Alicia Sometimes (eds), From the Outer: Footy Like You've Never Heard It, Black Inc., Carlton, 2016.

Bruce Hearn Mackinnon, The Liam Jurrah Story: From Yuendumu to the MCG, Victory Books, Carlton, 2014.

Russell Holmesby & Jim Main, SEN Encyclopedia of AFL Footballers: Every AFL/VFL Player Since 1897 (tenth edition), Bas Publishing, Seaford, 2014.

Garrie Hutchinson, The Great Australian Book of Football Stories, Currey O'Neill, South Yarra, 1983.

Mark Jackson (with Jon Anderson), Jacko: Dumb Like a Fox, M. Jackson, J. Anderson & R. Daubeny, Windsor, 1986.

Matthew Klugman & Gary Osmond, Black and Proud: The Story of an Iconic AFL Photo, NewSouth, Sydney, 2013.

Peter Lalor, Barassi: The Biography, Allen & Unwin, Crows Nest, 2010.

Chip Le Grand, The Straight Dope: The Inside Story of Sport's Biggest Drugs Scandal, Melbourne University Press, Carlton, 2015.

Garry Linnell, Playing God: The Rise and Fall of Gary Ablett, HarperCollins, Pymble, 2003.

Konrad Marshall, Yellow & Black: A Season with Richmond, Slattery Media Group, Melbourne, 2017.

Leigh Matthews, Accept the Challenge: The Autobiography, Ebury Press, North Sydney, 2013.

Janet McCalman, Struggletown: Public & Private Life in Richmond 1900–1965, Hyland House, South Melbourne, 1998.

Jason McCartney (with Ben Collins), After Bali, Geoff Slattery Publishing & Lothian Books, Docklands, 2003.

Glenn McFarlane, Jock: The Story of Jock McHale, Collingwood's Greatest Coach, Slattery, Docklands, 2011.

Bob Murphy, Murphy's Lore: Tales from the West, Black Inc., Collingwood, 2015.

Adam Muyt, Maroon & Blue: Recollections and Tales of the Fitzroy Football Club, The Vulgar Press, Carlton North, 2006.

Ross Oakley, The Phoenix Rises, Slattery Media Group, Richmond, 2014.

Titus O'Reily, A Thoroughly Unhelpful History of Australian Sport, Penguin Random House Australia, Melbourne, 2017.

Roland Perry, *The Changi Brownlow*, Hachette, Sydney, 2010.

Alan Ramsey, *A Matter of Opinion: Informed, Insightful, Unafraid ... From Over Two Decades of Political Writing for the Sydney Morning Herald*, Allen & Unwin, Crows Nest, 2009.

Lou Richards & Stephen Phillips, *The Kiss of Death: Memoirs of a Sporting Legend!*, Hutchinson Australia, Milsons Point, 1989.

Nick Richardson, *The Game of Their Lives*, Macmillan, Sydney, 2016.

Ian Ridley, *Urge to Merge: The Power, the People, the President and the Money*, Crown Content, Melbourne, 2002.

Michael Roberts & Glenn McFarlane, *In Black and White: 125 Moments that Made Collingwood*, Nero, Carlton, 2016.

Peter Rose, *Rose Boys*, Allen & Unwin, Crows Nest, 2002.

John Ross (ed.), *100 Years of Australian Football*, Penguin Books, Camberwell, 1996.

Leonie Sandercock & Ian Turner, *Up Where, Cazaly? The Great Australian Game*, Granada, London & Sydney, 1982.

Ian Shaw, *The Bloodbath: The 1945 Grand Final*, Scribe, Melbourne, 2006.

Geoff Slattery (ed.), *Grand Finals: The Stories Behind the Premier Teams of the Victorian Football League. Volume 2: 1939–1978*, Slattery Media Group, Docklands, 2012.

Jim Stynes (with Warwick Green), *My Journey*, Penguin, Melbourne, 2012.

Mark Thompson, *Bomber: The Whole Story*, Penguin Random House Australia, Melbourne, 2017.

Matt Watson, *Fabulous Phil: The Phil Carman Story*, Brolga, Melbourne, 2017.

Newspapers and periodicals

The AFL Record aka *The Football Record*
The Age
The Argus
The Australasian
The Canberra Times
The Emerald Hill Record
The Horsham Times
Inside Football
The Malvern Standard
The Prahran Chronicle
The Port Melbourne Standard
The Referee
The Sporting Globe
The Sportsman
The Sydney Morning Herald
Truth
The Weekly Times
Winner

Websites

www.adb.anu.edu.au
www.afl.com.au
www.afltables.com
www.aflua.com.au
www.aihw.gov.au
www.aph.com.au
www.australianfootball.com
www.awm.com.au
www.boylesfootballphotos.net.au
www.footyalmanac.com.au
www.footyindustry.com
www.footyjumpers.com
www.footyology.com.au
www.footywire.com
www.insidesport.com.au
www.nswfootballhistory.com.au
www.sportshounds.com.au
www.thehickeystand.com
... and all the AFL's official club websites.

Acknowledgements

I first had the idea of writing some sort of book about football while promoting a previous book in Australia in 2013. Among the interviews I gave was one to Billy Brownless on his radio show on Triple M in Melbourne. It occurred to me that I was much more interested in asking him questions than answering his.

Amusingly, I thought that a football-related book would be something I could knock off in a year or so, given a three-goal breeze. So a few people are due thanks for their patience. First and foremost, Helen Littleton at HarperCollins, who signed up on the basis of a proposal which – it turned out – offered little clue as to what *Carn* would eventually be. I'd also like to thank Scott Forbes at HarperCollins and Julian Welch for their work on the edit, and Bronwyn Sweeney for her proofread. Thanks also to my agent, Fiona Inglis at Curtis Brown, for her enthusiasm for the project, and to Gary Ayres and Mark Yeates, who agreed to be interviewed for the original speculative idea. Special thanks to Bruce Dawe and Liz Dawe for permission to use Bruce's poem 'Life-cycle' as the epigraph.

Many people who know far more about Australian football than I do, and who have any number of better things to do with their days, took time to answer questions when a particular fact was proving elusive. Thanks to Michael Lovett, Tony De Bolfo, Francis Leach, Rhett Bartlett, Col Hutchison, Konrad Marshall, Ricky Mangidis and everybody else who fielded my emails.

I'd like to offer a general thanks/apology to all my friends in London, who have mostly affected a more or less convincing patina of interest while listening to me wanging on about this book, and about Australian football in general, for what I'm sure seems like several geological epochs. A special salutation to Matthew Dupuy – and, latterly, Finch DeLand-

Dupuy – for bringing the muffins to what are, in London, the Friday brunch-time games.

I'm grateful to all those who have paid me for writing (or talking) about other stuff while I've been writing this, notably Jack Phillips and Nikolina Skoric at *GQ Australia*, Chris Harrigan at *Smith Journal* and most of all to everyone at *Monocle* and Monocle 24 – in particular the producers of *The Foreign Desk*, Joleen Goffin and Bill Leuty, who may not entirely understand why they've been assigned St Kilda and Fremantle respectively, but they're stuck with them now.

I'm grateful to my fellow members of The Blazing Zoos – Lara Pattison, Jeremy Jones and Gen Matthews – for not fidgeting or sighing or conjuring ear-splitting squalls of feedback too obviously when I spend too long outlining the premise of our song 'Bob Chitty's Blues' to baffled British audiences.

Thanks always to Dad, for taking me to Kardinia Park to see Geelong the first time, and – though she's no longer with us – to Mum, for the many Saturday afternoons I'm sure she'd rather have been somewhere other than on a couch in front of a television next to a nervous child in a blue and white beanie.

Finally, a note on facts, of which there are many in *Carn*. Though I solemnly promise that I have checked, double-checked, cross-checked and re-checked everything, like the miserable and forsaken pedant that I am, it is nigh certain that errors have nevertheless smuggled themselves into the text. Sometimes, this will be because the primary sources were themselves inaccurate. This is a particular hazard when many primary sources are contemporary newspapers. For all that most reporters work far harder to get things right than we're usually given credit for, we sometimes get things wrong, and not always because we're bone idle, incompetent, ignorant, drunk or part of a vast and sinister conspiracy to distract the people from the truth.

Sometimes, it will be because the internet has alchemised bullshit into truth – when one of those rare reporters who is bone idle, incompetent, ignorant, drunk or part of a vast and sinister conspiracy to distract the people from the truth endows some hogwash they read online with the imprimatur of their allegedly reputable masthead, and thereby does their little bit to subtract from the sum of human knowledge.

And sometimes, these things just happen: as late as the final read-through of *Carn*, I spotted that in one place I'd mistyped the margin of

Geelong's 2007 grand final win over Port Adelaide, a number I know better than my own birthday. Go easy, is what I'm saying.

Because even the most authoritative databases are fallible: on a few occasions during my research, I got to wallow in the rich, smug satisfaction that comes of correcting the official record. I would not wish to deprive anybody else of this singular joy. If you think you have caught me out somewhere, please email me via my website – or just call me a useless, bungling hack on Twitter, @andrew_mueller – showing your working, and corrections will be made in subsequent editions, should there be any.

Carn the Cats.